Dear Reader:

The book you are about to read is the latest bestseller from the St. Martin's True Crime Library, the imprint the *New York Times* calls "the leader in true crime!" Each month, we offer you a fascinating account of the latest, most sensational crime that has captured the national attention. St. Martin's is the publisher of bestselling true crime author and crime journalist Kieran Crowley, who explores the dark, deadly links between a prominent Manhattan surgeon and the disappearance of his wife fifteen years earlier in THE SURGEON'S WIFE. Carlton Smith's COLD-BLOODED details the death of a respected attorney—and the secret, sordid life of his wife. In Edgar Award–nominated DARK DREAMS, legendary FBI profiler Roy Hazelwood and bestselling crime author Stephen G. Michaud shine light on the inner workings of America's most violent and depraved murderers. In the book you now hold, THE FORTUNE HUNTER, *New York Times* bestselling author Suzy Spencer explores the tortuous twists and turns in the notorious case of Celeste Beard.

St. Martin's True Crime Library gives you the stories behind the headlines. Our authors take you right to the scene of the crime and into the minds of the most notorious murderers to show you what really makes them tick. St. Martin's True Crime Library paperbacks are better than the most terrifying thriller, because it's all true! The next time you want a crackling good read, make sure it's got the St. Martin's True Crime Library logo on the spine—you'll be up all night!

Charles E. Spicer, Jr.
Executive Editor, St. Martin's True Crime Library

St. Martin's Paperbacks True Crime Library Titles
by Suzy Spencer

Breaking Point

The
Fortune Hunter

A Story of Marriage, Murder, and Madness
in the Heartland of Texas

Suzy Spencer

St. Martin's Paperbacks

THE FORTUNE HUNTER

ISBN: 0-312-99619-5
EAN: 80312-99619-2

Printed in the United States of America

St. Martin's Paperbacks edition / January 2005

St. Martin's Paperbacks are published by St. Martin's Press, 175 Fifth Avenue, New York, NY 10010.

10 9 8 7 6 5 4 3 2 1

Acknowledgments

I thought I would never write another book as emotionally wearing as *Breaking Point*, the story of Andrea Yates. But *The Fortune Hunter* drained me even more.

Perhaps it was because I'd been following the case since November 1999, started pitching it in the spring of 2000, began covering it nonstop in the summer of 2002, and then spent well more than two years living with it every day, including traveling from the Gulf Coast to the Pacific Ocean and battling the Texas Department of Criminal Justice in order to do my research.

More likely, it's because I got to know, like, and truly care about the people on both sides of the case. Alas, those relationships will be tested with the publication of this book because I tried my darnedest to tell the whole truth, not just one side's truth. I hope that doesn't destroy some cherished friendships.

Simply because the State won their case, I will start my thank yous with them, namely Allison Wetzel. As she knows, I could not have written this book without her help, encouragement, introductions to the family and their friends, and willingness to show me her soul. I utterly admire her integrity.

Thanks also to Becky Beard, who got me through the trial with her humor, kindness, honesty, openness, and love. I miss our dinners at Ray's. You *are* my friend.

Thanks to Paul and Kim Beard for including me in their family, sharing their tears, and bringing me peanut butter fudge.

Ellen Halbert, Anita Ashton, and Jerry Inglis filled me in on background and set me up with the kids. Thank you. I was privileged to be around Jennifer and Kristina Beard and Justin Grimm almost every day for two months. I cannot express how much I loved that time. Y'all were a joy to be around. I miss your smiles, our shared meals, and the late night phone calls and emails.

Christopher Doose and Amy Cozart, I think you two know how much I like you. Thank you for being kids of your word and for sharing so many, màny hours with me. I'm speechless in how to express my gratitude and admiration. I know you make your parents proud. I wish you both great success and happiness.

Paul Weyland, Chuck Fuqua, Ray McEachern, Carolyn Jackson, Monica Davis, Gus and Linda Voclzcl, Ed and Joan Moore, and Bob Dennison brought Steve Beard to life for me, so much so that I began to think I truly had met the man. Thank you also, Bob Cole.

Travis County has the best-looking cops I've seen since Beverly Hills. Thanks to Lt. Paul Knight and Officer Alan Howard for their wee hours and hours long interviews. Thanks to Det. Rick Wines, officers Greg Truitt, Bryan Whoolery, and PIO Roger Wade. In the DA's office, gratitude goes to Glo Moncivais, Debra Smith, and Dawn McLean.

Thanks to my BookPeople friends—Jeremy Ellis and Trevor Patten, as well as those who didn't want their names mentioned.

And that brings me to Tracey Tarlton. As Celeste said to me, "I know you like Tracey." She was right. Despite it all, I find Tracey an admirable person. I thank her too for giving me her word and living up to it. Celeste also said Tracey was the smartest person she'd ever met. Everyone seems to admire her intelligence. I like her sense of humor.

Thank you to my Camp Longhorn buddies for sharing stories with me about Tracey and her family. Thanks also to fellow Camp alum, Judge Julie Kocurek, and her always smiling and helpful staff—Sally King, Michael Kinkaid, and Virginia Vasquez.

Thank you to former prosecutor Bill Mange.

Thanks to the Bratcher family—Jeff, Denise, Richard, and Kathy, too.

On the defense side, I couldn't have written a balanced

account without the kindnesses and continuing help of Marilou Gibbs, Dana Whatley, and Catherine Baen. The slams I heard do not match with the women I met. I like the fighter in you all.

I did not understand this story until I met Celeste. Then I understood. She is utterly charming and a blast to be around. I didn't want to leave our interviews because I was having so much fun. Thank you, Celeste, for sharing time and many letters with me. I can understand that you brought Steve joy. And I have a high regard for the loyalty you inspire—especially from Marilou and Dana, who believe in you down to their toes.

Thanks to Celeste's family—her mother, Nancy; her sister, Caresse; and her brother, Eddy, and his family. You are a fine man, Eddy. George and Flo Ragsdale and daughter, Linda; Gladys Timm; Susie Smith; Louise Lightfoot; Eileen Lightfoot; B. J. Gray; and Katy Nail, thank you.

Particular thanks to Cole Johnson, Jimmy Martinez, Doug Byers, Boone Almanza, Bo Blackburn, and Charlie Burton.

A BIG thank you to my editors Charlie Spicer and Joe Cleemann and their abiding patience. I hope you think it was worth it.

Nick Ellison, I can't tell you how much I appreciate you and your tough love. You're a blessing that my whole family appreciates.

To Louise Redd, you saved the day in a desperate time. This book is for you.

Prologue

Celeste Beard was good at sex, but she didn't like it.

At least she told people she didn't like it.

Every Sunday morning, Celeste brought the family dogs, Nikki and Megan, to her teenaged, twin daughters' bedroom at the opposite end of the house from the master suite.

Nikki was Celeste's little black-and-white, pedigreed cocker spaniel whom she rarely let out of her sight. They were a pair—both young, feisty, and fun.

Megan was her husband Steven's big, old, arthritic dog whom his first wife, Elise, had bought in a grocery store parking lot. Megan always slept near Steve's feet. They too were alike—solid, reliable, and loyalty-bound.

Steve looked and acted like a mustachioed Jackie Gleason with bloodhound jowls. His was a persona some believed he deliberately perpetuated.

Celeste was a mischievous charmer who swept her blonde hair into an up-do; painted on her makeup; wore fresh, pink, acrylic talons over her fingernails; and slipped gold jewelry around her fingers, wrists, and neck when she went out to pick up men.

She closed the girls' door so the dogs couldn't get out, walked back down the hallway, past the gourmet kitchen where a man-made brook flowed beneath the see-through flooring, past the bar filled with Steve's collection of Toby mugs, and by the huge living room cluttered with her pricey Staffordshire porcelain dogs.

On her right were walls of glass doors and full-length windows overlooking the limestone patio and swimming pool. Celeste turned right toward the adult wing where there was the office, separate baths—hers with a bidet—separate walk-in closets, separate dressing areas, and the master bedroom, which included a $6,000 dog-sized replica of their bed with a matching comforter, for Nikki.

The first time Celeste put the dogs in her twins' green, pink, and white bedroom, the teens asked what was going on. Jennifer and Kristina were a preppie-looking twosome who liked to wear blue jeans, khakis, or shorts, and T-shirts or tailored, cotton shirts in sweet, pastel tones. Unlike their mother, they didn't blatantly parade Steve's wealth.

Like their mother, they loved to belly laugh and relished raunchy humor.

So Celeste explained that her husband liked to have oral sex on Sundays and the dogs couldn't be in the room because they distracted him. If Steve became distracted, God forbid, she had to start over. She even told the girls how long the sexual deed took.

They named the task "the Sunday Suck."

Soon, not only the twins knew about the Sunday Suck, but so did their friends. Celeste told them that she and Steve had an agreement—if she performed the Sunday Suck, then she could have money to go shopping. She also said that a lawyer had told her she had to do the deed once a week to get the money.

Such talk was typical Celeste. Even before she married Steve, she flaunted a forty-two-diamond cocktail ring and proclaimed, "Well, he didn't give this to me for my cooking." And she breezed on, her scent of Christian Dior's Dolce Vita perfume lingering in the air.

When Steve was asked why he was marrying a woman nearly 40 years his junior, the 300-pound man growled through a wide smile beneath his dyed black moustache, "She gives the best head I've ever had."

1

There were only two ways to go.

She could creep her SUV down the winding road of Toro Canyon, scouting the curves through the oak and cedar trees that draped the asphalt edges, being careful not to drift off into the brushy grass that grew wild over the pavement. It was the route many residents took as they headed home from the downtown Austin bars, their headlights searching the woods near the Lady Bird Johnson family compound. then flashing against the security gates outlining the Michael Dell estate.

She could listen to the rumble of her big tires as they turned sixty miles an hour over the scenic Capital of Texas Highway, past the stadium where the Westlake High School football team had just hours earlier beaten Waco High. through the traffic light that after midnight flashed caution at Lost Creek Boulevard, past the future home of Dell Computers, and then right at Westlake Drive where Susan Dell had her designer boutique in multimillion-dollar Davenport Village shopping center. In 1999, folks in Austin still loved to shout the Dell name. It was as big and powerful a deity as Willie Nelson.

She could continue up the wide and concrete-curbed Westlake Drive, past the half-million-dollar homes that computers and politics had built, and turn right, back onto the blacktopped, curbless Toro Canyon, where the multi-million-dollar homes stood behind gates that were locked tight.

Either way, just before 3 A.M., there would be drunk teenagers speeding home from their football victory parties, their parents a bit tipsy too from their own little post-game adventures. It was a neighborhood known as Lexusland for its high-rolling Republicans who concentrated on their cell phone conversations as they drove, their self-absorption demanding that outsiders move out of their paths.

Their teen children drove SUVs, tricked-out pickup trucks with head-ringing stereos, and BMWs as they drank and talked and laughed on their phones, too. It was not a neighborhood where people were allowed to do only one thing at once. Multi-tasking, being too busy—they were things to boast about.

And then there were the deer. Some claimed they were the craziest residents of all, jumping over fences in the middle of the night, bounding into the road in the quiet darkness, smashing into windshields when caught in headlights, popping the airbag, blinding the driver.

There was really only one way to go.

She laced on her black sneakers, tied them tight, slipped two shotgun shells into the chambers of her 20-gauge and walked out to her 1999 mahogany pearl Pathfinder. The plastic she'd stretched over the floorboard and driver's seat crinkled when she climbed in. She lit a Camel Light, cracked a window, and eased onto the Capital of Texas Highway. Music played on her CD, as she watched her speedometer, making sure she didn't go too slow or too fast, just right as she turned onto Westlake Drive.

She clicked off her radio and headlights and backed through the chain link gate and up the hill that led into 3900 Toro Canyon Road, her tires spinning and crunching in the gravel. She parked her SUV, climbed out and into the clear October night, and closed her car door with a mere click. The fresh fall air was scented with cedar and ragweed. The wind was still, with only the voices of nature—the chirp of crickets, the scratch of a raccoon, a possum, an armadillo, the stirring of the crazy deer.

There really was only one way to go. She stole through the darkness, past the pool, into the silent house. There were pillars of faux marble in the entryway, cypress wood meticulously stained the color of coffee in the office. She sneaked into the master bedroom and stood at the foot of the bed. She lifted her 20-gauge shotgun, aimed close to the big belly sleeping before her, and squeezed, the blast ripping into the gut.

There was only one way to go.

She walked out the door.

The burst of burning light jolted Steve Beard awake. He looked down at his abdomen. "Goddamn!" He rolled to his wife's empty side of the bed, struggled to the security panic button and hit it. Nothing happened. He slapped the switch that was supposed to turn on every light in the house. Nothing happened. Just a smear of blood stained the switch. He fumbled for the phone and dialed 911. "I need an ambulance," he said breathlessly. "Hurry!"

He never thought he'd die like this. "My guts just jumped out of my stomach. They blew out, yeah, they blew out of my stomach." TV executives, real estate developers, they didn't breathe their last breath due to their guts mysteriously jumping out of their bellies.

"How did this happen?" the 911 operator asked.

"I just woke up . . ."

He had no idea why his guts had jumped out of his stomach. And worse, he had no idea if his wife was safe. He begged the operator to phone Celeste, who he said was somewhere in the house. He cupped the blood that flowed from his gut, cursed, waited, and worried.

Travis County sheriff's officers, Westlake firemen, and Austin EMS pulled up the long driveway to the 5,309-square-foot home that was barely visible from the street. They pounded on the front door, then wound back by the courtyard and smashed through the expensive glass on sliding doors.

Circling lights from their vehicles flashed into the twins' wing of the house. A frightened Kristina Beard dialed 911 in the dark, was told that officers were already at her home, then crept down the hallway, her mother trailing closely behind her, to discover a cop standing in her living room and EMS in Steve's bedroom, working on him, trying to stop his bleeding.

"Has he had surgery recently?" an officer asked.

"No," Kristina answered. She paced over to Celeste, who

cried hysterically. Kristina tried to soothe her mother, then raced back into the bedroom, checking on Steve again. This time, she overheard the word "shotgun shell."

"He's been shot?" she asked.

Yes, the officer confirmed, but instructed her to tell no one. EMS hefted the victim onto the stretcher.

All of his friends believed he'd die from obesity. They'd tried everything from begging him to teasing him into losing weight. "I don't want to carry you at your funeral," one friend had only half-joked. "I'm scared I'll drop you."

Steve peeled his hand back from his belly and stared at the blood coating his beefy fingers. It was as though he could look inside the black hole of his stomach and see the very guts that made him a man—a multimillionaire dedicated to hard work. No, he wouldn't die like this.

There was a sprinkling of stars in the fall sky, mixed with the red warning lights from nearby radio towers as Officer Alan Howard steered his brown patrol car up Westlake Drive. He was only half a block from Toro Canyon Road and thinking he was on his way home for the night.

Sergeant Greg Truitt, a TCSO supervisor, also was cruising the Westlake area, when they both heard the call over the radio—assist EMS. Truitt flipped on his flashing lights, turned his vehicle toward Toro Canyon, and pressed the accelerator to the floor.

When Howard steered through the open electric gate of the Gardens of Westlake, the Beard house was dark except for a bit of decorative landscaping light. He rushed up the limestone steps and banged on the frame of the beveled stained-glass front door. He yelled, breaking the silence of the morning. A lone lamp glowed in a hallway. Howard turned his face toward the radio on his shoulder. "Nobody's answering."

"Call the house back," Truitt told dispatch. "Tell them we're knocking on the front door."

Howard edged his way along the house, trying doors. Truitt rang the doorbell while red, white, and blue lights flashed in the night. A fire truck groaned up the driveway. Time and again, dispatch got the Beard answering message.

Howard rounded the left side of the house leaving footprints in the dew-covered grass. He eased through an open gate of a chain link fence and stepped onto a brick courtyard surrounded by a wrought-iron fence. Through glass doors, the light from a bedside lamp illuminated a bloody, heavy man dressed in white boxer shorts, a breathing mask on his face, the phone in his left hand, and his guts poking between the fingers of his right hand. *It's going to be a mess if the man lets go*. "Over here!"

The deputy tried to open the door; it wouldn't budge. He grabbed his baton, expanded it to its full length, and struck the double-paned, tempered glass with all his might. Nothing happened. He struck it again. The sound echoed through the quiet night and startled the deer eating acorns as the nine-hundred-dollar glass broke, then shattered, scratching deep grooves into his baton, and fell like rhinestone pebbles onto the carpet. He reached through, unlocked the door, and tried to swing it open. It didn't budge. He jerked on the door handle.

"It slides," Steve Beard rasped.

Howard slipped it open and walked in, followed by Truitt and the firefighters. The bed sheets were thrown back; the comforter was pushed to the end of the bed, draped to the floor. Pink intestines and blood protruded between Beard's thick fingers. Captain Stephen Alexander of the Westlake Fire Department went for his shoulder mike. "We need STARFlight."

Truitt walked out the bedroom and down the hall to unlock the front door for the next EMS crew. The mumble of his voice speaking to a female floated back down the hallway and into the bedroom. He'd flipped on the lights and heard, "Why are you in my house? Who are you? What's going on?"

He turned and saw a blonde woman wearing pajamas, and a teenaged girl in boxers and a T-shirt.

"Why are you in my house? What are you doing here?" The woman's voice was loud and deliberate.

The uniformed sergeant tried to answer, but Celeste Beard wouldn't give him the chance.

"Why are you in my house? What are you doing here?"

Finally, he managed to explain that he was there on a medical call, someone had phoned 911.

"Don't let him die! Is he okay? Don't let him die! Is he okay?" Celeste babbled.

Truitt told her that medical personnel were already working on him and an ambulance and helicopter were on the way.

"Okay, Mom, just settle down," Kristina soothed, as she reached over and hugged her mother. "Things will work out."

Celeste Beard calmed briefly, then erupted into hysteria again. "We're supposed to go to Europe in the morning. This can't be happening. We're leaving for Europe in the morning." Every so often, she acted like she wanted to walk into the bedroom.

Truitt placed himself between her and the hallway, blocking her access to the bedroom. "Come on, leave them alone," he urged. "There's glass and stuff all in there." He nonchalantly maneuvered her around the living room, noticing the big screen TV and a few easy chairs.

Officer Russell Thompson looked down at the bed. Beard was on his back, a half dozen men working on him. A tip of yellow peeked out between a medical box and the maroon comforter. Thompson picked it up with his bare hand and looked at it.

"You might want to put that back," Howard said.

Thompson put it back.

"That's probably a gunshot," Howard announced. "It's definitely a crime scene."

O. J. Simpson and JonBenét Ramsey—police scrutiny— ran through Truitt's head as he was told about the shotgun shell. He reached for his radio. He needed another supervisor and detectives from both the east and west substations, he told dispatch.

Celeste paced. Truitt asked her if they had an alarm system. She said they did, but they never used it. She paced some more, while swinging from calm to hysterical . . . until she asked if she could go outside and smoke.

Anything other than yelling or screaming is fine with me, Truitt thought.

Sgt. Bryan Whoolery stood on the front porch getting the rundown on the situation. No signs of forced entry, no suspects, Truitt reported. Whoolery watched Celeste and Kristina. Radios squawked; an officer stood at the front door.

"He's coming through!"

"Where're they taking him?" Celeste cried.

The men strained as they lifted him down the steps.

"Why are they taking him out of here? Is he dead? Why are they taking him out of here?" Celeste covered her face. "Oh, my God!"

Whoolery stared at the woman. *What a bad acting job. It's almost like she expected him to be dead.* The woman seemed to be trying to make herself shake.

"Is he dead? Oh, my God! I want to see him! Why are they doing this?" Her voice was breathless. Her questions ran together so that no one could answer them. "Is he dead? Why are they doing this? Where are they taking him?"

Whoolery and Truitt looked at each other.

Celeste briefly said something to her husband. And she cried, but there were no tears. Kristina, looking shell-shocked, quietly soothed her.

Silence filled the space between Whoolery and Truitt as they read each other's minds. Celeste calmed, rubbed her face, then moaned and abruptly cried again. "We need to go in there and find that gun and make sure there's nobody in this house," Whoolery said.

Steve was airlifted to Brackenridge Hospital.

Celeste and Kristina were loaded into a squad car and driven to the hospital.

Kristina's boyfriend stood outside the police perimeter and watched as they passed by.

Brackenridge Hospital was more than a few miles from Lexusland and Toro Canyon Road. It wasn't uncommon to stroll through its ER waiting area to the groans of the poor in pain and the grunts of drunks heaving on the floor. Gurneys of accident victims were often crowded against hallway walls, and the stench of blood and urine filled their lungs.

But as Steve Beard was rolled into surgery, and Celeste and Kristina walked through the emergency doors, Brackenridge was unusually calm. Then, Kristina's boyfriend, Justin Grimm, arrived. She pulled him into a quiet, private place. Football-player-tall, but computer-geek-slim, dark-haired, and naturally pale, he listened to her whispered instructions: Call her sister Jennifer, who was spending the night at the Beard lake house near Lake Travis, and tell her Steve had been shot, and not to mention Tracey's name to anyone. He reached for his cell phone and started dialing.

Even in the dark, Criminal Investigation Division supervisor Sergeant Paul Knight could see that the large house sat on a huge, tree-covered lot. *My God, that's going to be a big crime scene.*

Knight stood in the chilly air and dipped into his Skoal. Nothing fazed him. He'd been a working cop since he was 19 years old.

Forty-five minutes after he arrived, Knight was on his way to Brackenridge, taking the back roads, easing his vehicle down the hills, past the country store he'd frequented as a kid, over the low water crossing near Lake Austin, and finally into downtown and Brackenridge Hospital. As he drove into law enforcement parking, the helicopter that had transported Steve Beard sat quietly on its pad.

He crossed the drive and walked through the emergency room entrance. Only four or five people meandered in the lobby. Knight wanted to talk to Steve Beard. But he quickly learned Beard was in surgery.

Detective Holly Dillard stood outside the door of a private waiting room.

Knight walked over to her.

"You need to talk to this lady," Dillard said. "She's wearing a bra."

"Okay." Knight didn't understand.

"Nobody sleeps in a bra."

Celeste sat in a private waiting room that opened onto reception. Knight stepped into the room, which was cramped with a blue couch, a couple of chairs, a coffee table, a lamp, magazines, Knight, Celeste, and one other adult. Knight focused on Celeste, who was visibly shaken. "Start from the beginning and tell me what you know. So, you guys were out at the lake house tonight?"

Steve had gone to bed around 9:30 or 10 P.M., and Celeste had left for about an hour to go out to their lake house to see her daughter and boyfriend. She explained where the lake house was—on the other side of the Pedernales River. She gave direct answers and was coherent.

Knight asked her how long it'd taken to go to and from the lake house, what time she'd gotten home, who'd been with her, and when the last time was that she'd seen her husband. She gave the sergeant the impression that she'd checked on Steve when she'd gotten home and then gone to sleep in her daughters' room.

She stopped for gasoline at the Texaco off Bee Caves Road near Cuernavaca. Her gasoline receipt would prove the time, she volunteered.

"Do you have any idea who would do something like this? Is there a boyfriend, ex-husband, lover with a vendetta who could have done this?"

"I have absolutely no idea who could be responsible for such a thing."

Celeste told him she and her husband had planned on going on a trip. She'd cashed a check for the children and because of that, there should be about $1,000 in Steve's wallet. She described where the wallet would be in the bathroom. If the money wasn't there, she said, it must be a robbery.

"Why were you sleeping back there?" Knight asked, referring to Kristina's room.

The noise from Steve's sleep apnea machine bothered her.

• • •

Perfectly creased slacks draped to the upper heels of Detective Rick Wines' cowboy boots. He seemed to rock on the heels of those boots as he stood in the million-dollar luxury home, pebbles of glass dotting the floor, making the room look like the site of a convenience store smash-and-grab, not the attempted murder of a multimillionaire.

But on the bed linens was the proof—a few stains of blood, some the diameter of coins, a few the size of a fist, one about the circumference of a volleyball, as though it had been dipped in dark crimson paint and bounced hard against the mattress.

The sliding glass doors that led out to a courtyard were open just wide enough for a man to enter, the gliding plantation shutters that could cover them opened even farther.

Wines' sergeant was at Brackenridge Hospital with the victim's family and, according to the sergeant, no one had heard the shotgun blast. At least that's what the family members had said. Wines had no reason to question their word. One wing of the house stretched east, while the other went west. The victim had been the only one in his wing when he'd phoned 911 and said his guts were coming out of his stomach.

The phone, a lamp, a family photo or two, stacks of reading material, and a weird-looking gizmo with two long hoses sat on a messy but obviously expensive bedside chest. The only evidence that Wines could easily spot was a single spent 20-gauge Winchester Super X shotgun shell at the foot of the bed.

Wines and crime-scene technician Toby Cross climbed into Wines' vehicle, eased down the long drive, through the open security gates that led to Toro Canyon Road, and headed back to the sheriff's office. In his rearview mirror, red lights on towering TV antennas flashed high in the sky—reminders of Steve Beard's days as a media mogul.

Knight wanted hand swabs from everyone to test for gunpowder residue. It was standard procedure, he explained. "We do this all the time . . ."

"You don't think I did it?" Celeste asked.

"No, I don't," Knight assured. "It doesn't mean you're a suspect. We do it to eliminate people."

Crime lab technician Toby Cross arrived. He pulled out a cotton swab, wet it with solution, and carefully rubbed between Celeste's thumb and forefinger—the perfect place for gunpowder to stick.

Knight walked down the hall to a larger corner waiting room enclosed by glass on two sides. Kristina and Justin had it all to themselves. Knight introduced himself. He had a gut feeling that separating the two wasn't the right thing to do, not with this couple.

With Justin sitting silently, Kristina relayed the same story as her mother. Kristina didn't tremble. She didn't cry or panic. She just seemed concerned.

The room filled as Jennifer, Christopher, and their friend Amy Cozart arrived. In T-shirts and jeans, they too appeared calm—as if they'd already been through their *Oh, my God*s. They sat on the couches and chairs, while Knight sat on the floor wanting them to feel like he was someone they could talk to. Looking like an encounter group, they all faced him attentively. His squinty eyes and furry blonde arms were soothing. But they knew he was the law. He wore his black CID jacket. "So you guys were where?"

They told him they were out at the lake house.

"And Celeste left at what time?" Knight wasn't learning anything new. "So, who would've done this?"

They too said they didn't have any idea.

"Come on, you guys, this was done by somebody you know. This isn't a stranger. Ninety percent of these types of things are committed by people you know. By family members and people you know. This is the way the world works. This is not a 'stranger' type of crime."

Knight reminded Christopher of John Wayne. He seemed so nice that he made Christopher want to tell him what he really thought. "How about that crazy Tracey?" Christopher popped.

They all looked at each other with that look of "Nah" on their faces.

Knight eased his way back to Christopher's comment. "Who's Tracey?"

Tracey Tarlton, lives in south Austin, on Wilson, works at BookPeople, crazy, lesbian. "She's in love with Celeste." The boyfriends were more forthcoming than the twins.

"Have you had any trouble with her? Has she ever been a problem?"

There was a time when Kristina gave Tracey's guns to the police.

"You did what?" He was getting the impression that there was an obsessed woman. A suspect was born.

After forty-five minutes to an hour, with only one name, Sergeant Paul Knight walked to his blue Ford Taurus, passing Amy Cozart sitting outside on a bench smoking with Celeste. Knight stopped. "Tell me about Tracey," he said.

"She's nobody," Celeste answered. "She's just a friend."

Knight knew that conversation wasn't going to happen. He walked over to his car, got his clipboard with a consent-to-search form attached, filled it out, and walked back toward the hospital to have Celeste sign it. But he was cut off by a somewhat short, somewhat tubby, greasy-looking man with too-tanned skin who introduced himself as Phil Presse and said he was a friend and, by the way, a lawyer.

"Can I have a consent to investigate this crime scene at your house?" the cop asked.

Presse didn't object and Celeste signed the form, with Presse as the witness.

Authorities again crawled around, through, and in the house. The officers were stunned by the wrapped Christmas packages that lined the dining room floor and covered the dining room table; by Celeste's closet and the number of clothes with price tags still hanging on them; the hundreds of purses, the hundreds of shoes in plastic boxes, the sheets in dry cleaning bags.

On a vanity, there was a box they couldn't open. If this were a robbery, Truitt wondered, why didn't the burglar sweep all the jewelry boxes into a pillowcase?

Toby Cross processed fingerprints and took photographs. By then the shotgun shell was on the floor and the bedclothes had been removed.

Wines searched Kristina's bedroom and the attic.

Knight walked outside, studying the fence around the property, the wrought-iron gate that was ajar on the north side, and the closed construction gates to the driveway. He walked around inside and into the master bathroom where he looked for Steve Beard's wallet. It wasn't there.

The crime scene was unspectacular. The door to the extra bedroom that some people considered to be Jennifer's room was kept shut. But behind the closed door, the bedroom was immaculate, especially compared to Kristina's. Its bedclothes were rumpled and unmade.

He went into the garage and checked two Cadillacs and a Suburban. All three vehicles had cell phones installed, but one vehicle also had a loose Nokia phone. Knight went into the house and searched for the car keys, which he found on a rack behind the kitchen door.

Once he got into the car, he turned on the phone and ran down the list of recent calls. There were about twenty. He made a list for Wines. And under Tracey's name, there were two numbers—one for her cell and one for her home.

The days blurred into weeks as Celeste stood by her recovering husband's hospital bed and his friends gathered in the aisles of Randalls—considered the neighborhood's high-end gourmet grocery, with a bigger, better selection of wines, among other items—and vented their frustration, even anger, at the Travis County Sheriff's Office. In their opinion, TCSO didn't seem to be doing anything on their friend's case. On top of that, there was a news blackout on the story.

Every man standing there had the ability to get the news on the air. One anchored at the very TV station Steve Beard had owned. Other Beard loyalists still worked at the station. Another had managed the city's top radio stations and lived just down the road from Beard. Even Rich Oppel, the top-dog editor at the *Austin American-Statesman*, lived in the same neighborhood. He'd bought the house Steve had shared with Elise.

There was just no reason for the blackout . . . unless that's what Steve wanted—and his friends were respecting that.

If anyone knew that to be fact, they weren't confessing it there in the busy aisles of Randalls, where it was nearly impossible not to hear the juiciest gossip. After all, Westlake had lots of secrets that everyone knew but no one dared whisper to outsiders.

But as Westlakers stepped into the chilly dew on November 4, 1999, more than a month after the shooting, reached down into the grass for their newspapers and opened them, they were shocked to find the *Statesman* headline: "A Shot in the Night—Wife's friend charged in the attack on TV executive."

Prominent bookstore manager Tracey Tarlton had been arrested for shooting Steve Beard in the gut with a 20-gauge shotgun. She was an avowed lesbian who had met Celeste Beard at St. David's Pavilion, a local psychiatric hospital.

2

BookPeople, in downtown Austin, was a place that made sense of the nonsensical. Sandwiched between the eclectic G S D & M advertising agency and the home of the once–hippie-loving Whole Foods grocery store, it embraced the outcasts and the weirdos and gave them a place to fit in. At BookPeople, it was the norm to have primary-colored hair, be tattooed and pierced and gay.

Forty-two-year-old Tracey Tarlton was more of a preppie gay in blue jeans, plaid shirts, and black Doc Martens. No obvious tattoos. No purple hair. She was the general manager of the store, overseeing 150 employees, one floor of offices, and three floors of books.

Tarlton's staffers stared at the front-page story with the color photo of a proud Steve Beard standing next to his television station's logo. October 2, 1999, someone had walked into the Beards' $1.2-million Westlake home, as Celeste and one of her daughters slept in one room and Steve slept alone in another wing, the *Statesman* reported. The alarm system had been off. There was no sign of a break-in.

Celeste Beard spoke briefly with investigators, then refused additional interviews. Private security guards blocked sheriff's deputies and others from visiting the ailing TV executive. Outside the Toro Canyon home, a sign read: "No Trespassing. This property is armed and under 24 hour video surveillance."

On page 9, there was a postage stamp–sized black-and-white photo of a bespectacled, unsmiling Tracey Tarlton with blonde streaks in her short, brown hair.

Her dumbstruck employees murmured, "Really? That happened? Is that possible?" Tracey was at work that day. Her solid body seemed bolted to the floor as she parked herself at the information desk, right at the store's front double doors, her face relaying an unspoken message: I dare you, just ask me.

No one dared.

As the sun had risen and dried the dew on Saturday, October 2, 1999, the name Tracey Tarlton had been whispered repeatedly. Detective Rick Wines heard the name from his sergeant, Paul Knight. "Okay, we'll get to it," Wines told his decades-younger supervisor, then focused his attention on drafting an affidavit for a search warrant for the Beard house.

His work went unfinished when Knight phoned from the hospital. The victim's wife had granted permission to search the house and wanted to know if the investigators had found a large amount of money—$1,000—and her husband's wallet and watch.

A return to the Toro Canyon house found a lamp lying on a couch inside the main entrance. Wines thought it looked like the lamp had been laid down, not knocked over. In a

chair, there was a phone. Nothing else was out of place . . .
until he walked into a stone-tiled dressing area off the victim's bedroom.

Multiple drawers were pulled out from a dresser of rich,
finely polished wood. Clothes hung out of the drawers.
Other clothes lay in small, messy heaps near the drawers. In
the bathroom, more drawers and cabinets were open. And
there was no money, no wallet, no watch. Only a mural of
big-breasted nudes.

Tall, good-looking, sharp-witted, and possessed with a vocabulary of profanity, Sergeant Knight sat in his fourth-
floor office and ran an Austin Police Department check on
Tarlton. There were a couple of incidents on her, the latest
being a DWI—driving while intoxicated—and two addresses, one more recent than the other. He leaned back in
his chair to talk across the hallway to Wines, who had returned from Toro Canyon. "Here's this chick's address."
Knight reached for his black TCSO jacket. "Let's go over
there and give her a visit."

Depending on how one looked at south Austin, it was the
only place to live, or it was a place to avoid. Trendy Anglos
from the worlds of music and literature lived next to poor
Hispanics in a neighborhood bordered by cheap, popular
Mexican food dives; convenience stores that sold plenty of
beer; greasy car repair shops; and a Catholic university next
to a supposedly high-end strip club. Prostitutes and politicians were known to visit the area.

Knight drove past them all to a shotgun brick and frame
house at the corner of Alpine and Wilson. Cars could almost
scrape the mailbox that stood too close to the curb on two
skinny metal posts. A few scraggly rose bushes begged for
life in a small front yard. A concrete driveway led up to a
carport that obviously had been added when the garage had
been converted into an extra room. In the drive was a vehicle that matched the one on the APD report. An A/C unit
hung out of a side window. In the back, a big yard and a

large porch beckoned friends and dogs for beer and burgers.

Knight parked down the street and watched and waited for Wines. When the detective pulled up in his gray Ford LTD and eased to a stop, Knight joined him. The two officers knocked at Tarlton's front door.

As soon as she opened it, they recognized her from her APD booking photo: barely chin-length brown hair that just hung there, 5'7", a 175 pounds with the beginning of a double chin, puffy brown eyes. She was a bit sloppy in jeans and a ratty, long-sleeved T-shirt. And, she was on the butch side.

At the flash of a badge, Tarlton identified herself.

"Ma'am, can we come in and talk to you about a situation?" Wines had a face that looked as though he'd spent too many days in the Texas sun and too many nights in Austin's smoke-filled, country-western bars. His mostly white hair was straight and combed back on the sides as though he used that old-timey pomade.

She invited the officers in. Wines sat closest to her on a couch in the living room, as Knight stood near the kitchen next to some bar stools. Books were everywhere—about dogs, about wildlife, on history and natural history. The drapes were closed.

"Do you know Steve Beard?"

They were friends, she said, her eyes dead on Wines'.

"He was shot last night, and we're doing an investigation." His voice was cowboy-deep from age and cigarettes. "Your name came up."

Tarlton's eyes flittered. That was all. "Do you know who did it?" she asked.

Wines couldn't divulge any information—it was an ongoing investigation.

"How was he shot?" Still she stared straight into Wines' eyes.

"With a shotgun. Do you own one?"

She admitted she did—a Franchi, 20-gauge, which was in her bedroom closet.

"Do you mind if we take a look at it?"

She stopped. She thought. "Well, why?" She looked a bit like a trapped, panicked crawfish. "I don't know if I want you to look at it. Do I need an attorney?"

"That's your prerogative. If you don't let me look at it, I have no choice but to go downtown and get a search warrant and come back and seize it."

Knight plopped down on the bar stool, stretched out his long legs and crossed his arms. He was a polo shirt–wearing cop who'd grown up in Westlake and knew all the hidden roads that were best for necking. "I'm gonna wait right here."

Tracey thought for a couple of minutes. The room was still and silent even though it felt like they were listening to the sounds of a ticking clock. Finally, Wines started to stand as if he were going to leave.

"Okay, okay," she said. "I'll get it for you." The three walked down the hallway to the first room on the left. She reached into the closet and handed over the shotgun. She walked back into the living room and sat down.

Wines laid the shotgun on the kitchen counter, zipped open the carrying case, pulled out the firearm, checked to make sure it wasn't loaded, walked over to the back door for some light, and looked over the gun. It smelled of clean oil. "I think it'd be a good idea if you came down to the office and we had a visit."

"You want me to go to your office?"

Wines made sure she understood she was going in for a talk, not being taken into custody.

"You're going to take my shotgun?"

"Yes, ma'am."

At the sheriff's office Wines led Tarlton into his beige office and asked her if she'd like something to drink. Alarmingly calm, she requested some water. She was good at small talk. But her arms were crossed. And when he began to ask her about her relationship with the Beard family, her eyes started moving, searching, looking, even though her body remained relaxed and open.

"When did you last shoot your shotgun?"

She said she'd shot one box of 20-gauge eights on Thursday, September 30, at Austin Skeet Range.

A 20-gauge eight was what had been found at the crime scene. Wines practically salivated.

When he asked her where she'd been on Friday night, she looked at the wall, the window, the computer—everywhere but at Wines. And her eyes didn't stop moving. She'd had a pizza and beer, didn't shoot Steve Beard, and didn't know who did, she said.

Wines kept her shotgun for fingerprinting.

Tracey Tarlton was concerned.

Two days later, the gun was released to Calvin Story, the ballistics expert for the Austin Police Department. October 7, 1999, Story informed Wines that the spent shotgun shell found in Steve Beard's bedroom was fired from Tracey Tarlton's 20-gauge Franchi.

Detective Wines proposed a motive to *Statesman* reporter Laylan Copelin: "It appears there was an infatuation from Tracey's viewpoint toward Celeste."

". . . She said she . . . last spoke with Ms. Beard on either Thursday or Friday, 9-30-99, or 10-1-99," Wines had typed in his affidavit for Tarlton's arrest warrant. "She knew quite a bit about the relationship between Mr. and Mrs. Beard and blamed Ms. Beard's depression on the victim."

Steve Bercu, the lean, gray-haired owner of BookPeople, quietly called Tracey's fourth-floor employees to the receiving room and informed them that Tracey was accused of injury to an elderly individual. He forewarned them that they might be getting calls regarding the matter. Bercu, who had a law degree from the University of Texas, emphasized to them all that one is innocent until proven guilty.

The employees could already quote Tracey's profession of innocence to the *Austin American-Statesman*. They didn't need the newspaper to tell them the truth. Behind her back they called her "Shotgun Tracey."

The scandal spilled across the Austin Country Club dining tables and echoed around its faux limestone pillars.

Steve Beard had met his wife Celeste "while she was working as a cocktail waitress at the Austin Country Club, where
he was a member," Copelin reported.

Beard had hired Celeste as his house sitter before marrying her February 18, 1995. "Four months after the wedding, Beard filed for divorce," Copelin wrote. "By August
1995, Beard withdrew his divorce filing, and the couple
reconciled."

"Beard 'is crazy about his wife,'" the paper quoted
Steve's good friend and former KBVO co-worker Ray
McEachern. It also pointed out that just one year after
Steve's wife Elise had died, Beard and his fellow TV in-
vestors sold the station to Granite Broadcasting Co. for
$54-milllion, with Beard's take being 30 percent of that.

Radio shows fed on the news: crazy lesbian tries to murder millionaire senior-citizen husband of crazy, depressed,
young, blonde gold digger. The gossip didn't abate the next
morning as KVET country radio call-in show hosts Sam Allred and Bob Cole and their listeners discussed the hearsay.

The number one radio team in the city adjusted their
headphones and spoke into their microphones. "How are
you, sugar?"

"Hi, Celeste."

"We read about you yesterday."

Softly, sweetly, Celeste talked on her phone and said her
husband was still in the hospital and was about to have his
sixth surgery.

They would send their prayers to Steve, Sam and Bob
responded.

Celeste replied that Steve would be in the hospital until
after Christmas. Then she shifted to what really motivated
her to call in—the media reporting, she gently complained,
read like the *National Enquirer.*

But the media had stayed away from the story for a
month, the hosts defended, and added, "We're sure behind
you all the way." Their voices were respectful and caring,
not necessarily their usual on-air traits. They were trying to
keep her talking.

Celeste sadly returned to the "sensationalizing."

"They've really hurt our family. . . . I'm trying to hold up." She saw Steve five times a day. She and the kids were "holed up in one room" of their house because they were scared. They'd received threatening phone calls.

"God bless you, Celeste." KVET was a station that Beard friend and neighbor Ron Rogers had overseen for more than two decades. And everyone at the station knew Steve. "A lot's been heaped on you."

"I'm just glad he's not able to read the paper." Celeste was clicked off the air.

Bob Cole looked straight into the tinted lenses of Sammy Allred's eyeglasses. "Damn, she's good."

Tracey Tarlton's already ruddy face turned even redder when she came nose-to-nose with BookPeople employee A. J. Davis. The embarrassed look in Tracey's brown eyes relayed, "Oh, God, you know." A hint of shame shadowed her, too.

Shit. A. J. did know. She clearly remembered that early October weekend, just a month before, when boxes were stacked floor-to-ceiling in the receiving room, every inch of space crammed with books. It was more than receiving room employees could manage. Tracey came in to help. And out of the blue, she turned to A. J. and announced, "I went out skeet-shooting, and it was really good."

For a moment, A. J. was stunned into silence. Tracey never spoke at work about her personal life, at least not to A. J. "Wow, you skeet-shoot? That's awesome."

All most co-workers knew was that Tracey had a whippet dog that she brought in on occasion, she could be funny, and she had an intimidating temper.

But they also remembered—Steve Beard wasn't the first husband of a lover of Tracey Tarlton's who had died. There was Zan Ray. Long had rumors whispered up and down the four floors of BookPeople and throughout the gay community. Folks gossiped that Tracey had shot and killed Zan's husband so that they could be together.

Zan, a hairdresser, came home from New York to find her husband dead. Zan's friends and employees went over to her apartment to comfort her. Tracey opened the door. None of Zan's friends had ever seen or heard of Tracey Tarlton before. But suddenly she was there and wouldn't let anyone get near Zan.

"That bitch Tracey was controlling everything," co-workers complained. At the funeral, Tracey sat behind Zan with her hand on her shoulder, comforting the widow. The next thing everyone knew, Tracey had moved into an apartment above Zan's hair salon. Everyone wondered what was going on.

When Zan stood with her staff to tell them the truth about her husband's death—suicide—Tracey stood right by Zan's side. Zan and Tracey started appearing as a couple. Tracey was Zan's date at the salon's annual Christmas party. Then, Zan broke up with Tracey.

Soon, Tracey Tarlton too disappeared from the incense-scented aisles of BookPeople, and no one would say where she'd gone.

"Oh, she probably wanted to go get psychiatric help," employees guessed among themselves. "Anyone who acts like that is probably bipolar."

When Tracey eventually returned from her visit to a "spa," her movements were sluggish, her eyes unfocused, and her face expressionless. She was drugged into numbed oblivion.

Depression had haunted Tracey Tarlton for decades. It was an intimate relationship that she and Celeste Beard shared. Likewise, both had an intimate knowledge of the wealthy.

As a child of a prominent Fort Worth attorney and as a University of Texas co-ed, Tracey had attended the same summer camp as President George W. Bush, Senator Kay Bailey Hutchison, and, decades later, actress and pop singer Hilary Duff.

At Camp Longhorn, on the shores of Inks Lake in Burnet, Texas, the hot summer air radiated with the high-pitched sounds of children laughing. Motorboats groaned low and deep as their wakes rippled onto the shores to cool tanned feet. Saint Augustine grass butted up against pink granite boulders scarred with veins of quartz. At Longhorn, where a camper received an "Attaway to go" and a merit for a job well done and a demerit for a hurtful deed, Tracey Tarlton's inner core of ethics was being formed.

In 1966, she was a tow-headed tomboy with a toothy grin who could swim a mile with speed. One July night, as the sun began to set, and the moon began to rise, the campers started singing: "Hail to that campfire lighter, Hail to that Longhorn girl, Hail, hail to . . ."

The girls leaned forward with anticipation. A counselor yelled, "Tracey Tarlton! The camper of the day!" Tracey leaped from her seat with her Wren cabinmates, raced over to the counselor, who gave her a big hug, and walked over to a campfire pit filled with a teepee of cedar. Gingerly, Tracey struck a wooden match and reached to light the flame, as the campers continued singing.

"Hail to that campfire lighter . . . Hail, hail to Tracey Tarlton, the camper of the day." It was an honor that every Longhorn girl and boy dreamed of receiving. "Campfire lighter" meant counselors and staff honored you for being a good, fun, helpful camper who got along with everyone. It meant you were accepted.

By 1968, Tracey was in the Bluebird cabin, and her wide openness of being a happy little tomboy seemed to be replaced with an inner toughness. She was still swimming a mile and winning freestyle and butterfly medals in Longhorn's Siesta swim meet, but she was no longer a campfire lighter.

The next year, the 12-year-old's smile seemed strained. Back home, she suffered physical aggression from her two much older and very big brothers. Tracey was expected to act like them and defend herself. She fought, she cursed, she hunted, and she fished.

Her father was a physically powerful man, too. And everyone in the Fort Worth household frequented the liquor cabinet, especially her mother. Tracey was known as a camper with a rough life. But despite it all, she presented a happy façade—she was voted favorite camper in 1969. Again, she was accepted *and* popular.

Upon graduation from high school, Tracey became a Camp Longhorn counselor. Campers loved her because she was funny, generous, and kind, did crazy things, and played with them, rather than sit and gossip with the other counselors. Tracey was promoted to staff counselor.

On her nights off, she streaked in her new car under the camp's giant "So Long Horn" sign and down a narrow dirt road, puffs of pink dirt flying into her headlights. She shot across Highway 29 and parked at the Bluebonnet, nicknamed the "BB," the local dive bar where counselors gathered to swig Coors beer.

At first, Tracey was just loud to get attention, telling off-color jokes while using the most profane, inappropriate language she could think of. But as she slammed back more beer, the fun, easygoing girl transformed into an obnoxious drunk who positioned her strong body before any person who *she* perceived had done her wrong—telling her she was acting stupid or weird. At that, Tracey exploded like TNT.

She rolled back into camp around midnight in a besotted rage. The director of the girls camp counselors ran to Martha Cates for help. Martha was a guitar-strumming counselor with a big grin who was as calming as jasmine incense and a mentor to Tracey.

While campers slept, she and Tracey crept in the dark down to the swim bay and walked out onto the concrete diving pier, where they sat, smoked, listened to the night sounds, and talked.

"TNT. That's my initials," Tracey Nolyne Tarlton said, the hot ash from her cigarette floating like a scarlet firefly in the night. "That just sums me up, TNT." Her smoke drifted away with the breeze.

Tracey Tarlton was friendless and lonely. She was intelligent, but she didn't want anyone to know it. And she appeared to relish her role as a misfit. Anything the "popular" crowd did, Tracey didn't want to do. But in truth and in secret, all Tracey Tarlton really wanted was to be loved.

At the University of Texas, much to everyone's surprise, TNT pledged a sorority. As an active Kappa Alpha Theta, she spent long hours guzzling beer with her sorority sisters, listening to live music, going to parties—her sole obsession seemed to be finding the next best party—and smoking pot at the Armadillo World Headquarters, where Willie Nelson sang.

In those days, Tracey thought all girls were expected to sleep with boys, and that that was what she had to do, too. Still, she understood the truth about herself and admitted her homosexuality to Martha. By then, Tracey had slit her wrists at least once. She later quit UT and briefly used heroin and IV amphetamines in 1979.

But Tracey went to rehab and returned to college, enrolling at Texas A&M University in College Station. She was graduated in 1986 with a Bachelor of Science degree in biology.

She worked for the U.S. Fish and Wildlife Service for the next two years. From there, she moved to the Bat Conservation International where she was a staff biologist doing fieldwork and paperwork—advocating for conservation with other non-profits, other conservation groups, citizens' groups, and local, state, and federal governments.

Her work produced emergency protection for bat hibernation caves on Bureau of Land Management property in New Mexico. She testified before the Nevada Division of Minerals resulting in a change in the way the state closed old mines.

By 1999, Tracey had been working at BookPeople for five years. It was her dream job. As the largest independent bookstore in Texas, the general manager was high-profile—Tracey was regularly quoted in local newspapers, and she was interviewed on C-SPAN2's Book TV. Tracey Tarlton fed on her demanding, pressure-cooked, sixty-hour workweeks surrounded by all the books she could read.

But in February 1999, after a profanity-filled blowup in front of the store's staff, Tracey checked into St. David's Pavilion. By then, she definitely knew her type of lover—dark, heavy-set women with a bit of possessiveness about them.

Celeste Beard was neither dark nor heavy-set. But when

she shined the bright light of her eyes directly into someone else's, she could read right through them. And it felt good.

Tracey Tarlton and Celeste Beard were soon smoking cigarettes together on the patio.

3

At first glance, Celeste Martinez was simply tall and shapely, and had blonde hair. There wasn't anything striking about her . . . until she turned her face to someone who needed a tender touch. Then there were charming little dimples in her cheeks, a mischievous glint in her blue eyes, and a seductive, tasty, little grin around her young, pink lips.

There was a challenging fieriness to her and a blatant honesty that first shocked, then charmed. Yet she could act almost properly shy with a soft, lispy voice, while being engaging and talkative at the same time.

In the summer of 1993, she watched Steve Beard roll his wheelchair-bound wife into the Austin Country Club dining room. Wrought-iron chandeliers hung from the ceiling. A wall of picture windows looked out on perfectly green, perfectly manicured Saint Augustine grass. Steve always sat at table 99, a big round table at the back of the room next to the windows.

Most waitresses at ACC didn't like to wait on him because he was gruff, rude, and demanding. That didn't bother Celeste. She could give even better than she could take. Plus, she liked to watch the way Steve held Elise's scotch to her lips and helped her drink it.

"I just thought it was sweet how he would give her her scotch and stuff when she couldn't talk, you know, like dribbling down her chin. People always say that's terrible. I thought it was kinda sweet, because she was an alcoholic."

• • •

Others remember Elise Beard for her golfing, her love for Steve, her friendship, her ability to make guests feel welcomed and comfortable whether she was hosting dinner at her house, a restaurant, or the country club . . . and her singing. Elise always got people going with her singing at the annual KBVO Christmas party.

The year the party was held at Austin Country Club, she had a little too much to drink and was getting a bit obnoxious with the microphone. Still, everyone was enjoing it, except for Steve. He grabbed KBVO station manager Ray McEachern and an ACC waiter. "You serve my wife one more damn drink and I'll fire both of y'all," he roared.

Steve looked out for Elise. He begged her to quit smoking, and she refused. Her cigarettes were as essential to her as water and golf. She rarely wore anything but golf clothes, but when she needed a new dress, she phoned Steve and asked his permission.

Elise Beard was a frugal woman, loyal to her husband, who would do anything with him, whether taking a luxurious trip to China or bass-fishing in a skeeter boat on Lake Sam Rayburn in rural East Texas.

"But anyway, then she died."

On October 13, 1993, Elise Beard, the smoky-voiced, trophy-winning golfer with skin aged by sun and liquor, died of cancer. For more than half a year, Steve sat at Brackenridge Hospital watching Elise fade, and asking friends, "What's going to happen to me after she dies?"

After she passed, he still sat, desperate with loneliness and grief. He lost interest in his social life. He lost interest in his business. He went to the office. He glanced at the sales figures, but then he just sat and read magazines. His friends were worried.

Then Steve started going to the Country Club every day.

Steve invited Celeste Martinez to dinner less than two weeks after Elise died. His invitation worked out just fine with Celeste's plans—she was going to leave her husband, Jimmy Martinez, with whom she constantly fought.

All the fighting was driving Celeste to drink. Sometimes, she shared those drinks with Steve Beard, the lonely gentleman who yearned to be a young white knight again.

In late October 1993, as the sun slanted pale peach rays in the late afternoon and the evenings finally cooled with a hint of cedar in the air, 5 foot, 8 inch–tall Celeste Martinez dressed in black linen slacks and a black linen blouse underneath a beaded vest. She pronounced the beaded vest "b-eauuu-tiful," slipped her size 9 feet into her high heels, and walked into Mama Mia's Italian restaurant on the arm of 68-year-old, very recently widowed millionaire Steven Beard.

Despite having gained nearly fifty pounds in the past year, Beard looked pretty sharp himself. He wore navy slacks and a navy cashmere sport jacket over his rotund, 5 foot, 10 inch frame.

The couple sat down at a candlelit table and ordered vodka cocktails. They were compatible on that—Celeste was a vodka drinker, too.

After dinner, Steve asked her to his house. She accepted; he maneuvered his Lexus over the hills to Westlake and the Davenport Village subdivision, the exact same neighborhood as the Country Club. They walked into his split-level, Spanish Mediterranean home on Terrace Mountain overlooking Lake Austin. Everywhere Celeste looked, there were touches of Elise.

Celeste and Steve climbed into his hot tub, listened to the music of Frank Sinatra, Dean Martin, and Tony Bennett, and shared more cocktails. Around midnight, a little woozy from the evening and with a gentle yet passionate goodnight kiss on the lips from Steve, Celeste climbed behind the wheel of Steve's Lexus and drove herself home.

From then on, Steve was on his mobile phone to Celeste, asking, "What's going on?"

The next thing Ray McEachern knew, he was standing in

Steve's office and Steve got up and closed the door. Steve never closed his office door.

"Ray," Steve warned, "if you ever call the house at night looking for me or anything, I have a new house manager."

"A house manager! What kind of house manager?"

"Well, hell," Steve chuckled.

"It's a woman!"

Steve's mouth widened into that Jackie Gleason smile. "Celeste," he said. "I didn't want everyone in the neighborhood to think I'd turned queer."

"Big Daddy, I don't think anybody's ever going to think that of you."

Steve and Celeste both liked to travel. They both liked to shop. They both liked to eat. He enjoyed cooking, and she didn't cook. He enjoyed grocery shopping, and she didn't grocery shop. Celeste Martinez never worked as Steve Beard's housekeeper, and as far as she admitted, that was never the plan.

In December 1993, Celeste's 12-year-old daughter Kristina flew to Washington State to visit her father for Christmas. After Christmas, Kristina didn't come home. Celeste's first husband, Craig Bratcher, filed for custody. Furious, Celeste officially left her then husband, Jimmy Martinez.

"I thought I would never survive my broken heart. I thought I had lost my best girlfriend. Steve had me help with planning the lake house so that I would be busy and not dwell on my loss."

On Christmas Day, Steve and Celeste drove to Lake Travis looking for property on which they could build a house, despite the fact that Steve didn't want a lake view. He said they didn't need another; they already had one at Terrace Mountain.

He also gave her three gifts: a $3,200 Baume & Mercier watch, a $16,500 cocktail ring with forty-two diamonds, and a 1994 Ford Explorer to replace the Pontiac

Grand Am that Celeste drove and Jimmy Martinez had purchased.

"He kept on me to quit working at the club. It was embarrassing for him to have his girlfriend working there. I finally agreed and quit, effective January 1, 1994. This is also the day I moved in with him . . .

"We only had actual intercourse two times in our relationship. The first time was the day I moved in . . ."

"Steven said that I was "the 'lady of the house' now and needed to dress like one. It hurt my feelings. At one point, I was starting to cry. He hugged me and kissed me and told me that he loved me. He said the he was helping me. He sat on the bed and made me show him every garment, one at a time. This was on a Friday night. He gave all my clothes, the following week, to a charity for battered women."

The couple drove up Loop 360, crossed the burnt-orange Pennybacker Bridge over narrow Lake Austin, and to Talbots in the upscale Arboretum shopping area where they walked through the store's scarlet doors and Steve bought Celeste an entire wardrobe—slacks, sweaters, blouses, skirts, belts, shoes, and even socks.

Celeste never cherished her clothes, she claimed—she went through too many of them. Still, she felt she was being stripped of her identity.

"The clothes, to me, made me look 60 years old and I was only 30. I felt bad and didn't like it. . . . We came to an agreement. If he could choose the clothes he wants to wear, then I could choose the clothes I wanted to wear. But, they had to come from the stores he picked. I agreed."

The following day, they drove over to 35th Street and shopped the boutiques at Jefferson Square, including Leger Lingerie where he filled her arms with two weeks' worth of expensive, lacy, delicate La Perla bras with matching panties.

Twenty-five thousand dollars later, her closet was full

again. And, she hired a Country Club bus person to clean Steve's house, replacing his maid service.

"Like for my first birthday, he bought me the most b-eauuu-tiful ankle-length sheared beaver fur coat. He was just so generous. And for Christmas he gave me, uh," Celeste stopped and thought, *"he always gave me jewelry."*

February was Celeste's month for birthdays; her daughters, her first husband, her mother, and she all had been born in February. Time and again, Celeste let Steve know that she wanted a fur coat for her first birthday with him.

"You don't need a fur," he told her. "Austin's too hot for furs."

Still, she wanted a fur. Her friend Rita Phillips had a fur and wore it everywhere, she argued. "Rita always wears fur coats."

"Okay, I'll make you a bet," Steve said. "If Rita comes over tonight with her fur on, I'll get you a fur. If she doesn't have her fur on, you can't say another word to me about furs."

Celeste agreed, and that night, when Rita stood at the Beard front door, Celeste gasped in her sweet lisp, "Oh, bless you, Rita." Rita Phillips was wearing a fur.

Celeste thought Steve had forgotten their bet, but by her February 13th birthday in 1994, she was wrapped to the ankles in sheared beaver from Koslow's in the Arboretum, Austin's premiere fur boutique.

"Former Austin television executive Steve Beard Jr. died Saturday afternoon, almost four months after he was shot in the abdomen . . . He was 75," the *Austin American-Statesman* announced on Tuesday, January 25, 2000.

News of Beard's death didn't reach the public until three days after he had died in a local hospital. And then, it only made the B section, below the fold with a two-inch-by-two-and-a-quarter-inch photo of a smiling Steve Beard in a pale yellow shirt. Celeste Beard recognized the photo, which she hadn't provided, as one taken at a party given by Rich Oppel, the *Statesman*'s editor.

Reporter Laylan Copelin wrote, "His death surprised many friends because after seven operations, Beard recently was released from Brackenridge Hospital and appeared to be recovering, said Ray McEachern, a family friend.

" 'I saw him three weeks ago, and he looked like he was going to live another 100 years . . . He was learning to walk again. His spirits were great. He was ready to tackle the world and go on with life.' "

Travis County Medical Examiner Roberto Bayardo ruled the death a homicide—complications from a gunshot wound—the newspaper stated, and continued the story on page B3. There the headline was, "New charge possible against woman accused in shooting"—Tracey Tarlton.

Beard's obituary, with a slightly different, two-inch-by-two-inch, black-and-white clichéd photo of a fat and happy man ran on page B4.

"He attended Texas Christian University, Southern Methodist University, and the University of Georgia majoring in advertising and marketing," the obit read. But World War II interrupted his education. "In the Navy Air Corps, he was trained as a pilot and later as an engineer at the United States Maritime Academy . . .

"After the war he returned to his university studies, and soon to his career." In 1947, he handled sales and development of the first FM commercial radio operation at KRLD in Dallas. He later became assistant to the president of Tracey Locke Advertising, the largest advertising firm in the South. "After another two year period, he helped establish southwest regional sales operations for John Blair & Co."

The obit outlined his time in Austin—1981, partner and general manager of independent TV station KBVO, which became a Fox affiliate in 1985. Twice, his career was described as "illustrious," and the obit mentioned that upon his retirement "Steve became active in real estate investments.

"He established Broadcast Representatives of Dallas (B.R.A.D.); and he organized 'The Texas Showdown' as a Media Client function, while President of B.R.A.D. He was a developer and director of Town North YMCA in Dallas, as well as the Director of the Red Cross in Austin.

"He leaves behind his wife, Celeste and their twin daughters, Jennifer and Kristina Beard."

Two paragraphs down, the obit noted, "Steven is also survived by his children Steven III, Becky and Paul; his grandchildren, Steven IV and Kelly; and his great-granddaughter, Allison." There was no mention of Elise.

But the obituary closed with a personal tribute from Celeste: "You were truly a gifted, generous and strong man. Your family and friends will sorely miss you. These words can not [sic] begin to touch every aspect of your life. You were my darling husband and you brought nothing but joy to my life and I will love you and miss you forever."

" 'Celeste and Steve were as close and attached married partners as I've seen,' " Beard attorney Charles Burton told Laylan Copelin.

Five years to the month after Steve had cleaned out Celeste's closet and refilled it, Austin was frigid and gloomy. Gray winter clouds hung depressingly low. Oversized SUV after oversized SUV exited Interstate 35, traveled north on the feeder road, and turned right through the gates of Capital Parks Cemetery. Steve Beard's friends, former friends, and mere acquaintances eased down narrow blacktop roads neatly plotted around graves, and rolled to a stop in front of the Capital Parks Mausoleum.

Slim trees were winter-bare. Patches of brown grass sprouted in dirt. Mourners wore dark, heavy coats pulled snug against bone-chilling wind.

Inside the mausoleum's rotunda, they sat in brown pews, teal carpet beneath their feet, hard tile in the pathways, the solemn clicking of heels echoing against the crypts. Steve Beard's body, dressed in a pale yellow golf sweater adorned with a yellow rose boutonnière, rested in an open casket.

4

Steve Beard was a man who loved to wrap his big paws around his family and friends and give them long hugs. Boisterous and jovial, he roared with a grin when he ordered his Wolfschmidt vodka, "Don't bring me that expensive stuff. Bring me that cheap shit." His rough language and plebeian taste in vodka belied the palate of an epicure and a man with the heart of a teddy bear and hands as big as a newborn lion's paws.

Big Daddy's death hit Ray McEachern hard. Ray was a sweet-faced man aged only by his balding head and the strain of the TV business . . . and Steve's death. Big Daddy had been a second father to Ray.

In September 1983, before the KBVO building was even built, Steve had hired the then 26-year-old CPA and former savings and loan executive to be his financial officer. In May 1984, the independent station signed on the air running old movies.

Still, there was no money to pay the bank, and KBVO owed at least $10 million. Steve and Ray sat in Steve's office, scouring the accounts that owed *them* money, when Steve came to a name that stood out.

"Procter & Gamble," he bellowed. "They've got more Goddamned money than God! Get me the phone!"

Ray explained that he'd written ten letters to P&G begging for the money.

But Steve yanked the phone up to his ear, dialed P&G, and demanded to speak to the company's president.

The president's assistant insisted that the head honcho wasn't in.

"Well, give me the number of the son-of-a-bitch in charge! I'm Steve Beard, as in whiskers!" Steve's words blasted through the open office door and down the station corridors. "I used to be John Blair's assistant, and I own a TV station in Austin, Texas. I'm gonna tell you one damn thing—you're ninety days past due. That's three months!"

Oh, my God. Ray was about to twitch out of his chair. *This is our biggest advertiser and we don't even have any ratings. We're lucky to have* any *advertisers.*

"When I walk into the damned drug store to buy a tube of Colgate toothpaste, I pull money out of my ass pocket and pay cash for it!"

Ray motioned for Steve to calm down.

"If y'all wanna get back on this TV station, you'll be paying cash out of your ass pocket . . . To hell with you! I'll take you off the air!" Steve slammed down the phone.

Ray turned white. "Oh, my God, Steve. We just lost the biggest client we have."

"Right. That's how you deal with them damn New York Jews! I bet we'll have our money tomorrow," he growled, his voice raspy as ever.

The story blew through every office door in the building from executives to janitors, leaving behind a dust of fear that the station would soon be going dark. P&G wasn't simply their biggest advertiser; it was their biggest advertiser ten-to-one.

The next day, Steve phoned Ray. "I told you that's how you deal with those bastards," Steve chortled. P&G had just sent Steve the largest check the station had received in its first five years of business, along with a note of apology and a request to let them back on the air.

Twice after Steve was shot, Ray McEachern trekked to the hospital to see his friend. Twice, he was sent away. On his third try, he was being sent away again when Steve heard his voice. "Get in here, Ray!"

Ray walked into Steve's private room to find his friend dressed, lying in bed reading, and immediately asking about the TV business and everyone who'd worked at their station.

For two hours, the old friends visited.

"You know when we'd be going down the road and we'd

see these guys and they'd be jogging down the road?"
Steve's lips widened into a grin.

Ray's did too as he remembered. Steve always said,
"There ain't no damn way that stuff is good for you. Look at
that guy. He's turning solid red. He's gasping for air. He's
got the worst frown on his face. And they're saying that's
healthy for you? Hell, I got more friends that died on the
tennis court . . . Damn old fart out there trying to play tennis or jogging. That's not good for you!"

Steve's grin grew even bigger as he looked at his slim
friend. "I told you being fat was an asset. The doctor told
me that if, when the shotgun blasted, I didn't have so much
padding right here, it would've killed me. Remember what I
used to tell you about exercising?" he rattled on. "Now if I'd
been fit and trim, I wouldn't be here today. Don't listen to
those damn doctors."

Steve always had to be right and always had to point out
when he was right.

But he shocked Ray hard when he said, "I'm scared to
go home. Can you believe some lesbian had the hots for my
wife?"

Oh, my God. Ray knew Steve checked his locks and
alarms every night. He knew . . . he had to keep his
thoughts and emotions to himself. "Well," Ray finally said,
"the police haven't come up with anything." He asked if
Steve had seen anyone that night.

"Ray, all I heard was this huge sound and a burning in
my stomach. I didn't see anybody at the foot of my bed. It
was just totally dark, and I had my eyes closed."

"What happened?"

"I don't have a clue. Only what they told me. But when I
had that burning sensation in my stomach, I felt like my
guts were on fire. I grabbed the phone and I called 911. I
thought I was bleeding to death. I didn't see anybody with a
gun. I was just sound asleep."

"How in the hell did you find the phone in the dark?"

"It's just kinda like self-survival. It's amazing what you
can do and how your mind can read one, two, three . . . I felt
around for the nine and the one-one."

Ray asked his question again, emphasizing that Steve had been shot at the time.

"Adrenaline took over."

Steve talked about how the doctors wanted him to hire a nurse to help him at home. "Hell knows I can afford it. Isn't Celeste such a sweetheart? She's taking special training to . . . change my dressings. Isn't that sweet? She's been through hell."

Within two weeks of the funeral, Ray McEachern received a big box from Celeste. Inside there was a mahogany case with two framed license plates. One said FOX 42. Steve had always had those on the front of his car. The other said KBVO-TV. Steve had had those on the back of his car.

Celeste also included a two-page note saying she knew that Steve had always thought of Ray as one of his sons, and, of all the things Steve liked most, Celeste wanted Ray to have his license plates.

My God, maybe I'm wrong.

Ray thought of the days when KBVO was the only station in town with a kids' show—Fox Kids' Club. Little kids would see those license plates on Steve's white BMW, get excited, and start waving. Steve grinned back and waved, too.

"Ray, you need to get a set of those license plates!"

"Steve, I might pull out in front of someone and—" He gestured with his hand. "You know, I just don't want that."

Steve roared, "Oh, it's great advertising!"

Ray McEachern sat down and cried.

In 1994, Celeste whispered about the twins' father to Anita Ashton, a club member and lawyer who had befriended her when she was an ACC waitress, "You know, Craig calls the house all the time and makes threatening calls, and doesn't leave his name. But I know it's Craig. And look at this letter he wrote."

She showed Anita a letter written in block printing that said, "Steve, you do not know the woman you are with. You need to have her investigated."

The next thing Anita knew, Steve had financed Celeste's custody battle and Kristina was living in the Beard house.

Steve Beard was gaining a family again, but he was losing a TV business. Rupert Murdoch and friends of CBS were forcing him out. Steve didn't go around shouting that information. But Ray McEachern knew Big Daddy's dilemma.

Due to Murdoch, KBVO was going to lose its Fox affiliation, so Steve and his business partner, Darrold Cannan, wanted to become a CBS affiliate. But a CBS employee who met with them said they had to sell the station to friends at Granite Broadcasting because CBS wasn't going to give the affiliation to KBVO.

"You've got to be kidding," they replied.

He wasn't joking. He threatened to give the CBS logo to the Austin NBC affiliate "and then you'll be a nobody."

On October 3, 1994, five years, minus one day, before Steve was shot in the gut, the impending sale of KBVO to Granite Broadcasting was announced.

Steve had struck media gold. His decades of working two to four jobs, being away from his wife and kids, wearing himself out with traveling and entertaining had finally paid off. He could make sure his children would be taken care of forever. Rumors circulated, and Steve and Celeste perpetuated them, that he was worth $40 million.

On February 8, 1995, four months after the announcement of the sale, Steve and Celeste signed a premarital property agreement, which immediately gave her a gift of a half a million dollars—her second birthday with him was just five days away.

February 18, 1995, 32-year-old Celeste married 70-year-old Steve at a small ceremony held in what would eventually be named the Harvey Penick Room of Austin Country Club. Kristina attended. Jennifer, who had chosen to stay with her father, wasn't invited and didn't know about it.

Steve gave Celeste a Byzantine necklace for her wedding gift; they flew to New Orleans for their honeymoon, checking into the St. Charles near the French Quarter.

• • •

*"My favorite memory of my honeymoon was Steven telling
me that he has never loved someone as much as he loves me.
He said that included his first wife."*

*"The first time I had intercourse with Steve was on our wedding night. . . . I had to inject medication in his penis, being
careful not to hit a vein. He had to lie still for 20 minutes. It
was far from romantic. He wanted to make sure that our
marriage was consummated. It was very difficult for me. I
did the same thing the following night. It was kind of traumatizing, so we came up with the oral sex solution. I performed oral sex on him once a week as long as he hadn't
had a cocktail. This was usually on Sundays."*

5

Celeste Marie Beard had committed acts that were intended
"to result in physical harm, bodily injury, assault, or were
threats that reasonably placed JENNIFER LYNN BEARD
and KRISTINA ANN BEARD in fear of imminent physical
harm, bodily injury or assault." Celeste's acts "therefore
constitute family violence."

Edwin J. "Ted" Terry was a mustachioed, $350-an-hour-civil attorney who many wealthy lawyers and more wealthy
men, particularly those from Westlake, recommended as one
of the two best divorce attorneys in Austin. But it was Kristina and Jennifer Beard who hired Terry to file for, in essence, a divorce from their mother. On the twins' behalf, on
June 21, 2000, he filed for a protective order from Celeste.

"My mother has acknowledged to me that she slept in
the same bed with Tracey Tarlton," Jennifer's affidavit declared. "Despite the fact that Tracey Tarlton has been
charged with injuring my father, my mother, CELESTE
MARIE BEARD continues to be friends with Tracey Tarlton and continues to communicate with her."

Jennifer didn't believe her mother's denial that she wasn't involved in Steve's shooting. "I base this on the fact that two days before my father was shot, my mother announced to me that she wanted my boyfriend and me to spend the night at our family lake house. It was very strange and out of the ordinary for my mother to suggest that we spend the night away from the family home . . ."

Late Friday night, October 1, 1999, Celeste "unexpectedly" drove the thirty to forty-five minutes from Westlake to Spicewood, the small community where the lake house was, and brought Steve's big old dog, Megan, with her. This was "extremely unusual," Jennifer said, "because Megan . . . rarely left my father's side." She believed her mother had brought the arthritic canine to the lake house "so that Megan would not interfere with Tracey's plans to shoot my father that night."

The 19-year-old said that many times over the past two years she'd watched her mother put sleeping pills in Steve's food and switch his Wolfschmidt Vodka with 190-proof Everclear alcohol. "I sincerely believe that she wanted my father to become ill and die."

Since Steve's death, Celeste had "become more and more unstable." On February 11, 2000, she'd asked the twins and their boyfriends to "commit suicide with her." Three days later, Jennifer spotted her mother's and sister's Cadillacs parked behind Studio 29, a Davenport Village hair salon Celeste and Steve frequented. She parked her Cadillac there too and soon watched her mother pull "a kitchen knife out of her shirt" and threaten to stab a salon staffer. "A struggle ensued for the knife and during that struggle, my mother cut herself and the knife grazed my sister's leg, bruising the bone and drawing blood."

On April 5, 2000, Celeste told Jennifer and her boyfriend, Christopher Doose, "that she could physically kill my sister." Celeste then phoned Kristina and told her "she would regret making her mad." Jennifer had not seen her mother since that April.

"In addition, my mother, CELESTE MARIE BEARD, has arranged and paid for funerals for my sister and me. She asked us to pick out our caskets, but we were emotionally unable to, so she picked them out for us."

Jennifer swore that when she was a kid her mother hit her so hard with wooden spoons that the spoons broke. "I also remember that my mother drugged me as a child to the point to where I became severely ill. I became so ill that I was admitted to the hospital. My illness mysteriously disappeared when I left my mother to go live with my father."

Kristina's affidavit was similar. "My mother has acknowledged to me that she is involved in a romantic relationship with Tracey Tarlton, and that she and Tracey Tarlton have had sexual relations together. Tracey Tarlton has openly admitted to me that she and my mother are lovers. In September of 1999, I witnessed Tracey and my mother kissing passionately."

Since Steve Beard's death, Celeste Beard had phoned Tarlton from the Beard house, from pay phones, and from her cell phone. And like her sister, Kristina questioned her mother's denial of involvement in Steve's death. She doubted it because two days before the shooting, Celeste told the twins she'd be sleeping in their room over the weekend and Justin, Kristina's boyfriend, couldn't spend the night. Justin Grimm, Kristina swore, regularly spent the night.

She also said Celeste had claimed she was sleeping in Kristina's room the night Steve was shot. "However, I do not remember seeing her in the house until the police wakened me." Before Kristina was questioned by the police, Celeste "instructed" her not to mention Tracey Tarlton's name.

The day of Steve's funeral, Kristina said, Celeste mentioned that she'd bought trip insurance for the long European vacation she and Steve were supposed to take because " 'she knew they wouldn't go on the trip.' " Her mother had never before bought trip insurance, Kristina swore. "It is my belief that she knew in advance that my father would not be taking the trip."

The afternoon after Steve was shot, and after they picked up the family's Suburban from the Toro Canyon house,

Justin Grimm drove Kristina, Celeste, and Celeste's friend Dawn Madigan back to Brackenridge Hospital. As he eased the white Suburban close to ICU, Celeste yelled, "Stop the car."

He slowed the vehicle to a halt in an alleyway, and with Justin, Kristina, and Dawn watching, Celeste reached under the car seat and pulled out a book and an empty liquor bottle. She then jumped out of the car, laughing a bit, and said, "Those stupid idiots. They didn't catch this." And she tossed a copy of *The Poor Man's James Bond* and an empty bottle of Everclear into a nearby Dumpster.

Kristina recounted the hair salon incident, saying that her mother "began to cut her wrists" and Celeste's friend Donna Goodson stopped her. But in Kristina's affidavit, the knife grazed Jennifer's leg, "bruising the bone and drawing blood."

She added, "My mother, CELESTE MARIE BEARD has related to me in a telephone conversation that she has hired a hit man to kill Tracey Tarlton. I have recorded this statement."

Celeste had taken out "three large life insurance policies" on Kristina, the teenager swore, and she was scared for her "safety due to the large face amount of the insurance policies." The "large" face value was $50,000.

Celeste had spanked Kristina with a meat tenderizer when she was a kid and drugged her so that she "became severely ill. I was diagnosed with Grand Mal Seizures that mysteriously disappeared when I left my mother to go live with my father."

Both girls believed their mother was "somehow involved in the death of my father."

Celeste Beard told Andrea Ball of the *Austin American-Statesman*, "Everything the girls are saying is a lie."

"The best thing that Steven ever gave me was my children. I have always loved my daughters. Everything I did, I did for them."

. . .

On July 17, 1996, Craig Bratcher, the twins' father, sat alone in his apartment, placed a shotgun to his head, and squeezed the trigger. A bloodstained note lay on a pizza box. The note, which Craig had written to Jen on July 3, told her to be happy. Craig didn't leave a note for Kristina.

The twins, who had planned to go with their father to Disney World in a few days, were in California sitting on their paternal grandfather's couch when they got the news. As soon as Jen phoned her mother, Celeste flew to California to get her daughters.

When they arrived in Austin, Jennifer met Steve for the first time. The conservative businessman was more than cordial to the teen with punk, dyed-red hair.

Jennifer was a bit standoffish.

On July 19, 1996, just one day after Craig's body had been found, Celeste obtained legal custody of Jennifer. Craig's family packed up his apartment so quickly that Jennifer didn't have a chance to get her clothes. Celeste immediately took her shopping for bras and panties and preppie clothes. Steve paid.

Two years later, when the twins were 17 years old, Steve changed his will, giving Celeste a bigger inheritance, and adopted the girls. By the end of the year, 1998, Celeste's mother and stepfather had moved in to the Beard lake house.

Two months later, Celeste tried to kill herself.

St. David's Pavilion smelled of disinfectant and the odor of an old hospital, although its box-like, red-brick construction suggested that the building wasn't all that terribly old.

From the last few days of February 1999 and on into March, every day, and more than once a day, Kristina visited Celeste at St. David's, taking her food, clothes, whatever she needed. Kristina watched out for her mother.

Celeste had only spent two nights in the psychiatric facility, when Kristina, in the day room, loudly confronted one of the hospital's registered nurses. Patients always seemed to be screaming, arguing, and cursing in the back-

ground, almost becoming white noise. But not visitors. The
nurse eased the teen into the waiting area where Kristina
yelled, "I don't appreciate you offering my mother discharge and yelling at her like that!"

*"She's the one that wanted me to befriend Tracey in the first
place. . . . Kristina was watching her and she goes, 'Oh,
Mom, help her. She can't even tie her shoes,' you know, and
then she's all, 'I'm gonna go get some food.' So Kristina
went and got a pizza or something, you know, shared it with
Tracey. And then she just always made sure that, you know,
somebody was tying her shoes, helping her walk, because
she was so drugged up that she couldn't even walk. And
then that's how Tracey and I became friends with—through
Kristina. . . . That's the truth."*

Every time Kristina looked at Tracey, Tracey was crying.
Kristina felt bad for her. She sat at a mesh metal table out on
the patio, surrounded by a chain link fence that bent inward
at the top with razor wire, as the whoosh of traffic from I-35
floated through the fence. She wore a T-shirt, sweatpants,
and black, four-hole Doc Marten's. Nobody wore Doc
Martens with sweatpants. Her hair hung limply in her face
and a cigarette dangled in her hand. Tracey obviously
needed help.

Trevor Patten, a BookPeople employee, had visitors in the
store—Celeste Beard and her twin daughters. The young
deaf man looked them up and down. To him, Celeste looked
rather big-boned, with hunched shoulders, but very well
dressed in a flashy, elegant sort of way.

One daughter seemed friendlier than the other as she
used sign language to tell him to feed Tracey's two cats and
her dog, since Tracey was still in the hospital. Celeste
handed Trevor the key to Tracey's house and gave him the
Beard phone number in case there was a problem.

Trevor would do anything to help Tracey. She'd men-
tored him in the bookstore. They went out to happy hour together. She'd slap her hands on his shoulder, give him a

hug, and say, "You're a good man." He thought she was a good woman.

On June 11, 1999, when complete darkness never seemed to come until well past 9 P.M. and the crickets in Westlake seemed to chirp loudly all night long, Celeste phoned Kristina—Tracey was planning on killing herself. She has guns.

On her own, Kristina rushed over to south Austin, the neighborhood where country politicians went to buy time with inexpensive prostitutes. The night was late and dark when Kristina walked into Tracey's little house with the sole goal of calming the woman who helped her with her homework.

For Tracey Tarlton, the darkness rarely seemed to leave. Two handguns sat on her kitchen table as she talked about shooting herself. Then she walked out to the back porch for a cigarette, where she could curl her fingers into her dog Wren's warm fur and feel a Hill Country wind caress her face.

Kristina grabbed the pistols and ran out the front door.

She stashed the revolvers in the back seat and phoned the cops to find the nearest police station, but couldn't understand the directions, so she drove until she spotted some officers who'd pulled someone over. She turned the guns over to the police.

On June 15, Tracey's therapist, Barbara Grant, discussed the role of suicide in Tracey's life. She suggested it was "providing a way out and a sense of control." Tracey told her about Kristina coming over to her house and taking away her pistols. Grant's solution was to suggest that Tracey needed to identify alternatives to suicide and recommended *The Woman's Comfort Book*.

Tracey Tarlton cancelled the following week's appointment.

One year later, on June 15, 2000, that time of the year when the grass was still green and growing, despite the early summer heat working to beat out life, Beard neighbor Bob Dennison was walking down his driveway to the mailboxes when Celeste drove her Cadillac through the gate. Bob stopped her.

"I've been trying to get ahold of you," he said. He glanced over his shoulder and saw a dark red SUV. "Celeste, there's somebody else trying to get in here. . . . Why don't you pull up about ten feet, and we can continue our conversation?"

Celeste glanced in her rearview mirror. "Oh, my God!" She looked frightened. "That's the woman that killed my husband!"

"Why don't you drive up my driveway," Bob said, "park in my drive, and go in my house?"

Celeste gunned her Cadillac up her driveway. Tracey whisked in behind her. Bob trailed them up the drive. Celeste got out of her car, and Tracey, with her hands on her hips, marched over to her. The two stood face-to-face, loudly talking. Tracey moved toward Celeste. Celeste, standing near her car door, backed to the front of her car.

Thirty seconds later, Tracey turned, stomped back to her SUV, and left.

"Are you okay?" Bob asked.

"Yes." Celeste got in her Caddy and whipped around to her garage.

Tracey sped home, rushed into her house, pulled open the freezer door, and grabbed a bottle of Stoli vodka. At 3:30 that afternoon, she paged her psychiatrist. "I wonder whether it's worth it," Tracey said, while promising she wasn't suicidal. She wanted to know if she could take an extra Xanax to calm herself. She could.

"Fuck her. I'll just drink her vodka." Tracey filled her stomach with a half a bottle of expensive vodka and 120 even more expensive pills—60 Valium and 60 Seroquel.

At 9:20 that night, Dr. Christine Warmann phoned Tracey to check on her. No one answered.

By the time EMS arrived, Tracey was unconscious. She was placed on oxygen and given an IV. She vomited in the ambulance. At South Austin Hospital, she was strapped down, her stomach was pumped, and she was put on a ventilator. She didn't rouse at all until the following day; then she repeatedly moaned and asked where she was.

Three days later she was transferred to St. David's Pavilion.

Tuesday, July 11, 2000, was a scorcher in Austin, Texas. Temperatures burned 99 degrees. In downtown Austin, it felt even hotter.

Ted Terry and Celeste Beard attorney Karl Moeller stood in the hallway outside District Associate Judge John Hathaway's courtroom. Four deputy sheriffs hovered close to Kristina and Jennifer and Ellen Halbert, their victims services representative from the district attorney's office. The twins had a second attorney there, too—$250-an-hour Karl Hayes.

Summer sunlight beamed into the narrow courtroom as they took their places before the judge, the twins cautiously glancing around the courtroom, their faces a straight line of seriousness. Only a few spectators filled the worn, brown gallery chairs.

Celeste Beard wasn't among them.

"She was quite understandably devastated . . ." Moeller told the judge. "And her response to it was to pack up and go to Colorado where she still is, I understand." He said he'd spoken on the phone to Celeste that morning, at 7:30.

"Was she in Colorado then?" Terry asked.

"I don't know. She called me." Moeller sat in the witness box. "You know, I certainly did not tell her not to be here." Celeste was an emotional lady, who had been hysterical about the allegations, and she'd just needed to get out of Texas for a while, he explained.

Terry's thick eyebrows arched like dark caterpillars as he countered, "And you understand, do you not, that she threatened to commit suicide when she was served . . . with the citation?"

Judge Hathaway entered the protective order, and Jennifer Beard rose from her seat next to Ellen Halbert and took the stand, purportedly to testify about attorneys' fees.

She was a pleasant-looking, typical teen with braces on her teeth. But she had a strained look on her face that was marked by a tiny mole under her right nostril. That and her braces were all that distinguished her from Kristina. Her shoulder-length blonde hair hung loosely. "We are afraid of our safety," she whispered. Beneath her clothes was a small, new good-luck four-leaf-clover tattoo on her belly—a rebellion against her mother.

"Have you been hiding out from your mother the last few months?" Terry asked.

"Yes, we have."

"Why are you afraid for [sic] your safety?"

"Because she is violent and scary."

Moeller tried to object.

Terry persisted and moved into Celeste's relationship with Tracey Tarlton, which Jennifer called "romantic."

Again, Moeller tried to object. "We are way beyond attorneys' fees here."

But Hathaway was fascinated and overruled again.

Jennifer spouted the facts from her affidavit, and then Terry asked, "Is your mother a multimillionaire?" A gold Rolex Presidential watch gleamed from his left wrist.

"Yes, she is."

Terry asserted that the Toro Canyon home was worth $1.75 million.

Kristina, who had been sitting close to her redheaded victims' services representative, stepped into the witness box.

". . . You also have some knowledge of things that your sister does not have, is that correct?" Terry asked.

"Yes, it is." Like Jennifer, her blonde hair draped just over her shoulders. Like Jennifer, she wore a dark-colored blouse. And like Jennifer, she had a new tattoo on the right side of her tummy. Kristina's was a flower.

"Did your mother in your presence tell you that she had hired a hit man to kill Tracey Tarlton?"

"Objection," Moeller cried.

"Yes, she did," Kristina answered before Hathaway had the chance to rule. She'd even recorded the three-minute-long conversation.

Moeller pleaded, "Again, Your Honor, I will object to the recording of the conversation, it has nothing to do with anything at issue here today."

Terry didn't wait for Hathaway. "Why do you want the judge to hear this?" he asked Kristina.

"Because I am afraid of her and what she might do to me."

"All we are talking about here is the attorneys' fees," Moeller begged his objection.

The judge turned to his court reporter and instructed her to stop transcribing.

And the tape was played. Celeste's voice said, "I hired somebody to kill Tracey."

6

"I find that Ms. Celeste Beard has committed family violence against Jennifer Beard and Kristina Beard and that Celeste Beard is likely to commit family violence in the future," Judge Hathaway ruled.

As Jennifer and Kristina stood before the judge, Terry's arm around a weeping Jennifer, and Ellen Halbert protectively looking at Kristina, Hathaway added, "Y'all are survivors of incredible violence. I see no family dysfunction. I see a dysfunctional Ms. Celeste Beard—but not you two.

". . . In addition from [sic] being prohibited from committing family violence, Ms. Celeste Beard is prohibited from going within two hundred yards of Jennifer Beard or Kristina Beard at any time for any reason. That Ms. Celeste Beard is prohibited from touching any part of Jennifer Beard or Kristina Beard's body with any part of Ms. Celeste Beard's body. And that Ms. Celeste Beard is prohibited from touching any part of Jennifer Beard or Kristina's body with any object whose movement in any way has been generated by any part of Celeste Beard's body.

"In other words, not only can she not get within two hundred yards of you, but she can't shoot a spitball at you, she can't use a knife or a gun, she just can't get anywhere near or touch you in any fashion."

Hathaway awarded Ted Terry $13,500 in attorneys' fees, which Celeste had to pay.

The day after the twins won their restraining order, Celeste twice phoned Dr. Michelle Hauser. She was "very concerned" that she hadn't heard from the psychiatrist. Most of all, she hoped the doctor did "not believe she played any part in Steve's death."

Celeste said she was leaving town for two weeks, but she wasn't running away, she emphasized.

By 8:10 that evening, when the sun still shined and the heat and humidity made a body drip sweat, process server Jerry Melber rang the doorbell at 3900 Toro Canyon Road. A white woman answered the door, and he asked if she was Celeste Marie Beard.

The woman said she wasn't, hadn't talked to Celeste in a couple of days, and didn't know Celeste's plans.

Melber drove away, unsuccessful in his first attempt to serve Celeste with notice that Steven F. Beard III, Becky Elise Beard, and Paul Ellis Beard, with Kristina Beard and Jennifer Beard as intervenors, were requesting a temporary restraining order against Celeste to stop her free-spending of the estate's millions, as well as to try to take control of the estate from the young widow.

The children claimed that Celeste "aided and abetted Tracey Nolyne Tarlton to willfully and unlawfully cause the death of Steven F. Beard, Jr." and that she would be "unjustly enriched" by acquiring property from his death.

As Steve filed his will on July 30, 1998, the twins were to be treated like his own children, even if their adoption proceeding had not been completed at the time of his death.

He gave Celeste $1 million, of which she'd already received $500,000—the premarital gift. He also gave her the lake house and Toro Canyon house with a combined worth of well over $2 million; their Austin Country Club membership, worth $25,000 if they turned it in but $50,000 if brand new; the cars, including a limousine; boats; furniture; silverware, china, crystal, jewelry; and his partnerships and stocks.

On November 23, 1999, after he'd been shot, Steve changed his will again, giving Celeste half of his entire trust, plus his complete partnership in Davenport Village shopping center, the location of her favorite beauty salon and Susan Dell's designer boutique. In essence, Celeste would be Dell's landlord.

Steve also created a provision that revoked all gifts and benefits to anyone contesting the will, "regardless of whether or not such proceedings are instituted in good faith and with probable cause."

On July 17, Celeste and Dr. Hauser sat down for their first therapy session since April 14. Celeste thought the children were trying to push her "over the edge." She was having suicidal thoughts, and she told Hauser she was staying with a man named Cole, whom she'd been dating since March.

The next morning, Travis County Probate Judge Guy Herman granted a temporary restraining order preventing Celeste from depleting the estate, but still allowing her her $10,000-a-month allowance.

By August 7, 2000, Celeste was upset, depressed, anxious and hopeless—Kristina, she said, had sent her a threatening letter. She couldn't sleep despite taking six Sonata. She suffered back pain, she urinated frequently, and she had a problem with her skin touching at night.

Celeste was renowned for sleeping with toilet tissue between her toes and wearing gloves while she slept so that her skin didn't touch.

Hauser prescribed more meds for her patient.

Four attorneys for Celeste Beard crowded the right side of Judge Herman's courtroom on Tuesday, August 29, 2000. Two attorneys sat on the left representing the natural-born Beard children, while Karl Hayes returned as the lawyer for the twins.

Nearby were Steven Beard III, Becky Beard, and Paul

Beard in his dress Navy whites. Just the night before at T.G.I. Friday's, Paul and Steven had set eyes on their adopted sister Jennifer for the very first time.

The twins stood with Ellen Halbert, a deputy nearby, terrified to see their mother for the first time since April. They averted their blue eyes as Celeste walked in.

At first glance, Celeste looked like a friend of the twins—young and innocent with her slimness, white tucked-in blouse, and hair pulled back in a ponytail and tied with a scarf. There was a thick vein of vulnerability to her. It was the very trait that Tracey had found so magnetic.

But at closer look, Celeste's ponytail was perfectly coiffed. Her makeup was expertly done. And as she sat at the defense table, her mannerisms and the way she leaned over and talked to her attorneys seemed to show a hardness in her eyes and face that made it obvious she wasn't a teen.

Once again, Jennifer was called to the stand. The night after the funeral, she had come home to find Steve's personal effects gone. "Our mom told us that everything in that house was of our mom and Steve, and when she passes away we would get that. But, you know that we didn't get really anything."

She specifically stated that since Steve's death, she had not taken any money from Steve's or Celeste's bank accounts, nor had she taken any of Celeste's personal property, including address books and calendars. But before his death, she heard her mother say she wished Steve would die. "It was usually when she was mad."

Celeste's tall, dark, and good-looking attorney, Boone Almanza, turned his attention to Jennifer. She turned her face to the wall.

"You are just guessing, aren't you, that your mother was involved in the shooting of your father?"

"I'm not—"

"You're guessing about it, aren't you?"

"Can you rephrase the question?" She still didn't look at the lawyer.

"Well, you are speculating and guessing that your

mother was involved in the shooting of your father?" `

"No, I am not." But under cross-examination, she conceded that her mother had never admitted to being involved in the shooting, and she'd never heard her mother and Tracey talk about it.

"So you are essentially just guessing about it, correct?"

"Am I supposed to say, 'Yes, I'm guessing?'" she snapped.

"You are guessing about it, aren't you?"

"I haven't—Well, I guess so." And, with great reluctance, Jennifer confessed that her mother had always denied having a sexual relationship with Tracey Tarlton.

"And as a matter of fact," Almanza pounded, "it's really just kind of your belief that it's a romantic relationship. You don't have any hard evidence of it, do you?"

"No."

Celeste Beard walked toward the restroom and reached out her arm to open the door. A uniformed deputy sheriff blocked her. She looked into his face. Brett Spicer. She'd hired him many times and paid him many dollars to watch and protect her home and family. Now he was guarding the girls and preventing her from going to the bathroom just because her own daughters were already in there.

Celeste glanced at the twins' victims' services rep. *I'm the victim here.*

A few long-forgotten, but solid, dark wood chairs seemingly straight out of Andy Taylor's Mayberry sheriff's office lined a wall. Old, tan movie seats furnished the gallery. Seven ceiling fans with dark wooden blades hung low from worn acoustic tiles.

With afternoon heat rising from the asphalt streets just below Judge Herman's courtroom, Kristina Beard took the witness stand and talked about Celeste's relationship with Tracey Tarlton.

"At one time I saw Tracey kiss Mom. And then another time I saw Tracey kissing her in Jimmy Martinez's bedroom."

Celeste shook her head in disgust.

Kristina then waffled on the second kiss and said she hadn't seen them actually kiss that time. "They were just kind of—Tracey was kind of fondling my mom."

Kristina's attorney questioned her about writing checks on her mother's account.

She'd stopped writing the checks in April after she quit speaking to her mother, she answered.

"Did you have any concerns about the manner in which your mother was handling her financial affairs?"

"I started realizing that some bills weren't legitimate." Kristina claimed that Celeste had paid Jim Madigan, a builder and the husband of Celeste's best friend, Dawn, $21,000 for work he'd already completed at the lake house. She told Bank of America about it. "But I don't think anybody listens to me. So it was paid and now the money is gone," she beefed.

"And she overpaid Jimmy Martinez for security work at the house so she could have the money back for herself." A $75,000 Bank of America check to Jimmy was deposited in Celeste's account.

Kristina insinuated that Celeste had ordered items from Louis Shanks, a swank furniture store, had the invoices backdated to before Steve died, submitted those invoices to Bank of America for payment from Steve's trust, then returned the furniture, making sure the money was refunded directly to her rather than the bank.

Kristina admitted she'd written checks on her mother's account, one for $12,500 and another for $7,500, most of which went to pay her own attorneys' fees. Those checks equaled the selling price of Steve's car, which her mother said she and Jennifer could invest, she explained.

Kristina closed her personal account at Bank of America after Celeste phoned the bank, posing as Kristina, and transferred approximately $21,000 out of Kristina's account and into the joint account, then went to the bank and withdrew the money.

As a result, Kristina filed a forgery claim against her mother.

The muffled groan of street traffic filtered through the

second-story windows. Wide, white blinds with yellowed ribbons were raised high. Judge Guy Herman sat so deep in his big, brown leather chair that he was almost hidden behind his bench.

Hayes asked Kristina if she'd ever talked to Celeste about putting sleeping pills in Steve's baked potato, even before Celeste and Steve married.

"No, not really, because she told me not to say anything. And I didn't think she would hurt him. I don't really know how to say no to my mom."

Twice during her testimony, Kristina explained her inactions or actions to her inability to say no to her mother. And throughout much of her time on the stand, she referred to Celeste as her mom rather than by her first name. It was a slip she didn't intend. So when she told the court that her mother had said Tracey was in love with her, Kristina carefully called her mother Celeste.

Hayes had Kristina state that Celeste had told her she'd hired a hit man to kill Tracey Tarlton, that she'd talked about what she and the girls would do if Steve were no longer around, and how life would be so much better without him.

Hayes inquired about Kristina's conversations with attorney David Kuperman regarding Steve Beard's estate.

". . . Just sounded to me like we weren't getting anything, so—it was mostly going to my mom."

Celeste lowered her head, feeling like the biggest dope. She'd thought her daughters weren't speaking to her when she was calling and calling and calling them back in April because they were angry she'd yelled at Kristina.

"I had no idea that they thought that I had actually had any involvement in Steve's murder. But now I believed that they didn't really think I had any involvement. I think they know I wasn't involved with the murder. I think they just wanted the money."

Boone Almanza loomed over the teenaged witness. "Am I bothering you?"

"Not at this moment," Kristina stated.

He showed her the affidavit in which she'd claimed Celeste had acknowledged a romantic and sexual relationship with Tracey. Then he pulled out the transcript of her July testimony for the restraining order. There Kristina had stated her mother denied being lovers with Tracey.

"So your affidavit where you swore to tell the truth and your testimony before Judge Hathaway conflict, correct?"

"Well, apparently it does."

"You had a key to [Tracey Tarlton's] house, didn't you?"

At first Kristina denied that, saying it was simply on the key chain to the car she drove. Under pressure from Almanza, though, she admitted she did have a key.

They argued over why she'd graduated late from high school. He claimed it was because she'd gotten caught cheating. She insisted it was because she'd never finished her courses.

They bickered over the "three large-face life insurance policies" that Kristina said Celeste had bought on Jennifer and herself. Almanza said they were for a mausoleum Steve intended to build. She contended they were "payments on a burial." He insisted they were payments for caskets and burials Steve had prearranged.

"No, my dad did not prearrange that."

Almanza insisted that Kristina had moved out of the house because Celeste revoked the power of attorney she'd signed over to her daughter.

"No. Why don't you listen to the tape?" Kristina pouted.

He stated that Celeste verbally revoked the power of attorney in front of her psychologist with Kristina present during an April 1, 2000, counseling session.

"I don't recall," she claimed. "It wouldn't have mattered to me anyway if she revoked the power of attorney anyway. I didn't care."

He pointed out a $12,500 check and a $7,500 check she'd written on May 4, 2000, on Celeste's account. "And did you talk to her on May first or May fourth about writing these two checks?"

"No, I did not." She whipped over seven March 13,

2000, checks she'd signed claiming power of attorney, after earlier testifying she'd never used "Kristina Beard POA" on her mother's bank accounts.

On redirect, Kristina described Celeste's demeanor on the day of the funeral.

"Well, on the way to the funeral she was, you know, kind of normal, quiet and all that. And then at the funeral she was kind of crying and all that. And then when we were in the limo going back she was laughing."

"And did anything about that seem to you to be inappropriate?" Karl Hayes asked.

"Yeah."

"Why is that?"

"Well, because I wasn't too happy at the time. So I didn't feel like laughing or having a good time."

One last time, Almanza took over. He handed Kristina the life insurance policies and showed her that they were purchased April 28, 1997. "Now, are these the policies that you testified in your affidavit about being the large-face-value policies?"

"Yes."

". . . I always thought that blood was thicker than water. And for the first time, you know, it just slapped me in the face that my kids are evil. And I just felt like everything I've done for them, you know, I thought I'd lived my whole life for them, I thought, you know, how could they be so hateful to me?"

On Wednesday morning, August 30, Jason Panzer, attorney for the natural-born Beard children, called Tramex Travel agents Stacey Sadler and Rose Marie Hagman. They were supposed to bolster the children's case that Steve and Celeste had never before purchased travel insurance. Instead, they helped the defense by stating that the Beards had bought travel insurance in the past—it was cheaper usually than what they'd paid for the European trip, and Steve usually did the purchasing.

But Hagman also stated that in March 1999, Celeste had purchased round-trip tickets from Kansas City to Dallas for Tracey Tarlton.

The heat was climbing toward 100 degrees when Bank of America's Janet Pinkerton was called to the witness stand just after lunch. As vice president of private banking at B of A, she was the administrator of Steve Beard's estate.

Pinkerton reported that the Toro Canyon house was on the market for $2.5 or $3 million, and the lake house was worth about $300,000. She outlined Celeste's inheritance, adding memberships at Barton Creek country club and the Headliners Club, as well as ACC, but estimated the value of that membership price to $10,000–$19,000.

After all debts and taxes had been paid, a marital trust was to be established. If the marital trust were funded that day, it'd be worth only $100,000, *plus* the value of the high-end Davenport Village shopping center on some of the most valuable real estate on the west side of Austin. The shopping center was producing approximately $10,000 a month in income.

"Since Mr. Beard's death, how much money has the bank distributed to Celeste and for Celeste's benefit?" Panzer asked.

"In excess of five hundred thousand."

In the six weeks between February 11, 2000, and March 31, 2000, Celeste had spent more than $100,000. Pinkerton believed that Celeste Beard was squandering her funds, and she said she'd told that to Celeste.

"Since those conversations has Ms. Beard shown any propensity towards frugality or otherwise saving money?" Panzer asked.

"Actual evidence?" Pinkerton replied. "No."

On the third day of court, the street heat seared the courtroom windows just like Steve Beard liked his steak seared on both sides after being rolled in cracked pepper. The temperature was 106 degrees outside. But Celeste remained cool as attorney David Kuperman took the stand.

She was on sedatives. Boone Almanza was the one who was burning.

Kuperman had been, first, Steve Beard's attorney, for sixteen years helping him with his prenuptial agreement, postnuptial agreement, and setting up his trust and estate planning. Then, he'd been Celeste's attorney, helping her with estate planning. On this sweltering day, he was testifying against her.

The tall, gray-haired attorney stated that after Steve was shot, all of the Beard bills were sent to him, then were forwarded to Bank of America for payment. From October to November of 1999, bills totaled approximately $321,000. By December 10, a new stack of invoices added up to $249,000.

On December 14, 1999, Kuperman stood in Steve's hospital room and reported the half million dollars in expenditures.

Steve wasn't happy. In fact, he was downright upset. In his deep, raspy voice, he instructed Kuperman to talk to Celeste and tell her to slow down her spending—she was eating into the principal of the trust.

Kuperman and Celeste did talk—several times.

"David Kuuu-perman calls me and tells me that I'm spending too much money and blah, blah, blah, blah." She says "blah, blah" almost like a baby blowing bubbles out of her mouth. "And so I'm thinking Steve sicced *David on me because Steve can't tell me himself, which it turned out it was true—because he did sic David on me.*

"And that really upset me, and so I, I, I said things to David on the phone out of frustration, anger, hurt, not getting my way, that I didn't mean.

Her politer comments, Kuperman testified to: Steve had never complained about her spending before, so if he now had a problem with it he should be the one to tell her, not Kuperman.

She went to the hospital and informed Steve, "If you want to divorce me, go right ahead."

Just before Christmas, Celeste left Kuperman a few similar voice mails. Kuperman's secretary transcribed the mes-

sages, which Kuperman relayed to Steve. "And that afternoon I got another voice mail to the effect . . . that it's not
right for me to be transcribing her voice mails and talking
with Steve about stuff without her being present, the eco-
nomics without her being present, and then reiterated again
her desire to be divorced." He told Steve about that, too.

*". . . I always thought, you know, when he was mad at me
that it instantly meant divorce. And that's not what he said.
And that's not what he wanted. And when he explained to
me that I was spending way too much money, that I was
spending the principal, which—I did not understand that,
you know—I tried to back off a little bit."*

Bob Powell, the natural-born children's attorney, stepped up
to read a portion of the videotaped deposition Celeste
Beard had given just days before.
    "Question: Since his death have you remarried?
    "Answer: Yes, I have."
    On July 3, 2000, Celeste Beard married Spencer Colon
Johnson in Aspen, Colorado. Cole, she said, was a carpenter.

The next morning, Tracey Tarlton read the newspaper. Then
she read it again and again and again. *Charade. Setup. Bullshit.* She couldn't believe what she was reading.

7

*"You know, I don't understand how they say I don't love
them. I did everything for them. I gave them credit cards."*

Celeste's lisp was often as prevalent as her tears as she
talked about and thought about her daughters. When the
girls were little, every day after work she took them to the
beach, where they loved to play in the sand. When they

moved to Arizona and were in school, every Friday night she took them to Peter Piper Pizza. They spent hours there eating and playing video games.

When Kristina was in elementary school and Celeste was married to Jimmy Martinez, Celeste would come home late wanting to watch *Designing Women* and would ask Kristina to watch with her. Kristina would say she couldn't stay up that late—she had school the next day. Celeste would tell her she could skip school. They watched *Designing Women*.

Kristina loved those nights with her mother.

Just after Celeste and Steve's third date, Kristina met her future father. The three of them went to the chain restaurant Macaroni Grill. Celeste thought it was a casual and fun evening. Twelve-year-old Kristina told her mother she didn't want her with Steve—he was fat.

What Kristina thought mattered. For all of Kristina's life, she had been the one person on whom Celeste could always depend.

Then her favorite daughter had sued her. Celeste felt like she was being punished for her love.

"I went to all their softball games, their basketball games, their volleyball games. I was the team mother. I threw parties for them. You know, I did all that stuff. So they make me sound like I'm this horrible mother that never did anything."

Judge Guy Herman, she believed, had seen the truth.

He had peered through his glasses and said, "I'm going to grant the motion for judgment. I find the evidence to be insufficient at this time for the Court to render a temporary injunction."

Celeste phoned Dr. Michelle Hauser on September 1. She was excited. She'd won in court, she said, and wanted to see Hauser that day. Hauser wrote, "Judge will not put restrictions on her spending." Court was okay, but seeing her daughters lie in court about her upset her. She felt betrayed.

• • •

"You know, I basically taught them how to lie. But I wanted to be their friend. You know, I wanted them to love me, and so I would do all those things for them even if it meant that I had to stay up until three o'clock in the morning doing homework."

When Steve found out she was doing her daughters' homework, he insisted they get a tutor. Everybody could see how much Steve loved the twins and Celeste. He called Celeste "Princess" or "Darling." She called him "Big Daddy." He said she was the one great love of his life.

Sometimes, though, Celeste wondered if she pushed and pushed and pushed Steve just so she could see how much he loved her. But he did the same with her, she thought. The morning after he'd been drunk, loud, and rude in the night, he would turn to her and say, "Darling, was I a bad boy last night?"

In mid-January 2001, Celeste and her new husband Cole boarded a jet for Africa for a belated honeymoon. They stopped in England, visited Kenya, where they were on the first anniversary of Steve's death, moved on to Tanzania, where they were on the first anniversary of his funeral, visited Nairobi and Uganda, and returned via England and Ireland. Along the way, they loaded Celeste's credit cards with gifts for almost everyone they knew, including Boone Almanza.

When they arrived back in Austin, Celeste took out a $60,000 loan against her cars to pay Almanza a portion of his attorneys' fees.

At the same time, Jennifer and Kristina were applying for and obtaining their own loan for $208,250 to pay for real estate they were purchasing on Jim Hogg Avenue in Austin. Picked out by Anita Ashton and her husband Jerry Inglis, it was a not-very-nice triplex in a not-very-nice part of town. They obtained a second deed of trust for $64,250 on the same property.

• • •

On February 16, 2001, the grand jury quietly indicted Tracey Tarlton for the murder of Steven Beard—a death penalty charge with bond set at $500,000. An arrest warrant was issued. Tracey's attorney was notified.

That weekend, she waited around her house, with her dog Wren close by, expecting an arresting officer to show up at her doorstep. No one came.

Her attorney then informed her she would be arrested in court at her next pre-trial hearing. Tracey arrived for the hearing on February 27 and was taken into custody. She had no way to raise the half-million-dollar bail. Tracey Nolyne Tarlton went to jail . . . while Celeste Beard Johnson lived "the good life."

Celeste sold the Frank Lloyd Wright–inspired Toro Canyon Road home and the lake house for well more than $2 million and on March 9, 2001, moved with her new, young, blond husband to Southlake, a ritzy suburb of the Dallas–Fort Worth area.

Despite the fact that the Yeargin Court home was brand new and cost more than $500,000, Celeste and Cole gutted the brick house and, for the entire next year, they remodeled it. They ripped out the kitchen cabinets and bathroom fixtures, and added a pool and landscaping, among a multitude of other things.

One year later, on Saturday morning, March 30, 2002, Westlakers again stepped out their doors, picked up their *Austin American-Statesman*s, and nearly spewed their coffee in shock.

"Wife is indicted in 1999 slaying," the headline read. "Celeste Beard is arrested in the shotgun killing of her husband, an Austin TV executive."

"It has taken two years to unravel this mystery surrounding the death of Steve Beard," District Attorney Ronnie Earle said in a prepared a statement for the media. "This indictment is the result of the dogged persistence by Bill Mange and the sheriff's office. They never gave up."

Tracey Tarlton was set to go on trial the following Monday, April Fool's Day, 2002. But Rosemary Lehmberg, the first assistant district attorney, refused to tell the *Statesman* whether the trial would go forward. "It's set for Monday, and we expect she'll be in court on Monday," the *Statesman* quoted Lehmberg. "I have no other comment."

On April Fool's Day, Tracey Nolyne Tarlton stood before Judge Julie Kocurek. Tracey was an orange-and-green-jail-house-clad Theta standing before a black-robed Pi Phi. Both were former University of Texas co-eds. Both were Camp Longhorn alumni.

Tracey pleaded guilty to murder and was given a 20-year sentence in exchange for her testimony against Celeste Beard Johnson. After being incarcerated for more than a year, Tracey had finally turned state's evidence against her former lover.

". . . I never, ever had a clue that I was going to be arrested for Steve's murder. Never. Even when they came to arrest me in Southlake, I never suspected."

Celeste Beard Johnson believed that it was stupid of her to think that, especially after everything the kids had done to try to get her money two years before. Still, it never occurred to her to keep tabs on the natural-born Beards after their father's death.

Bill Mange had pressed the elevator button for the second floor of the Stokes Building on the frigid Wednesday morning of Steve Beard's funeral, January 26, 2000. Mange was a tall, thin man with a long neck, a face that came to a point at the chin almost like it was giving direction, and graying hair. If he wore black horn-rims rather than gold wire-rims, he could have passed for Dennis the Menace's father.

And while he was a man with one child, a man who told his wife "I love you" at the end of every phone conversation, Bill Mange was far from a cartoon. Some considered him humorless and plodding. But he was a man whose soft voice could become loud and passionate when he was angered.

As the elevator door opened, he was mere hours away from anger. Mange stepped through the crowded corridors to the sound of "Hey, Bill!"

"What?" He glanced into an office where Detective Rick Wines and two prosecutors sat, despite the fact that the time clock hadn't yet struck business hours.

"Sit down. This is gonna be your case!"

A faint look of guilt covered the face of the detective as he moved a small folder from his lap to Mange's lap.

Mange flipped through the folder. "This is the original file. Rick, you know how this works." Mange placed the folder back in Wines' lap. "You give us original documents. We *lose* original documents. So you *keep* your originals and give us copies. That way when we lose *those*, we can make more copies." Irritation rose in Mange's voice. "Right? That's how this works."

Later that morning, Mange sat bored in magistrate court reading the Steve Beard case file. Just before his mag court shift ended, near lunchtime, he received a page—"Ronnie's looking for you. It's about the Beard case."

I haven't had it very long; I can't be in trouble, Mange thought. *There's not enough time for me to have made a mistake.*

But the one thing the prosecutor knew for fact by having read the file was that there wasn't much to work with in order to assure a conviction.

He conveyed that thought when he sat down with Ronnie Earle, a scrawny, gray-haired Democrat with slightly crooked, graying teeth, who'd held his elected position nearly twenty-five years, since 1976. Earle's greatest claim to shame was that he had unsuccessfully attempted to prosecute Kay Bailey Hutchison, whose defense attorney had been Houston powerhouse Dick DeGuerin.

But on January 26, 2000, Earle wanted to know what was going on with the Beard case.

"Quite frankly, I don't know if Celeste was involved in this. I've read an offense report during mag court. We've got Tracey Tarlton, we've got her shotgun, and we've got a shotgun shell, same gauge."

Earle believed this was a real whodunit.

Mange laid out to Earle, First Assistant DA Rosemary Lehmberg, and Prosecutor Claire Dawson just exactly what Rick Wines had done on the case *and* what he'd left undone.

There was blood spatter on the walls of Steve Beard's bedroom, but there were only three or four photos of blood on the bed and on an alarm pad. The bloody bedclothes had been removed before they were photographed, but there were pictures and pictures of a tiny red dot on the floor of the garage, which was never tested for blood. All other photos were of the kitchen, the study, porcelain figurines throughout the house, items that had nothing to do with the crime scene. There wasn't a single diagram of the home.

The lack of crime-scene documentation eventually sent Mange into a profanity-laced rage. "When you have a body, or something with a lot of blood in it, start there. It might be important in a murder investigation . . ." he ranted. "I sound angry, because I am, Goddamnit! That's not how you do it!" The crime-scene work was a disaster, he believed. It struck Mange, as kinda funny—Steve Beard's intestines were literally falling out of his gut, and a deputy sheriff didn't declare the bedroom a crime scene until someone accidentally discovered the shotgun shell.

His guts are all over the bed. What'd you think happened? He scratched himself wrong?

Mange wondered why the officers didn't immediately worry whether the shooter was still in the house. And once they got Steve Beard out of the bedroom, they shouldn't have removed the bloody bed linens. "There was nothing, zip, zero, nada from TCSO! What kind of crime-scene documentation is this?"

Wines also didn't talk to Steve Beard. In fact, Mange felt Celeste Beard and her attorneys at the "red brick house"—the building across the street from the courthouse that was home to her law firm Minton, Burton, Foster & Collins—had buffaloed Wines. When the Beard family "lawyered up" the very same day Steve Beard had been shot, that should have been a red flag flying in the face of the veteran detective, Mange thought. The detective should have immediately gotten a grand jury subpoena and served it on the victim, but he hadn't. There were just too many should've that weren't.

Mange understood Ronnie Earle to say, "This Rick Wines guy, his head's gonna be on a pike."

8

"Do you know anybody I can hire to help me return some clothes?" Celeste said as she visited with Ray McEachern at Austin Country Club, where the family and a few friends gathered after Steve's funeral.

"How many clothes are you talking about?" Ray asked.

"The last time I took back one set it was over twelve thousand dollars. I probably have that much or more to return."

"Good God! You need a moving van!"

Celeste moved on; Ray glanced at Steve's real kids. "Somebody's gonna take a swing at Celeste before it's all over."

Around four that afternoon, Steven Beard III and his younger sister Becky walked into Bill Mange's office. They were sad, angry, and convinced that their stepmother was making a public display of faked grief. With utter certainty, they said that Celeste Beard had murdered their father.

Bill Mange wanted and needed proof.

Becky spilled what she knew.

In 1993, when the summer heat made I-35 sizzle like hot tar, Becky had frequently driven to Austin to visit her dying mother. On one of those trips, Steve took Becky to dinner at Austin Country Club and introduced her to maître d' Fer-

nando Von Hapsburg. Fernando stood next to table 99, his
back to the windows overlooking the Saint Augustine grass,
as he promised to help Steve find a housekeeper—a mature
woman, which Becky interpreted as elderly, probably His-
panic, and live-in.

The following October, Elise died. "Then, next thing I
knew, shortly before Christmas, Celeste moved in as the
housekeeper." Becky found that out when her dad phoned
her and said he'd helped the new housekeeper move in.

"Where's she living?" Becky quizzed.

"Up in the upstairs bedroom on the left, not your room."

"And how old is she?"

"Thirty."

A thirty-year-old housekeeper?

Many, many months later, when Becky made her usual Sunday phone call to her father, a little girl's voice streamed
over the phone line.

"Who are you?" Becky asked.

"I'm Kristina."

"Kristina who?"

After a sentence or two more, Celeste grabbed the phone
and yelled, "What are you doing talking to my daughter that
way!"

Becky hung up.

Celeste called back.

The one time Becky had met Celeste in person, Celeste
hadn't mentioned anything about kids. There were just too
many surprises with this woman.

Two months before Celeste and Steve wed, Steve called
Becky and told her about the impending nuptials.

"Why do you need to marry her?" Becky's voice was
deep from decades of cigarettes and cheap vodka.

"She does a lot of things for me. She takes care of me
good . . . and she's got cancer."

"What do you mean she's got cancer?"

"Well, she's had cancer in the past. They think it's been
cured."

"What kind of cancer?"

Her father didn't know. But Celeste had a lot of medical problems, he explained. He could help her financially with them. He hadn't been able to help Elise with her cancer because it was too late, so if he could help Celeste, he wanted to do that.

The night before the wedding, Becky, her boyfriend, Celeste, Steve, Steven III, his wife, Nancy . . . and Kristina gathered at Austin Country Club for dinner. It was the first time any of the natural-born Beards had met Kristina in person. She was a cute, sweet little kid who was good at softball.

But Celeste—the first thing Becky noticed, though she kept her rage held in—had Becky's mother's diamond watch wrapped around her wrist.

The next day, Celeste wore an off-white beaded suit that Steve had picked out for her as she stood next to him and exchanged their vows under an archway. Becky cried tears of fear throughout the ceremony. After a lamb chop wedding dinner, Becky walked out the Country Club doors.

"His daughter Becky wouldn't even speak to me. Not a word the entire time. We got married, and, uh, had, a luncheon at the Club. It was real nice. But his son, uh, Paul didn't come. And his son Steven came. There was just about forty people there."

When the twins were 15, Steve mentioned to Becky the possibility of adopting them. After talking to his attorney David Kuperman, though, Steve changed his mind. Jennifer and Kristina were so close to 18, when they'd be legal adults. Why do it? Kuperman had persuaded.

The next thing Becky knew, two years had gone by, the twins were 17, and her dad had adopted the girls.

The Wednesday after Steve was shot, Becky sped down I-35, past Hillsboro, Waco, Temple, and Belton, her thoughts whirling chaotically in her mind.

She remembered the phone call she'd made to her dad just a few months before—May, she believed. It was her usual Sunday morning call. But that particular day, every time she asked him a question, he just mumbled something and that something had nothing to do with what they were discussing.

"Dad, are you okay?"

"Yeah, yeah. I'm fine."

She immediately dialed Steven III. "Something's wrong with Dad. You need to call him and talk to him and see what you think."

Steven dismissed her worry with a *there's nothing wrong, he was probably asleep and you just woke him up.*

When Becky phoned her dad seven days later, he didn't even remember talking to her the Sunday before.

On top of that, she believed the trip to Europe was to be the last chance to work things out, or her dad was going to file for divorce from Celeste.

Already, Becky had spoken a few times and exchanged emails with Detective Rick Wines, who had quizzed her about her dad and Celeste, even asked her to be probing when she talked to Celeste, and suggested that Becky tape her conversations with the new wife . . . just in case.

So once Becky got to the hospital, she asked Celeste who Tracey Tarlton was.

Celeste answered that she was a friend who was crazy.

What did Celeste promise her? Becky wondered.

When Steve was finally moved out of ICU, Celeste called Becky. She thought it'd be fun to have a 75th birthday dinner for Steve in his hospital room, she said. Paul and Kim were coming. Steven III was busy, though, and couldn't make it. She would order Thanksgiving dinner from ACC and bring in tables and chairs.

Becky agreed—after all, her mother and father had always ordered Thanksgiving dinner from ACC.

About two days before the holiday, Becky accidentally let it slip to Celeste that Steven was coming after all.

That same night, her dad phoned her. "Celeste is just too

stressed out and she just doesn't think she can handle all the company," he rasped. "So I think we'll just postpone it and do something later."

"Dad, Paul and Steven already have plane reservations," Becky begged.

"She's just too stressed out. She doesn't think she can handle it at this time."

"Well," Becky sighed, "you know, it's up to you. I mean, it's your birthday, and we would all really like to be there for your seventy-fifth birthday. And we've all planned it." She'd already sent the girls money to buy some koi fish that they were all going in on. "Everybody was really looking forward to it." But no matter how long and hard Becky talked, her father wouldn't change his mind—Celeste just couldn't handle the stress.

"I remember that, um, I had planned for—I, uh, before Steve was shot, I had planned a seventy-fifth birthday party for him at the Country Club. And, um, I had arranged rooms for his kids . . . And so, they still had all those plans and [were] gonna come out for Thanksgiving, because Steve's birthday's around Thanksgiving, while Steve was in the hospital and visit him.

"But his kids were so nasty to me and cussing me out and everything, that Steve called each one of them and told them to stay home, that he did not want to see them. And, uh, that's why I bought Kaci, the little cocker spaniel that Kristina stole—um, that was Steve's birthday present. And then there's a picture of him kissing her.

"And Kristina, of course, lied and lied and lied and lied and said that was her dog, [that] it wasn't Steve's birthday present, in the 2000 hearing."

The week before Christmas, Becky once again journeyed to Austin to see her father, deliver presents, and bring him the sugarcoated pecans he'd specifically requested.

Just like a little kid wanting to show his mother how high he could jump, Steve showed off for Becky, proud of what all he could do and how well he could get around.

As they shared lunch together in his room, Becky yearned to ease him into talking about Celeste and whether she was involved.

But her dad bragged about how wonderful Celeste was, how well she was taking care of him, and how she was working so hard remodeling the house so that it would be ready for his return home.

". . . I was doing all those repairs to the house. I thought, you know, Steve was gonna be pleased. And I did—you know, I spent like $26,000 for the bronze handrails. And I did go overboard. I mean, I think I spent like, I don't know, I think they said over $500,000. But I was looking at it as I'm doing all this stuff for Steve because I wanted the house to be different for him when he came home, because I didn't want him to be traumatized.

"I redid the bedroom colors and everything. I changed— well, it was more, it was more yellows and tans and greens, and I changed it—well, like the wallpaper in the bathroom, I made it gold and burgundy. And, um, I just had a new duvet made and, oh, all kinds of stuff."

This makes me sick, Becky thought. She knew, though, that her dad's health was the most important thing, and she was worried about his mental state. Prodding him about Celeste would just have to wait until their next visit.

Just after Christmas, Celeste informed Becky that her dad's medical power of attorney had been changed. It was no longer joint with Celeste and Becky. Celeste had sole authority.

Becky was pissed, but she kept her mouth sealed shut.

The Sunday night before Steve was finally to return to Toro Canyon, Becky called her father. "I'm worried about you going home," she said. "I just don't think you're ready."

The doctors had removed a tube from his heart, he was awake during the whole procedure, and it was pretty neat, Steve told her. He was excited about going home.

"Okay, you're going home. I'll give you a couple of

days, you know, to give you time to get settled in, and I'll call you then. I love you, and I'll talk to you in a few days."

Becky did try to call him at the Toro Canyon home a couple of days later. But there was no answer. She left a message. And she left more messages as she phoned continually for three days. She was beginning to panic. She called and left one more message—"I want to talk to my dad now! I don't want to wait any longer. If I don't talk to him, I'm going to show up there on Saturday and find him!"

She walked into her home at 4:30 P.M. on Friday and noticed a message on her answering machine. She hit PLAY.

Celeste's hateful voice shouted from the speaker, "Your father's back in the hospital! I wasn't going to call and tell any of you that, but if you're insisting on coming down here, I just want you to know that your father is back in the hospital and he's not doing well. He's at Brackenridge."

By 5 P.M., Becky was telling her dad, "She didn't even bother to call and let anybody know you're back in the hospital. What's wrong with you?"

He'd had some chest pains, the doctors didn't know what was wrong with him except that he had an infection, they were still running tests, but he was on potent antibiotics.

A doctor walked into Steve's room.

"Well, I'll let you go. I'll talk to you tomorrow," Becky promised, "to see if they know anything more."

"I love you, Becky," her dad said. "I love you." His voice seemed frantic. "I'll talk to you. I love you, Becky. I love you. I love you."

Saturday, Becky was rolling an orange cart down the concrete aisles of Home Depot when her cell phone rang. It was Celeste—Steve was getting worse, they didn't expect him to live.

Becky rushed out the Home Depot doors, leaving her cart in the aisle. By the time she got home, her father was dead.

. . .

If Detective Wines had been able to interview their dad, Steven and Becky said to Bill Mange, all he could have told him was that there was a loud boom, a bright flash, and he may have seen a figure at the end of the bed.

Mange reached for his code of criminal procedure and flipped to the accomplice witness rule. "We've gotta do more than say we think she did it. We've really got to tie her to it."

"We can't give you what you need."

Becky didn't give a hoot about the money. "Do whatever you've got to do to get the right thing done."

But when they left the DA's office four hours later, at 8 P.M., Bill Mange didn't know whether Celeste Beard was guilty or innocent; he just wanted to do justice. His mind was open; his body was exhausted.

Mange started bugging Rick Wines—get copies of the photos, get copies of the statements. He studied verbal statements from Kristina and Jennifer Beard and their boyfriends, Justin Grimm and Christopher Doose. Mange reached over, picked up the phone, and called Christopher. *Don't hit me over the forehead with a two-by-four. Maybe I ought to ask the kid what he knows.* Christopher had been the first one to pull an officer aside and say that Celeste might be involved.

By February 22, 2000, at Rosemary Lehmberg's suggestion, Mange also contacted Tracey's attorney, Keith Hampton, a good-looking, bespectacled, dark-haired preppie boy.

"Look," Mange understood Hampton to say, "obviously, shooting somebody—if that's what my client did—is very bad. But in the grand scheme of things, that looks white compared to the blackness of pure evil that was done by others."

Tracey Tarlton knew something. But Hampton wanted transactional immunity for his client. Neither Bill Mange nor Ronnie Earl would agree to that. *Not even in a parallel universe.*

After more than two months of pestering Christopher Doose with once-a-week phone calls, Mange finally got a response the first week in April 2000. Christopher's attorney called the prosecutor, and after a game of telephone tag, they arranged a meeting.

Friday, April 7, 2000, at 4 P.M., Mange stepped out of his office, looked up, and was astonished. There was a gallery of kids and attorneys—not just Christopher Doose and his attorney, but Justin Grimm and his attorney, and Jennifer and Kristina Beard and their attorney.

This is a little more than what the average bear has. Mange blew a silent whiff of air through his lips. Christopher was the only kid he'd planned on meeting that day. He led Chris and his attorney into his office.

Mange pulled his computer keyboard into his lap and looked over at the potential witness.

Christopher was a little on the short side for his age, blondish hair, nice build, a bit acne-faced, perhaps an oomph effeminate and a bit stiff in his body movements. Formal, perhaps. Some might consider it pompous . . . if they didn't know the boy well.

But despite his rigidness, Christopher let loose with an account of how Celeste had manipulated Steve Beard. He described cards and letters he'd seen between Tracey and Celeste that expressed a relationship between two women who were more than just friends. "It's two women who are sexual partners, lovers." He talked about photos of the two at a party.

Mange reached under Christopher's chair, pulled out a box of evidence that had been seized from Tracey's home, thumbed through it, and pulled out a picture. "You talking about this photo?"

"Holy cow!"

Mange held a picture of Celeste sitting in Tracey's lap.

"Yeah, this is the party." Celeste had thrown it at the lake house for Tracey and her BookPeople employees. They called it the "Fashion Victim" party.

Mange pulled out greeting cards written between the two women.

There were more cards than that, Christopher said. Celeste had had him clean out a storage closet full of paperwork and personal cards. He'd found similar ones there.

Why bother to trash all that stuff if you're not involved?
Mange thought.

One and a half hours later, the prosecutor walked out of
his office to face the rest of the kids. *It's like trying to get a
drink of water out of a fire hose. It's not possible.*

"I don't trust you," Kristina announced.

"Where are you living now?" he asked.

The twins refused to tell him.

"How can I get in touch with you?"

"You're a lawyer. We don't trust you." Their lives, and
especially the past year, had taught them not to trust anyone.

"Okay. Well, then don't tell me. Tell someone else who
you do trust. Then if I do need to get in touch with you, I'll
contact that person."

They agreed.

Justin Grimm and his attorney followed Mange into his office at 5:30 p.m.

Normally with Celeste, your schedule was not yours, it
was Celeste's, Justin explained. In fact, Celeste showed up
where she damn well pleased when she damn well wanted.
But on the evening Steve was shot, and that evening alone,
it was imperative that Celeste be back at the Toro Canyon
house by midnight. And Justin went on and on.

He shows a lot of curiosity regarding Celeste. Mange rapidly typed on his keyboard. *He expresses his suspicions of
his girlfriend's mother with an amazingly detailed memory.*

Still, there was no real obvious evidence on which the
prosecutor could nail a guilty verdict. Mange kept typing.

Justin explained that Celeste had had Tracey use a shotgun because Celeste had read *The Poor Man's James Bond*,
which, according to Justin, said that if you're going to murder someone, use a shotgun, because ballistics can't be
traced on a shotgun shell.

"That's not even true," Mange said.

"What?"

"That's not even true. You can too use the shell."

"Huh?"

Finally, a grave-faced and serious Justin Grimm played a tape recording of Celeste screaming and raging over the phone at Kristina, before turning confessional.

"I hired somebody to kill Tracey."

Mange's skin went prickly. "Hired." He focused on the past tense. "This is all I can do," he said, putting down his keyboard. He was beat. Justin Grimm didn't simply have a staggering amount of detail; he had an excruciating amount of detail.

At 8:30 P.M. on that Friday, April 7, 2000, Bill Mange shook the hands of Justin Grimm and his attorney, and they all finally went home.

Mange went home to think, ponder, and worry. The kids were afraid of someone who was scary and abusive. Christopher Doose's opinions of Celeste had come to light with the audiotape Justin had played. Phrases from the tape reeled through the prosecutor's mind. *"Come pick me up!" "You think it was fair when my dad was sticking his dick up my ass?"*

This is unbelievable. It's awful, but it obviously happened.
"I hired someone to kill Tracey."

Either Tracey Tarlton knew something and Celeste had to have her killed, or Celeste wanted Tarlton dead because she had killed Celeste's beloved. Mange was running out of alternative explanations. *This is awkward.*

He picked up the phone and called Rosemary Lehmberg at home.

Lehmberg told Mange to call Rick Wines.

Immediately, Mange phoned Wines and told him to talk to Tracey's attorney, Keith Hampton. "Tell him to tell his client to be pretty damned careful, but don't tell him what we know or how we know it."

Wines reached Hampton the next day. It was a cryptic conversation, but Hampton understood.

9

What Keith Hampton had understood in April 2000, Tracey Tarlton didn't realize until she read in the newspaper that Celeste had gotten married. Suddenly she saw her world differently.

Tarlton's lawyers, Keith Hampton and Stuart Kinard, the latter a soft-spoken man with a distinguished snow-white beard, repeatedly told the prosecutor that their client could give him Celeste Beard.

"I don't care," Mange responded each time.

But the defense attorneys kept dangling that in front of Mange, who combed through the photographs, cancelled checks, and records the kids gave him, and spent time on the phone with the twins, his headset on, his computer keyboard in his lap.

By Christmas, Mange admitted to colleagues that the Beard teens and their friends were handing him his case, but that didn't stop him from grousing about how they were pestering him with constant calls and visits. Their Christmas gifts to him didn't ease his complaints.

Still, he delved deeper into the case, and more and more often he found himself saying, "Huh? That's kinda weird. I can see how it's consistent with her being guilty, but it could also be consistent with other things."

He *could* find possible other explanations.

Finally, he made of list of eighteen to twenty "coincidences." *This is a lot of coincidences, Batman.* But Mange believed he would never have probable cause against Celeste Beard for the murder of Steve Beard unless Tracey Tarlton flipped on her lover. And the way to do that, Mange knew, was to put a case together against Tarlton and try her.

• • •

February 15, 2001, an alleged drug dealer shot and killed Travis County Sheriff's Deputy Keith Ruiz. The next day, Bill Mange got his indictment against Tracey Tarlton. But the high-profile, high-pressure deputy sheriff's case had been assigned to Mange. It would take up all of his 2001 thoughts, time, and energy.

By early 2002, Tracey Tarlton's lawyers were saying more and more often, "She can give you Celeste, you know."

"Yeah, yeah, I know that," Mange answered. "I don't care. We're fixing to go to trial. Either rack it up or don't."

While Mange knew Tracey Tarlton was the shooter, Mange also knew Tracey had told Detective Wines, at the very end of her first statement, that Celeste had a key to her house. It was a back-door escape for Tracey—someone else could have used her gun.

Bill Mange had to be prepared for anything.

Defense attorney Keith Hampton focused his astonished eyes on boxes and boxes and binder after binder of research. One binder had Celeste's psychiatric records from Timberlawn. Another binder had Tracey's.

Celeste and Tracey were on suicide watch at Timberlawn, Mange recounted to the defense attorney, so every fifteen minutes, a nurse walked into their room to check on them. About 8:15 at night a nurse walked in and saw Celeste with her shirt off and Tracey's hands on Celeste's back giving her a back rub. The nurse stopped the action and rebuked the pair for their behavior.

"Oh, I'm sorry," Tracey said. "I didn't know."

Half an hour later, the same thing happened with a different nurse, and Tracey responded the exact same way as before, Mange said.

"Did you have that memorized?" Hampton remarked, taken aback again.

Mange swiftly pulled out the answer anytime Hampton asked him a question. Hampton realized that Bill Mange truly intended to try his client.

And Tracey Tarlton realized it wasn't fair that she was going to do that much time—life—for someone else's crime.

Dawn McLean was a thin-lipped investigator with shaggy,
frosted blonde hair and legs that jittered non-stop when she
was nervous. Brown eyes shined behind wire-rimmed
glasses. Small gold hoop earrings looped through her ears.
A silver-toned watch wrapped around her wrist. Rings
adorned the fingers of tiny hands. Dawn McLean, who often wore khaki slacks, packed a pistol on her right hip.

Her office was crammed with a small refrigerator full of
Diet 7-Up, a computer, and a desk with one end pushed
against an interior wall, its top covered with tape recorders,
pens, and CDs—Marc Anthony and Carole King. A "things
to complete" list was outlined neatly on a white board near
the room's only window, while the Law Enforcement Code
of Ethics hung on a wall.

In a movie, she'd be the proverbial tough cop with the
heart of gold.

Bill Mange asked the white-collar crime investigator of
the DA's office to help him with Tracey Tarlton. So in mid-
March, Dawn drove the twenty to thirty minutes from
downtown to Del Valle and the Travis County Correctional
Complex.

Her brown hair short, big glasses over her eyes, Tracey
stood with her shoulders squeezed in and bunched toward
her chin like a linebacker set for the hike. Despite body language that could be intimidating sometimes, Tracey Tarlton
appeared withdrawn and scared as she climbed into the
back seat of the unmarked vehicle. She acted as though she
didn't trust anyone and didn't want to talk about anything,
as she sat seat-belted in behind tinted windows. Tracey was
riding to her first meeting with prosecutor Bill Mange as
her attorneys tried to work out a plea bargain.

After spending hours with the investigator with the sweet,
comforting smile, the unlikely two started talking—about
dogs, life, police work, Tracey's previous work, the famous
writers she'd met, landscaping.

Tracey began to relax. "Do you know what I did?"

"No," Dawn answered.

"You aren't going to like what I did." Her voice was deep and hesitant, as if she thought long about each word before she spoke. But at the same time it reflected a remorseful earnestness.

"People make mistakes," Dawn said. "Whatever you've done, you've got to live with it."

"I can't believe what I did." Tracey was worried about what others would think of her.

Her attorneys milled in.

Over weeks, Bill Mange and Keith Hampton ground out the terms of Tracey's plea agreement. As final negotiations began closing, Hampton said, "Nothing personal between you and me, but my client really doesn't like you. Is there somebody else who can do the debriefing?"

"Hell, no."

Still, the plea agreement was hashed out—Tracey had to pass a Department of Public Safety polygraph test, debrief the prosecution as many times and as long as the State wanted, give truthful testimony to the grand jury, plead guilty to murder, give truthful testimony at Celeste Beard Johnson's trial, and not be sentenced until Beard Johnson's case had been disposed.

Stuart Kinard flanked Tarlton's left, while her third lawyer, Michael Maguire, a tall, dapper-dressing Irishman with trendy eyeglasses, flanked her right.

As always, Mange sat with his keyboard in his lap, ready for his first debriefing session with Tracey Tarlton. "Start at the beginning, and tell me what happened."

Tracey was so smart and articulate that there was no need for Mange to ask any questions. By the end of their interview, he realized that Celeste Beard Johnson had put meticulous thought into the murder plan. He knew he had enough against the widow Beard.

After debriefing Tracey for a second time, Mange understood that she hadn't shot Steve Beard for money. She'd done it for love—she thought she was saving Celeste from suicide.

Tuesday, March 26, 2002, Dawn McLean again picked up Tracey Tarlton in Del Valle and drove her north on I-35 to the Austin district office of the Texas Department of Public Safety. Tracey was nervous, but ready to get the polygraph test behind her.

Dawn walked her into a break room, got her a Coke, and stepped away so that Tracey could talk in private with her attorneys.

Tracey was introduced to Walt Goodson, the man who would be administering her polygraph test, and she and Dawn sat with Goodson in a tiny side room containing a desk and a chair.

Watching through a one-way mirror were Mange, Rick Wines, and Joe Martinez, an investigator from the DA's office.

About an hour later, Goodson rose out of his chair and walked into the adjoining room where everyone watched. "I haven't scored it yet, but I think she's telling the truth." He then assessed the test; and his gut had been correct.

Tracey Tarlton turned to Dawn McLean and said, "See, I told you I was telling the truth."

"I never doubted it," Dawn replied.

The next day, with the temperature hovering in the 70s, Dawn picked up the witness from Del Valle. Tracey was nervous. But Tracey's mind always worked over time mulling the ins and outs from every conceivable direction and searching for any possible angle that wasn't readily imaginable. After all, it still wasn't conceivable to her that she'd done the horrible deed—shooting a human being. She walked into the grand jury alone. Two hours later, she walked out knowing all through her soul that she'd done a wrong she would never forget and for which she could certainly never forgive herself.

. . .

On Maundy Thursday, March 28, 2002, Celeste and her husband, Cole, stood in the front yard of their half-million-dollar Southlake home and smoked cigarettes in the fresh spring air.

They'd finally finished remodeling their now—one-year-old, two-story brick home. As they smoked, Celeste glanced down the cul-de-sac. There were only about nine houses she counted . . . and a cop car at the end of the block. She didn't think anything of it. Celeste had other things on her mind. She needed to pick up her two cocker spaniels from the groomer's.

Cole said he'd go with Celeste to pick up the dogs.

"No. I'll go by myself. That's all right."

She got in the car, pulled out onto the street; suddenly there was a different cop in her rearview mirror. She kept driving, and another police car pulled behind her. She turned the corner, and there were two more cops. She drove about another hundred yards when all the cops flipped on their emergency lights and surrounded her.

What the hell's going on? She watched the cops walk up to her vehicle.

"Get out of your car!"

"Why?"

"You're under arrest."

"For what!"

"Capital murder."

"You're kidding." Then it dawned on her why the cop had been sitting at the end of their cul-de-sac. She looked at the cops. "Why didn't you just knock on the door?"

They gave her a look like she was crazy, she thought. "I need to go get my dogs!"

"You aren't going anywhere." They grabbed her purse.

"And then at the station, they finally let me call my husband and tell him to go get the poor dogs. That's all I cared about. I mean, everybody makes a big deal about Tracey's love [for her dog], but that's all I care about is my dogs. I feel like I gave birth to them."

. . .

Rick Wines notified Mange. "Do you want me to have transportation go up and get her?"

She's not the Goddamn Queen of England. She's a criminal. "No. Send the bus up."

Happy and tired, Mange went home to a young daughter who asked him what he'd done that day.

"I've been doing the right thing," he said.

10

Celeste Beard Johnson pulled on faded green pants and a faded orange tunic, marking her a maximum-security inmate at the Travis County Correctional Complex in Del Valle. Her new home was a dorm-like setting of narrow steel beds bolted to the walls, a dayroom with tables and stools bolted to the floor, and an open toilet.

It was in the same neighborhood as Austin-Bergstrom International Airport, an area once filled with lots selling mobile homes, fleabag motels, and low-end strip joints. But it was also the neighborhood that had once been her gateway to China, Australia, and Europe. At ABIA she'd freely walked wide corridors filled with music and vista windows of "the world."

At TCCC, a khaki-clad guard shuttled her along a narrow concrete path bordered by cream-colored cinderblock walls with accents of dark gray-blue lines marking her path. The yells of inmates, the screech of security radios, and buzzing and clanging doors echoed against the hardness. The antiseptic scent of ammonia permeated the air like cheap perfume.

The day after Easter, Celeste was considered friendly, cooperative, and stable at her intake health screening. The completed initial health/classification form stated that the last grade Celeste completed was the twelfth. It asked, among other questions, "Have you ever received MHMR services or other mental health services?" and "Have you ever attempted suicide or had thoughts about hurting yourself?" To both questions, "No" was marked.

At that point, Celeste was assigned to Building 3's "GP, open psych"—general population, with psychological problems, but stable. On weekdays, she had to have her bed made by 8 A.M. with no crawling under her loosely woven white blanket until 5 P.M. On weekends, she didn't have to have her bed made until 10 A.M.

Celeste quickly mingled with the other inmates and made friends, including Katina Lofton, considered a tough troublemaker. And Celeste immediately set up a regime of filling out slips of paper spelling out her requests and complaints.

"I need to be able to start taking my medications, but I need to see a doctor first," she wrote on April 4. "I need to start taking my medication please," she penned on April 5. April 6, she marked through the word *nurse* on the medical request form which had a box stating that the inmate needed to see a nurse and wrote in *doctor*. "I think I have a U.T.I. [urinary tract infection]. I also need to start taking my medications. I have been off my medication for almost two weeks."

"I have dropped several slips," she wrote on April 8, again marking through the word *nurse* and replacing it with *doctor*. "I am in terrible pain, in my back, my stomach, and when I use the bathroom it burns & hurts so bad. I can't take it anymore, plus I've been feverish, chills & sweats at night."

Celeste continued scribbling medical slips at 7 A.M., on April 16. "This is my 5th request to see the Dr. I need to see the doctor—not the nurse!" She underlined *doctor* three times. "I have medical insurance that can pay for my visit. I am having night sweats, irritability—because I need my meds. I do not want to see the nurse!"

Celeste couldn't seem to adjust to the fact that jail life wasn't run on her schedule.

At 10:30 in the morning of April 18, she scribbled, "My

nerves are bad and the shampoo & conditioner is causing my scalp to break out & my hair is falling out. Sores are coming up on my head."

She complained to other inmates that her hair was frizzy because of the jail's bad shampoo and conditioner, and she bragged that before she was arrested she used to spend $50–$60 on those products.

At 7 P.M., on April 21, she again wrote, "I have medical insurance. Why am I being ignored?" Her writing shouted, "*I would like to see the Doctor!!!" and underneath that, she emphasized, "!!! No one else!!!"

On April 22, 2002, Cole Johnson phoned the jail trying to urge the authorities to get Celeste her meds. That same day, he mailed his wife a letter saying he was trying to raise her bail. "Your kiss is missed," he wrote.

Celeste was referred again to the jail doctor for sweats and irritability, hot flashes, and a broken-out face. She was led down the cinderblock corridors, half moon–like mirrors eyeing her at every hallway intersection. She passed sergeants sharing a cramped office, then another small office stuffed with a copying machine and refrigerator. Finally, she was led outside, down the concrete sidewalks and to the medical facility where the doctor ordered an extra mattress and a lower bunk due to Celeste's osteoporosis.

On April 25, Registered Nurse Story wrote in Celeste's record that she had spoken with the inmate's husband. "He stated to me that she was not getting any Premarin according to her . . ." So Story checked with the jail's pharmacy. Celeste's Premarin had been sent out on Monday evening, April 22.

At 7:30 A.M., April 26, Celeste continued slip-dropping. "I need to see the psychiatrist. I am very depressed. I am also have [sic] extreme panic attacks. I can't sleep at night. I am NOT suicidal."

Suicidal inmates were placed in a padded cell, no sink, no toilet, only a trench for relieving oneself, and a trustee clad in a pale blue jail uniform posted outside the door twenty-four hours a day, with a guard checking every fifteen minutes.

Celeste did not want to be considered suicidal.

At 10:44 A.M., counselor Merry Fiske jotted notes regarding her meeting with inmate Johnson, housed in Unit 3, Post E, Cell 5B. Dr. Michelle Hauser had said Celeste was bipolar, Fiske wrote.

Celeste said her mother was bipolar too and had been hospitalized several times. "She does crazy things like strip naked and bang on people's doors not knowing where she is. I don't do things like that," the inmate said.

On May 1, 2002, approximately six weeks before Celeste Beard Johnson's first bail hearing, Rip Collins wrote Dr. Hauser a letter. "Ms. Johnson is presently incarcerated in Travis County jail and may be there for an extended period.

"She has informed me and I have observed that she is in need again of her anti-depressant medication. Since you were her most recent counselor that treated her and prescribed for her it is hoped that you could provide a letter or prescription that would assist her in obtaining anti-depressant medication at the jail."

Hauser replied the very next day. "Celeste Beard Johnson was last seen in this office on 12/01/99. She is not currently an active patient and her case file has been closed."

Three days later, B.J. Gray of Manor, Texas, tried to cheer up the inmate she referred to as her "best friend." Gray constantly jotted notes and typed long, neat letters assuring her incarcerated friend that everything would be okay. "They will let you out and clear this whole thing up," she wrote on May 4. "They have nothing against you other than just knowing that crazy woman."

Gray continued, "And it's not your fault you have two insane children that think . . . 'if Mom's out of the way they will inherit everything.' This has been their plan since day one. They thought they could drive you crazy . . . that in an insane hospital or if you committed suicide, they would get everything . . . when that didn't work . . . Now they are trying to imply your connection to this, to have you locked up forever . . . So they will get everything. They just see the $$ signs.

"I'm sorry . . . But they are just 2 MONEY HUNGRY
CONIVING BRATS. I'm sorry I said that about your daughters . . . I love you and I'd do anything in the world for you.
You are one of the sweetest persons I know. How did your
children turn out to be so cold hearted? It has to be their father's genes."

On May 30, 2002, Celeste rocked in her seat, never stopped
moving, was "very anxious," and complained of her inability to sleep. She was provided 50 mg of trazodone. Her bail
hearing was two weeks away.

11

Celeste Beard Johnson was the queen of Building 3 at the
Travis County Correctional Complex. She had her meals
alone, recreation alone. She had other inmates watching out
for her because, officers believed, she padded her commissary—purchasing extra items such as candy bars to use as
payoffs. When Celeste maneuvered down the hallways and
sidewalks to get her medicine, everyone knew who she was.

Paul Knight of the Travis County Sheriff's Office was
walking through Building 3 when he spotted Tracey Tarlton. He knew she had a reputation in the jail for being a
well-respected bull who had surrounded herself with some
hardcore inmates. He walked over to her. "Do you remember me?"

Of course she did. He was one of the cops who had
knocked at her door the first day they suspected her. The
killer and cop exchanged pleasantries.

"I bet we really surprised you when we showed up at
your house the very next day," Knight teased.

"That fucking bitch was supposed to pick up that shotgun shell," Tracey growled.

• • •

May 31, 2002, Bill Mange gave Ronnie Earle notice that he was leaving the district attorney's office, effective July 31, 2002.

Since Judge Julie Kocurek had been sworn in as the very first judge of the brand new 390th District Court in Travis County, Texas, on Friday, October 1, 1999, the day before Steve Beard was shot, she'd been assigned the same two high-profile, possible career-killer cases as Bill Mange.

About the same age as Celeste, and blonde like Celeste, Judge Julie, as many people called her, looked like she belonged at sorority rush rather than in criminal court, her dark robe hiding her figure.

Two weeks after Bill Mange submitted his resignation, he sat at the State's table in Judge Kocurek's courtroom and glanced over at what he referred to as "Team Celeste"—Celeste's staff of attorneys including Charles Burton, Rip Collins, Sam Bassett, Boone Almanza and more. Her attorneys swarmed like rich fire ants.

Is this how you create the impression you're poor? Mange thought. *It's not working. It's not working at all. It stinks!*

Celeste Beard Johnson thought it stank that she'd been wearing nothing but jailhouse scrubs every day for two and a half long months. The baggy, faded orange pants and shapeless green tops weren't becoming to her pallor. She craved a facial, manicure, and pedicure, and was in bad need of a root job on her blonde hair. Celeste desperately wanted out of TCCC, also known as Travis County Country Club.

Finally, on Friday, June 14, 2002, she wore her own comfortable clothes as she was escorted into the sterile courtroom. Under the fluorescent lights, the unscathed blond wood of the judge's bench barely shined. Black office chairs with turquoise-green backs and seats neatly lined two rows in the jury box. *Modern bland* described the décor.

"We're here for this application of writ of habeas corpus that has been filed by the defense," Kocurek said. "Let the record reflect Ms. Beard has been charged in Count 1 with the offense of capital murder; Count 2, murder; and Count 3, intentional injury to an elderly individual."

The air-conditioning blew hard. Just outside the courtroom, there were floor-to-ceiling windows that had picture-perfect tourist views of Lake Austin and the multimillion-dollar arts centers under renovation and construction. The centers were to be the pride of the capital city. But fundraising was at a standstill. High-tech finances were no longer booming.

Neither were Celeste Beard Johnson's. She'd reportedly paid Charles Burton $75,000 after Steve was shot, with a promise of $200,000 more if there were problems. There were problems.

Burton rose. A tall, bearded man with rugged skin and dark heavy bags drooping under his eyes, he had a voice deep and rough like a gravel road, in which he stated they were "here requesting reasonable bail. We represent a lady who's been a long-time resident of this community, about nine years, with community ties, and there's no reason to—that we're aware of, the State may differ with us—to show that she would either flee the jurisdiction or be a danger or a threat to the community if she were released on bail . . ."

Burton didn't mention that his client had been arrested in Southlake, nearly four hours north of Austin, where she'd been a resident for the past year.

Mange didn't mention it either. He argued that Beard Johnson was a flight risk *and* a danger to herself.

"Would you please call your first witness, Mr. Burton?" Kocurek instructed.

Cole Johnson stepped into the witness box to the right of Kocurek. He'd already had a bit of a hard day. When he'd gotten dressed for court, he'd pulled out an Armani suit and cufflinks for his shirt, and slipped on his big diamond wedding band. Since marrying Celeste, he'd taken to wearing $35 socks.

"Cole, you can't go down there like that," Marilou Gibbs said in a quivering voice thick with a Southern accent. Marilou was an old country woman with teeth that looked like she'd come straight out of the bayou.

She was also a kind-hearted Catholic who draped a cross over her hefty bosom and embraced the role of Celeste's loyal surrogate mother. "For God's sakes, we're going down there asking for a reasonable bond for her to get out on and you've got your diamond watch and the whole schmeer."

Marilou and Cole's mother picked him out something "pretty decent."

"C-o-l-o-n is the actual middle name," Johnson stated, but he went by Cole.

He said that in the daytime, he was a carpenter. At night, he said, he worked in Club 311 as a bartender.

The downtown bars along Austin's Sixth Street were filled with drunk and horny college students who rubbed body to body, along with underage Westlake High students, and a few fortyish men urgently seeking a young lay.

As Cole Johnson worked the bar at 311 in late February 2000, he heard the voice of his most obnoxious customer bellow through the long and narrow club. *Pain in the ass.* Donna Goodson had a voice as overwhelming as her bust line.

Amazonian tall with thick red hair curling to her shoulders as though she were auditioning for the Opry, Donna walked beneath the green-and-white–striped canopy over 311's door and entered the dark club. Usually, she arrived with a couple of girlfriends, when the hours were early and Motown oldies blasted over the speakers—before the tight-bodied college students with dewy, fresh faces crowded in for the live rhythm and blues bands.

Cole knew to pour Donna a double and charge her for a single or she would bitch so long and loudly—he could hear her voice thirty feet away—that he couldn't wait on the customers who actually paid their tabs and tipped.

That night, just a month after Steve Beard had died, Donna yelled to Cole, "This is my friend Celeste! She has money! Be nice to her!"

Donna and Celeste each had one drink and left, but before Celeste walked out the door, she leaned over the long, wooden bar and asked Cole what time he got off from work.

"I won't get out of here until three at the earliest."

"Well," she responded, "I'll send a limo for you."

Sure. Cole had heard that before.

Around 3 A.M., a limo *did* pull up to 311. Donna poked out her head and hollered, "Come on. Let's go!"

Cole grabbed his black leather biker jacket and looked over at John, the bouncer. "What are you doing?"

"Nothing."

"I don't know these chicks. Get in this limo with me!"

The next morning, Kristina and her boyfriend Justin took Cole and John back to Sixth Street, Justin racing the vehicle down the hills of Westlake and around the curves, their overgrown cedar borders limiting his visibility. Cole wondered if Justin thought he was Mario Andretti. Still, he tried to ignore the tall teen who acted like he was the man of the Beard house—and who apparently did control the three Beard women.

Back at 311, Cole jumped on his Italian motorcycle and rode down South Lamar to his tacky moss-green duplex. There were a few nice homes in his neighborhood. There was even a nice old home across the street with a well-maintained front yard. But two carports leading up to front entrances covered by cockeyed storm doors dominated Cole's small front yard. What greenery there was was a mixture of gray dirt and weeds that looked like the hair of a mangy dog.

The large backyard, which was surrounded by a hurricane fence, bloomed with overgrown weeds. In nearby yards, there were cars. In driveways were tow trucks. Under the carports were cars without tires. A few blocks down the road were small auto repair shops.

Cole Johnson's shared duplex was two million dollars away from the home Celeste Beard owned.

· · ·

Quickly, he maneuvered Donna Goodson out of Celeste's life and saw the wealthy widow Beard every day. One March day, Celeste asked Cole if he wanted her to go back into the psychiatric hospital. The girls wanted her to go. They promised they'd be good. They'd watch everything. Cole watched them talk to her. They just wanted their mother to be healthy.

Celeste turned to Cole. "What should I do?"

A few days later he gave her his answer. "I think you need to go up there and work really hard."

By then, Celeste had started joking to Cole that he and she should get married. Then her joking became serious. "I know I love you," she said. "Let's get married."

"Hold on," Cole laughed. He wanted to wait until the chaos in her life passed—or at least until they were in the eye of the storm.

The storm worsened, though, while Celeste was at Timber-lawn. The twins moved out and visited Bill Mange. After Celeste was released from Timberlawn, she and Cole drove straight to an Eckerd pharmacy to pick up $617 worth of prescription drugs—for sleeping, for anxiety, for anything and everything. She had so many pills that it seemed like she had to take a pill just to urinate. She could barely walk.

By May, Cole couldn't handle it anymore. "What's the damned deal with all these drugs?"

"Do you want me to get off of everything?"

"Yes, I do. I want Celeste. I don't want Celeste on drugs."

She went cold turkey.

"When everything was going on regarding the restraining order from the girls, Cole and I left town on the advice of my attorney Karl Moeller. We decided to drive to Aspen. We had driven about ten hours when Cole asked me if I wanted to get married in Aspen. I said yes."

Celeste pressed the OnStar button on her Cadillac and asked the concierge to set up a wedding ceremony in Aspen.

After being married to the well-respected, socially accepted, obese, multimillionaire media mogul Steve Beard,
Celeste was about to marry a nice-looking man who had
dropped out of the University of Oklahoma, eventually
earned a Bachelor of Science in education from Central
State University, then spent seventeen years tending bar,
playing in bands, and picking up women.

The concierge called back. Flowers had been ordered. A
photographer and a preacher had been booked. A church
had been reserved—the small, interfaith Aspen Chapel.
Cole loved it. He'd seen the stone chapel on the hill with
the tall steeple that reached above the evergreens twenty
years earlier.

Around mid-afternoon, on Monday, July 3, 2000, they
stood under the wood beams of the chapel, sunlight flooding through the stained-glass windows. Cole's dark blond
hair was combed straight back. A neatly trimmed goatee
adorned his face. A new navy blue, three-button Armani suit
covered his protruding beer gut. The gold tones of his tie and
handkerchief complemented Celeste's cream-colored Prada
suit, which she wore with gold Prada high-heeled sandals.

Gold jewelry hung around her neck and her wrists. Her
blonde tresses were swept into an up-do. Slim and pretty,
she held a small bouquet of pink and white flowers, which
matched the boutonnière on Cole's lapel.

Only an organist and the photographer were there to
watch.

Cole Johnson knew there was a risk his bride would be
arrested. But as far as he was concerned, he hadn't seen any
evidence that she'd done the dreadful deed, only hearsay
from a crazy shooter facing prison and some accusations
from a couple of money-grubbing twins.

That first night of marriage, Celeste and Cole shared a
bubble bath in a hotel designed by a protégé of Frank Lloyd
Wright. Celeste took a sip of champagne, altitude sickness
set in, and she climbed into bed.

Cole told the court, "I would do everything I could to make
sure we followed the rules set down by the court and to fin-

ish this out. And I would help her both physically and emotionally to get through all this. Yes, sir, I would."

"He's a really nice guy. I mean, he saved my life. He did."

"And I'll work two jobs if I need and—so we can finish paying off the attorneys and the bail and get this taken care of, see this all the way through."

The couple was reliant solely on the income of the unemployed Cole.

On cross-examination, Bill Mange began with Celeste's long history of marriage—first Craig Bratcher, then a man named Harald Wolf, Jimmy Martinez, Steve Beard, and most recently, Cole Johnson. Mange emphasized the quickness of the wedding to Cole.

He entered a copy of a *Dallas Morning News* ad promoting an upcoming weekend sale of the couple's expensive Southlake home's furnishings. The sale was being held to raise money for Celeste's defense.

Mange directed the husband to mark the items in the ad that he brought into the marriage.

"On this list there are none," the witness said.

Defense attorney Rip Collins, a tall man with broad shoulders and a head full of white hair so thick that it looked like a wig but wasn't, proceeded to introduce in his deep, rich voice a long line of Cole's relatives, near and not so near, all of whom had met Celeste after she became the wealthy widow Beard.

Everyone, from a lawyer to a Firestone store manager, from a preacher to a single working woman, from a mother to realtors, stated basically the same thing: Celeste Beard Johnson is "a very caring type of person," who was not a danger to society. "I couldn't ask for a better person to enter my life," Cole's brother, Hill Allen Johnson, stated.

Mange was getting fed up with the redundancy and offered to stipulate "that she's nice and she won't flee."

The judge insisted on letting the defense have its say.

Celeste bought blankets and heaters for a cold Spanish-speaking family in the winter of 1995. She fed the deer and the wild feral pigs, purchasing 100 pounds of food almost every day.

"She's very honest, very giving, very forthright. I'd trust her with my life," said Eileen Lightfoot, Celeste's childhood best friend. In their late teens, Eileen had lost contact with Celeste and had reconnected with her only in the last year. "I have never seen her run from anything."

"She's honest and forthright?" Bill Mange questioned, a tinge of sarcasm in his voice. "Do you know that she was convicted in 1992 of a felony offense in the State of Arizona, and specifically that was for fraud, running a con game?"

"For what?" Eileen was stunned.

Celeste Wolf had been indicted in the Superior Court of Maricopa County, Arizona on October 10, 1991, for the felony charges of fraud and theft against Sentry Insurance, Farmer's Insurance, and Century National Insurance.

She confessed in front of friends that she'd burned her own car for the insurance money.

"Sure you did," Lue Thompson laughed.

While Lue and her husband Gary were in California for a funeral, Celeste dialed them up around 3 or 4 in the morning to breathlessly, hysterically scream that their home had been burglarized. "Everything's gone," she shrieked.

Then, in the spring of 1991, Celeste and Air Force jet mechanic husband, Harald Wolf, divorced.

". . . I was devastated. I started going out with my . . . attorney and was drinking heavily at night. . . . My . . . attorney asked me to marry him, but then I found out he had been seeing a flight attendant for over five years. This is when I met Jimmy."

Besides a divorce, Celeste got silicone breast implants, paid for by her attorney.

In May, Celeste informed the cops that Lue and Gary Thompson had submitted a fraudulent insurance claim. But on January 2, 1991, the cops learned that Celeste had pawned jewelry and a Philco camcorder that the Thompsons had reported stolen.

Celeste was supposed to sit down and talk with the police again. She didn't show. She was later located at a Laundromat and taken into custody, along with her dog.

With the dog waiting in a holding cell, Celeste explained that the Thompsons were the ones who had stolen her property. So she stole their property. She then added several items of her own to their insurance claim.

Furthermore, she admitted driving her Ford Taurus into the desert and torching it because she was fed up with it—it had mechanical problems. The insurance company had paid her $13,000 for the car.

Celeste took the cop to a storage unit where he found seventeen items, most of which belonged to the Thompsons. The remainder were items Celeste had reported stolen. "How did the Thompsons' property get into your locker?" the detective asked.

Celeste suddenly became confused and couldn't answer.

In total, the cops collected nearly $18,000 worth of stolen items.

When the Thompsons found out what had happened, Lue called Craig Bratcher.

It wasn't the first time, Craig said—Celeste had stolen from him, his mother, his father, and his brother. On top of that, Celeste's mother wasn't dead. She'd disowned her daughter, Craig said.

The Thompsons located Harald Wolf. He'd gotten a restraining order against Celeste and had kept her gun because he didn't know what she was capable of doing.

Suddenly, the stories the Thompsons heard about Celeste seemed never-ending. A friend said Celeste had told her that she slept with lawyers and older judges and anyone else who could pay her rent, get her a new car, or buy her good jewelry.

Their niece, Lori Said, told them that when she had moved in with the Thompsons, Celeste told her that if she didn't leave, she'd hurt her. And if that didn't work, she'd get Lori's son. Lori was terrified. Celeste said she'd fed the twins speed to kill them, then chickened out, rushed them to the hospital, and blamed Craig.

On February 13, 1992, Celeste's 29th birthday, she was arraigned on the felony insurance fraud and theft charges.

Ten days later, Celeste was waitressing at the Discovery Inn in Tucson. When she reached into an Ice-O-Matic for a bucket of ice, the door of the machine shut, and hit her left breast. "Ow," Celeste said and kept on working.

But she demanded an immediate mammoplasty—there was raging publicity that gel implants were unsafe.

A doctor examined her and determined that the implant had not ruptured; her breast was only bruised—but it was also smaller than her right breast. Celeste insisted on surgery to make sure the implant hadn't ruptured. She was so panicked that her employer handed her $2,000 for the operation.

The doctor replaced the intact left silicone implant with a saline implant, which was 50 cc larger than the original gel implant. The doctor believed Celeste was then in perfect symmetry.

A month later, Celeste and Jimmy Martinez sued the Discovery Inn and Coldmark, the maker of the Ice-O-Matic, for negligence, claiming Celeste "was seriously injured." And Jimmy had "been deprived of the society, companionship and congenial affection of his spouse," and he would "continue to be so deprived for an undetermined amount of time into the future."

The following November, Celeste agreed to a plea agreement regarding the insurance fraud charges. In return to pleading guilty, some counts would be dismissed and she would pay the various insurance companies approximately $20,000 in restitution.

To the probation officer doing her pre-sentencing investigation, she blamed the crime on the Thompsons and an attorney she'd been dating. The attorney, she said, was the one who'd told her to inflate her insurance claims.

Celeste also denied burning her Taurus. She said she'd admitted to that crime only because she was worried about her dog, who was locked in the holding cell—the investigating officer had threatened to send the dog to the pound. Also, the officer had told her she could leave to go to Dallas to be with Jimmy, if she'd just confess.

". . . She has sincere remorse for what she did, and she desperately needs counseling," the probation officer wrote. "She would also like to be granted an opportunity to prove to everyone that she can be an asset to society. In the future, Ms. Martinez will return to school, and finish her education . . . She hopes the felony conviction in this matter will not impede her chances of becoming a licensed practical nurse."

Celeste got 4 years probation and 3 months in jail.

In March 1994, after Celeste and Jimmy had separated and she had moved in with Steve, Celeste and Jimmy's breast implant case was dismissed with prejudice.

She was discharged from felony probation in October 1995, after Steve paid her restitution in full.

On June 14, 2003, Bill Mange turned to Celeste's childhood best friend, and asked his question again. "Were you aware she was convicted in 1992 of fraud for running a con game?"

"No, I was not," Eileen Lightfoot answered.

Dana Whatley, a Diane Feinstein lookalike with Amelia Earhart dreams, a realtor in the spot-in-the-road lake town of Spicewood, as well as Marilou Gibbs' daughter, took the stand. ". . . She will be in court and she will prove that she is innocent," Dana stated.

"Are you confident enough that you would be willing to sign a bond?"

"I would sign a bond. I would put up my net worth for her, uh-huh." Her net worth, Dana said, was "around a million and a half" with real estate holdings and her part ownership in an airport. It was the tiny, one-strip Spicewood Airport, directly across the street from her tiny, brown frame home.

Still, Bill Mange smiled in his state's chair. *Thanks for coming. I wish I could find four or five more like you.*

Dana Whatley had just proven that Celeste needed a high bail. And with the Delta Airlines ticket he was going to introduce, which proved Celeste had a credit with the airline so that she could stroll out of the Del Valle jail, walk next door to Austin-Bergstrom airport, and skip town, well, he felt like he'd just won his case without putting on a single witness.

Collins asked Dana if Celeste was a danger to the community.

"She's never been a danger to the community, and you know, she wouldn't injure or hurt anybody. So I don't even see that as a real question in my mind."

Judge Kocurek called the attorneys to the bench and asked if the grand jury had recommended a bail figure.

"They recommended no bond," Mange stated.

"But they didn't have an amount?" Kocurek asked.

"At that point, the number they came up with was twenty million."

12

Bill Mange stood to call his first witness—Janet Pinkerton, now Janet Hudnall, of Bank of America. In total, she said, Celeste had received in excess of $3 million, plus the personal property since Steve's death.

Charlie Burton faced Hudnall and asked how much money Celeste was currently receiving from the trust.

"Nothing."

"Have any debts been found to not be true and correct debts?" Mange returned.

Hudnall noted an $87,827.03 diamond ring that she believed was purchased in February after Steve's death, but according to Celeste, "Steven had committed to buying the diamond prior to his death."

"So essentially . . . what you are telling us is that she was trying to steal out of the pocket of the estate to increase the money that was in her pocket?" Mange said.

"I'm not sure I would phrase it that way," the banker replied, "but yes . . ."

Mange called Detective Rick Wines of the Travis County Sheriff's Office. "Tell Judge Kocurek about the nature of the offense and the circumstances under which it was committed."

Late in the day on October 2, 1999, Wines and Knight stepped off the elevator at Brackenridge Hospital and walked into the Intensive Care Unit. Steve Beard lay in bed, relaxed and alert, despite being on life support with tubes running out of his mouth.

"Can you hear me?" Wines asked. "If you can, blink your eyes once. If you can't, blink your eyes twice."

Steve Beard blinked his eyes as his wife stood in the doorway watching.

"Do you have any idea who could have done this?"

Celeste Beard shook her head in disgust.

"Do you know a Tracey Tarlton?"

Steve Beard's face contorted. His hands clinched tight. He swallowed repeatedly trying to utter yes.

". . . It appeared that his arms tightened up as best they could with him in the condition that he was in. His eyes began to flutter, and it looked as if he was trying to say something, even though that tube was down his throat." Soon thereafter, Celeste made clear that she didn't want the cops talking to her husband anymore.

October 8, 1999, Detective Wines typed up an affidavit for an arrest warrant for Tracey Tarlton. That very same day, she was arrested and released on $25,000 bond, with the stipulation that she have no contact with the victim and that she continue seeing her therapist.

Detective Wines drove to the Capitol La Quinta motel, near Brackenridge Hospital, where Celeste Beard was staying with her two daughters. He wanted to give the victim's wife the good news. He walked into the lobby and instructed the desk clerk to ring Ms. Beard and ask if he could speak to her.

Celeste Beard said no.

Wines rang the room again. "I need to talk to you in reference to the case. We've made an arrest."

Celeste Beard and her daughters finally came down to the turquoise lobby and walked outside with Detective Wines.

"He was lying—or mistaken when he said that . . . it was Jennifer and Kristina."

Celeste rolled her blue eyes. The detective couldn't even get his facts right. It was Kristina and Dawn Madigan who were standing with her outside the La Quinta.

"Ms. Tarlton has been arrested and charged with injury to an elderly," Wines said to Celeste. It was a first-degree felony.

Celeste Beard took the news "with a grain of salt," Wines thought. He looked over at her children. They weren't elated, but they did show more emotion than their mother.

"I didn't even talk.

"Kristina kept asking him, 'Where's the watch, ring, and wallet?' And Dawn said that Kristina was getting almost belligerent about it. And it upset Dawn because she thought that it was inappropriate and that's all she cared about.

"And I didn't say anything."

On the Tuesday morning after the shooting, Wines returned to Brackenridge's ICU. He stood outside the door and stared. Off-duty officers guarded the door. A handwritten sign was stuck to the door: "Absolutely no entrance, including police."

"Who put this up here?" he asked in disbelief.

Celeste Beard, he was told.

Wines could do nothing but leave.

• • •

"Yes, there was a sign on there. That was from—that was at the beginning because I thought that they didn't give a damn, you know, about Steve's care and condition and that he wasn't physically able to speak and give a statement to the police at that time. Well, I'm talking about anybody. And, um, so, yes, there was a sign on there.

"And that was at the recommendation of, um, Charles Burton. And Charles Burton's name and phone number was on the sign for them to call if they had any questions concerning the sign. They chose not to call, and I'm talking they now as the police, because they're the ones that had the problem with it.

"But once Steven was, was better and was moved to— to—um, out of ICU and got the trach [a tracheotomy tube] and stuff, because he can't talk, um, I took that sign down and it wasn't in his other rooms. It was only in the ICU for the period of time that he was in critical condition."

On Monday, June 17, 2002, Detective Wines walked back up to the witness chair. He had the tiny, compact butt of an aged but active cop with legs that looked like hard, thin branches of mesquite.

"Did something happen after this that led you to believe there was probable cause to arrest Celeste Beard?" Prosecutor Mange asked the detective.

"In March of this year I was a witness of an interview that was held by Ms. Tarlton and Sergeant Walt Goodson of the Department of Public Safety," Wines reported. "And in that interview it was learned that Ms. Beard was a party to the offense."

"What is your understanding of Celeste Beard's role in planning the shooting, the murder of her husband?" Mange asked.

". . . She set it up."

Rip Collins retorted, "During your investigation, Detective Wines, have you interviewed anybody or do you have any video recordings or videotapes of anybody saying—of Celeste Beard saying that she was involved as a party to Steven Beard's murder?"

"No, sir."

"Up until the time that you interviewed Tracey Tarlton in March of 2002, did you have any probable cause to arrest Celeste Beard for the murder of Steven Beard?"

"No, sir."

Cole Johnson returned to the stand to explain that he'd netted only $370,000 from the sale of the Southlake house because he and Celeste had taken out a mortgage on the home in February so that they could pay bills such as credit cards and renovations. He also said he would give "every penny, every dime . . . for her defense, because I believe that my wife is totally innocent, and we're going to fight this. We would like closure."

At that, Burton hoped to close his case. But Judge Kocurek had a question for the husband. "Mr. Johnson, since you have known Celeste Beard, where have you traveled with her?"

"Let's see." Cole thought for a moment. "We have been to Africa and Ireland and Scotland and then we have been to Canada, Colorado, and at this point in time that's all I can remember. That might be it."

Bill Mange grinned inwardly. He couldn't have provided a better answer if he'd typed it out himself and given it to Cole to read.

Judge Kocurek asked that Celeste's passport be turned over to the clerk of the court.

If the judge was asking for Celeste's passport, Cole reasoned, that meant she was going to set a reasonable bond. He could get his wife back! She could help with her own defense!

". . . The bond," Kocurek ruled, "is set at eight million dollars . . ."

You bitch! Cole's spirits crashed against that ass Kocurek's courtroom floor.

He had trusted Charlie Burton. He had liked Charlie Burton. Charlie had told him that he'd contributed to Julie Kocurek's judicial campaign and he thought he had a good chance of getting Celeste a decent bail. Celeste wasn't a flight risk. She and Cole were active in Eileen Lightfoot's church, where 3,000 people gathered each Sunday to listen to Christian rock and watch Christian dramatizations on giant TV screens.

When Celeste called Cole collect that day from the jail, she couldn't speak because she was crying so hard.

Bill Mange couldn't stop smiling. Eight million was the highest bail in the history of Travis County. He didn't think Celeste was a gold digger. He thought she was a slaughterer—she'd had Steve Beard slaughtered like livestock.

Some people were just blind to Celeste's charisma. Others could see it. Those who could see it like a beacon in the fog were often those who were lonely and hurting. To them, that beacon of charisma seemed like it could fill a cold void in the soul. They just wanted to be near her, see her.

Steve Beard had felt it. Tracey Tarlton had touched it.

Marilou Gibbs bathed in it. She was furious about what had just happened to her "daughter" and at Charlie Burton. One day, as Marilou sat at TCCC, watching Celeste through a window as she talked to her over the jail phone, Celeste said, "They're trying to get me to say I did it."

"Who?" Marilou said sharply. "The prosecution?"

"No. Burton."

"Don't admit to something you haven't done," Marilou scolded.

"I'm not going to," Celeste answered, her tiny lisp sweet, soft.

Marilou Gibbs walked out of the bond hearing so white in the face that Dana was concerned. "Mother, what's wrong?"

"Celeste is going to prison for life if we don't get her another attorney," Marilou answered. As she rode back to Southlake, she talked to Cole and tried to knock some sense into the boy. "Cole, Cole, for God's sakes, can't you see?"

But Steve had used Charlie Burton as his own lawyer for so long, Cole defended.

"What do you mean?" Marilou sounded like a schoolteacher with a ruler. "Steve didn't even know him. Steve hated his guts on sight. He said, 'I hate those fucking drugstore cowboys.'"

Men in suits, cowboy hats, and Stetsons just didn't impress Steve Beard.

Renowned Houston criminal attorney Dick DeGuerin was a man who first created his image in Thomas Thompson's *Blood and Money*. A protégé of Percy Foreman, DeGuerin was a lawyer who embraced the limelight and never shunned controversy. When the Department of Justice and the FBI tried to take down the Branch Davidians, Dick DeGuerin represented cult leader David Koresh.

Marilou and Cole sped down Interstate 45, passing the Huntsville state prison where Texas inmates were given their lethal injections, and on into downtown Houston.

DeGuerin's offices were on the top floors of a small historical building that looked ready for Doc Holliday and Jesse James to walk in and hang their guns on its brick walls.

Thursday morning, June 20, 2002, Marilou and Cole, toting documents they believed proved Celeste's innocence, rode up the tiny, rattling elevator and walked into DeGuerin's shockingly junky office.

Although the office was large, it was claustrophobic and didn't look like it'd had a good cleaning or a paint job in decades. Cubicles and files seemed everywhere.

With the exception of the framed news clippings of DeGuerin that plastered the waiting area walls, it was far from the image of an egotistical, multimillionaire, hard-drinking, hard-cussing, hard-fighting, exorbitant-priced Texas attorney. There wasn't one smidgen of overindulgent luxury, or any luxury at all.

Marilou Gibbs couldn't talk about Celeste without urgent passion in her country voice. Like an Elvis fanatic arguing that the King never used drugs, Marilou frenetically chattered about the injustices done to Celeste and her complete and utter innocence.

"Wait a minute! Wait a minute," Dick tried to interrupt.

Marilou was talking so hard and fast, he couldn't make heads or tails out of what she was saying. And he told her that.

She flipped through her notes until she grabbed the protection order hearing. "Here!" She jabbed it into his hands.

Dick DeGuerin couldn't help but mind Marilou Gibbs. He took it, and as he opened it, he said, "I'm going to tell you two things. I don't sue other lawyers and I don't criticize other lawyers."

Everybody who knew a lawyer with Minton, Burton, Foster & Collins—or even the spouse of a lawyer there— knew the firm would be thrilled to get rid of Celeste Beard Johnson. "Sit down and shut up," they told her all the time. Simply put, she was a pain in the ass who threatened suicide whenever she disagreed with her attorneys' advice, which was often.

DeGuerin skimmed the document. "*Damned* incestuous Austin attorneys."

But he had to end the meeting. Dick DeGuerin had a TV appearance to make.

Assistant District Attorney Allison Wetzel flopped down in a chair in the office of her supervisor LaRu Woody.

"Your name has come up," LaRu said as she eased their conversation toward the Celeste Beard Johnson murder trial and the possibility of Allison replacing Bill Mange as its lead attorney. "What would you think about it?"

"That doesn't sound like a good idea." Allison was a child abuse prosecutor with an overflowing docket of cases, including child homicide cases, one of which was a capital murder case set for October.

"It could be a lot of fun," LaRu tried to coax.

Allison didn't see that.

But she thought about it as she puttered home to her Westlake subdivision, just ten minutes or so from Toro Canyon Road. And she thought about it more as she sat down with her husband, an attorney in the Court of Criminal Appeals.

"They just might give it to you anyway," Rick Wetzel warned.

She knew he was right—she wouldn't have a choice in the matter.

Judge Kocurek wanted a December trial. With a capital murder case just six months away, Allison would need the best in the DA's office.

Dick DeGuerin took the case.

Marilou and Cole began scraping together the money.

Texans joked that all one had to do—when it was cheaper to kill a spouse than divorce one—was wire Dick DeGuerin $50,000. Celeste Beard sent him $500,000, a mere down payment.

Friday, June 21, Celeste's jailhouse buddy, Kathy Marie Flowers, raged against Kocurek, who prisoners called "the Wicked Witch of the West": ". . . That bitch lost her mind giving you an eight-million-dollar bond." Flowers closed with a request for money from Celeste.

Allison sat in her third-floor corner office overlooking a small portion of roof when an email popped up from LaRu. She was being assigned the Beard case. *Why me?*

While Allison certainly realized that if she won the case, everyone in the courthouse would know, she also believed that if she didn't win, everyone would know she was just a big, ole loser.

But that wasn't what the inmates in Del Valle thought. They'd nicknamed her "the She-Wolf."

During those early days of July, Cole Johnson, who had moved to Austin to be close to Celeste, sent his wife photographs of the new house and noted, ". . . it won't be a home until you grace its doorstep."

On July 15, Cole wrote, "I dream about the times we will be together again and that keeps me going. Be strong for us my dear; I could not make it without you. We will fight to the end and free your mind and body. God willing truth and justice will prevail."

As almost always, he signed the letter, "Your husband Cole."

And, he included the lyrics to a song he'd written—"Teardrops for Celeste":

> *Soulful teardrops falling close to my heart*
> *Reflecting memories of the time spent apart*
> *Faded colors of red white and blue*
> *Pooling teardrops with ripples of you*
>
> *Thoughts of combing your long blonde hair*
> *Is something that I'll never share*
> *Time without you seems oh so long*
> *Soulful teardrops bring you back home*

When Cole talked to Celeste, he said, "Honey, I'll send it to Willie Nelson. We'll make some money maybe, you know, put it in a fund toward you."

Celeste wrote Cole: "I just wanted to write you and let you know how much I love you! I hope you never give up on me. I need you so much. I feel bad because I feel like I am putting too much pressure on you. I would give anything to have you just hold me. I feel like, if I could just have kissed you good-bye instead of being taken away like I was—that I wouldn't feel like this. I doubt it though. I have all the time in the world to think about would have, could have, should haves. I realize that is not healthy. Anyway—I just want you to know that you are deeply loved and deeply appreciated. Pray for my return. I pray everyday for God to protect you. Give the babies," she wrote referring to their dogs, "a hug and kiss for me. I hope our separation won't be for much longer. I will always love you!"

On July 16, Dick DeGuerin wrote Major David Balagia, who oversaw Celeste's unit, "I understand that all of Celeste Johnson's books have been taken away from her and she is not allowed to have anything to read. Since she is in segregation . . . I request that she be allowed to have her books."

Balagia emailed DeGuerin that Celeste had received six

books in one day when the jail rules allowed her to possess
only two books at a time. "We have relaxed this rule for Ms.
Johnson and have allowed her to maintain three (3) books at
one time." He closed, ". . . I believe she is only telling you
half the story."

13

Allison, her co-counsel Bill Bishop, Jennifer and Kristina
Beard, Ellen Halbert, and Anita Ashton sat in the third-floor
conference room of the DA's office. The long, narrow room
was dark with closed blinds and chilly with air condition-
ing. There was no decoration, unless white legal boxes
lined against a wall were considered décor.

The twins' heads were lowered, but their eyes shyly
watched Allison. They seemed so much younger than their
21 years—a vulnerability, an innocence, as if they needed
protecting.

Ellen and Anita believed they were there to do just that.
Anita, an obese fifty-something woman who wobbled with
her cane when she walked, and spoke with an excited,
breathless burst of words like a teenager spilling the latest
gossip, thought of herself as the girls' mother. Kristina and
Jen asked Allison questions; Anita answered them.

Jennifer stated unequivocally that she could testify
against Celeste. Kristina said she could too, but it'd be
hard—the last time they'd seen their mother, at the August
2000 hearing, she'd looked so mean and mad.

After the meeting, Allison walked down the file-crowded
corridor back to her office; she knew the kids could do it.
And despite the fact that Allison was what Kristina called a
Bible-thumper—Jen said she didn't know how to pray,
while Kristina said she could fake-pray with the best of
them—they got Allison's dry sense of humor. Allison en-

tered her sun-filled corner office carrying the girls' email addresses; they wanted to meet next time without Anita.

On August 20, 2002, Celeste looked a bit mousy as she sat in the courtroom. Allison Wetzel towered over Dick DeGuerin, despite his cowboy boots and Stetson. She wasn't going to let the drugstore cowboy intimidate her.

DeGuerin informed the judge that he couldn't go to trial in December; he had a conflict. But Bill Bishop had a January conflict—the arrival of new baby in the family. And he planned to take time off after the birth.

On October 1, 1999, when Judge Kocurek stepped behind her bench for the very first time, a black robe draped over two new lives in her swollen belly. She plopped down on a plastic doughnut in her big, black chair to cushion her pregnant derriere. And she had 600 criminal cases on her docket.

Despite Bill Bishop's predicament, Judge Kocurek set the trial for early 2003.

A few days later Celeste requested she be placed on the list for nail clippers. When Steve was alive and they lived just blocks from Studio 29 salon, she'd gotten a manicure and pedicure every week.

Celeste's request made Allison Wetzel laugh. She desperately needed a good laugh. After Kocurek's ruling on the trial date, Allison had to find a new second chair . . . fast.

While Allison looked for a second chair, Celeste requested Bible studies, immediately answered them, and returned them to be graded—almost always scoring a perfect 100. And she complained to the mailroom that her books were missing and she wanted to know where they were.

Allison Wetzel made public reams of Steve Beard's medical records on September 12, 2002. With the exception of sleep apnea due to his obesity, asthma, and high blood pressure, Steve had never experienced repeated illness until he married Celeste Martinez.

In July 1995, he'd wanted help with his history of erectile dysfunction. His first wife wasn't interested in sex, Steve told Dr. John J. Horan. So that made him feel that he'd been "out of it" for some time, and he wanted to change that now that he'd remarried, despite the fact that he'd already filed for divorce from Celeste. They were living at the Terrace Mountain house at the time, the home Steve had shared with his first wife.

"But everywhere I looked it had Elise in it. And I couldn't stand it. I mean, I thought I could, but after a while it was driving me crazy. So that's when we decided to sell it in '95. That's actually what—when I left him in '95, when we were gonna get divorced. I just couldn't stand it anymore. I just felt like, I felt like he was trying to turn me into Elise. He wanted me to cut my hair short. He wanted me to dress in old lady clothes. And it just—and everywhere I turned it was Elise this, Elise that, Elise this. And so I just—I handled it inappropriately.

"By, um, you know, telling him I wanted a divorce and everything instead of just—and then I went into the, um, went into, uh, a psychiatric hospital for depression instead of just telling him. Because as soon as he found out what the problem was, he was all, 'Fine. We'll sell the house. We'll build another house.' I mean, he was just so nice about it.

"Steve's the one that filed, but it was at my insistence.

"But, anyway, we worked it out, and it was withdrawn. Steve withdrew it."

Steve had tried an over-the-counter remedy called yohimbine, which only had mixed results. He could obtain a 25 percent erection with sexual activity. And he had rare nonintercourse or morning erections. By 1996, Steve was taking testosterone. He called it "vitamin T."

In 1994, 1995, and 1996, 100 tablet prescriptions for Tylenol with codeine were being filled in Steve's name almost like they were three-a-day multivitamins. In January 1996, Steve was using Restoril as a sleeping aid. Suddenly, time after time, Steve was confused and disoriented after eating or drinking; often he passed out and was rushed by ambulance to the emergency room.

On Sunday, January 19, 1997, when the darkness seemed to fall too early, he sat in the living room, an old-fashioned glass filled with clear-colored liquor and ice in his hand. Steve drank his cocktail and started on a second. He only swallowed about half of that one before he moved into the kitchen and sat down to dinner.

During dinner, Steve began to act "weird" and became groggy. Around midnight, one of the girls found him back in the kitchen, confused and sitting in a chair. They gathered around and tried to rouse him. When they finally did, his responses were incoherent. And he'd wet his pants.

For the next two hours, they maneuvered Big Daddy to his bed. Around 5 A.M., he was found on the opposite side of the house. His pants were wet again, and he'd urinated in other places in the house, too. "I move my leg. I move my leg," he mumbled. They put him back to bed.

He was still out cold the next morning when Jen heard her mother say, "Let's go pick me out a Cadillac for my birthday." They jumped in a car, sped over to I-35, took a right on the feeder road and pulled into Southpoint Cadillac. They test-drove Cadillac after Cadillac after Cadillac, until Celeste finally found what she was looking for—a pricey but sporty and very fast STS. Celeste drove it right off the lot.

When they finally rolled home in the new vehicle, Steve was still passed out. At 2:30 P.M., well more than twelve hours after he first fell, they called 911. EMS arrived. Steve came to just enough to worry the Beard girls, so when EMS rolled Steve out of the house, Celeste and Jen stood in front of the new Caddy trying to hide it from Steve's blurry eyes.

By the time he arrived on a stretcher at the Austin Diagnostic Medical Center emergency room, he was back to normal.

Dr. Michael Martin recorded that the confused state might have been caused by Steve's sleep apnea and mucous buildup in his sinuses. "Of note is that the patient had been drinking probably at least 4–6 ounces of alcohol every evening . . ."

Celeste let Dr. Robert Emerson know that several times over the past two weeks she'd found Steve sitting on the commode in a confused state or disoriented in the opposite end of the house. "He has in recent weeks had increasing snoring to the point where his wife leaves the room," Emerson wrote.

Dr. Martin discharged Steve around 11 A.M. on January 22, 1997. At 4, Steve still waited for Celeste to pick him up. She told his nurse she wouldn't be able to get there until 6.

She arrived in her new birthday STS, telling Steve that he needed to send Southpoint a check for the car. She'd driven off the lot without paying for it.

Steve wasn't happy with a solid five-figure expenditure that he hadn't okayed first. In fact, he was upset, but he sent the check anyway.

A month later, Celeste didn't like the car, so she gave it to her girls. They got so many speeding tickets in it that Steve took the car away from them.

On September 12, 1999, Celeste found Steve passed out on the kitchen floor, in a pool of saliva. EMS rushed him to North Austin Medical Center where his blood alcohol level was measured at 168 mg percent. He told social worker Sally McCracken that he "drinks what wife pours. . . . He also says his wife has been drinking more recently, so he drinks more to accompany her."

On the 14th, Steve was to be discharged, but Celeste didn't want that. She didn't think he was ready. Plus, she had plans to go out that night and she didn't want him left alone at home. Still, he returned home on the 14th, and then returned to the hospital on the 15th. He'd passed out on the kitchen table while eating breakfast and reading the morning paper.

Celeste was enraged. She stormed through the ER screaming that he'd been discharged too soon, and she was going to get a camera crew out to the hospital. Two days later, Steve was discharged again, and no camera crew ever came.

• • •

Appoximately three years later, on September 19, 2002, Celeste busied herself corresponding with inmates. She wrote Laura Dow that she would talk to Dick DeGuerin about a parole attorney for Dow.

"Money & possessions used to mean everything to me before I came to jail," the inmate with the million-dollar lawyer penned. "After spending so much time in this cell—I realize that's not important at all. I am studying my bible and really trying to do what God wants me to. I used to make fun of people that turned to religion just because they are in jail. If it weren't for my circumstances, I too wouldn't have turned to God. I realize now that it is a wake up call. Until you have to face something horrible, people won't ask God for help. I am glad that He has been a comfort to me. I honestly will not turn away from Him, if I do get to leave this place."

Her correspondence continued with a note slipped to medical—"I need 2 Milk of Magnesias please. It has been three days since I have had a B/M." Medical responded two days later by telling her to increase her water intake; no over-the-counter drugs were available until after October 1.

Wednesday, October 2, 2002, the third anniversary of the shooting of Steve Beard, Allison Wetzel sat quietly in the gallery of the Third Court of Appeals. Three judges sat at the front of the room. Not one looked up as attorneys introduced themselves . . . until Dick DeGuerin said his name. Then, all three judges looked up.

They're impressed with him, Wetzel thought.

DeGuerin griped that Celeste's $8 million was the highest bail ever set, not just in Travis County, but in the entire state of Texas. He claimed his client was not a flight risk and deserved a $50,000 bond. He argued that the prosecution had no evidence to corroborate Tracey Tarlton's accusations. "[Tracey Tarlton] is a lesbian," he stated, "and she was obsessed with Celeste Beard."

Assistant District Attorney Sally Swanson reasoned Celeste Beard Johnson *was* a flight risk. Judge Kocurek had recognized that and the court of appeals judges should too.

Beard Johnson was so untrustworthy, Swanson maintained, that even the inmate's own twin daughters had been forced to get a restraining order against her.

"I love you so much and care for you beyond belief," Cole Johnson wrote Celeste that day. ". . . We will come through this and be together again."

Tracey was calm as the county vehicle eased through the electric gate and drove up the stone drive of 3900 Toro Canyon. The neighborhood looked different. When Tracey had been there, there were only two houses and one house under construction. Now, the small housing edition was complete with a handful of expensive homes.

But just like it had been three years before, it was a warm day in Westlake. Allison and investigators met Tracey as she crawled out of the back seat and stood in the ritzy neighborhood in her maximum-security orange and green jail scrubs.

The new owner of the house, whom Allison had had to coax into the visit, watched as Tracey talked about how Celeste had hired Pooper Scoopers to pick up the dog poop from the yard and how the yard had been manicured, pointing out bushes that hadn't been there in 1999.

From inside, the homeowner's wife nervously watched. The family had completely remodeled the home into a Zen-like oasis, telling others that they didn't want one speck of Celeste Beard's DNA left in the house.

Tracey led everyone to the back of the house where she sat and talked for an hour, explaining exactly what she'd done that night. "This is where I leaned against the wall and took a deep breath." She seemed distant and hollow like a victim of child abuse forced to recount the shame—where she'd entered, where she'd exited, where she'd stood when she'd pulled the trigger.

Allison Wetzel was up early, as usual, and steered her dark blue Volvo along Loop 360 and turned left to enter Loop 1, headed for the district attorney's office. October 11, 2002, was her 40th birthday, but what occupied the assistant district attorney's mind was the case against Celeste Beard Johnson. Wetzel would be spending the morning interviewing Justin Grimm.

"Justin's just a—turd."

Justin was a little bit weird, sometimes humorless, stiff, and a bit blank-faced, sort of like former prosecutor Bill Mange—but Justin could also be somewhat witty, with a profane vocabulary when he wanted, sort of like Bill Mange. Justin provided Wetzel with a brightly colored photograph of Celeste Beard Johnson about to shove a foot-long hot dog into her wide-open mouth. Wetzel had it stuck to her computer monitor to give her laughs and inspiration.

That day, it was more than the photograph that gave her laughs and inspiration. Her crew of co-workers started her day with gifts and a crown. She socked the paper crown onto her fluffy red hair and began her interview with Justin. It lasted all morning. The crown on her head lasted all day.

But as the clock ticked close to midnight, and Wetzel was curled up with her non-stop reading for the case, she was about to be given one more birthday present.

14

At 11:30 P.M. on October 11, 2002, Celeste sat on a gray stool at one of the three tables in the day room of Del Valle's Building 3, Post C, Unit I, referred to as "Ida" by inmates and deputies. Mere steps away was her private cell, number 2, called Ida 2.

Sitting across from her was a deputy who, like Celeste, straddled the stool as if riding a pony. One circular black metal pipe curved like a horse's neck from underneath the table to the bottom of the stool seat and then went straight into the concrete floor.

The deputy scattered before them the contents of a paper bag, Celeste's commissary requests, purposely delivered late at night so as not to stir up inmate problems.

The two of them counted the candy that was cast along the table's shiny metal top to make sure Celeste had received her ordered items. Suddenly, the deputy noticed a dazed look in Celeste's blue eyes. Celeste dropped from the gray stool onto the hard floor. She lay there and cried.

"Medical emergency," a radio squawked in the Health Services Building at 11:40 P.M. Two nurses rushed to 3C and found Johnson, as they called her, lying on the dayroom floor.

"My leg hurts," Celeste wept. "My right leg hurts."

Already, four or five officers had arrived, pulled Celeste's mattress out of her cell, and carefully laid the inmate on her back on the mattress, trying to make her comfortable.

"I was sitting at the table getting my commissary when I started feeling hot, started touching my head, and next thing I knew, I'm on the floor feeling a lot of pain on my right leg."

Her leg was swelling and bruising.

"Don't move your leg."

One nurse left the cellblock to get an immobilizer for the leg. While she was gone, the second nurse continued trying to reassure the crying inmate.

Fifteen minutes after she first hit the floor, Celeste began calming. "It feels like it's throbbing and burning right now."

Five minutes after midnight, splints were placed around her leg. She was hoisted onto a gurney, and twenty-five minutes after it started, she was wheeled to the Health Services Building trauma room. Celeste was calm but "very talkative."

At 12:20 A.M., a nurse phoned EMS. Twenty minutes later, EMS arrived and immediately started an IV. With Celeste still chatting non-stop, but cooperative, the EMS techs placed their own immobilizer on the inmate and started another IV for pain.

Before the clock struck 1:30 A.M. on October 12, 2002, Celeste Beard Johnson was rushed by EMS from the Del Valle jail to South Austin Medical Center, where she arrived twenty minutes later, accompanied by TCCC security.

"I think I broke my ankle when I passed out." She was given 25 mg of Demerol.

Celeste was in X-ray by 2:50 A.M., and a TCSO officer was phoning Cole Johnson.

South Austin wasn't far from Cole's rented house. He was standing next to Celeste in the ER before she'd even seen a doctor, an officer posted beside them, Celeste cuffed to the bed in shockingly good spirits. Cole hugged her, kissed her and told her he loved her. At 3:56, Celeste was in emergency room six.

At approximately the same time, a sergeant for Building 3 back at Del Valle phoned and woke her captain at home to report Johnson's accident and departure to the hospital. The sergeant immediately heard her captain express belief that Johnson had purposely broken her own leg and that it possibly was an escape attempt. After all, not only was Del Valle just a few minutes away from the airport and Interstate 35, but so was South Austin Medical Center. The captain instructed the sergeant to alert the TCCC security about Johnson's history.

At 4:40 A.M., South Austin medical personnel decided Celeste would be admitted to the hospital. As they filled out her admission form they noted that she was Methodist, she was slightly obese, she'd quit tobacco six months prior, and she suspected that she'd caught her leg in the stool as she fell. "The patient is currently w/out any significant pain." The notation was signed by Dr. Hien X. Duong.

At 6:10 A.M., she was admitted to room 445.

Constantly Celeste complained of pain and was given more and more pain medication. Regularly, she phoned her attorneys.

The morning of October 13, Officer J. Segura needed to use the restroom. Segura cuffed Johnson's right hand and left leg to the hospital bed, then walked into the bathroom.

Suddenly, the officer heard clanking and yanking against metal bed rails. Segura rushed back to Johnson's side and checked the restraints. Scratches and indentations that hadn't been visible before were on Celeste's right wrist.

"Were you moving your hands or foot around?" Segura asked.

"No," Celeste answered.

The officer washed her hands and then removed Johnson's handcuffs. Segura knew the cuffs weren't too tight. After double-locking them, she could still fit a finger between the cuffs and Celeste's wrist.

At 9:08 A.M., a nurse came in with more pain medicine.

Celeste began crying. "Don't let anyone, police or nurses, do anything to me," she begged.

That afternoon, Segura warned the next shift of Johnson's complaints and advised them to carefully watch the inmate because of her "manipulative behavior."

At 3 P.M. on October 15, 2002, D. Rosas added to Celeste's chart. "Johnson claims I was rude to her when I asked her to lift up her foot so I could remove the leg iron. Johnson is very manipulative and passive aggressive in her behavior."

Seventeen minutes later, D. Rosas wrote, "Johnson back in bed. She is displaying an attitude of helplessness. Very strange."

The last notation on the Brackenridge Security Hospital Duty Log for October 15, 2002, was that one handcuff, one belly chain, and clothing that would fit over a leg cast would be needed because Johnson would soon be released from South Austin Medical Center.

She was released from the hospital that day and transferred to Travis County's downtown medical facility. And from 2:30 P.M. to 10 o'clock that night, prosecutor Allison Wetzel sat with Celeste's former assistant and friend, Donna Rose Goodson. Allison listened to Donna tell story after story about Celeste. Donna loved to gossip. She told Allison how Celeste had had seven men in seven days, didn't use condoms, and had picked up a yeast infection when they partied in New Orleans.

Wetzel typed Donna's formal statement, leaving out the non-pertinent details.

Dressed in black-and-white jailhouse stripes, Celeste Beard Johnson lay on the pale blue plastic mattress on top of her concrete bed and read romance novels. Attached to the bed was a tiny metal stool. The stool hooked to a tiny metal desk attached to an inside wall. Another wall held a stainless-steel sink, combined with a stainless-steel toilet. Over the sink was an aluminum mirror.

A blue rectangle of a telephone was wheeled in for calls. As long as no other inmate wanted the phone, between 8:30 A.M. and 10:30 P.M., she could make as many collect calls as she wanted, and talk as long as she liked.

On October 16, staff discussed Johnson and her broken right tibia. The South Austin doctor had wanted to pin the break but was concerned that it would become infected at Del Valle. So he simply put a cast on it.

Just as Celeste was getting used to her new quarters, a new arrest warrant was issued for her.

On October 17, Judge Julie Kocurek signed Detective Jim Anderson's affidavit stating that "on or about the 13th day of February 2000," Celeste Beard Johnson "did commit the offense of criminal solicitation of a capital murder," which was a first-degree felony. Celeste Beard Johnson had ordered a hit on Tracey Tarlton, Anderson claimed.

The basis for the detective's affidavit and arrest warrant was the October 15 sworn statement of Donna Rose Goodson, who Celeste had asked to hire a hit man.

October 21, Celeste was indicted for criminal solicitation of capital murder. The notice of her indictment was delivered two days later on October 23. That same day, Dick DeGuerin filed a motion "to quash Count 1 of the indictment" and another motion "to suppress all evidence stolen from defendant's home by her own daughters."

Thursday, October 24, was a dreary, rainy day in Austin. Traffic backed up on the freeways as the city was warned of possible flooding. From Washington, D.C., there was word that the D.C. sniper may have been caught. On that day, the Third Court of Appeals gave Dick DeGuerin what he wanted. It reduced Celeste's bail from $8 million to $500,000.

"Capital murder is a serious crime," the Third Court of Appeals ruled, "but it is not an uncommon one in Texas. The murder of which Beard is accused was neither more violent in its commission nor more abhorrent in its alleged motive than other capital murders that come before the courts of this state. Although Beard is accused of a violent crime, there is no evidence that she has been a violent person in the past. She has a criminal record, but for a single nonviolent property crime committed ten years ago and for which she successfully completed probation. Although the agreed protective order is evidence of hard feelings, and perhaps physical violence, that have characterized Beard's recent relationship with her daughters, we find no evidence in this record that Beard is a serious threat to community safety."

The court further noted, twice in fact, that the $8 million bail was the largest ever set in a Texas criminal case. But that wasn't true. Dick DeGuerin had another client, Robert Durst, who was residing in the Galveston County jail under a bond of one penny shy of one billion dollars.

With a double backhanded swipe at Judge Julie Kocurek, the Third Court of Appeals also wrote, "Such a dramatic departure from prior practice is at least suggestive of an abuse of discretion," and "we conclude that the district court abused its discretion by setting Beard's bail at $8,000,000."

That same day, Celeste was scheduled to appear in Judge Kocurek's court for the bail hearing on the solicitation-of-murder charge. Dick DeGuerin wanted his client's $5 million bail reduced to a "reasonable" sum of $50,000. "Although the caption of the indictment states that Defendant has been charged with criminal solicitation of capital murder, a first degree felony, the body of the indictment actually charges her with a second degree felony, i.e. solicitation of solicitation of capital murder," his motion read.

Celeste, who was housed just steps away from Kocurek's courtroom, was a no-show. She waived her appearance because she would have had to wear her jailhouse black-and-white stripes to court rather than street clothes. And she refused to appear in the county stripes with TV cameras in the room.

15

October 27, 2002, Dick DeGuerin filed another motion—to quash a subpoena for the records of Barbara Grant, LMSW, ACP. He filed more motions on October 28—to prohibit cameras in the courtroom and to permit the defendant to appear in street clothes *and* makeup at *all* court appearances.

That same day, Allison Wetzel filed 147 pages of medical records for Celeste Beard and Tracey Tarlton, including those that DeGuerin wanted quashed.

Susan Milholland, a masters degree intern at Timberlawn psychiatric facility in Dallas, had phoned Barbara Grant in Austin on April 23, 1999. Tracey Tarlton had been discharged from Timberlawn and Grant would be doing follow-up therapy. Tracey, Milholland reported, didn't think she was fixable.

Tracey had spent two months in various psychiatric facilities—one week at St. David's, two weeks at Menninger in Kansas, three weeks inpatient at Timberlawn, and two weeks in day hospital at Timberlawn. She believed she'd run off all of her previous therapists.

As a kid, her father hadn't rescued her from her mother's abuse. As an adult, she reenacted her childhood abandonment. She tended to overgeneralize and minimize her issues. She played Russian roulette.

She got involved with married women who left their husbands. And at Timberlawn, she'd roomed with a married friend. Tracey's current married woman said she had no intention of leaving her husband for Tracey.

On April 28, 1999, Tracey walked into social worker Grant's office on Spicewood Springs Road. Grant was a bit hunched over, which, when combined with her gray hair, made her look little, old, and dowdy. But she also had black, droopy eyebrows that made her seem sweet, and her conservative clothes along with her eyeglasses gave her a bookish appearance, almost like a librarian.

When she was 10 years old, Tracey said, she figured out the sexual abuse and that she was "nuts." She phrased it, though, that the emotional abuse was so intense, and "Oh, by the way, there was sexual abuse." But Tracey's main concerns, she said, were how to relate to people, suicide, and Celeste.

She returned to Grant's office on May 5, two days before her 42nd birthday "struggling with an emotional flatness and lack of passion in her work." She also talked about the "person she is in relationship with."

Tracey and Celeste walked into the City Grill on May 7, 1999. On Waller Creek in downtown Austin, surrounded by empty beer bottles and homeless men on the outside, the City Grill was a trendy upscale restaurant with a strangely workable Austin–New York feel inside. To the left was a long, dark wood bar where cold martinis and hot appetizers were served. To the right were white-linen–covered tables where many of Austin's more prosperous gays dined on fresh grilled fish and fine California wines.

Tracey and Celeste were with Tracey's friends, Pat Brooks and Jane Smith. Tracey and Pat had known each other since childhood. The two couples shared dinner, on Celeste's credit card, to celebrate both Tracey's and Pat's birthdays.

Celeste gave Pat a gift certificate for the high-end hardware store Breed & Company, which also sold crystal, china, and the most expensive cooking utensils. Pat did catering and event planning.

Tracey showed off the Swiss Army watch Celeste had

given her. She'd also given Tracey a birthday card—"To the One I Love" signed "Love, Celeste."

The following week at Barbara Grant's, Tracey was concerned about her niece's upcoming wedding in Atlanta. And she was surprised to notice a pattern in her relationships. "Many of her relationships have been with people who were initially in another relationship when they met and that they were all also 'high fem,'" Grant wrote.

"I want to go. I want to go with you," Celeste said, when she heard Tracey mention her niece's wedding in Atlanta.

"You don't want to go," Tracey replied in her deep and husky voice, which was quite contrary to Celeste's soft, sweet, lisp. "It's a family wedding. I'm going to be down there two days and come back, and who wants to go to a family wedding?"

"No," Celeste protested. "I really want to meet your family. I want them to meet me. I'm going to go."

Tracey grinned, her dimple showing in her left cheek. She had a very sweet smile.

Celeste told Steve she was going out of town for a wedding with a friend. She didn't mention the friend's name. She took Tracey to St. Thomas, a designer women's wear store in the Arboretum, to get a suit for the wedding. Celeste paid for Tracey's atypical new clothing.

By May 19, Tracey's anxiety over the trip to Atlanta was increasing. She predicted only the worst with her family. She was also concerned that Celeste insisted on monogamy, though Tracey often dated others while in a relationship. Tracey talked about the book *The Ethical Slut*, the so-called bible on open relationships.

In Atlanta, they visited the hot nightclub the Leopard Lounge, charging hundreds of dollars to Celeste's credit card.

On May 26, Tracey was distressed over a "current disconnect within current relationship." She said she and Celeste had never had a fight before, so she didn't know if it was a permanent breakup or just the way Celeste fought.

Tracey asked for some benzodiazepine for anxiety on

June 4. Grant wondered if the drug request was really a way for Tracey to run off her therapist and psychiatrist.

Finally, on June 8, they began delving into Tracey's childhood. "Discussed mother's abuse, beginning with sexual abuse; digital penetration, salving on ointments in genital areas for long periods of time," Grant wrote. "Stated that in comparison to the physical abuse, this wasn't bad."

"Tracey said that she would feel guilty because she couldn't help being aroused by what her mom did sometimes. She would actually climax when her mom masturbated. Tracey said the counselor told her that this was not unusual behavior. Tracey told me that she only had sexual intercourse with one male that she worked with on the oil fields; all the rest were female."

"By about 10, she was on her own and raised herself," Grant noted. "I discussed learning to nurture herself, objected to concept of becoming her own mother. Idea of mother as positive unavailable to client."

Tracey soon stopped seeing Grant.

But in July, she phoned the therapist and asked for an appointment. She walked into Barbara Grant's office on July 21, 1999, with Celeste by her side. They were there to discuss "issues in their relationship."

Tracey loved Celeste and believed Celeste loved her. At least, Celeste spent a lot of time letting her know she loved her. They were having sex together, at least that's what Grant understood. But there were issues with their sex life. Celeste had to drink to be sexual. And Celeste wasn't sure she was a lesbian.

Tracey didn't want her lover to be uncomfortable. Nor did Celeste want Tracey to be uncomfortable. They'd both invested a lot of emotion in their relationship, despite the fact that neither one of them, they both admitted, was very good at staying in relationships. And Celeste was about to go on several long trips. Tracey was anxious. She was scared that one of them was going to leave for someone else. They said they wanted to get some grounding before Celeste left town.

"Grounding"—that was more of a Tracey word than a Celeste word.

Celeste told the therapist that when she was 17 her first husband had raped and beaten her. She couldn't have any more kids because she'd had ovarian cancer. She never drank until her present marriage. And she and Steve had a no-sex agreement.

Grant told Celeste she could benefit from therapy focusing on her incest history. She referred her to the Austin Rape Crisis Center and suggested she read *The Courage to Heal*.

Grant recommended Tracey read *Allies in Healing*.

Two damaged souls, two books on healing. They left, having completed their one and only session of couples counseling.

On October 24, 2002, the day Celeste refused to attend court, she met with a jail counselor. "Been in jail since March—Conspiracy to commit murder—appears possible—histrionic—dramatic in presentation," the counselor wrote.

With TV cameras focused on her, Celeste slowly crutched across the stark, gray courtroom, her face purposefully strained with pain. Her hair proved eight and a half months in jail. Its long ends were honey blonde. Then there was an abrupt halt and eight and a half inches of mousy blonde roots.

She wore a long dark skirt, gray blazer, and one expensive loafer, at 2:00 on Tuesday afternoon, November 12, 2002. Her face was jailhouse pale and void of makeup as the cameras clicked and she was seated to argue for her second bond reduction. She propped her right foot on a cardboard legal box as another box set on the defense table with "Beard Johnson" written in red ink. A third box sat on the floor with "Beard Johnson" written in green ink.

DeGuerin sat at the far end of the defense table opposite his client, but close to his beloved size 7⅛ 4x beaver Stetson. Sitting between DeGuerin and Johnson was assisting attorney Catherine Baen, known for her black-frame eyeglasses, which she seemed to wear only for court, designer clothes, and tall, thin body. Two Catherine Baens would not have made one Dick DeGuerin, and DeGuerin was not a rotund Texan.

Behind them, in the gallery, sat Celeste's supporters—Cole; Dana Whatley, who was busy taking notes before court even started; Marilou Gibbs, who wore all black, which was accented by the cross hanging around her neck; and Jimmy Martinez, Celeste's good-looking, dark-haired ex-husband.

On the other side of the courtroom, as if the gallery were divided like a wedding with groom's side and bride's side, were the Beard family supporters—Anita Ashton and her husband, Jerry, who had his own felony conviction; Ellen Halbert; detectives from the Travis County Sheriff's Office; local reporters; and workers from the DA's office.

At the prosecutor's table was Wetzel's handpicked second chair, the dapper-dressing assistant district attorney Gary Cobb, and Wetzel herself. She'd picked Cobb because he and she went together like potatoes and butter. She was the methodical researcher who planned her cases and abhorred dealing with the press. He was the flavoring, a lightning-fast thinker on his designer shoes who loved to schmooze and flirt with the press.

Wetzel stood, turned around to the gallery and studied the spectators. "Who are all these people?"

Tracey Tarlton anxiously sat in a holding cell, subpoenaed by DeGuerin. The twins and their boyfriends anxiously sat in the DA's office, subpoenaed by DeGuerin. Most in the crowded gallery were also witnesses subpoenaed by DeGuerin.

In contrast, Wetzel had not subpoenaed one witness.

DeGuerin, in his de rigueur white shirt and striped tie, dark blazer with a white hankie in the breast pocket, gray slacks, and expensive cowboy boots, stood and began his opening statement. He was a man who bobbed in his boots, as if he weren't used to wearing them, despite the fact that he always did—he had a self-admitted complex about his height. But he was smug enough to boast a love for Texas' most hated insect, the fire ant, and affection for roping, tying, branding, and castrating cattle.

"The facts of the case are very weak," DeGuerin stated, and he quickly outlined the solicitation-for-murder case. "Miss Goodson is not to be believed," he claimed. "Her credibility is zero."

Despite the State knowing about Celeste's claims for two years, DeGuerin argued, the DA's office didn't pursue the case until it looked like the court of appeals would reduce Celeste's $8 million bond on the Beard murder charge.

He rapidly moved to the audiotape recorded by the Beard twins in which Celeste said she'd hired someone to kill Tarlton. "This audiotape has been altered." DeGuerin didn't bother with any substantiation.

Wetzel didn't bother with an opening statement.

Instead, DeGuerin began proving Goodson's lack of credibility by calling her attorney, Allan Williams.

Williams, a tall, slender, white-headed man who looked like he was always leaning into the wind when he walked, testified that Goodson previously had been charged with a drug offense, had been placed on probation and was currently on probation for unauthorized use of government documents, a felony. She had also been arrested for assault and possession of drug paraphernalia.

DeGuerin pointed out that in the spring of 2000, a search warrant was issued for Goodson's house and Detective Henry Schuessler recovered "stolen and valuable jewelry" belonging to Celeste. Sporting gold rings on both of his hands, DeGuerin said that Goodson had been arrested and a motion was made to revoke her community supervision.

Allison Wetzel casually passed on questioning the witness.

In uniform and with a bit of a belly sticking out, a gray-haired and mustachioed Detective Schuessler walked up to the witness chair. He explained that "in Celeste's own words," her daughters, Kristina and Jennifer, and Kristina's boyfriend, Justin Grimm, were the prime suspects in the jewelry theft. But some of the allegedly missing jewelry was found in the safe in the Toro Canyon house. At Goodson's house, Schuessler found pawn tickets. He later recovered some of the reported stolen items, including a diamond necklace and a necklace of the Dallas skyline, in pawnshops in Austin and Louisiana.

Wetzel didn't bother with cross-examination.

"No gum in the courtroom!!" read an eight-and-a-half–by–eleven–inch sign posted on the swinging courtroom doors. Donna Rose Goodson walked through those doors, smacking chewing gum, and headed to her seat in the witness chair. She wore a proper black suit with cream blouse over her big bones and carried a matching little black purse with Chanel-like gold ornamentation. She had an innate cockiness that matched the boldness of her honky-tonk red hair.

Dick DeGuerin immediately asked her if she'd been convicted of a felony.

"Yes, I have," she answered in a voice as strong as her demeanor. She seemed as comfortable in that witness chair as any $1,000-an-hour professional expert witness.

Quickly, the defense attorney implied that the felon had stolen valuable jewelry from his sweet and innocent client, Celeste Beard Johnson.

"It was given to me," Goodson forcefully replied.

"That's your claim," he retorted.

"That's my claim," she answered.

DeGuerin stated she in fact did steal the jewelry.

No, she said, chomping her chewing gum. Compared to Goodson, DeGuerin was about the size of a fire ant. She could easily stomp him, and maybe even use his own cowboy boots to do it. At least she'd try to outwit him. That was just the way Goodson was.

Celeste watched with arms crossed.

Goodson admitted that just two or three weeks prior to this bond hearing she had accepted an immunity agreement from the State, which cleared her of any involvement in hiring someone to kill "the lady" who killed Steve Beard. But, she said, she never had any intention at all to hire someone to kill Tarlton.

So DeGuerin asked the witness why she took Celeste's money to hire a killer.

"If she wasn't going to give it to me, she was going to give it to someone else to get it done."

Allison Wetzel stood to enter State's Exhibit 1—Goodson's statement to the cops about the murder for hire.

In the last few days of September 1999, Celeste Beard zoomed her bronze mist-colored Cadillac into the back parking lot of Davenport Village shopping center. It was a small center, by shopping mall standards, with clusters of two-story, stone complexes in a Mediterranean style that sat a few blocks from Riverbend Church, which some claimed was the fastest growing church in America. Willie Nelson and Larry Gatlin frequented Riverbend's stage. Jaguars, Suburbans, and Lexuses filled its parking lots.

Davenport Village was also a few blocks from Lake Austin, Austin Country Club, and Celeste's multimillion-dollar home on Toro Canyon. She zipped her car as close as she could to Studio 29 hair salon and parked. Celeste popped into the salon at least twice a week, either to get her pink or red talons perfectly manicured or have her blonde locks twisted and twirled into an "up-do." And in her own calendar, on Thursday, September 30, two days before Steve was shot, she had jotted the notes "Joseph 6:30" and "Lilly [sic] Tomlin concert w/ Tracey." She plopped herself into hairdresser Joseph Prete's chair and said, "I don't know how I'm going to last three months. I wish the bastard was dead."

Donna Goodson, the salon's receptionist, eavesdropped. A few minutes later, she eased over to Prete. "What's up?"

Prete told her Celeste owned the shopping center.

". . . Financial partners in Davenport Village are West-lake residents, Celeste and Steve Beard," the *Austin Business Journal* had reported just the year before.

Goodson maneuvered herself over to the wealthy woman and started chatting about Halloween and shoes.

As their conversations progressed, Donna learned that Steve had given the teenaged twins Cadillacs and that Celeste was running out of cash, which irritated the hell out of Celeste. She was being forced to resort to travelers' checks because, according to Celeste, Steve's bank had frozen his account. Celeste informed Donna that she was going to get Steve's will changed after he got out of the hospital so that that wouldn't ever happen again.

Donna Goodson and Celeste Beard were starting a friendship.

"Using the traveler's check had nothing to do with Steve's will. It was more convenient."

In late January 2000, when the temperature could plummet from 95 to 35 within mere hours, Celeste walked into Studio 29. Steve was to be released from the hospital, and she wanted to make an appointment for him to have a manicure, pedicure, and haircut as soon as he was released.

The next day, Jennifer and her boyfriend, Christopher Doose, carefully maneuvered the wheelchair-bound Steve into the salon. Steve was in such pain that his stylist, Charmaine Richards, tried to finish fast to get him home.

"I brought Steve in for his haircut on the way home from the hospital. Jennifer and Christopher watched him while I ran home to make sure everything was ready for him."

That day, the temperature soared close to 90 degrees, then plunged the next day to near freezing. As the cold front swept in, Celeste phoned Donna, saying "Steve's back in the hospital." She started to cry. "I don't want him to die at home. I don't know why they released him."

Donna thought Celeste seemed put out. She'd phoned the salon only because Studio 29 had previously warned her that she was going to be charged for her appointments whether she showed up or not, since she missed so many. "Don't worry about your appointments," Donna told her. "Calm down. Just take care of whatever you need to do."

"I never cancelled my appointment saying Steve was going to die. He was ill and I wanted to be at the hospital with him, not getting my hair done."

Saturday, January 22, 2000, Steve did die. Suddenly, Donna Goodson had a cold feeling about Celeste Beard.

Before the funeral, Celeste returned to Studio 29 for another "up-do." After the funeral, she complained to Donna that no one was talking to her.

On another visit to Studio 29, Celeste carped that she was going to have to go to Dallas on some bank business. Celeste said the Dallas bankers were probably going to tell her she was poor. To that, Celeste said, she was going to tell them "they are going to have to learn how to lick [my] asshole and like it."

Donna warned Jennifer that she needed to watch out for her mother "because sometimes people get real depressed when they lose someone."

Celeste Beard's actions didn't insinuate she was a widow in mourning. In early February, Jennifer phoned Donna and said her mother wanted to get away and go party. Jennifer invited Donna to go with Celeste, Kristina, Justin, and herself to the Houston Livestock Show and Rodeo, held each year in the Astrodome. Donna said yes.

Around 2 P.M. on Friday, February 11, 2000, Jennifer and Celeste picked up Donna, with Celeste driving her new Cadillac, and following Kristina and Justin's car. It was a quick trip to Houston, with Celeste driving 100 mph.

"How could I drive 100 mph following another car all the way to Houston?"

As the hills of Austin zoomed into the pine trees of Bastrop, Texas, and the gold Cadillac sped past La Grange, home of

The Best Little Whorehouse in Texas, and finally turned onto Interstate 10 heading into Houston, Celeste admitted she'd gone into the psych hospital "because she hated Steve and it was a way to get away from him."

Steve had paid more than $200,000 in medical care for her and told her she needed to come home. She had told the twins not to say anything about Tracey to the police.

"Stay away from her," Donna advised. "Don't talk to her. And if you didn't have anything to do with it, don't feel guilty. Let the police do their work."

Celeste steered the Cadillac into the driveway of the Doubletree Suites Hotel in Houston's ritzy Galleria. She'd made plans to meet three guys she knew from the lake at Sullivan's Steakhouse, the overpriced eatery frequented by singles with gold and platinum credit cards. As Celeste sat in their hotel suite firming up the evening's plans, she fumed—one of the guys couldn't meet them.

When they showed up at Sullivan's, there were two men and a woman, a girlfriend of one of the men. Celeste was only interested in one, Lucky Leggett, a man who had a house near the Beards' Lake Travis property, who had another place in Houston, and who drove a Jaguar. She believed he was rich. She said she thought he'd be her next husband.

"Don't make me get that gun," she teased her "next husband." "Don't make me shoot you."

Lucky Leggett appeared a bit afraid of Celeste.

"Celeste, you need to watch what you're saying," Donna warned. "You need to lose that from your vocabulary."

They joked about stunts Celeste had pulled out at Windemere. They went dancing at a "hole-in-the-wall." As Celeste and Lucky sat at the bar, Donna accepted a ride back to the hotel with another man. She left him at the door, she said, and climbed into bed for some sleep with Jennifer.

Around midnight, Jennifer and Donna were still awake when Lucky and Celeste entered. Celeste bent her head down to Lucky's groin and performed oral sex on him. An infuriated Jennifer threw on the lights. Naked, Lucky grabbed his clothes and fled. Celeste laughed. Her husband had been dead for three weeks.

The next day, Celeste wanted to go to Lucky's house. He didn't want that.

"Lucky was not scared of me. I never said I'll shoot you, and I never gave him oral sex. That is absurd. Lucky and I were friends. I never wanted to marry him nor am I impressed by a Jaguar."

Sunday morning, the kids returned to Austin. Celeste and Donna planned on going to Lake Charles, Louisiana, to celebrate Celeste's birthday.

Before they checked out of the Doubletree, Donna lit a joint. She and Celeste shared it and got stoned. Celeste stared at Donna's extra large bosoms and remarked about how big they were.

They're real, Donna said.

Mine aren't, Celeste responded. She invited Donna to feel them . . . as she lifted up her shirt and exposed her enhanced glands.

Donna said she didn't accept Celeste's offer.

"I never commented on the flabby, saggy things Donna calls breasts."

Celeste thumbed through Houston's thick phone book until she found Lucky's address. They drove over to it. It was an apartment. As they drove away, they passed Lucky. Celeste didn't slow down. She didn't want to have anything to do with a man who lived in an apartment.

She phoned her bank; Bank of America had deposited her $10,000 monthly allowance. She and Donna headed east for Lake Charles and its riverboat casinos.

As they drove the two hours on Interstate 10, passing Houston's refineries, crossing the Old and the Lost River, and headed into Beaumont, Celeste obsessed about Tracey Tarlton—wondering why Tracey wasn't in jail. And she wondered why she herself hadn't been questioned. Celeste admitted her Arizona felony conviction, saying she'd burned a car.

With that, Donna confessed she too had been in trouble with the law and was on five years probation. She also mentioned a man named Modesto, who had gotten busted for marijuana possession. Donna then advised Celeste to watch what she was saying about Steve and his death because she came across as making herself sound guilty. Donna didn't see one iota of sadness in Celeste over Steve's death.

She certainly didn't show any grief as she told Donna that at noon, sharp, every Sunday, everyone, including the dog, had to be out of the house because that's when she gave Steve a blow job. Everyone had to be out because if the kids or the dog made a noise, she had to start over. And she hated doing that.

Again, Donna advised Celeste to watch what she was saying—Tracey could be working with the police to build a case against her.

Celeste said her attorney told her it would take two things to convict her—the gun and Tracey. If she could get rid of Tracey, she could justify her husband's death.

"Your guilt is going to eat you up."

Her attorney had lost only one murder case, Celeste claimed.

"You need to trust your lawyer, shut up, and stay calm, because one thing's for sure, this ain't going away."

"I'm not going to get caught, because they won't find my clothes in a Dumpster." She pointed out that the murderer in the case Burton had lost had left his clothes in a Dumpster. "And I'm no Anna Nicole Smith."

Celeste then put the big question to Donna—How much would it cost to get Tracey Tarlton killed? And she asked about the previously mentioned Modesto, inquiring how much he would charge to kill Tracey.

For $500, anyone could do it, Donna answered.

16

"I never discussed my case with Donna."

"Donna kept bringing up the shooting. She kept saying that if someone shot her husband, then she would hire someone to kill them."

Celeste Beard and Donna Goodson arrived in Lake Charles, walked the wide plank to the dockside riverboat, entered the Players casino, and sat down at the bar. As they did, Celeste locked eyes with a light brown–haired man with a moustache, and dressed in jeans and a T-shirt. He moved over and sat down beside them. He and Celeste began to drink and talk. He was from Houston, looked like a blue-collar worker, and was about Jimmy's height.

Donna walked off with $500 Celeste had given her and began gambling. As slot machines chinged and dinged in Donna's ears, she still plainly remembered Celeste's response to the $500 price tag for a hit on Tracey Tarlton.

"When can we do it?"

"Are you ready to go?" Celeste called over the flashing slot machines. "We're going to the other boat."

Donna climbed behind the wheel of the Cadillac and Celeste and her new beau of the minute lay down in the back seat. Donna listened and watched them in the rearview mirror as she chauffeured them to the Isle of Capri. She heard the sounds and saw the sights of sex.

Celeste and Donna ate from the buffet as the new man gave them his only two free meal coupons, while he sat and talked with them. Afterwards, he showed them how to play craps with Celeste's money, losing it all in a matter of minutes.

Celeste and Donna sped out of the town filled with blue-collar workers and air thick with the toxic smells of petrochemicals. As they blew west on Interstate 10, Donna phoned her friend Steve Regan, who was going to be alone on Valentine's Day, and invited him to V-Day dinner.

Celeste overheard and asked if there was something going on between Donna and Steve.

No, Donna said, so Celeste wanted to go with them.

Five hours later, back in Austin, Celeste and Donna stopped at a grocery store off of Highway 71 and got $500 out of an ATM, which Celeste promptly handed to Donna to pay Modesto to kill Tracey.

Donna's signed "Judgment of Community Supervision" regarding her probation on the third-degree felony charge of misuse of official information specifically stated she was to have no contact or association with Modesto Jaimes.

She was also supposed to report for "intensive outpatient treatment" at Cornerstone, a drug rehabilitation facility; attend two Alcoholics Anonymous, Narcotics Anonymous or Cocaine Anonymous, meetings a week; and report to the Austin Stress Clinic for its domestic violence prevention program.

"Donna never told me that she was on probation. I never told her . . .

"We went straight home from Houston. We never went to Lake Charles."

The Cadillac veered off Ben White Boulevard and turned toward Tracey's house on Wilson Street. Celeste wanted to point out the dinky house on the corner and Tracey's red-toned SUV. Ten, fifteen minutes later, Celeste and Donna drove through the electric gates at Toro Canyon, walked into the million-dollar home filled with overpriced figurines, changed clothes and went out drinking and partying. As they drove, Celeste asked Donna when she would talk to Modesto.

She'd probably see him at the bar, Donna replied. She didn't. But that didn't stop Donna from telling Celeste she'd seen him and given him the money. Don't worry about it, she told Celeste—it's taken care of.

When the bar closed, they went back to Toro Canyon without a hit man hired.

The following day, Valentine's, Donna went to Studio 29, picked up her paycheck, and immediately walked out on the job. She drove up Westlake Drive, turned onto Toro Canyon, and went to Celeste, to moan to her.

Donna could go to work for Celeste doing bookkeeping for $400 a week. Donna accepted the offer, and the two started drinking. Eventually, Donna went home, but later picked up her friend Steve Regan. The two of them returned to Toro Canyon.

Steve looked at the fancy house. "Are you sure this is it?" They walked up to the front door. He rang the bell.

"No, wrong house," Donna said.

"Shit!"

"Not," Donna laughed.

As soon as Celeste opened the glass front door and took one glance at Steve, an electrician, she appeared to fall in love with him.

With Donna in the back seat and Steve in the driver's seat, they rushed down the hills to Sixth Street and Louie's 106, a restaurant frequented by Republican lobbyists and wealthy University of Texas sorority girls.

The threesome followed dinner with a trek to Spiro's, a club that tried to portray itself as a hot, elegant bar for young professionals who liked to drink martinis and smoke cigars. It was just another joint to pick up a quick lay.

Celeste and Steve kissed . . . until Nick Gikas, a bar manager, eased into their group. Suddenly, Celeste's interest wandered, but only momentarily. She left with Steve and Donna. The three spent the night at the Toro Canyon house—Donna in Kristina's room, Steve and Celeste in Celeste's room, two nights after Donna and Jennifer had to watch Celeste give Lucky Leggett a blow job, not to mention the Lake Charles encounter.

Lucky's name was really John Leche.

• • •

"The incident in the hotel never happened. John never even took his clothes off. . . . I was never interested in him for anything more than a friend."

Donna finally wandered back to her house, which was really her mother's home.

There, on February 16, Donna got a hysterical call from Celeste—Justin's mother had a friend who'd overheard someone at Studio 29 gossip that Celeste had put Tracey up to killing Steve. Donna sped over to Toro Canyon to find a furious Celeste wanting to know "who was running her mouth." Donna had her suspicions—Kim Chandler, a woman who did Celeste's nails.

Donna drove Celeste over to Studio 29, where they found Kim standing outside. Celeste immediately opened her purse, yanked out a six-inch-long knife, and scrambled toward Kim. Kim ran too, but disappeared as Donna raced over to Celeste. Kristina swung into the parking lot, jumped out of her car, and both she and Donna screamed, begging Celeste to put down the knife. Celeste took the knife to her own body and started stabbing herself.

With blood oozing from her left arm, she walked through the back door of the salon and into its kitchen, where she encountered another Studio 29 employee. Donna and Kristina followed and overheard the employee telling Celeste "she was sorry about anything she had to do with this." The employee then left, and Celeste stabbed herself several times in the leg. Blood poured from Celeste's hip and thigh. Donna yanked the knife out of Celeste's hand.

Three uniformed officers allowed Donna to take Celeste to Austin Diagnostic Clinic, one of the hospitals that Steve Beard had frequented before he was shot. They walked in just after 3 P.M. Donna told the attendant that Celeste wasn't trying to kill herself, she was just frustrated, and was cut during a struggle over the knife.

"I wanted everyone to know in Studio 29 how hurt I was by what they were saying. I was devastated. I saw a knife in the

*break room and stabbed myself in the leg. I wanted them to
know I was hurting."*

Ten minutes later, Celeste disappeared. Staff finally found
her in the lobby. They took her to room number nine, and
sutured her skin back together. "Chief Complaint: L groin
puncture wound." It was two inches deep. Celeste was admitted for observation.

Steve Regan showed up at the hospital to take care of
Celeste. The girls came by with hamburgers. Donna left to
run errands, as Steve stayed by Celeste's side.

Celeste was released the next day, and Donna returned to
Toro Canyon where Celeste was trying to reach Robbie
Mayfield, the brainchild behind Davenport Village and
Steve's partner in the business. Robbie wasn't taking Ce-
leste's calls. Neither were many other people.

"They're probably working on getting a restraining order
against you," Donna offered.

And once again, Celeste wanted to go out. They went
and got manicures, came home, and took showers. When
Donna got out of her shower, she went looking for Celeste.
She found her in Steve's office, on the phone, saying, "Oh, I
shouldn't have called you." And she slammed down the
phone.

Donna thought Celeste was talking to Tracey. She felt
even more certain of that when Celeste later said to her, "It
hasn't been taken care of."

"Don't worry about it," Donna responded. "Take a chill
pill."

They hooked up with Steve Regan and went downtown
to a bar on Red River. Donna felt Steve was being awfully
possessive. He said he wanted to know everything.

Celeste and Steve started to leave, but Donna refused to
go with them, telling Celeste she wasn't going to ride with
Steve since he'd snatched the keys out of Donna's hands.
Donna rode back to Toro Canyon with two other friends, one
of whom was Jeff Willet, who worked at the bar and at Studio 29.

When Donna and her friends arrived at Toro Canyon, Steve had locked the doors and wouldn't allow Donna into the bedrooms. Finally, she told him she just wanted to get her things and leave, and he let her in, while retorting, "Celeste and I are going to Las Vegas to get married."

Donna's friends walked into the bedroom, and she reported the marital update.

"Hell, no, they aren't going to get married," Jeff erupted.

Kristina and Justin walked in.

As Celeste watched and listened to it all, Steve Regan told the teens that Donna was beating up Celeste.

Donna told them about the Vegas marriage.

Justin pulled Steve into the hallway. Moments later only Justin returned, reporting that he had asked Steve to leave, and he had.

Celeste slept until 5 P.M. the next day.

"I did not fall in love with the electrician Steve Regan. We were not a couple."

That night, Celeste and Donna returned to Spiro's, where Celeste picked up the bar manager she'd fancied a night or two earlier, Nick Gikas.

"I can hide you out on a mountain where they grow grapes in Greece," Nick cooed. Nick and Celeste spent the night together.

A few days later, the phone rang in the Beard house. Donna answered it. Charles Burton was on the line—Petra Mueller, the owner of Studio 29, had gotten a restraining order against Celeste. She was also suing Celeste for $100,000.

But Celeste didn't want to be served with the restraining order. They spent their time avoiding the constable trying to serve the directive, sometimes ducking out the back while he came up the front. Once, Donna faced the officer and told him Celeste was at a "nut house" in Arizona. Four days later, they called the constable and told him Celeste had flown back just for him—meet them at the house and only *you* come.

While they waited, Celeste pulled her full-length mink over her pajamas, socked on a fur hat, slapped on her sunglasses, and stuffed a clear purse with thirty bottles of pills.

They laughed their asses off as they watched the constable come up the driveway.

He rang the bell, and damn it, it wasn't the same officer. He'd tricked them.

But Celeste and Donna played on as Donna announced over the security speaker, "Who is it?"

He gave his name, and she asked to see his badge, which he put up to the surveillance camera. She made him wait another five minutes, then walked over to a side door, slid it open, stepped out onto the front porch and told him to have a seat. "I'll get her," she said formally, trying to stifle her laughter.

When Celeste finally walked out to the porch, a Marlboro Light 100 in one hand, the purse of pills in the other, the constable's eyes bugged.

"Would you get me a vodka, Donna?" Celeste asked. "I need to take some pills."

The officer read the restraining order to Celeste, as Donna handed her her vodka and Celeste slugged it back along with a fistful of pills. When he turned the page, a staple fell out.

"Oh, you can't leave that down there," Donna said. "You must find it."

The pair complained that it might get stuck in a dog's paw.

The officer got down on his hands and knees and searched for the staple.

"You're good at that," Donna said.

He crawled around the porch until they told him to be on his way. And the two thirtysomething women with felony criminal records walked into the house screaming, jumping, and rolling with laughter like 10-year-olds. They ran to the security VCR so that they could watch the video, when Kristina and Justin came home. They watched it together.

"I wish I could remember what all I took," Celeste said of her handful of pills. "I had a damn good buzz."

. . .

Celeste and Donna kept going out drinking every single night.

And every single day, Celeste asked Donna when Tracey was going to be killed.

"It's supposed to be taken care of," Donna answered. Finally she said, "It's going to be taken care of while we're in New Orleans." They were going to New Orleans, the site of Celeste's fourth honeymoon, to continue their birthday partying. "But they need more money to do it."

"How much?"

"Twenty-five hundred."

Celeste told Kristina to go to the bank and get $2,500.

With Kristina, Justin, Celeste, and Donna standing in Celeste's bathroom, Celeste handed the envelope to Donna.

"The money—$2,500—she had . . . was for our trip to New Orleans."

On March 2, 2000, Celeste bought some Viagra and slipped it into Nick's drink.

The next day, March 3, Donna got behind the wheel of Celeste's Cadillac and the two of them streaked over to New Orleans, staying at an elegant hotel for one night, then moving to a Ramada Inn on Interstate 10 and phoning Cole, whom Celeste had known for only a few nights. She invited him to join them.

"No," Cole answered. "I'm working. I don't have the money."

"There's a plane ticket waiting for you . . . Can you be on that plane?"

"I'll be on the plane."

There was nothing like the voodoo cocktail scent of bourbon, rum, and urine on humid pavement to lure one into the dark side.

They drank, they partied, and they shopped. Celeste liked to spend money, and Donna liked helping her.

They walked past a wig shop, its windows filled with wigs of many colors. Celeste said she wanted a wig. She and Donna slipped in. Cole waited outside. And he waited.

And he waited. He walked into the shop. "Come on. Let's go. I didn't come here to do this." He stood on the sidewalk and waited some more.

When Celeste and Donna walked out, their arms overflowed with pink, purple, and platinum blonde wigs. Cole counted ten wigs each in every possible color.

A day later, Celeste stuffed $200 into Cole's jacket pocket, and he was gone.

"Let's party!" Celeste said.

They moved to the Bienville House, a boutique hotel with lacy, black wrought-iron balconies located in the French Quarter and not far from the Hard Rock Cafe, House of Blues, and Saks Fifth Avenue. But it was an Eckerd drug store across the street that they walked to first so that Celeste could buy a phone card. She wanted to be able to make calls that couldn't be traced back to her.

Yet she made sure to use her credit card for all of her other purchases to prove she was in New Orleans when, she hoped, Tracey Tarlton would be murdered in Austin.

They drank. They picked up men. A 6-foot, 6-inch–tall bellman plopped Celeste on his shoulders and carried her up to her room. Donna slept by the small courtyard pool or in the lounge to give Celeste her intimate privacy.

Celeste turned to Donna and asked her to call and find out if Tracey "had been taken care of." Donna dialed a number and acted like she was talking to someone. Upon hanging up, she told Celeste that it still hadn't been done.

"When we were in New Orleans, Donna kept bringing up hiring a hit man and I got scared and talked to Cole about it. He said to just ignore her, that she was crazy."

Celeste and Donna got robbed and took a cab back toward the hotel despite not having any cash. A block from the Bienville, they jumped and ran. They raced up to their room, laid some tampons, douche, and fifty pennies outside their door for his pay if anyone came knocking on their door. Then they locked it shut.

Celeste repeatedly asked Donna to find out if the deadly

deed had been done. Donna phoned, then told Celeste that Tracey might be getting killed right then, because no one answered.

Celeste phoned Tracey's work and home to find out if she was still alive.

Donna didn't think that Celeste ever spoke to Tracey. So as Donna and Celeste sat in a New Orleans restaurant, she broke the news to Celeste—Modesto needed more money to pull off the hit. "Another guy is going to kill Tracey. We need to get some money for him now." Sam was his name, she said. He was going to pull off the hit that night if he had the money.

Celeste tore out of the restaurant and ran for the hotel. Barreling through its doors, she ordered the six-foot-six bellman to have her Cadillac packed and ready to go in five minutes—she had an emergency. Fifteen minutes later, on March 9, 2000, Celeste Beard and Donna Goodson were on their way back to Austin with receipts for $11,000 worth of partying and shopping in New Orleans.

When they drove into Austin, they stopped again at a grocery store on the outskirts of town to get some ATM cash.

Celeste got $500 and handed it over to Donna. They drove to Toro Canyon, where Donna dropped off Celeste, told her she was going to meet Sam, and went to her own home. The next night, Donna told Celeste that they needed more money for Sam and she was supposed to meet him at Waterloo Brewing Company at 10 P.M.

Donna drove Celeste and herself to the downtown brew-pub in Celeste's Cadillac. Waterloo was filled with loud, shorts- and jeans-clad young people throwing darts, shooting pool, playing pinball, and eating burgers while drinking too much beer on its second-story deck. Soon Cole and a friend showed up. Despite Cole's attentions, Celeste kept a close watch on Donna . . . until Cole started playing with Celeste, which distracted her. So the very next time Celeste asked Donna if she'd seen Sam, Donna answered yes.

"Damn, I missed him," Celeste replied.

"The five hundred dollars is going to take care of it," Donna responded. "You have to be patient. He needs to go down to Mexico to take care of some family business. He'll take care of it when he gets back."

At 12:20 in the afternoon of January 25, 2001, one year to the day after Steve Beard's death was reported in the *Austin American-Statesman*, Dr. Christine Warmann phoned Seton Shoal Creek hospital.

By 5 P.M., Tracey Tarlton was being checked into the psychiatric facility on emergency referral from Dr. Warmann. At the time, Tracey was a temp employee at Dell Computer doing customer telephone support . . . and she was suicidal. Tracey planned to slit her throat.

Her intake nurse thought Tracey was misstating her level of suicidal thoughts because Tracey stated she'd simply leave Shoal Creek if she wanted to kill herself.

The same nurse noted that Tarlton was experiencing auditory and visual hallucinations. She saw a cat running alongside her SUV, but there was no cat. She saw a car blocking the freeway and swerved to miss it, almost wrecking her own vehicle. Then she realized there had been no car there.

At first, the whispering voices she'd heard seemed malevolent. Later, they seemed practical, "telling her to kill herself, she's not a good person, and she's a drain."

Tracey was so confused when she signed the hospital's various release forms that she frequently put the wrong date beside her name. But she was coherent enough to remember those "TNT" initials when she instructed the staff, in writing, not to notify any of her family members. In fact, she left blank the space for a family member's name. Instead, she listed her emergency contact as Deborah Wiley, friend.

Her goal, she wrote, was "to get through this psychotic episode."

By 7 P.M., a polite Tracey Tarlton had completed her admission paperwork and left the consultation room. Restless, she went to her room, then to the dayroom, back to her room. She roamed the hallway, went back to her room, and again to the dayroom, where she watched TV for a few minutes before returning to her room to read. She was asleep by 10:45 and was supposed to be checked every fifteen minutes due to being on suicide watch. The nurses skipped checking her for one hour.

At 10:45 A.M. on January 26, Tracey's every-fifteen-minute suicide watch record was marked DISCHARGED. Her thoughts were organized, her insight limited.

About that same time, Dr. David W. Brown dictated notes regarding Tracey—her psychosis had been worsening for the past two days. "She . . . describes intense tactile hallucinations of 'my skin erupting.'" For two weeks, she'd been suffering racing thoughts, had little need for sleep, and was "feeling 'despairing.'" And, he noted, "She describes auditory hallucinations, feeling that someone is behind her, and that someone 'has a hit out on me.'"

Wednesday, March 15, 2000, Donna and Celeste partied and fought. The fighting continued into the next day, resulting in a car chase up Loop 360, Celeste tossing away a five-carat ring that Donna was wearing, Celeste begging Donna to return to Toro Canyon, and Donna calling the cops on Celeste.

"The ring Donna is talking about . . . is the ring she pawned. It is the diamond cocktail ring."

They partied and fought again the next night. With Donna wearing a green St. Patrick's Day wig that Celeste had provided, Donna handed Celeste an envelope filled with $2,500 in cash. "It's the money I owe you."

Not much later, they were in a limousine with Cole that pulled into the Dog & Duck, a dimly lighted dive of an Irish pub with dark, low ceilings, cozy corners, thirty beers on tap, more darts and pool, and lots of cigarette smoke. It was a hangout for jazz musicians, writers, and photographers, and folks who liked to joke about their drinking and drug use. Donna started feeling a little weird. She thought somebody had slipped her some Ecstasy. Then Celeste reached over and kissed Donna. Donna thought Celeste was on X, too.

The next thing Donna knew, Celeste and Cole were gone, leaving her at the Dog & Duck.

They were down the street at Waterloo Park listening to a Patti Smith concert. During the concert, Celeste's cell phone rang—Donna calling, enraged that they'd left her. She bitched at Celeste. Celeste handed the phone to Cole. Donna bitched at Cole. "Hey, hey, I'm losing you," Cole said. "I'm losing you. Bad reception," and he hung up.

Donna phoned and phoned Celeste's house, leaving perhaps as many as five messages. In her last message, Donna said she and Celeste had "some unfinished business to take care of."

17

"Donna told me that she beat her husband up to a pulp with his knight [sic] stick. He was A.P.D. [Austin Police Department] That is why I was scared of her."

"If I don't hear from you in an hour, I'm going to call Laylan Copelin at the *Austin Statesman* and sell those pictures we took in New Orleans," Donna threatened. She was damn pissed about St. Patrick's Day. Plus, she was flat broke. She'd given back the $2,500, only to string more out of Celeste. So she had to resort to a few topless photos.

On March 19, with Kristina talking in the background, Justin Grimm turned on his tape recorder and played the cell phone message into it.

"I'm gonna wait about thirty more minutes and then I'm not going to contact you anymore 'cause I know her games. And then I'm gonna go take these pictures to the newspaper and sell them. Then we can play real ball," Donna said.

Celeste called Donna within five minutes wanting her to come over.

They met the following day at Baby Acapulco's, a Pepto-Bismol–pink and flowered Mexican restaurant with a noisy outdoor, wrought-iron–fenced patio facing the busy, smoggy traffic on Barton Springs Road. But it had cheap frozen margaritas that were easy to suck down on a spring day.

"If you really want this done," Donna said, referring to the hit on Tracey, "you need to give me the twenty-five hundred dollars back."

Celeste handed her an envelope and told Donna she was going back into Timberlawn. Her attorney, she said, told her she needed to go the psychiatric facility because no one could touch her there. Plus, she thought it'd be a good alibi for when Tracey was blown away. Celeste asked Donna to drive her to the airport.

"I never met her at Baby Acapulco's."

Donna drove up to the Toro Canyon house, walked in, and handed the pictures to Celeste, who turned them over to Jennifer. In return, Celeste gave Donna a check for $2,400, enough to keep her employed for six weeks. The check was dated March 20, 2000. Another check to "Donna Godson" was dated March 20, then marked out and changed to March 17. That check, on Celeste's account, was signed by Kristina.

Celeste also gave Donna a Texaco card and her cell phone so that she could call Donna. Donna already knew the code to the phone—1002, the day Steve Beard was shot. Celeste had told her that as far as she was concerned, that was the day Steve died.

Soon, Donna drove past the stone fountain leading in to Austin-Bergstrom International Airport, circled the long drive to the terminal, and waited in the no parking zone while Celeste walked into the airport and got $200 out of the ATM.

A week later, Nick Gikas, the manager of Spiro's, told

Donna he wanted to visit Celeste at the hospital. The following Monday, his day off, they drove to Dallas.

Timberlawn, from the outside, was a serene antebellum home with a large lawn of healthy green grass and shady trees. In the 1960s and '70s, it was the place for wealthy drunks and addicts to go and dry out—a place of whispered prestige.

Celeste, Nick, and Donna visited for a bit, then Donna turned to Nick. "Celeste and I need to talk for a while in private." She waited for Nick to leave the room. "This is the total amount needed to do the job." Donna reached for a piece of paper and pen and wrote down *$10,000*. She knew Celeste had given Nick $10,000, and he was only sleeping with her. "It will be taken care of before you get out of the hospital."

"I had given Nick a check so that he could bring his wife and son here to the States. He loves his family very much. Nick and I were just friends."

Celeste scribbled out a check to Donna Goodson for $7,650. The date was March 27, 2000. They told Nick the check was for Celeste so that she would have some money when she got out of the hospital—Kristina had frozen all of her accounts.

"Nick says nothing like that happened at the hospital. I gave several patients money to pay their bills, taxes, etc. About $5,000 went to patients. The money I gave Donna is what she said I owed her for the next months and for expenses. At that time I thought I would be in there for a couple of months. I was heavily sedated and forgot I had already give her some money."

That April Fool's Day, Donna went to a bank, cashed the check and got $2,500 in cash, the rest in a cashier's check. She called Celeste to report that she had the money.

Celeste told her to get someone to do it, it didn't matter who.

Donna headed to Lake Charles to gamble.

• • •

Upon Donna's return to Austin, Kris wanted to know about the checks and money Celeste had given Donna. And out of the blue, she asked, "Who's Sam?"

"I don't know. Ask your mom." Donna hung up, called Celeste, and told her she didn't think the plan to kill Tracey was going to work because Kristina was "asking too many questions. She wanted to know who Sam was. This is not going to happen."

"Goddamn it. I'm checking right out of here," Celeste screamed. "I'll fix that little bitch!"

Kristina and Justin held a micro-cassette tape recorder up to the cell phone as Celeste talked to Kris from Timberlawn.

"Keep your Goddamn mouth shut," she ordered. "Who in the hell do you think you are? Huh?"

"I don't know," Kris meekly answered.

"You get in my fucking Cadillac right now and you drive up here and you pick me up. Do you understand?"

"I'm not driving to Dallas," Kristina said.

"Oh, yes, you are."

"Why?"

"If you don't drive up here, then get your shit out of the house and move!"

"Fine," Kris said.

"And leave your car. Are you driving up here?"

"No, I'm not driving up there."

"Yes, you are! You sat there and you fucking told her about the tux and the ring and, um, that you never played that tape for, um, Burton that I did. And about—"

"No, I never said you did."

"You liar."

"No, I did not," Kristina pleaded.

"You liar!"

"Whatever. Oh, fine. Believe Donna."

"I will, because you are nothing but a little liar. I want you to get in my car and get up here now. Do you understand English, Kristina?"

"Mom, no!"

"Kristina, I'm not, I'm not asking you, I am telling you. Get in my car and get up here. If you make me take a cab home, I will never forgive you. And you better call Donna right now and you better get everything straight as to what you said and didn't say, you big-mouthed little bitch."

Kristina begged her mother to stop calling her a bitch. "You're constantly lying to me."

"That's right, Kristina. I am. And I want you out of my house. But you better get my car up here now. Do you understand? Do you understand!"

Kristina sighed.

"Are you going to answer me!"

"I'm here," Kris whispered.

"Are you going to get in my car and get up here now? Or do I have to take a cab home?"

Again, Kristina sighed and there was silence.

"And you did this. Opening your big fat trap. Kristina, Goddamn it, answer me! Are you coming or not?"

"I don't think it is right for me to come up to Dallas."

"Well, that's too bad. Kristina, I'm leaving this hospital whether you come up here or not."

"I know you are."

"How I get home is up to you. When did you decide to call Donna?"

"Donna called me."

"Are you coming up here or not? You are wasting time."

"Mom, I'm not com—I'm not driving to Dallas at eight o'clock at night."

"Yes, you are!"

Kristina protested. "What about school tomorrow?"

"I don't give a *crap* about school. Who pays for it? I do!"

"I give a crap about school."

"Well, then you are just going to have to be tired. Aren't you? Are you coming?"

"I—No."

"Yes, Kristina, I swear to God I will make you pay for this if you do not come up here."

Kris asked her mother if she was "going to beat the shit" out of her.

"Oh, I will make you pay," Celeste replied.

"How?"

"Oh, I have a hundred thousand ways I can make you pay."

She and Kristina argued back and forth over whether Kristina was a brat.

"I'm not a brat," Kristina protested.

"You're a nosy, good-for-nothing daughter. That's what you are."

"Thanks."

"You don't know when to keep your mouth shut and when not to. All you do is hurt me and hurt me and hurt me."

"You hurt me."

"How am I hurting you?"

"All the time. By lying to me."

"I hurt you by buying you a forty-thousand-dollar car?"

"You didn't buy me a forty-thousand-dollar car," Kris retorted.

"Kris, whatever you say. I don't care. Where do you live? You live in a Goddamn mansion."

"Yeah."

"You want to know what hurt is? Why don't you go get a job at McDonald's and pay your own way through school?"

"Fine."

They argued again about Kristina coming to pick up Celeste, with Kristina repeating that she wouldn't do it—"because I am tired of you treating me like this."

Celeste shot back that she treated Kristina the way she did because Kris was "always" saying things she wasn't supposed to say—like talking to Donna.

"She called me."

"You don't know how to hang up the phone?"

But Kris had learned at her mother's knee and knew how to respond. "Mom, you are just as bad as your molesting father." She continued, "You treat me just as bad."

"Oh, I do? How do I do that?"

"By the way you talk to me."

Celeste wanted to know if that's what Emily Grimm, Justin's mother, had said.

"No."

Once again, Celeste ordered her daughter to Dallas. Once again, Kristina simply sighed. Finally, Kris added, "I don't know why you are doing this to me."

"Why are you doing this to me, big mouth?" Celeste responded.

"Because you are making bad decisions."

Celeste argued that she was old enough to make her own bad decisions and she didn't need a 19-year-old brat telling her what to do.

"So I can watch you go to jail?" Kris said.

"For what?"

"For what? What do you think for?"

Timberlawn patients interrupted the conversation. Celeste suddenly thought she heard another voice on Kristina's end—Justin taping the conversation. Kris declared that she was the only one on the line.

". . . I am *not* going to jail. But you are making it worse. If you would just shut your fucking mouth, it wouldn't be that bad. But no, you keep making it worse and worse and worse. So now we gotta put up with more of Donna's shit because of you."

Twice, Kristina asked her mother what she had to put up with.

"You don't know?" Celeste screamed. "I don't have to explain to you. Thanks a lot, Kris. That's all I can tell you. Thanks a fucking lot. Now get in the car and pick me up."

"No."

Celeste ranted and demanded to know why Kris had done what she'd done—talked to Donna and butted into her mother's business.

"I don't know why," Kris answered.

" 'Cause you're a Goddamn little bitch. Get in the car and pick me up. And I appreciate you saying that I am just as bad as my molesting father."

"Well," the teen responded, "you treat me like shit."

Celeste defended that that was because her daughter didn't do what she was told. "I thought we made up on Saturday," she said, referring to when she and Kris had had a joint counseling session on April Fool's Day. "I thought you were going to quit your shit. But no."

"Why don't you quit your shit?"

"Why don't you get in the car and pick me up? Or I swear to God you are going to live to fucking regret it. If you do not get in the car and come pick me up, I am going to make your life hell!"

"It is already."

"Well, it's gonna be worse," Celeste swore and demanded one more time that Kristina come pick her up. "Don't you dare bring Justin with you. Why do you hate me so much?"

"I don't hate you," Kris said. "I love you. You are the one who hates me."

"If you loved me, you would butt out of my business."

"No." Because of Kris, Celeste claimed, Donna thought she had lied about everything.

"You are lying about everything, Mom."

Celeste wanted to know one thing she'd lied about.

"Like, oh, you didn't even—You told—You didn't tell us that you came home from New Orleans early and made us believe you were in New Orleans."

Celeste insisted that they were in New Orleans.

Kristina argued that she was in Austin. "And then you bring Cole and lie to me and tell me that you didn't bring anybody from Austin. You fly him back and forth. You're still seeing Nick. What do you think the DA is gonna say about all of that?"

"Well, a lot," Celeste responded, "since you're the one that has to keep your big mouth open to tell everybody."

"No," Kris said. "Everybody already knows."

"No!"

"You don't think they're watching you?"

"Oh, shut up! Are you going to get in the car and come get me or not?"

"I can't."

"Why not?"

"Because I'm scared of you."

Celeste begged, pleaded, implored, and begged again for her daughter to come get her. She demanded that Kris phone Jennifer, while staying on the phone with her, and tell Jennifer to drive to Dallas and pick up their mother. But Celeste had one more sentence of caution for Kristina. "You are going to regret not picking me up."

18

"Donna had just finished talking with me at Timberlawn and was threatening me. She said that she was going to sell my pictures from New Orleans to the paper. I was very upset, because she had just visited me a few days earlier and got a check for $7,000 to work for me. She even told me that she would never return the money and that she had no intention of working for me. From what I recall, what set Donna off was a police officer called regarding her returning some items of mine and trying to get cash when they were purchased on my credit card. This was at Dillard's.

"Donna said I was trying to have her arrested. I knew nothing about the incident until a few hours earlier when Kristina called and told me about it. At that time, I instructed Kristina to forget about it until I got home and could find out what was going on. I had begged Kristina not to talk with her. Donna told me that she had just gotten off the phone with Kristina. That is why I was so livid with Kristina."

Two weeks later, Donna's cell phone rang. It was Celeste. She wanted her $10,000 back and she wanted to make the exchange at Chuy's on North Lamar, a local Tex-Mex restaurant that was obsessed with Elvis décor and closer to Jimmy's neighborhood than Toro Canyon Road.

"Sure," Donna said, despite the fact that she no longer

had the money. Around 8 P.M., their appointed meeting time, Donna drove by Chuy's and she kept on driving.

Ten minutes later, Celeste phoned Donna again. "Where are you?"

"You weren't there, so I left."

Celeste started crying frenetic tears. "I was just a few minutes late."

"You can still meet me, but not alone."

Celeste fell from frenzied to furious.

"Meet me at Waterloo."

Donna sat at Waterloo with friends when Celeste drove up and phoned her to come outside. Donna walked out to Celeste's Cadillac, a friend watching from nearby. "Looks like you got ripped off," Donna said.

Celeste's body shook in the late spring heat.

"They got scared and ran to Mexico," Donna said. "Celeste, you will be okay. I just can't have anything to do with this. Whatever you do will be okay."

"No, I won't. I'm going to kill myself."

"Well," Donna responded, "I'm not going to hang around to see that. Goodbye." She got out of the car and went back to drinking at Waterloo.

"Her entire story about Modesto, Sam, and the money is a complete fabrication."

May 13, 2000, Celeste wanted to meet. Donna agreed. They'd meet at Baby Acapulco's, this time the I-35 location. Donna lived on the far north side of the city, while Celeste lived on the far west side. Baby Acapulco's was somewhat in the middle, though it leaned toward Donna's side of town, as well as Jimmy Martinez's, again.

Celeste said she'd been traveling with Cole, that the twins had left, taken everything, and were in hiding. She thought they might have gone to New York to attend a wedding. She wanted to locate them.

Celeste checked Donna into the Red Lion hotel on I-35, just an exit or so away from Baby A's so that Donna could call New York and find the girls. Then Celeste wanted to drive to New York.

"What are you going to do?"

"I'm going to take care of them," Celeste answered.

Donna tried to find out if Celeste and Cole had gotten married. She never found out. And she never made the calls. But she stayed at the hotel for three days.

"Donna came by the house and told Cole and I that she had moved out because her mom kicked her out and she had no place to go. I didn't want her in the house, so I told her I would follow her to the Red Lion and rent her a room for the weekend. At that time, I told her about all the jewelry that had been stolen from the house and not once did she say she had it because I gave it to her. I specifically told her the pieces. She only said she had my banking records and cancelled checks to Steven's account."

A week or so later, Celeste and Donna met again at Whole Foods. Donna climbed into Celeste's car, and Celeste asked why Sam hadn't returned the money.

"He's gone, and I don't know how to get ahold of him anymore."

In closing her affidavit, Donna Rose Goodson stated, "All I did for Celeste was drive her, took her phone calls, brushed her hair, waxed her eyebrows, and just catered to her. I didn't have any type of sexual relationship with her."

"She was paid $400 a week to basically hang out with me. The girls were too busy with their boyfriends and I was extremely lonely."

Donna had pages and pages of both typed and hand-scribbled notes about her days with Celeste. Her cursive writing was giant-sized as though it were from a large-print book. Both sets of notes overflowed with misspelled words. Some of the notes agreed with her affidavit. Some of them had slight differences. The gist, though, was the same throughout all.

Dick DeGuerin called Travis County Sheriff's Office Detective Jim Anderson.

Sporting a moustache, buzz cut, and drill sergeant look, Anderson had been assigned to the Goodson case on October 14, 2002, and took her statement after talking to her "for hours and hours and hours."

Again, DeGuerin outlined Goodson's past crimes—four assault charges, one charge for damaging property, two charges for possession of dangerous drugs, and then there was the killing Tracey Tarlton episode.

Wetzel objected that DeGuerin was the one doing the testifying.

He soon passed the witness.

Wetzel entered State's Exhibit 2, the three checks to Donna Goodson—one for $2,400 signed by Celeste, one for $400 signed by Kristina, and the big $7,650 check signed by Celeste for payment to find a killer for Tracey Tarlton.

The checks were stolen from the defendant's home by Jennifer and Kristina Beard or Kristina's boyfriend, Justin, DeGuerin argued. He objected twice, he said. He objected once by saying that the three had met with former prosecutor Bill Mange, then started bringing things to Mange that belonged to Celeste Beard Johnson, when they weren't authorized to do so. He objected a second time on the basis that it was hearsay from Donna Goodson.

He was overruled.

He argued that the items wouldn't be admissible in trial because they were taken without authority.

"And those are your objections?" the judge responded, in an incredulous tone of voice. "This is a bail hearing, and I don't believe the rules of evidence apply."

The rules of evidence do apply, DeGuerin responded.

The judge let his comment pass until Wetzel entered State's Exhibit 3, one of the audiotape recordings of Celeste talking to Kristina. When DeGuerin objected to the exhibit, the judge informed the defense lawyer that the rules of evidence *don't* apply in a bond hearing. DeGuerin kept arguing, while Wetzel set up her tape player, and the judge simply nodded to him with each objection.

"It's obviously not a valid tape. It's been edited."

"Overruled."

Wetzel pressed the PLAY button on the boom box.

"I'm tired," a young voice moaned.

"What?" Celeste answered, irritated.

"I said I'm tired," Kristina replied.

"Well, you need to get in the car and go home and go to bed. . . . Are you listening?"

"Yeah," she said, weakly.

"Kristina, just because you're nineteen doesn't mean you don't have to do what I tell you to do. You want to move out, is that what you're telling me?"

"I don't know."

"What?"

"I said I don't know."

"You *might* want to move out and move in with the Grimms?" Celeste asked.

"No, that's not what I'm saying."

"Then what are you saying?" Celeste demanded.

"I don't know."

"Make up your mind right now, because I asked you to do something and you're not doing it." There was a long silence. Finally, Celeste filled the air. "Is that where you want to live, at the Grimms'?" Again, there was silence. "Kristina?"

"I'm here," the teen moaned.

Her mother soon asked, "Then what are you saying by deliberately disobeying me? Is Mrs. Grimm sitting right there?"

"No."

"What are you saying by deliberately disobeying me? I want you to answer that question. I am not yelling at you, but I expect an answer."

"I'm not saying anything."

"Then why did you not go home when I told you to? Huh?"

"I don't know," Kristina replied.

"Kristina, let's get something straight right now. Are you listening? Are you wide awake? Can you hear me?"

"Yeah."

"If you want to continue going to college, if you want to continue to have your expenses paid without working, then you better get your ass home tonight. Do you understand?"

"Yeah."

"Because if you don't, I'm gonna come over there tonight and get your car keys and I'm gonna take your car away, and you can have the Grimms buy you a new car, and they can pay for your clothes, because I will lock you out of the house. I will change all the locks tomorrow. I am not playing games with you. You live at home. Do you understand what I am telling you? And I am not going to change my mind. Do you understand?"

"Yeah."

"And you're willing to just say *Fuck it*?"

"I don't know," the teen said.

"What do you mean, you don't know?"

"I don't know."

"What don't you know? What don't you know? Because I'm, I'm a worse person than my father who molested me, is that what you don't know? Huh? Did I deserve an old man's dick up my ass when I was four years old? Is that what you don't know? 'Cause I've been cruel to you? Answer me. Answer me, Kris. Are you still there, or did you hang up?"

"I'm still here."

"Then what's the problem? I realize that you're angry with me, but not half as angry as I am with you. That still doesn't give you the right to disobey me."

"Uh-huh."

"What?"

"I said I didn't say anything."

Celeste asked her daughter if the Grimms had talked her into staying at their house.

"No."

"Did they know you were told to go home?"

"Yes, I said that you wanted me to go home."

Celeste asked what they said.

"Do what I want to do."

"Well, Justin's not allowed over at our house anymore."

"Fine," Kristina stated.

"So I guess that means that you're staying over there?"

"I don't know."

"Why? Because they're telling you one thing, and I'm telling you something else?"

Kristina eventually answered, "No."

There was more conversation and more long silences. And Celeste asked, "Why are you doing this to me?"

Kristina replied, "Why are you doing this?"

"Because, Kris, I am not going to have my life run by a nineteen-year-old teenager who thinks she knows everything in the Goddamned fucking world. I am an adult. I am your mother. You are not going to tell me what to do, and you are going to do what I tell you to do. And if you don't like it, you can talk to me about it. You don't go behind my back and do what I ask you not to do. You—Ever since— You and Justin have been so high and mighty. You think the Goddamned house is yours. Well, it's not. It's mine. If I want to piss away every penny, I'll do it. But I thought that's what I was going in there for help with. But obviously not, because I can't even trust my own kids to keep their Goddamned mouths shut long enough for me to get out and get everything taken care of. And then you're gonna threaten me about you don't know if you're gonna stay at Justin's or not. I'm telling you right now, I am not kidding and this is not impulsive." Celeste got even angrier. "You choose to stay over there and you will be sorry. I will get a restraining order first thing in the morning. You will not be allowed at my house, ever. You know how Christopher feels at his dad's house? You're going to feel worse at our house. And you aren't getting any of your stuff either, 'cause I'm gonna make you, I'm gonna make you feel what it feels like what I had to go through when I was seventeen and had nothing and you'll be nineteen and have nothing. Let's see if you can make it up the ladder to success. And you're lucky. You didn't have your father sticking his dick in you when you were four years old for eight years."

Celeste Beard Johnson sat in the courtroom, her head down, scribbling on a yellow legal tablet.

"But I'm mean—I'm so mean, I'm, I'm worse than that. And you're not going to be able to pay Peggy to go to counseling either. You just better stop and think exactly [about] everything you get. And I don't ask that much of you. Oh, do I?"

"Yes, you do," Kristina responded.

"Like what?" her mother retorted.

"Everything. You ask me to run here, run there."

"Well, if you resent it, you little bitch, then you should have said something, instead of just doing it. That's what you call *communication*. I would've gotten somebody else to do it. If you had a problem with it, you should've said, 'Mom, I really don't want to do this,' instead of holding all this resentment and hatred inside of you. And then it comes out to people that I've asked you not to speak with. That's the adult way to do things. You talk about it. You just don't do it and then get pissed off until all this resentment builds up and then, boy, when you get a chance to slam-dunk me, you do it. And then you think you can do it while I'm in the hospital and can do nothing about it. And your little power-of-attorney trick didn't work either, because it's all revoked. You are not going to run my life, do you understand that? You are nineteen and you are not worldly enough to run my life. You're a nineteen-year-old acting like a twelve-year-old."

"Oh, whatever," Kristina replied.

"That's how twelve-year-olds act."

"You're the one that's acting like a twelve-year-old."

"How am I acting like a twelve-year-old?" Celeste bit back.

"Walking around doing what you want to do, hurting yourself to get what you want."

Celeste screamed, "I was fucking depressed, you Goddamned little bitch! I was fucking sick! You think I did that because I wanted to do that? What the hell is wrong

that I have all these mental problems. But you at least get
the dog home tonight. Do you understand? If the dog...
home, I'm gonna have th...

Suzy Spencer

168

an y

"No, that s ...

"Then why did you say
my dad hurt me?"

"Because you do."

With that, Celeste screamed again about her own childhood. "Do you know what it feels like when you're four
years old, you aren't even in kindergarten, and some guy
has a big dick sticking in you? Do you know what that does
to you?" She began crying. "Don't you ever, ever say that to
me again! Do you understand?" She raged more. "How dare
you say that to me? I protected you and your sister from all
that shit." She said that Kristina's words hurt her. "Just because you enjoy it with Justin now doesn't mean that I enjoyed it when I was four years old. You just sit there and
think about it. Think about somebody you know that's four
years old, and how, how much they would enjoy being tied
down and forced to do something they don't want to do for
eight years. You know that fucks with your mind."

There was a long silence.

Marilou Gibbs' chin rested on her chest as she listened to
the tape.

"Are you still there?" Celeste asked.

"Yes," Kristina answered.

"Bring the dog home, if you're not going to stay. I want
the dog at the house. And if you don't stay, I don't give a
shit. After what you just said to me, you can just forget anything. And when you go to sleep tonight, Kris, you start
your dreams by dreaming about how would you like it if
your father was on top of you, fucking you every night, and
then beating the crap out of you? I never laid a hand on you
guys. I never beat you. I never did anything to you except
try to raise you to be nice young women. And I am sorry

the dog isn't
the police go over there and I'm
gonna tell them that you stole it. Do you understand?"

"Yes."

"I don't think I can ever, ever, ever forgive what you have said to me tonight. Because as soon as I get home, I feel like just fucking sticking a knife down my throat, you bitch."

Prosecutor Allison Wetzel then played a few voice messages from Celeste, one of which was left for Justin's parents.

"Emily, Peter, I hope that you're not influencing Kristina on staying at your house and moving out, because that is not in her best interest—unless, of course, you're willing to support her. Um, I want the dog brought home tonight, and I want her at home tonight. And I don't want you or anybody else to try to influence her otherwise. I am not psychotic and I am not abusive and I am not going to hit her. And if she doesn't come home, then you can have an extra guest forever. And you can pay her college tuition."

And there were more conversations between Celeste and Kristina, with Celeste once again asking Kristina why she hadn't brought the dog home and when she was going to bring it home.

Finally, there was one last conversation between Celeste and Kristina.

"Kristina."

"Uh-huh?"

"Why are you doing this?"

"Why are you doing this to me?" Kristina replied.

"Because you belong at home. You don't live over there. You live at home. And I am not sick anymore."

"I never said that," Kristina answered.

"Then why are you doing this? You said you're scared of me. You think I'm going to beat you up or something? I never even laid a hand on you. When have I ever hit you?"

"I don't know."

"I have never hit you. What do you mean you don't know? Don't you care about me at all?"

"Yes, I do care about you," the daughter said.

"Then why don't you come home? Why? Why wouldn't you come down and talk to me?"

"'Cause I didn't want you to throw a scene."

"I wasn't gonna throw a scene. You think you know me, but you don't. I was not gonna throw a scene. What are you so frightened of?"

"'Cause I'm tired of you hurting yourself."

"I wasn't gonna hurt myself, Kris. What the hell do you think I went to the hospital for? I'm not gonna hurt myself anymore. I'm not gonna throw a scene anymore. I know how to talk and have a conversation with somebody without doing that. I've gotten over my grief and my trauma. And what you said last night just about killed me."

"Well, I'm sorry, but that's how I feel when you call me names."

"Do you feel like I'm worse than my father?" Celeste said.

"When you call me names, like *you little bitch*, and you always say that I'm worthless and selfish, when all I ever do is do everything for you."

"So it's okay that you said that to me?"

"No," Kristina answered, "but I wanted you to know that it's mentally abusive."

Celeste responded, "I just wanted you to know that I do not appreciate you butting into my business when I asked you not to. And I was gonna—When you came home, I was gonna tell you exactly why. Exactly what Donna has on me."

"What does she have?"

"I'm not telling you over the phone," Celeste said, "'cause you'll just go tell Justin and everybody else. Right?"

"No."

"What?" Celeste said.

"No."

"I hired somebody to kill Tracey."

19

To Celeste Beard's "I hired somebody to kill Tracey" comment, Kristina Beard simply responded, "Okay." Then abruptly, the tape ended.

In a mere whisper, Detective Anderson explained that Kristina had told him she was so shocked by her mother's words that she immediately turned off the tape recorder and told Celeste she didn't want to speak to her ever again.

On redirect, DeGuerin tried to defuse the tape's power by emphasizing that the detective didn't know whether the tape was the original, he couldn't date the tape, he didn't know where Celeste was when the tape was recorded, and the tape had been in evidence for two years, but never pursued.

As the November afternoon sun slanted into the courtroom, Coalter Baker walked up to the witness box. He was a gray-haired, bespectacled CPA with a thick Texas accent who had been hired by Celeste to prepare a financial statement for Spencer Cole Johnson and Celeste Beard.

Baker understood that Celeste Beard Johnson did not have any assets available. She had only $7,300 in cash and a net worth of $62,431.

Celeste listened attentively, watching, leaning over to her attorneys and commenting.

On cross-examination, Wetzel pointed out that the Johnsons' financial condition would be different in November than it was in July.

"It's possible that they have other accounts they didn't tell you about?" Wetzel demanded to know.

"It's possible," the witness returned.

She asked about property Celeste and Cole sold for cash and wondered where that money had gone.

Again, the accountant didn't know the answer to her question.

By the time the courtroom clock ticked close to 6 P.M. there was talk that Celeste still had some furs and jewelry. DeGuerin disagreed. "They're mine now."

Just before 1:30 P.M. on November 13, 2002, Celeste sat in a wheelchair and was guided into the courtroom, her broken leg sticking straight out like a steel girder. The deputies acted as her crane as they eased her into a comfortable chair at the defense table. She wore a black sweater and a long charcoal-gray skirt.

Allison Wetzel wore a charcoal gray suit that complemented Celeste's outfit. Only Allison accented her suit, with pearl earrings and a watch with a powder pink wristband—Celeste's favorite color.

Five minutes later, the attorneys stood at the judge's bench as DeGuerin grumbled that the State was insinuating that Celeste's money had just disappeared, when that was only hearsay.

Wetzel answered that hearsay was admissible. Wetzel knew that Celeste had told Tracey Tarlton she'd stashed money all over the world.

Dressed in her usual earth tones, Dana Whatley tromped into the courtroom, sat down in the witness chair, turned, and smiled at the judge, then at DeGuerin. Unofficially she was overseeing the sales of Celeste's assets, Whatley testified, her forehead wrinkled as she spoke. She was selling Celeste's jewelry and furs for DeGuerin. She'd sold the lake house for Celeste and any remaining property had been deeded to DeGuerin. The Southlake estate sale had produced less than $37,000. She'd held hangar sales at the Spicewood Airport in order to sell Celeste's furniture and artifacts. So far, Celeste had realized nearly $38,000 from the hangar sales. Dana was also selling things on eBay.

. . .

Celeste hadn't known anything about eBay, until Dana showed her. The next thing Dana knew, Celeste was saying, "I want that! I want that! I want that!"

"Celeste," Dana had to interrupt, "you're here to sell, not buy."

Celeste's obsessive-compulsive shopping made Dana shake her head. Celeste had spent many moonlit mornings stuffing a shopping cart full of Wal-Mart goods.

Dana allowed Cole a $2,500 a month allowance, which paid his $1,000-a-month rent and the minimum due on their $89,000 in credit card debt. Currently, in the account Dana had set up for Celeste, there was a mere $16,000.

DeGuerin, looking relaxed and in control, stood next to his witness as she tried to explain where Celeste had spent every penny—nearly $200,000 remodeling the Southlake house, nearly $224,000 to American Express, business expenses, credit card payments, donations, entertainment and travel, legal and professional fees.

Wetzel and her co-counsel, Gary Cobb, giggled at the State's table. Whatley began to giggle herself as she reached into her pants pocket for a piece of paper that had Celeste's account balances written on it. Then Whatley simply stated that there was no money left in the account.

But Dana Whatley was ready. She and her mother had pulled together enough money to meet Celeste's bail, as long as it was reasonable—$1 million.

DeGuerin tried to make sure Dana understood that if Celeste jumped bail, Dana would lose everything.

"Yes, that would be devastating." But Dana wasn't worried about that. "I think she's fighting mad to defend herself. . . . She won't run." Dana Whatley kept her plane across the street from her house, only a few blocks from Celeste's former lake house.

Wetzel asked her if she saw any emotional instability in Celeste.

"She's always seemed normal to me," the witness answered with a straight face, while those in the gallery snickered.

Wetzel quizzed Dana about Celeste giving money to other inmates.

"Celeste has a big heart and has asked me to send twenty-five dollars to an inmate there."

Wetzel asked for the inmate's name, to which DeGuerin objected. She argued that Celeste claimed she was broke, yet she was sending money to other inmates.

DeGuerin looked frustrated again.

Just after 4 P.M., Wetzel submitted document after document—the probable cause affidavit for the solicitation of capital murder charge, the indictment for that charge, the protective order for the twins, the application for the protective order, Detective Rick Wines' June testimony, a fax from Galveston County verifying that DeGuerin's client Robert Durst had received a $1-billion minus a penny bail, and the warranty deed, contract, and settlement for the Southlake house.

Celeste looked bored and miffed, but finally the bail hearing ended. The pre-trial hearing on DeGuerin's motion to suppress evidence the kids had "stolen" began with the testimony of Dr. Bernard Gotway, Celeste's psychologist at Timberlawn.

Gotway, a short, stocky man with curly gray hair, looked like he belonged on the original *Bob Newhart Show*. He wore eyeglasses and a moustache, and had cheeks puffy like a squirrel's.

On April 1, 2000, he, Celeste, and Kristina met in a counseling session, he testified. At the time, Kristina held Celeste's power of attorney. He was concerned, he said, about the emotional affect of the 19-year-old daughter having control over her 37-year-old mother, "which I thought was inappropriate." So, she and Kristina had a tense and difficult meeting where Celeste revoked her power of attorney, he said.

DeGuerin introduced Defendant's Exhibit 1—a letter from Gotway regarding the April Fool's Day meeting: "During this meeting, Celeste did express and convey to Christiana [sic] that she did *not* want her to serve as power of attorney for her. (I do not remember the exact words used, but Celeste's indications were clear.)" The letter was dated July 10, 2000.

On cross, Wetzel stated she didn't see anything about the revocation of a POA anywhere in Gotway's notes about the April 1 meeting.

Gotway didn't make any notes about the POA because he was more concerned about the lack of trust between mother and daughter, the role reversal, and Celeste believing Kristina hated her.

Wetzel asked whether Kristina actually had taken advantage of her mother or had Celeste simply expected Kristina to take advantage of her?

"I'm not sure."

Wetzel wanted to know what made Gotway think Celeste wanted to revoke the power of attorney.

"I don't want you in charge of my life. I don't want you doing these things," he quoted her as saying, despite the fact that two and a half years earlier he'd written that he couldn't recall her words.

At that, Wetzel introduced Celeste's year 2000 progress notes from Timberlawn.

"The patient reports a competency hearing is being held because of her inability to function." The Timberlawn records showed that Celeste entered the facility on March 22, 2000. She had an ulcerated toe, "which I bet has not healed because I suspect she keeps manipulating it," and tested positive for methamphetamines and marijuana.

Two days later, on March 24, Celeste said, "she slept poorly last night because she was upset by receiving a phone call from the person who reportedly shot her husband. She says that she did not talk to the person, but hung up as soon as she realized who was on the phone . . ."

Celeste met with Gotway on March 27 and told him she didn't want to acknowledge or accept Steve's death. Gotway suggested she write a letter to Steve.

On March 28, 2000, Kristina and Jennifer walked through Timberlawn's doors for a counseling session with their mother. There, Kristina said Celeste's "lawyer recommended that they proceed with gaining guardianship" over Celeste.

To Gotway, Celeste complained about her daughters trying to control her. On March 29, Celeste stated that her strengths and resources were "she's a survivor, intelligent, wealthy." Other records stated Celeste said she had $50 million, didn't like sex, was a CPA, was being stalked by Tracey, and didn't have any strengths.

Gotway's notes from April 1 showed that he thought Kristina was truly concerned about Celeste, despite his testimony.

On April 4, Celeste was overheard screaming, "You're a liar!" on the phone to Kristina. Celeste then signed a letter of release to get out of Timberlawn, despite the fact that she was "on suicide precaution due to erratic behavior."

Celeste returned to Timberlawn on April 17. When she sat down with Gotway, she told him she came back because her daughters were afraid she'd kill herself. The next day, she confessed to Gotway her fear that her daughters would never talk to her again, "like I did with my mother."

Looking nervous, Christopher Doose entered the courtroom on Thursday, November 14, 2002. He was short in stature and short in hair, which was cropped close, but with long sideburns. He seemed to tuck his head and neck deep into his business suit, a bit like a young turtle trying to decide whether it was safe to come out.

When Christopher Doose first met Celeste, he'd liked her a lot. She was cool. She was charismatic . . . when she was "on." But when the bad Celeste stepped out, it was better to get out of her way.

She was a storm brewing. But she was an exciting, enticing storm, like a hurricane that young men just have to stay, watch, drink through, and ride out for the experience—as well as the rush from the brush with the high winds of death.

Quickly, Christopher realized how to work Celeste—ask her what she wanted done, do it, and then she'd give Jen and him permission to do what they wanted. Celeste Beard took a liking to the responsible Christopher Doose.

So did Steve.

Christopher loved to be around the bossy old man who was always trying to teach him something. It didn't matter if Steve was having Christopher set the table and telling him how to cook or ordering Christopher to drag three hookups of water hoses around the house to water the trees.

"No! No! You're doing it wrong!" Steve yelled across the big yard. "Lay it down on the ground!"

Just thinking about Steve brought a smile to Christopher's lips. He loved to go over to the Beard house to be around Steve. There was never a time that the kids visited that Steve didn't have them doing chores, whether it was picking up dog poop, filling the bird feeders, or putting out corn for the squirrels. It made them feel like family.

Christopher truly did consider Celeste and Steve close friends.

December 1999, Steve was getting better, David Kuperman was chewing on Celeste about her spending, and they were all talking about divorce. Celeste didn't know when Steve was coming home, but she feared it might be soon. And the Toro Canyon house was a wreck inside and out with remodeling and just junk. "Stuff" covered every surface of the more-than-5,000-square-foot home.

Container Store crates full of cards, photographs, bank statements, and credit card receipts were stacked high in what they called the third storage, a walk-in closet in the garage, as well as hidden in the girls' bedroom, the guest bedroom, and the attic. For too many years, Celeste had gotten the mail from the lake house and two post office boxes that she kept secret from Steve, and stashed the mail where she didn't think he'd find it.

Single out pictures, bank statements, bills, anything referring to money, Celeste told Christopher. He and Jen pulled everything out of the third storage, into the garage, and sat on the concrete floor sorting it.

He put Bank of America statements into one file. First American Bank statements into another pile. Celeste seemed to have as many secret bank accounts as she did secret post office boxes. One bank was near Tramps hair salon on Burnet Road, which was a tiny salon across town that only she went to, unlike Studio 29, which both she and Steve frequented. She also had secret safe deposit boxes.

Celeste climbed through a crawl hole into the attic, scooped her hands through the paperwork and tossed it down onto the garage floor like a snowstorm of paper that became an avalanche as she pushed down furniture, too. She laughed wildly, like Chris had never seen her laugh before. She tossed down Beard family photos from Steve's years with Elise.

Christopher looked at Jen. "Oh, my God. I cannot believe she's throwing this stuff away."

"Oh, they don't need it," Celeste said from the attic.

He picked through the photographs. "Let's not throw this stuff away. Let's at least send it to them," he said to Jen.

Celeste tossed out Kristina's moped. She pushed down an antique table with a thick, back-straining, heavy marble top. It crashed like a car to the garage floor, breaking, then chipping the concrete.

"Oh, my God," Christopher yelled to Celeste. "Kristina wanted that."

Celeste just laughed and in her thick lisp said, "I guess she's not going to get it now." She pointed out the things she wanted tossed and told them to take them to the dump near Highways 620 and 71, which they passed whenever they went to the lake house. There was so much trash, they had to rent trucks to haul it to the dump—a white, dual-wheeled pickup once, a U-Haul truck another time.

They filled up the U-Haul until it was three feet deep in trash. And as Christopher shoved the trash out of the truck and into the dump, he pulled out things he found interesting, peculiar.

Tediously, they went through three boxes of trash the kids had collected with Christopher identifying three Mead black-and-white marble composition notebooks as Celeste's journals, and a couple of greeting cards from Tracey to Celeste.

Christopher Doose planned on being the governor of

Texas one day and perhaps even President of the United States. He had no motive to testify against Celeste—nothing to gain, only a career to lose. Unlike the twins, he wouldn't make any money from a guilty verdict. Besides, he was from a wealthy west Texas family and had every material possession a college boy could want—an Expedition, a big bank account, credit cards, expensive clothes, expensive cowboy boots, world travel, his own apartment.

Chris Doose posed trouble for Dick DeGuerin.

As the day stretched into an exhausting late afternoon, DeGuerin questioned Christopher about picking up Celeste at Timberlawn on April 4, 2000.

Celeste was very much in control when Chris and Jen arrived late in the night at Timberlawn. But as soon as she saw the kids, she jammed her suitcase into Christopher's hand. They speed-walked for the elevator, trying not to draw attention. Uniformed Timberlawn nurses were trying to stop her. She told Chris, "Hit that button. Hit that button." And the elevator doors closed before the staffers could get there.

They hoofed it to the Cadillac, jumped in, and Celeste yelled, "Go!"

Chris and Jen thought Celeste was breaking out of Timberlawn. They didn't know she'd signed a letter of release and packed everything but a missing leather coat.

Then, on I-35, there was that screaming, cursing phone call to Kristina.

Christopher looked in the rearview mirror at Jennifer, who sat in the back seat. He knew that wasn't good. He was scared for Kris, Jen, and himself. He knew they had to get out of there. When his eyes locked with Jen's, he knew she thought the same thing.

As soon as Celeste dropped them out at Christopher's apartment, he and Jen left again to get Kris.

They were on the run.

In the next week, Celeste left more than twenty messages on Christopher's answering machine. Twice she pounded on his apartment door looking for the girls. Other times she followed him. Christopher started carrying a knife for protection.

The courtroom was silent when a heavy-set, round-faced, 21-year-old Jennifer Beard took the stand and glanced over at her mother, who held her gaze firm. During the year they hadn't seen each other, Jen's blonde hair had grown long. And she'd started parting it down the middle so that she looked like a plain, country girl.

DeGuerin grilled her as to whether she'd stolen evidence from Celeste, which she'd then turned over to the district attorney's office. Sometimes near tears, but always articulate, Jen testified that her mother had instructed her, her sister, and their boyfriends to clean out storage closets and the attic, and they had simply kept things that "looked interesting." Those things included photos of Celeste and Tracey, love letters from Tracey to Celeste, bank statements, and more.

Kocurek rubbed her eyes as DeGuerin insisted on going through the three boxes of trash once again. Envelope after envelope, Jen said she didn't remember. Kocurek yawned. Wetzel offered to bring the next box over to DeGuerin to speed the process.

"I'd get it myself, but the last time I tried, you snapped my head off," he retorted.

Many of the items in that box Jen recognized, but she said it was her sister who had turned them over to the prosecutor—a 1999 appointment book, Steve's address book, documents from Celeste's computer.

Repeatedly, DeGuerin asked her how many times she'd seen Bill Mange and when was the last time she'd seen him.

Each time Jen answered the same way—she couldn't remember.

Kocurek looked like she was about to drop, and recess was finally called until the next afternoon.

DeGuerin eased over to Wetzel, who towered over him. "I'm only going to say this once," he muttered, almost under his breath. "I have this offer and it's good only until tomorrow."

20

Dick DeGuerin apparently believed he was in trouble—he made an offer to the prosecution that if the State dropped the Steven Beard murder charge against Celeste, she'd plead guilty on the solicitation of Tracey Tarlton's murder.

"Of course, we'd want her to do maximum community service," Wetzel cracked, her prim lips never hinting that she was joking.

DeGuerin didn't laugh.

A few blocks south of the courthouse, at the noisy and smoke-filled Star Bar on Sixth Street, Steve Beard's friend, Paul Weyland, and Chuck Fuqua, Beard's former banker, gathered at a small, round cocktail table for happy hour and reminiscence about the man they loved and the woman they never trusted.

"She took advantage of the kindness of a vulnerable old man," Paul said, his voice deep and rich from years of radio. She was a classless bitch, trailer trash, and everyone knew it, just like everyone knew about and talked about Sunday Suck Day.

At first they'd tried to accept her. "Hey, Steve, we hear you have a girlfriend."

"House manager, Goddamn it," he growled.

But even before she and Steve married, Celeste was pulling her shenanigans. She tried to cash a check on Steve's account. Chuck didn't let it go through. Celeste called him up and chewed his ass for five minutes.

"Celeste," he said, when she quieted for a moment, "are you through?"

"Yes."

"Well, you and I don't have anything else to talk about." Chuck hung up on her.

Right after they married, Celeste sneaked into Steve's safe deposit box and stole Elise's silver, then hocked it at a local pawnshop. That was the reason for their near divorce, Chuck said. When Steve confronted Celeste, she at first denied involvement. Then she said someone else had stolen it. Finally she acted confused.

Steve simply told Chuck, "It has been returned."

Steve had planned to build his young wife a $750,000 home. But the price soared as she demanded faux painting on the walls, the cabinets, the pillars, everywhere. Paul had a relative who'd done some of the faux painting and complained about how Celeste grabbed the asses of all the workmen, including his.

"He's just a drunk and horrible old son-of-a-bitch," Celeste used to tell Paul.

Steve complained only slightly about Celeste, confronting her about credit card charges made in Las Vegas and Reno. Then there were the charges to the Austin gay bars Oilcan Harry's and the Rainbow Cattle Co. that were made while Celeste was supposed to be in Dallas at Timberlawn.

Paul heard them fight like characters in *Who's Afraid of Virginia Woolf?*

The Wednesday before Steve was shot, Chuck had lunch with him. Steve was excited about the trip to Europe and bought $10,000 worth of travelers' checks for it. But there was something inside Chuck that made him believe Steve was going to have to cancel the vacation. He'd seen Celeste shake her head when they talked about it.

The moment he heard Steve had been shot, he knew—he'd even said out loud—Celeste had done it.

And as soon as Steve was shot, Celeste had tried to get on her dying husband's bank account, because she said she needed money. "What about the travelers' checks that Steve bought?" Chuck asked.

"I have them in the vault," Celeste answered.

"Well, use those."

Ray McEachern knew she'd done it, too. As soon as he'd found out Steve had been shot, he called the cops and said, "You've got your number one suspect right there."

"She didn't have gunpowder on her hands," the cop answered.

"I'm just telling you, you write down in the notes in big letters, 'She was involved in it.' "

The cops never talked to Ray again, didn't even try to.

The radioman and the banker needed one more round of drinks.

Steve took all of his money out of the joint checking account he'd had with Celeste after there was a $40,000 to $50,000 overdraft. He placed the money in a new account on which only he could sign.

The Monday or Tuesday after Steve died, Kristina had brought a signature card signed by Steve allowing Celeste on the account. Chuck had refused the card.

"I miss him, and I'm angry," Paul said of the man he too called "Big Daddy," whose vodka rocks drinks they called Whitey Loud Mouths, and who always talked like a Chinaman when he was drunk. "When I say we loved the guy, we *loved* the guy. . . . He truly wanted this woman and her kids to have a wonderful life. He wanted to give them money and happiness. He wanted to help them become a normal real family."

And Paul swallowed the last of his drink.

On November 15, 2002, on the seventh floor of the Blackwell Thurman building, Jennifer Beard returned to the stand to try to help convict her mother of capital murder.

Allison Wetzel picked up item after previously trashed item and asked Jennifer if she recognized each one and who had told her to throw it away.

"Celeste," she answered.

When Jen found trashed items with her own Social Security number on them, she saved them, eventually discovering that Celeste had opened at least one credit union account using Jennifer's Social Security number long before Jen even arrived in Texas.

There was also a to-do list that Celeste had written, after Steve died, for Justin and the girls to carry out.

"1. Janet at the bank needs to be called regarding the

$75,000 that is owed to me for Abercrombie Jewelers. The ring was given to me before Steve died. Tell her I only paid for it because he kept bugging me for payment."

"6. Schedule new carpet installation for living room & both hallways."

"11. Hire a new maid."

The list went on for three pages.

"13. Pick up Jewelry [sic] from Kirk Roots." She also wanted them to pick up paintings, bronzes, lamps, artificial flowers, and patio cushions. She wanted to get windows tinted and have Doug Byers paint in "my courtyard" because the paint job "looks bad on left side looking out my sliding glass doors."

There was also a letter Celeste had written to Jennifer and Kristina while she was in Timberlawn. "I am typing this letter to you because I no longer can write. I am falling a lot too. I do not know why I am even telling you because after not speaking to you for almost a month, I realize you no longer care about me. . . . This will be my last attempt at communication with you."

She asked the kids to take care of the house until she got home from Timberlawn. She complained that they wouldn't give her the code to her own safe. And if she didn't hear from them soon, "you will leave me no choice . . ." She would cut them off financially. She said she loved them both and scrawled in drugged-out, child-like writing, "Mom."

Wetzel asked Jennifer if she'd gathered the items as evidence against Celeste.

"No."

Continually fluctuating among angry, nice, and antagonistic, Dick DeGuerin pointed out that Celeste never gave Jennifer permission to give the items to Mange, she never told Jennifer to throw out various items that became State's exhibits, nor had Celeste told Jennifer to keep various State's exhibits.

DeGuerin read from Celeste's letter: "I will tell you you have completely broken my heart." "I verbally abused you and I am deeply sorry. I was hoping you would be an adult, accept my apology and realize that I was sick. It will never happen again."

He showed Jennifer photos of the filthy kitchen Celeste and Cole found upon her return from Timberlawn on May 5, asking her who did it.

"I don't know. I didn't."

He pointed to Whataburger remnants on the kitchen table and asked if she'd done that.

"I don't even like Whataburger," she snapped, and the gallery laughed.

Celeste scribbled on her yellow legal pad.

Just before 4 P.M., Justin Grimm entered the courtroom, and Celeste immediately wondered when he'd gotten so fat. The kids joked about the "Celeste 30"—the thirty pounds they'd gained since going into hiding.

And Celeste knew just where to strike the insecure young man. He, and others, felt that his mother constantly put him down, about his weight for one thing, and continually chipped away at his self-esteem, while his older sister could do no wrong.

Justin wore eyeglasses, a pale blue Ralph Lauren shirt, about which he bragged, a darker blue tie, and no jacket. He looked like a young, nerdy lawyer, stockbroker, or accountant. And he did have the hope of going to law school.

Justin's mouth was a straight line as he waited several seconds to answer each question, and then reply that he couldn't remember. Someone had advised him to count to three before answering. The slowness of his answers made him come across as a liar.

DeGuerin grilled the witness about the tapes of Celeste's phone conversations and messages.

"They're as original as they can get," Justin said.

Regarding the documents he'd turned over to Mange, Justin said that over Christmas break they'd picked out love letters from Tracey to Celeste that were supposed to be thrown out, and other items that looked "curious." Then he'd hidden them in various places around his parents' home.

Soon after that, Justin returned to his "I don't remember" answers, sounding more and more like a liar.

DeGuerin asked Justin from whom was he hiding the items.

"No one."

DeGuerin went through the three boxes of trash one more time, utilizing his own tone of voice and Justin's hesitancy to insinuate that the scared, nervous young man was indeed lying.

Justin had found a card with a heart on the front of it from Tracey to Celeste. "I do want to work on expressions of intimacy between us, and then on sex." Tracey was reading a book on sexual abuse, *The Courage to Heal*, which she'd bought for Celeste and hoped she'd read—there was a section "addressed to the partner on sex."

Tracey wanted them to be able to talk about sex and be honest so "that we can pick our way through this mine field. . . . There may even come a day when you like sex— that probably scares you to death. Let's just say there may even come a day when you can tolerate it without discomfort!

"But, short of sex, a certain amount of intimacy is important to me. I love you so much, I get so turned on, that I want to find some avenues of intimacy that will work for both of us, that are acceptable for both of us." She wanted them to explore together "ways to make you comfortable being intimate with me. I love you, T."

Justin had had computer printouts from Celeste's computer that he'd printed when she and Donna were out of town. Everyone in the house, he said, had access to the computer. And being the "Code Meister," he repeated the codes to the computer—Mickey1 and Nicole1.

Three times, after April 17, Justin said, he went back to the Toro Canyon house—to clean the pool and koi ponds, to help the girls get their clothes, and to get the FedEx package Celeste had told him was coming—the one with the three-page to-do list. He claimed that the list was for Kristina, not him.

At that, DeGuerin had Justin read the last page of the list.

Celeste specifically wrote to Justin: "I don't know if you are doing this or if the girls are. I really appreciate everything you are doing. I hope the girls will help you—if they don't I am forever indebted to you. Please believe I appreciate and care about you. I know you will make sure things will get done before I get home. I really can't thank you enough! I love you!"

DeGuerin insinuated that Justin was a bad, disobeying, little boy who didn't carry out even one item on the list. Like a child, Justin slowly swiveled in his chair as he admitted he'd changed the security code on Celeste's safe.

But he claimed in court that she'd never asked for the code. He seemed to forget the contents of the very messages he'd recorded.

DeGuerin asked about the video surveillance tapes. Every day, Jennifer was supposed to change the tapes. There should have been thirty of them. But no one claimed to know where a single one was.

On cross, Wetzel wanted to play some of the tapes Justin had recorded.

"I don't understand the purpose of playing the tape unless it's to get on the news tonight," DeGuerin beefed. He was the only lawyer who stood outside the courtroom for the cameras every day. The prosecutors exited through a locked hallway and private elevators.

The judge overruled DeGuerin. He sighed and sat down.

He should have smiled, though, at the sounds coming over the boom box.

"Justin. It's Celeste. I want the safe code."

And she threatened, ". . . I don't know what they're scared of, but they have no reason to be scared, but they will have a reason if they don't show up at five."

Eight minutes later, Justin saved another message where Celeste proclaimed she wasn't psycho, but she would report the girls for stealing the keys and "everything else" and she'd hire a private detective to "track them down," if they didn't return her "stuff." "And if they don't do it tonight at five, they will be sorry."

By 6 P.M., Justin saved another message—Celeste had

gotten into Jennifer's cell phone, listened to her messages, and changed the pass code.

She phoned again and said she wanted back her telephone book that Kristina "stole from the house," she wanted the combination to the safe, the master safe key. "And if I don't get it back tomorrow, then I will call the police."

Justin sat in the witness chair looking stressed, while Celeste kept her head down and sifted through papers.

She left more telephone messages, finally crying and saying, "I love you guys very much and I'm really hurting, because I want to see you. Please call me."

The next day, Justin recorded more. ". . . Since the three of you think this is funny, and you, you, you think, you know, it's hilarious to hurt me and just steal from me, you leave me no choice. And I really wish the girls would talk with me before I have to have them arrested."

DeGuerin propped his head in one hand.

The judge turned her chair so that she faced her court reporter rather than the gallery. Still, she looked shaken. Her toddler twins, who had been born just a few days after Steve Beard died, were blonde like Kris and Jen.

Celeste continued to threaten the girls with arrest as she accused them of stealing a $10,000 necklace, her printer, laptop, and digital camera. She begged for the girls to meet her at Michelle Hauser's. Then she said she wouldn't pursue them anymore; she loved them. Then she threatened Kristina with arrest again. "She is going to jail, because I've had it." She screamed, "What have I done to deserve this? She took twelve thousand five hundred on the first and seventy-five hundred on the fourth. Why? What are you guys doing to me?"

Justin looked frozen in fright in the witness chair.

There were just too many angry, threatening, confusing messages to count. Finally, Celeste stated there was a warrant out for the girls' arrest. ". . . And if I have to, I'll get a, I'll get a damned billboard and put the girls' pictures on it and say how they're stealing from their mother whose, um, husband was murdered. So I'm not playing around with them."

• • •

Wetzel proceeded by showing Justin another card from Tracey to Celeste. ". . . and I want my madness and my destiny to be with you. I love you with all my heart."

DeGuerin sat with his arms crossed defensively. The clock ticked close to 6 P.M. with the judge looking tired and Wetzel showing Justin an anonymous letter from a friend of Celeste's written in 1999 to the *Austin American-Statesman*. For two pages, it talked about what a good woman Celeste was, the hardships she'd suffered and conquered, and her deep love and loyalty for Steve. Justin had found the letter on Celeste's computer.

Justin was renowned as an untrustworthy snoop whose big claim to fame was the phrase, "I've got your code." He knew the code to the house, all the cell phones, even Steve's code to access the porn movies—3900.

Wetzel brought out a letter from Celeste to Steve where Celeste said she was writing because she and Steve "obviously" were unable to communicate. "When you called me this morning asking if we should just get divorced, it completely took me by surprise."

Steve had been drunk the night before, she wrote, and awakened her to scream at her because the girls had left the lights on. ". . . And when I yelled at you, you told me to go back to Dallas if I did not like it. That was at 10:00 P.M. So I left. I slept on the side of the road when I got tired along the way.

"Steve, I love you with all of my heart. If you truly want a divorce, then please tell me on Thursday when we meet with Dr. Gotway. I will have shown him a copy of this letter, so that he is apprised as to our current status. Please don't have me served while I am in the hospital. Tell me face to face on Thursday. I think I at least deserve that much."

The letter was written May 9, 1999, two days after Celeste had taken Tracey to City Grill for her birthday and given her the "To the One I Love" card.

Wetzel handed Justin a letter dated nine days after Steve's death, written to Celeste's mother. "I am only writing this because I have nothing but time on my hands now and was wondering what I did for you to never speak with me again? I would really appreciate it if you have the time to write and let me know what I did."

The pre-trial hearing did not reconvene until Thursday, November 21. Justin Grimm returned to the stand with Wetzel producing a thank-you card Celeste had given him along with a $1,000 check. "We really couldn't have survived these last 2 months without you! Love, Celeste."

Justin testified that over the weekend he'd discovered more tapes of voice mails from Celeste that he'd recorded between April and June 2000.

Wetzel played them. Justin's head was bowed as he listened, as was Celeste's, who flipped through pages. They were the same old threats. But with Wetzel doing the questioning rather than DeGuerin, Justin explained that Celeste had asked him to change the safe code because of Donna Goodson, and that he had stopped speaking to Celeste by the time she asked for the code.

Wetzel wondered aloud if Justin didn't give Celeste the code because he feared she'd remove items and report them as stolen.

DeGuerin objected that the prosecutor was leading the witness.

The judge's eyes fluttered.

But when DeGuerin returned to questioning, Justin softly admitted that he chose not to give Celeste her safe code.

DeGuerin accused Justin of signing checks on Celeste's account, which the boyfriend denied, and of entering the Toro Canyon house and accessing Celeste's computer long after Justin claimed he was last in the house. DeGuerin had alarm access records that he believed proved his point.

Justin continued frustrating the attorney with "No" and "I don't know" answers. Then, when DeGuerin slightly rephrased one of his questions, asking Justin if he'd signed Celeste's name to checks, Justin thought at length, before responding, "I don't remember."

Celeste crossed her arms over her stomach.

DeGuerin picked up the to-do list and started going over it.

The judge begged him not to name every chore on the list.

DeGuerin persisted, his face turning redder as the morning dragged on, and repeatedly asked if a single one of those chores mentioned that Celeste had wanted Justin to take anything and give it to Bill Mange. "You were fooling her, weren't you?" DeGuerin pronounced.

"Yes."

DeGuerin and Wetzel stood before the judge, DeGuerin arguing that evidence the kids gave Mange should be suppressed because the chain of custody couldn't be followed. The arguing between the attorneys was relentless, and Kocurek kept getting more and more annoyed. She was in for a hellacious trial if this was just a pre-trial hearing.

Soon, Celeste was wheelchaired up to the witness stand, and calmly claimed in her soft lisp, under oath, that her daughters had stolen her photos, letters, bills, and more.

Then Wetzel's second chair, Gary Cobb, walked over to the witness. Cobb had a build that any woman would wish for her husband. And he draped those muscles in *GQ* clothes.

"So why did you have your husband killed?" Gary Cobb gunned.

"I did not murder my husband. I'm not guilty."

"When did you kick the girls out of the house?"

"I never kicked the girls out of the house."

He fired questions so rapidly that Celeste couldn't keep track of her answers, eventually contradicting herself, realizing it, stating she was confused, and breaking into tears, with a tissue covering her entire face.

DeGuerin constantly objected, arguing that Cobb's questions were beyond the limited purpose of his client's testimony.

"Well, Mr. DeGuerin," the judge tersely replied, "you asked those questions in great detail, and I'm going to allow the State to ask her about those as well."

Cobb asked her about Justin. "Did you ever do anything to restrict his access?"

"What do you mean?" Celeste asked.

"Did you tell him, 'Don't come to my home'?"

"Why would I do that?"

DeGuerin wanted a clearer definition of the time frame to which Cobb was referring.

"Any time after you had your husband killed."

"Sustained," Kocurek said without DeGuerin having time to object.

"He could come into your home without your daughter?"

Celeste became angry, then calmed herself. "He could, yes."

But as Cobb continued with his raging-paced interrogation, Celeste brought her hands up to her head and asked, "What was the question?"

Cobb asked about receipts that she said were stolen from her by her children. He asked her where the receipts were the last time she'd seen them.

"In my purse."

"In your purse where?" he shot back.

"In my purse, one of the purses that I had from Mardi Gras, and it had a bunch of receipts in my purse that I hadn't filed yet."

"Where was your purse at?"

"In my closet."

"Was this the purse that you use all the time?"

"I have over three hundred purses."

The judge's jaw dropped open.

Cobb later showed Celeste a letter she had allegedly written, but she said she didn't recognize the letter. "I'm not denying that I wrote it. I just don't know."

"You don't know?"

"I was on a lot of medication when you're saying that this was written, so I don't know."

"So there could have been stuff that you could have done or said that you may not have been aware that you said or did?"

After DeGuerin objected, his client answered, "Let me think." She eventually said she did write the letter. When it became clear under more questioning that Celeste was contradicting her own testimony, she broke into tears again forcing questioning to pause while she composed herself.

Gary Cobb poured a glass of water as if he were getting it for the witness. He drank it himself. Then he questioned her more about her medication-fogged memory, to which she finally tersely answered, "I remember what I did in May."

Finally, Celeste was excused from the witness stand. She was wheeled back to the defense table and court proceeded . . . until Sally King, the court reporter, rose from her chair, her finger pointed toward Celeste, who was slumped over the defense table, supposedly passed out.

The judge was concerned. The court reporter was worried. DeGuerin wanted to proceed. It was late in the evening and well past cocktail time. Celeste's friends and family responded as if nothing had happened.

But Dick DeGuerin didn't get what he wanted. His client's bail was reduced only to $2 million and his motions to squash the purportedly stolen evidence and capital murder indictments had failed.

And he'd never called Tracey Tarlton to testify.

21

Celeste rarely talked about her past. If she told the truth, no one believed her . . . except for Tracey. "I believe you, Celeste," Tracey scribbled in her notebook one day when they were in group therapy.

"We just, um, we just became friends in the hospital. I mean, I don't know if you've ever been in one of those places, but you just look for—look for someone to latch on to, I mean, because you don't have your family there, you don't know anybody there. And just the fact that she was abused also, uh, kinda was like a magnet for a friendship for me."

• • •

To most people, Celeste just spilled the stories of her physical health—ovarian cancer, Legionnaire's disease, tubal pregnancies, osteoporosis, the list was endless.

There were people who did know the stories of her past, people who loved her no matter what. They were the ones she'd left behind. But even they didn't know the whole truth. Some didn't know because they didn't want to believe it. Some didn't know because they didn't want to take responsibility for their part in it. And some didn't know because they just couldn't comprehend it. It was too preposterous.

Celeste's adopted parents, Nancy and Edwin "Johnny" Johnson were a pair twisted between the days of *Leave It to Beaver* and Woodstock. But before Celeste was born, it was simply a grade-C horror movie.

Johnny's baby brother had drowned while his dad was taking Johnny to a public restroom. His dad had committed suicide, and his mother—who was a descendent of a Queen of England, married his dad's brother, a General Electric executive. At least that's the story Nancy believed.

She also claimed her family was so poor, her grandmother made her underwear out of potato sacks, that her dad was a card-carrying Communist, and her mother was an alcoholic prostitute who spent her days staring at the wall and her nights in bars.

Married on Christmas Eve in 1955, Johnny and Nancy had visions of great wealth and three children. But after the births of three babies who didn't live, they started adopting. In 1961, they adopted a son, Cole Johnson—the same name as the man Celeste would marry nearly 40 years later. In 1963, they learned a girl was available.

Two days after Celeste was born, they picked her up. Nancy felt as if she and Celeste bonded as she helped the baby through non-stop crying, feeding Celeste plenty of protein to help her newborn nerves.

Eight months later, the Johnsons were contacted again about another girl. They adopted Caresse, who would grow up to look the complete opposite of Celeste: short, stocky, dark. But they would share a magnetic sense of humor and propensity to talk about their ill health. Two years later, in 1965, Johnny and Nancy adopted their last child, Eddy, who seemed to get lost in the insanity of the house. He clung to Celeste for love and protection.

During those fast adoptive years, Johnny washed dishes at the Colonial House restaurant, drove a cab, sold photograph albums, and worked as a mechanic with Oxnard Volkswagen. Nancy did babysitting to bring in extra money.

Two years later, Johnny opened his own Volkswagen repair shop in Camarillo, the same town that housed the infamous Camarillo State Hospital. In those days, Ventura County seemed to be best known for the psychiatric hospital that was once home to jazz musician Charlie Parker and was allegedly the inspiration for the song "Hotel California."

But Ventura County was a comfortable little area along the Pacific Ocean, its beaches and military bases and golden fields of vegetables sliced by Highway 101. With Nancy dragging the four kids around the county as she picked up car parts her husband needed, made the bank deposits, and took a dollar a day out of the till to buy a pound of hamburger for the family of six, Johnny became known as the best mechanic in the area.

He was a handsome man with closely cropped hair that hid his receding hairline, and who always wore sunglasses due to light-sensitive eyes. He also started going to Alcoholics Anonymous and held Bible studies every morning with his employees. The Johnsons became very involved in church.

Still, no matter how successful Johnny appeared, money was always in short supply. Nancy never saw any money beyond the dollar a day for ground meat, she told friends. Then, one day she went down to the repair shop, asked the bookkeeper for her dollar, and was told she couldn't have it.

Celeste watched it all—her mother always frightened about money, her mother getting teary-eyed as she talked about it, the stress sending her mother into a nervous breakdown and Camarillo State Hospital.

When Johnny had his wife admitted to the psychiatric hospital, he simply said, "She's nuts."

After Camarillo, Nancy started selling soap products, natural vitamins, and then her plasma, three times a week, $25 a time. She wanted her kids in a Thousand Oaks private Christian school where her best friend, Louise Lightfoot, who was also Eileen's mother, was the principal.

Principal Lightfoot bumped the straight-A, second grader Celeste Johnson into the third grade, and Celeste continued earning top marks, while also swimming and winning on the local YMCA swim team.

Around age 11, Celeste became withdrawn, started grinding her teeth, had nightmares, kicked and thrashed in her sleep if anyone tried to touch her, screamed, and fell out of bed.

Life in the one-story, three-bedroom stucco house on the corner with oleander trees in the front yard was careening out of control. Ed was losing his business. Nancy was breaking under the stress of work, commuting, and life at home. It was either quit work and put the kids in public school, or go back to the insane asylum. She enrolled the kids in public school and sent Celeste to Europe and Hawaii with the Lightfoots.

More and more, Celeste wanted to be with the Lightfoots. She spent every weekend at their house. When her father dropped her off, Celeste was stiff and backed away from him. When he left, she relaxed and ran off giggling with Eileen.

Everyone just figured it was Johnny's weirdness. By the mid-seventies, he'd lost his business, shucked the suit he'd worn every day at work, pulled on dungarees, slapped on a toupee, grown a beard, and enrolled at Pepperdine University in Malibu. He wanted to be an intellectual professor. He eventually changed his name to Jedidiah.

Outsiders could only judge the Johnsons on what they saw: a family of great swimmers with Celeste the shining star—a great debater, softball player, and cheerleader.

Rarely was anyone allowed inside where Johnny struck his children with his fists or boards, forcing Caresse to call the cops on her dad.

Late at night, he held Celeste and Caresse in his lap, hugged Caresse and kissed her. As the Johnny Carson show ended, he put Caresse to bed, but kept Celeste up with him. When Celeste came to bed, Caresse heard her crying.

Celeste downed a bottle of aspirin. Nancy never understood why Celeste tried to kill herself, even though she knew Celeste hid in a closet until she came home. But Nancy was rarely home. The kids took care of themselves with Celeste getting the meals on the table and acting as the mother to Caresse and Eddy. Celeste was about 14 years old at that time.

By then, her parents had separated—on Christmas Eve 1977—but Johnny always seemed to be around. Caresse seemed to always be getting pregnant. Eddy got in trouble with the law. Nancy kicked him out of the house and forced him onto the streets before finally letting him come home again. At one point while on the street, Nancy had him arrested. Nancy believed Cole was selling drugs and had him arrested, too.

Meanwhile, Johnny visited friends' homes, scavenged through their medicine cabinets, and stole their prescription drugs. He asked friends for money. He became sarcastic and derogatory.

Celeste popped Valium, broke a window in the house, and took a hammer to the kitchen tile. Nancy called the cops and had her daughter hauled away to the Ventura County youth facility. Nancy chose to leave Celeste there for a week. In 1979, Nancy filed for divorce from Johnny.

Celeste started wearing heavy makeup, like a streetwalker, her mother thought. She drank. She did drugs. She went to parties that the police broke up. After coming home from one party, Celeste said she'd been raped, and washed and washed herself.

Each time she and her mother fought—once Nancy screaming and pulling Celeste's hair and both of them punching each other—Celeste left home, sometimes staying with friends, sometimes sleeping in front yards. Her grades plummeted. She dropped out of school her junior year, hooked up with Craig Bratcher, and got pregnant.

In 1980, Nancy and Johnny's divorce was final, with the girls siding with Nancy and the boys siding with their dad, an act Nancy would never forget. She refused to see or even speak to her sons for decades. Celeste went to Nancy, who helped arrange a tiny evening wedding ceremony at the Four Square Church in Thousand Oaks. Celeste was very pregnant in a cotton dress, her skinny legs sticking out like sticks. Craig was so casually dressed that he had to borrow a jacket when the Lightfoots hosted the wedding dinner at the Westlake (California) Country Club.

On February 6, 1981, the twins were born by C-section at Pleasant Valley Hospital in Camarillo. They were six weeks early and were airlifted to a neonatal unit, where they stayed for six months, while their grandparents continued fighting over the paltry property they'd collected in twenty-two years of marriage.

At one property hearing, where Nancy and Johnny fought over the house, Celeste testified that she "loathed" and "hated" her father. Johnny got the house, but by then it had urine on the rugs, doors off the hinges, a toilet ripped out. And he couldn't make the payments. He turned to his son Eddy. "That's it, baby. You're on your own."

For a while, Eddy slept in an athletic equipment room, then dropped out of school. Flo and George Ragsdale took him in. He called them Mom and Dad.

Every Johnson kid seemed to adopt a different family to stand in for their parents. Eddy eventually joined the Army, then Circus Vargas as a roustabout.

But the Ragsdales cleaned out the Johnson home to fix it up and sell it. Inside, pill bottles were scattered everywhere. The dust was so thick it was like cat hair. Sections of the kitchen countertop were unusable, destroyed by a hammer. The bed sheets hadn't been changed in months. Used condoms were tossed around Cole's room.

• • •

By 1983, Celeste's mother had a plan for saving the United States government, which only she could save. Nancy sat down and wrote a manifesto to send to Washington. A few months later—a Sunday afternoon in October 1983—she dropped by a friend's house wanting to go out to lunch. Nancy was dressed up for an outing.

But when her friend said she couldn't go, Nancy's face contorted and her eyes fired wild. She paced up and down the family room. She clomped around the house in a walk that wasn't her walk and shouted, "Yeah, I wuz being o-ppressed. Yes, they'z o-ppressing me." She yelled with a Southern black accent straight out of *Gone with the Wind*.

Nancy stomped into the kitchen and went for a block of knives on the countertop. She grabbed a butcher knife, pointed it at her friend, and ran at her.

The friend screamed for help.

Her daughter raced in. "What's the matter? What's the matter?"

Her mother struggled with Nancy, trying to get the knife away from her. "I'm fighting off Nancy. Quick, go get your dad."

The friend swung at Nancy to slap her, hoping to bring her back into reality. She missed, but knocked Nancy's glasses off her face.

"Nancy, stop it!"

Nancy stopped, stood there, and stared.

The friend took the knife from Nancy's hand and grabbed her arm, while her husband took the other. They pulled Nancy out to the back porch and locked the door.

Nancy screamed and kicked the door, then pounded on it, wanting back in. Finally she got in her car and left.

She drove to Oxnard, stripped off her clothes, and, naked as a woman could be, beat on a stranger's door demanding to be let in. The police were called. Nancy was hauled off to a psychiatric facility where she stayed for three days, heavily medicated.

When she got out, Nancy didn't remember a thing she'd done. But she told her friend, "It's all your fault."

• • •

"As far as my childhood—they never should have let me be adopted. I couldn't wait to get out of that house at 15. Pregnant at 17 and married at 17. He abused me daily, so for me I went from an abusive home to another abusive home. I never stood a chance. My brother Cole also sexually abused me. He is 1½ years older. He did this when I was 13 & 14."

Yet, nearly twenty-five years later she married another Cole Johnson, a man with the exact same name of the brother she said sexually abused her. But that alleged abuse has never been verified independently, and her father denied to Eddy that Johnny ever molested Celeste.

June 26, 1996, Celeste Beard typed a letter to Ann Landers saying she'd hired a private detective to find her birth mother and he'd succeeded. She then wrote the woman a letter. "I enclosed a stamped self addressed envelope and also my telephone number. I made it clear that I did not intend to disrupt her life or cause her any turmoil. I just wanted to put an end to the search.

"She responded with a letter stating that she was only my incubator for nine months, not the birth mother. She wrote if abortions had been legal 33 years ago, she would have had one."

Her mother, she told others, was a rich hotshot in the Republican Party.

"Then she said it may be hard for me to accept that, but that is it!" Celeste continued, "I am deeply hurt and devastated by her letter. . . . I really need your opinion. Should I honor her wishes and not contact anyone? I respect your opinion and would deeply appreciate a response. Thank you."

After that letter, Celeste told Marilou Gibbs, she'd received a phone call from the woman's husband inviting Celeste to visit.

Celeste said she'd flown to California, dressed in her best designer clothes, climbed into a limousine, gone to a jewelry store, bought a diamond tennis bracelet, and then met the woman at a restaurant with the dream of tossing her

mother the bracelet and receiving a long, hard embrace in
return.

Instead, her mother said, "I've met you. That's what I
promised my husband I would do. I don't want to ever hear
from you again."

In 1994, Craig Bratcher and his brother Jeff were living in
Stanwood, Washington, when they heard Celeste was dating a rich old man. Craig phoned Steve Beard. "You'll be
dead," he warned.

Jeff made a follow-up call. "She's trouble. Get out. Get
rid of her while you can."

22

*"I was always hiding from [Craig]. One time in Oxnard,
California in about 1984 he broke in and stuffed cat poop in
my mouth while I was sound asleep. In 1983, he broke my
wrist and arm. In 1986, I moved to Arizona. He broke in
and raped me. I became pregnant and gave her up for adoption. She is 100 percent twins [sic] sister. One time he
shoved a shotgun through the living room window in California and ended up shooting my next door neighbor in he
leg. I think he always wanted the girls to try to get me
back."*

Jeff Bratcher was no fan of Celeste's. "Her mouth, her irritating voice, her demeanor, the way she acted. I couldn't
stand her immediately." She was skinny, no ass, and not
much of a chest.

"She came home from work one day and told me and
Craig and a few other guys that were around that her boss
was just molesting her and manhandling her. [She] got all
of us to go over there and basically we tore the store apart."

Celeste's boss reached for a hammer and slammed it

into Craig's face. And Jeff was arrested. "That's just the manipulation."

"She never worked for anything. She slept for everything," Jeff believed. "[She and her girlfriends] used to go out to the naval base and pick up Navy officers and see who could come home with the most hotel keys."

Craig said he often walked into his home to find Celeste with not just one man, but two or three "just going at it."

"Come on, Craig, join us," she taunted in a sexy, seductive voice.

Celeste and Craig's marriage officially ended on September 22, 1983, but in 1985, Celeste was still applying for restraining orders against him.

By then, Jeff Bratcher hated Celeste so deeply that he frequently, literally, spat in her face. All the Bratchers believed Celeste had had something to do with Craig's death. Kathy Bratcher, Craig's estranged wife at the time of his suicide, claimed "without a doubt" Celeste was in Stanwood the day Craig shot himself.

Jen believed it. After Craig's death, she planned on running away from her mother as soon as she turned eighteen.

On December 2, 2002, Celeste was cheerful and talkative in MOO, the jail's medical facility. She spent part of December 6 writing letters. "I haven't seen a chaplain in six months. I really miss that," she wrote to Texas Department of Criminal Justice prisoner Bobbie Coy. "My trial date is coming up quickly—I am scared—please pray for me," she wrote to Alicia Mayfield, also a TDCJ inmate. She asked Kathy Flowers about Katina Lofton and signed the letter, "I love you & miss you." To friend M. Michelle Hill of Lago Vista, Texas, Celeste said they could play golf when she got out. "I am anxious to use my Callaways!"

Dick DeGuerin and Catherine Baen walked into the office of Zan Ray's attorney on Thursday, December 12. Baen clicked on a tape recorder as DeGuerin began to question Zan, focusing on her breakup with Tracey.

Was Tracey distraught, did she take the breakup hard,

did she try to get you to change your mind, did she stalk you? he queried. He also asked if Tracey was involved in the death of Zan's husband.

He'd been depressed recently, Zan had told the APD in July 1995. She'd been in New York, come home, and found her husband with vomit coming out of his mouth. Tracey then ran upstairs to the apartment and confirmed he was dead.

Medical Examiner Dr. Roberto Bayardo verified that Zan's husband had died by suicide—an overdose—about a day before his body was discovered.

Zan told Dick DeGuerin she wasn't afraid of Tracey and she didn't think Tracey was dangerous. She and Tracey had had a "trauma bond." She'd broken up with her because Tracey had begun drinking again.

On December 16, 2002, Celeste's leg X-rays showed good alignment. She needed to be weaned from her crutches.

"Can you wait to make any changes until I talk to my lawyers?" she responded.

Monday morning, January 6, 2003, attorneys gathered in Judge Kocurek's court. Dick DeGuerin still wanted the indictment squashed—trial was set for February 3.

DeGuerin was also upset with the "Notice of Intent to Introduce Evidence of Extraneous Offenses in Case-in-Chief, as Impeachment and for Punishment" that Wetzel had filed. He expressed his displeasure as Celeste sat nearby with a new green cast on her right leg. The motion was too detailed, he complained.

In 1993, the motion outlined, Celeste had hit and cut herself and blamed Jimmy Martinez. It didn't note that the twins said she had done the same thing with their dad. They'd be outside playing, see a cop car roll up, and say, Oh, Dad's going to jail again.

Celeste had maintained an ongoing sexual relationship with Jimmy Martinez, the man she'd divorced to marry Steve, and had a pet name for his penis. The document didn't spell out that name, which she'd used to her girls, but it was BMW—Big Mexican Weiner. According to the court filing, Celeste Beard had often had sex with Martinez and Tarlton on the same day.

When she'd performed oral sex on Steve Beard, she referred to it as "time to go make some more money." She'd also performed oral sex on a cop to get out of a speeding ticket.

"On or about March 20, 1999, in Travis County, Texas, the Defendant shaved off all of her pubic hair except for a little patch."

"On numerous occasions between on or about March 20, 1999 and on or about October 1, 1999, in Travis County, Texas, the Defendant touched Tracey Tarlton's genitals with the Defendant's hand, allowed Tracey Tarlton to touch the Defendant's genitals with Tracey Tarlton's hand, penetrated the vagina of Tracey Tarlton with the Defendant's finger, and allowed Tracey Tarlton to penetrate the Defendant's vagina with Tracey Tarlton's finger . . ."

"On numerous occasions between on or about March 20, 1999 and on or about October 1, 1999, in Travis County, Texas, the Defendant contacted the vagina area of Tracey Tarlton with the Defendant's mouth, and allowed Tracey Tarlton to contact the Defendant's vagina with Tracey Tarlton's mouth."

Judge Kocurek explained to the big city attorney that such detail was the norm in Travis County.

As the hearing wound down, a TV cameraman entered the courtroom toting his heavy equipment. Celeste, who had been laughing and joking with her attorneys prior to the hearing, suddenly placed her hands over her face and turned her chair away from the cameraman. The man hadn't even set up his equipment, but Celeste Beard Johnson didn't want her face on TV—she wasn't wearing any makeup.

"Halle-fucking-lujah!" Allison Wetzel yelled on January 10, 2003. For two days, all of her evidence that had been in possession of the sheriff's office had gone missing, including the shotgun shell. For two days, people had searched the evidence room with no luck. For two days, Allison had yelled, cried, and cursed. Finally, the evidence room was torn apart, and all was found.

It wasn't the first time evidence on the case had disappeared. Before Wetzel was assigned to the case, a tape of a phone threat from Celeste to Harold Entz, a district court judge in Dallas and very close friend of Steve's, had vanished after Entz handed the tape to Travis County. Both Mange and Wines had refused to admit responsibility for the tape.

Such mistakes were what motivated Wetzel—besides the typically spouted "getting the bad guy and justice for the victim." Wetzel admitted to what few wouldn't. "Fear of failure or looking stupid keeps me up worrying at night a lot more than justice for the victim."

On January 14, 2003, records from Cook-Walden funeral home were filed with the Travis County District Clerk's Office. They showed that on January 28, 2000, two days after Steve Beard's funeral, Celeste bought Jennifer and Kristina matching brush lilac coffins with pink velvet interiors, wood memorial books, and 200 personalized acknowledgment cards and addressed envelopes at a cost of $7,652, each. She then purchased the twins burial insurance for the exact same amounts.

Friday, January 31, 2003, Paul and Kim Beard sat in the courtroom, Kim's right hand on Paul's sweatpants-covered knee. Kim wore a Disney T-shirt, a gold watch, a silver charm bracelet, and diamond and emerald rings.

A rambling Dick DeGuerin once again argued that the "hit man" audiotape had been altered, edited, and spliced, and he had proof. His proof was Doug Morrison, a tall, gray-haired assistant director of the Dallas Sound Lab School who hadn't outgrown his hippie days. His long gray hair parted down the middle combined with his drooping moustache made him look like an old member of Three Dog Night.

"There's data that's been left out," Morrison testified. He pointed out possible edit after possible splice. He thought there was a splice just before, "I hired somebody to kill Tracey." His proof was a "bump" sound just before "I."

Allison Wetzel asked the witness if he was 100 percent sure the bumps were edits.

DeGuerin looked miffed.

Morrison explained that an analog tape, which was what the original tape was, was harder to edit and splice than a digital tape, which was what he'd transferred the originals onto and was playing in the courtroom. And, he added, on an original analog tape the edit could be seen on the actual tape.

So Wetzel asked if he'd looked at the original tape.

He hadn't.

Suddenly, network cameras rolled as Celeste Beard Johnson slowly crutched up to the bench and, leaning on her crutches, stood before Judge Julie Kocurek. At 10:55 A.M., Celeste Beard Johnson was arraigned on the capital murder charge of killing Steve Beard.

"How do you plead?"

"Not guilty. I was not involved in my husband's murder."

Allison Wetzel stared at Celeste's toes; Celeste needed to request those nail clippers again.

Paul Beard held a cigarette between his fingers as he stood outside the Travis County Courthouse. His wool sport jacket was snug around his arms as warm, gray clouds hovered above. "I'm not nervous," he said.

"It's the beginning of justice," smiled Kim Beard. She lifted her cigarette toward her round face as attorneys, accused criminals, and deputy sheriffs hustled past.

By 9 A.M., on Monday, February 3, 2003, Judge Kocurek's courtroom was packed with Beard family members and friends, court watchers, reporters, supporters from the DA's office, and attorneys who had come to watch "the master," Dick DeGuerin.

Attention swayed to the right at 9:10 A.M. as Celeste crutched in in eyeglasses and a pale pink sweater, which all matched attorney Catherine Baen's outfit, and a khaki-colored skirt. Her left leg was covered in light-colored hose, her left foot in a shoe. The toes on her right foot peeked out of the green plaster cast. With the help of deputies, she struggled into a chair.

Jurors filed into the courtroom, notepads in their hands. Gary Cobb read the three-count indictment, and the capital murder trial of Celeste Beard Johnson began.

Allison Wetzel stretched to her full height and then some as she stood in her black pumps and walked over to the jury. "Figuring out who shot Steve Beard was not too difficult, but it took more than two years to answer the question, Why did this happen? To answer that question, we have to go back to the fall of 1993, to the dining room of the Austin Country Club, where a lonely, rich, older man met an opportunistic young waitress."

A photo of Steve beamed at the jurors, while Wetzel looked into their eyes, her hands held together, close to her body, her forefingers lightly touching, slightly pointing. Celeste Beard Johnson bent over the defense table and scribbled on a legal pad, not looking at or acknowledging the jury or the prosecutor.

Wetzel's notepad lay on a narrow table pressed against the jury box. She rarely glanced down at it, as she stood as close to the jurors as she could get, her body barely moving, her voice calm and measured. "Three weeks after his death, she went to Houston with her daughters and some other friends. On that trip she laughed about Steve being dead, and she bragged about how, now that he was dead, she was a millionaire."

A juror jotted that down.

"The evidence will show that what happened here is a simple case of a greedy, manipulative defendant who took advantage of a mentally ill woman who was in love with her. The defendant married an older guy with a lot of money. She got tired of waiting for him to die. She encouraged, directed, aided, and attempted to aid this mentally ill woman to shoot him. And the defendant's motive to kill him was the money. And we expect when you hear all the evidence, you will agree that this defendant is guilty of capital murder."

Dick DeGuerin took a sip of water and, with his yellow legal pad in his hand, he walked to the middle of the courtroom, standing several yards from the jury. "This is a case of fatal attraction. It's a case of obsession. Tracey Tarlton was psychotic. . . . She's been diagnosed as having delusions, as hearing voices that aren't there to command her to kill herself, as seeing things that aren't there as auditory and visual hallucinations.

". . . Tracey Tarlton is an avowed lesbian. She's predatory, she is aggressive, and Tracey Tarlton became frustrated and obsessed with Celeste Beard. . . . So Tracey, we believe the evidence will show you, shot Steven Beard for her own selfish and sick reasons because she feared that Steven and Celeste were going on with their lives . . ."

Brightly colored Post-it notes hung from each side of DeGuerin's legal pad. "Tracey Tarlton is now saying, contrary to what she said before, that Celeste put her up to it. Tracey is testifying in order to avoid a possible death sentence or life in prison. Tracey is testifying because she has been promised that the most she'll ever have to spend in jail for brutally shooting Steven Beard is twenty years, a sentence from which she could be paroled in as little as ten."

DeGuerin moved to Steve, and Celeste reached a finger under her eyeglasses to wipe away a tear. As DeGuerin spoke of Steve's generosity to Celeste, she took off her glasses and used both of her hands to rub away the wetness.

With his left hand to his face, Gary Cobb looked bored.

"He adopted Celeste's twin daughters, and he did so happily, even though the kids hated him and they spoke about him behind his back. . . . After their graduation from high school in the summer of 1999, Steve gave them matching—consider these are eighteen-year-old kids, spoiled brats—gave them matching Cadillacs for graduation."

The twins sat uncomfortably.

"I believe the evidence will show you that the sexual relationship existed solely in Tracey's mind." Dick DeGuerin was not charismatic in his presentation as he moved to the twins' high school graduation party, held at their ex-stepfather's house. Celeste had passed out on Jimmy Martinez's bed, DeGuerin said. ". . . And Tracey was, as Kristina described it then—she's changed her story, because the twins have turned against Celeste. The twins know that if Celeste is convicted, they get the money. The twins have turned against her and Kristina has changed her story, but originally what she said was, 'Tracey is molesting Mom.'"

His voice rising in tenor, he seemed to be wrapping up. "We believe the evidence will show you that on the early hours, unencouraged, untold, undirected, uncommanded, unasked by anyone, on her own, Tracey Tarlton entered Steven Beard's bedroom with a twenty-gauge shotgun loaded with birdshot.

"If you're going to plan a murder, you don't shoot someone with a twenty-gauge shotgun. You shoot them with a twelve-gauge. You don't load it with birdshot. You load it with buckshot. You don't shoot them in the stomach. You shoot them in the head."

DeGuerin wasn't wrapping up after all. Rather, Celeste was revving up, first with wet eyes, then sobbing. "Celeste married Steve for security and for money. . . . Celeste didn't want Steven Beard dead."

Judge Kocurek warned the attorney that he had only ten minutes more.

DeGuerin announced that the State would try to make Celeste look bad. "Making her look bad is not enough. Celeste Beard is not guilty. Thank you."

At 10:25 A.M., court recessed briefly. The twins and their friends left the courtroom. They wouldn't be allowed back in until they sat down in the witness chair.

Allison Wetzel, with her arms crossed, moved over to the natural-born Beards and told them she was about to play their father's call to 911. "Don't react," she said.

They were handed tissues.

"Beard. It's thirty-nine hundred Toro Canyon Road. Hurry!" Steve Beard breathed heavily, his voice deep on the scratchy recording.

LEFT: Convicted murderer Celeste Beard, shown here on a 1999 graduation trip to Australia. *Courtesy Marilou Gibbs and Dana Whatley*

BOTTOM: The man she married and later had killed: millionaire Steven Beard. *Courtesy Becky Beard*

Steve and Elise Beard's wedding photo. *Courtesy Becky Beard*

The natural-born Beard family—Steven III, Becky, Steve, Elise, and Paul—at the Terrace Mountain home, Christmas 1991. *Courtesy Becky Beard*

TOP: Celeste and Craig Bratcher's December 6, 1980, wedding. Celeste was already pregnant. *Courtesy Marilou Gibbs and Dana Whatley*

LEFT: Celeste's twin daughters, Jennifer and Kristina. *Courtesy Marilou Gibbs and Dana Whatley*

BOTTOM: Celeste, Jimmy Martinez, and the twins at Christmas. *Courtesy Marilou Gibbs and Dana Whatley*

Celeste, Jen, Steve, and Kris at the Continental Divide, June 1998.
Courtesy Marilou Gibbs and Dana Whatley

Celeste Beard and Tracey Tarlton at the July 1999 BookPeople Party.
Some said they were lovers. *Courtesy Trevor Patten*

Steve's at-home office. *Courtesy Travis County District Attorney's Office*

Steve's bedroom after the shooting. Note the broken glass in the upper left-hand corner. *Courtesy Travis County District Attorney's Office*

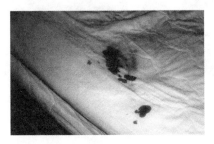

The mattress on which Steven Beard lay when Tracey Tarlton shot him. *Courtesy Travis County District Attorney's Office*

Tracey Tarlton's mug shot. *Courtesy Austin Police Department*

Donna Goodson and Celeste in New
Orleans during Mardi Gras 2000.
Courtesy Donna Goodson

Celeste and Cole Johnson on their
wedding day in Aspen.
Courtesy Celeste Beard Johnson

LEFT: Jennifer and Christopher Doose on the night of their May 1999 prom. *Courtesy Christopher Doose*

BOTTOM: Justin Grimm and Kristina at Texas Stadium, July 1999, for "All Girls Weekend." *Courtesy Christopher Doose*

Celeste Beard's mug shot. *Courtesy Austin Police Department*

Prosecutor Allison Wetzel.
Photo by Suzy Spencer

Judge Julie Kocurek. *Courtesy Julie Kocurek*

Celeste wrote on her legal pad.

"Thirty-nine hundred Toro Canyon Road." He began giving the 911 operator directions.

Celeste wept, shook her head, and put her hand to her forehead.

"What is your telephone number?"

He gave it, stunning the pin-drop–silent courtroom with his composure.

"My *guts* just jumped out of my stomach. They blew out. You know, they blew out of my stomach. They're—they're laying on my stomach."

"Okay. They're laying on your stomach?" the operator responded almost in disbelief.

Celeste bit her lip.

"I'm in awful pain."

"How did this happen?"

Nothing happened, Beard said. "I just woke up."

"Okay. Are you there by yourself?"

"My wife is somewhere in the house. I can't find her."

Celeste shook her head.

"When did this—when did this happen?"

"It just happened. I woke up. I just woke up."

"Okay. Can you tell me how they came out?"

"They just blew out of my stomach."

Celeste appeared to take a deep breath.

"Okay, can you tell me how? I'm having a hard time figuring out what happened."

"I don't know what happened. I've never had this happen before."

Celeste's eyes fluttered, then closed briefly.

"Okay. And—and you can see them?"

"Honey, I can't move. Yes, I've got—I've got ahold of them."

Celeste lowered her head, then raised her left hand to her face.

Friends in the gallery quietly wept.

"Call—call a number," he begged.

"Okay. They're on their way."

"Call another number," he begged again.

"Okay. What do we need to do?"

He gave her a phone number. "Tell my wife. She's in another part of the house."

"I'm going to call you right back," the operator said.

"Thank you," Beard responded.

In the stunned, still courtroom, three more words were spoken: "Pass the witness." Celeste Beard Johnson wept and wrote on her legal pad.

24

When TCSO officer Alan Howard took the stand just after 11 A.M., the gallery was only half-full. It stayed that way as Captain Stephen Alexander of the Westlake Fire Department, TCSO deputy Russell Thompson, Sergeant Greg Truitt, and Lieutenant Paul Knight, who had been a sergeant at the time of Beard's shooting followed him.

On the afternoon of October 2, 1999, Knight picked up some birdshot pellets and wadding from Brackenridge Hospital—evidence. He later spoke with Deputy Brett Spicer, who said one of the daughters had told him she'd just remembered there was a shotgun in the Beards' attic.

Knight returned to Toro Canyon, climbed into the attic, filled with camping equipment and too much junk, and found the previously overlooked shotgun, still in the box, covered with dust, and all taped up.

Jennifer had bought it as a one-year anniversary gift for Christopher. They were inseparable. He was what had kept her from running away from Celeste long ago. "This isn't a coincidence," she said to Knight. Christopher stood nearby. "My father died from a shotgun."

Monday, October 4, 1999, Knight tried to revisit Toro Canyon, but was told he couldn't go in the house. Celeste had strictly forbidden it.

"You know what this motherfucker did?" Knight yelled to Wines. "We're not allowed to come back in this house!"

"Just leave it alone," Wines said.

The two headed for Brackenridge, when they got a page that said Steve wanted to talk to them. But as they walked toward ICU, Celeste stopped them. "I don't want you anywhere near my husband." Her blue eyes were icy daggers as she cursed them. But the cops walked into Steve's room anyway.

The following morning, Charlie Burton phoned Knight and informed him that he was the Beards' attorney and the sheriff's office was not to communicate anymore with Steve Beard. Knight told him to go fuck himself.

On February 4, 2003, as Dick DeGuerin cross-examined Knight, he immediately focused on the October 4, 1999, encounter with Celeste. He stated that Steve, not Celeste, didn't want the cops there because they'd so upset Steve on their first visit.

Knight denied almost everything DeGuerin argued.

Around 11:25 A.M., the jurors saw a young, chunky bleached blonde with a face so round that she almost looked like a *Peanuts* character. She wore a steel-blue–colored sweater set that topped a black skirt fringed with dangling black beads, cream-colored hose, and carried a small, black Kate Spade handbag. Her mouth was lipstick-free.

Amy Cozart was a 21-year-old college junior, an advertising major at the University of Texas, and she was very nervous, she testified. Her junior year in high school, she met Kristina Beard at a yearbook convention at UT. October 1998, Steve and Celeste took a nearly month-long trip to China. While they were away, Amy and the twins would play.

Dick DeGuerin suddenly griped that Allison Wetzel was leading her witness.

"Is he objecting or is he going to object?" Wetzel retorted.

One of the first times Amy met Steve, she and Jen had wanted to swim. But Steve had wanted them to play volleyball in the pool and demanded that they put up the volley-ball net. Jen stood on one side of the pool putting in a pole while Amy was on the other side trying to tie off the net.

"You're tying it the wrong way!" Steve bellowed, standing right in front of the short, stout young blonde, his beefy body casting a frighteningly large shadow over her. "You don't know how to tie this thing! Just let me do it." He shoved her out of the way and started doing it himself.

It was the first time Steve treated her like his own daughter; she loved him for it.

"Steve often told me I was like a third daughter to him," Amy testified.

The first time he said it, she didn't know what to say back. They sat in the kitchen talking about the advertising business. He told Amy how proud he was of her for going to college, having plans, and taking steps toward her plans. Then he said it: "I love you as if you were another daughter."

Amy spent the night at the Beard house two or three times a week.

Wetzel asked Amy about her observations of Celeste and Steve's relationship.

DeGuerin objected seemingly non-stop.

"Celeste made it very obvious that she had married Steve for his money." Celeste had said it on many occasions.

"Did the defendant tell you that she had lied to her husband, yes or no?"

"Yes." Amy began talking about Celeste's relationship with Jimmy Martinez.

Again, DeGuerin harshly objected, until he was ordered to approach the bench. While the attorneys and judge conferred, Amy poured her first glass of water.

Afterwards, Wetzel returned to Jimmy Martinez.

"It was a sexual relationship," Amy stated.

Over and over, DeGuerin objected.

Either in the fall of 1998 or the spring of 1999, Amy wasn't sure which, she and Kristina had climbed into the car with Celeste, who was driving, and ran errands. And on that errand run Celeste told them that if Steve found out she was sleeping with Jimmy that that would nullify her prenuptial agreement and Celeste wouldn't get any money.

"Did Celeste Beard ever ask if you would lie for her?" Wetzel asked.

"Yes, she did." Celeste had asked Amy to lie about Jimmy, about Celeste's spending, about the parties they had, and the trips they went on.

DeGuerin fiercely objected again. His objections were so frequent and forceful that the defense attorney's very outcries seemed to give the prosecution more credibility. And with that, Judge Kocurek went ahead and released the jury for lunch.

With the jury in recess, the attorneys argued over what the prosecution could and could not enter. There could be no discussion of sexual positions, whether condoms were used or not, or a mention of Celeste's pet name for Jimmy Martinez's penis.

But so much of Amy's life with Celeste revolved around sex. They talked about sex as they smoked cigarettes together. They watched porn together. Celeste complained to Amy that she had trouble getting her nipples erect. She had Amy touch her breasts, which were stunningly hard. When Celeste lay down, her breasts didn't move at all. All the kids noticed it. Then again, Celeste had everyone touch her breasts. She loved to flash them, just like Kristina loved to talk about how she herself had beautiful nipples.

Celeste blabbed to Amy the details about her sex life with Jimmy. Jimmy's BMW was eight inches long. After having sex with him, she'd sit on the toilet and let his cum dribble out of her. It'd go plop, plop, plop into the water and she watched it sink to the bottom. Her knees were skinned because she'd given Jimmy head all night long.

She told Amy she'd had her tubes tied because she didn't want to have any more kids, but she wished she hadn't done that. She wanted to have another child because she needed someone to love her. Kristina was graduating. Everyone was abandoning her. She offered Amy a million dollars to have a baby for her. All she had to do, Celeste said, was lie there while they squirted Jimmy's semen up her.

Amy turned her down.

Celeste didn't know what to do. She'd already been to Christopher and Jennifer and made them an offer too. She'd pay a million dollars for a boy from them. If Christopher would impregnate Jen, then Celeste would pay for them to live in Europe for nine months. When the baby was born, she'd fly to Europe, pick up the infant, and fly home. At that point, Christopher and Jen could return to the States.

Eventually, Celeste resorted to making an offer to Justin and Kristina too, who also turned her down.

Amy still sat in the witness chair as DeGuerin argued that the prosecution was just trying to disparage his client, that the jury would lose sight of the real case, and that the State was trying to convict Celeste because she was a bad person.

Amy Cozart sat slump-shouldered as she poured her second glass of water. The tiny stud in her left nostril faintly glinted under the fluorescent lighting. The piercing in her tongue was barely visible.

Amy had decided two things before she took the stand—she was going to tell the truth and she wasn't going to look at Celeste. But when Amy had to point out Celeste Beard Johnson, identifying her by the headband and eyeglasses she wore, Amy also decided to give her a burn-in-hell look.

Celeste simply turned to Catherine Baen and started talking. Amy read her lips: "She's lying. None of the things coming out of her mouth are true."

You bitch. You're going to jail and I'm going to do everything I can to put you there. At the very beginning, Jen had warned Amy not to get too friendly with Celeste—*You'll get burned.*

As testimony resumed after lunch, Wetzel asked Amy what secrets Celeste wanted kept from Steve regarding Tracey Tarlton.

"The degree of their relationship, I guess."

DeGuerin objected and was sustained.

While giggling and calling Tracey a dyke, Celeste had shared with Steve the cards and letters she'd received from Tracey. Steve didn't laugh. He asked Celeste if she was a lesbian.

"She's a lesbian and in love with me. Isn't that funny?" Celeste had laughed. "She's my friend, but I don't really like her."

Amy said Celeste often called Steve names.

When Wetzel asked her witness for examples, DeGuerin objected again.

Kocurek overruled him, so Amy repeated the words—"asshole, fat fuck"—always said behind Steve's back. Celeste had also flipped Steve "the bird," again, behind his back, made faces at him, and on several occasions said she hated him.

Amy swore that Celeste had told her she'd switched Steve's Wolfschmidt with Everclear so that he would pass out earlier and she could do what she wanted. She said she'd witnessed Celeste mixing sleeping pills in Steve's food so that Celeste could go out.

Wetzel asked about Celeste's demeanor when she talked about pouring in the Everclear.

"She found it very amusing."

Amy had been on the stand a little more than thirty minutes that afternoon, when testimony finally turned to October 1999.

When Celeste had arrived at the lake house, she'd paced nervously. No one thought much about it, because with Celeste there were always a billion things going on. Constantly, Celeste looked at her watch. She said she wanted to get home at the exact same time as Kristina, at midnight.

Celeste asked Amy to take care of Megan. "Sure," Amy said. Thirty minutes to an hour after Celeste arrived, she left.

Amy described Megan as an old dog with fat tumors all over her body, who didn't like to ride in a car.

DeGuerin objected. "State of mind of a dog."

Amy modified her testimony—Megan resisted riding in a car.

After Celeste left, Amy went to the girls' room and pulled Megan into bed with her—with difficulty because Megan was so arthritic.

Jen and Christopher retired in the king-sized bed in the master bedroom.

In the wee hours of night, Christopher woke Amy. Within minutes, they were out the door and streaking toward Highway 71 and Brackenridge Hospital. Amy led in her Honda Accord. Jennifer, watching the road through tears, was at the wheel of Christopher's Expedition; he knew he was too drunk to drive.

All the way into town, and the hospital was at least an hour away, Jen and Christopher were on and off the phone with Justin. Then they'd call Amy in her car and relay the information.

By the time they got to Brackenridge, Christopher was stone sober. Amy had been calm until she got to the hospital and phoned her parents. With her dad on the line, as soon as she said, "Steve's been shot," she fell apart.

Christopher, who'd been crying along with Jen on the way into town, pulled Amy into a restroom and shook her. "You've got to control yourself."

The three kids spotted Celeste. She seemed frantic with crying. But it came across as a calculated upset. "Absent hysterics," Amy described it.

Amy and Celeste walked outside and sat on a bench near the sliding door into ER. They talked about "just everyday inane bullshit that didn't even matter," things Celeste needed to do. There were no more tears. In fact, Celeste seemed downright serene.

As they sat there smoking, it hit Amy—Celeste had said if anything happened to Steve, no one would ever know she wasn't in love with him. Amy and Kristina had been in the car with Celeste. It was one of those days when Celeste said, "I wish he would die already. How much longer is he gonna stick around?" Then she specifically stated, "When he dies,

I'll be so upset that no will ever know that I never cared about him." She would only *act* like she was mourning.

Celeste interrupted Amy's thoughts when she said she had a headache and asked Amy to get her some Tylenol.

Amy went to the hospital gift shop, gave Celeste the Tylenol, then went to be with the kids, who sat in a waiting room with two officers. One swabbed their fingers and hands for gunpowder residue, while the other asked them questions.

Suddenly, the name Tracey was blurted.

But Amy couldn't get Celeste's words and behavior out of her mind—how she treated her husband, the mean things Celeste had said about Steve, and what she would do if Steve died. In Amy's mind, there was definitely a second suspect.

Tears crept into Amy's young eyes as she spoke about her visit with Steve, two days after the shooting. She walked into Steve's room, crowded with people trying to get in their few minutes with him, when Steve tried to push everyone aside and grabbed toward Amy repeatedly. She eased through to him. He grabbed her hand, pulled her to him, looked straight in her eyes, and tried to say something.

She couldn't figure out what he was trying to say. When he was better, she wanted to ask him what he'd said. The opportunity never arose.

But from that day on, Amy never questioned Steve.

She was by Steve's side again the day his trach was removed. Again, he grabbed her hand, squeezing it tightly as she sat down with him. For five minutes they sat there communicating through their hands.

Doctors came in. Steve asked her to wait outside and come back in.

She did. He took her hand into his bear paw again and held it firmly while she told him what was going on in her life.

It was the last time Amy saw Steve Beard alive.

• • •

Dick DeGuerin began his cross-examination about 2:10. She admitted that Justin Grimm didn't like Steve's character, and Steve didn't like Justin. But as DeGuerin pushed Amy and tried to force the girl into saying that Justin was controlling, she wouldn't give in. The more DeGuerin tried to pressure her, the more determined she became.

He did the same regarding spending October 1 at the lake house, insisting that Celeste had said the kids *could* stay out there, not that they should.

Amy was equally determined—no, Celeste had said "should." But whereas DeGuerin's insistence was wrought with passion, Amy's rebuttals were matter-of-fact, in a tone that practically dismissed the senior lawyer's accusations.

DeGuerin brought up the twins' 18th birthday and mentioned that there were male strippers there, which Amy had requested.

"I don't know if I requested them," she said, "but I wouldn't be surprised."

A juror laughed.

Court ended with Amy's testimony. It'd been a stressful few days, and would continue to be stressful until the end of the trial. She hadn't seen the twins for years. In a way, it felt good being with them again. The girls just didn't understand why Amy had had to leave. The twins felt betrayed by her moving on—when it was the hardest thing she'd ever done in her life.

For their daughter's safety, her parents had insisted—no more Beards. Amy had gotten phone calls from Celeste after the girls went on the run. "Don't ever call me again!" Amy shouted into her cell. "If you ever fucking call me again, I'm calling the police."

One of the things Amy had loved so about Celeste was that Celeste was so different from Amy's parents—who were God-fearing, stable, loyal, loving. She'd never seen an adult act the way Celeste did. At the time, it was fascinating. Now . . . she just felt the girls were so used to drama in their lives that if Celeste didn't create it for them, they'd create it on their own. She didn't want that for herself. She owed that to Celeste—Celeste had taught Amy what *not* to do. Amy Cozart would become everything her parents and Steve Beard wanted and knew she could be.

Sometimes, she could just feel Steve's energy.

25

The third day of the trial of Celeste Beard Johnson was tedious as the State spent its time primarily calling employees of Bank of America. C. W. Beard, a senior vice president of Bank of America, as well as Steve's cousin and best man at his wedding to Celeste, testified that Steve had opened a trust account for Celeste in February 1997 with Celeste as the trustee. Steve deposited a half million dollars' worth of stocks and bonds in the account. Six months later, there was nothing left—empty.

A juror shook his head. The gallery laughed.

David Kuperman stated that Steve had been worth between $11 million and $12 million. Their premarital agreement separated their income, making it unlikely that there would have been any community property. And the $500,000 Steve gave Celeste in 1997 settled his divorce obligation as etched in their prenuptial agreement. Therefore, if Steve and Celeste had divorced, she would have gotten nothing more.

Around 8:30 A.M. on a chilly, rainy Thursday, February 6, 2003, an elevator to the seventh floor was filled with attorneys for Bank of America complaining that this was far from the first battle they'd had with Celeste Beard Johnson. In fact, it was at least their fourth.

That morning, David Kuperman returned to the stand. In September 1999, when Steve had been in North Austin Medical Center, Kuperman stated, "He was pretty down in the mouth about his marital relationship." So he asked if

Steve wanted him to recommend a divorce attorney. Kuperman had made the same recommendation in 1995 when Steve did file for divorce. But just days before Steve planned on leaving for Europe with Celeste, he simply said, "I'll think about it."

In early November 1999, when Kuperman stopped by Brackenridge Hospital to visit Steve, Steve was so groggy that when Kuperman returned three days later, Steve didn't even recall their previous visit.

Around that same time, Kuperman was presented with a letter Steve allegedly signed stating, "I'm coherent and Celeste Beard read this entire letter to me." Kuperman believed Celeste had prepared the letter. And the signature, there was something just fishy about it; it didn't look quite like Steve's normal signature.

Kuperman mentioned divorce again in December 1999, right at the time Steve was upset about Celeste's free spending.

The afternoon sun rapidly slipped down the sky that December 1999 when Kristina had dialed 911. Her mother was attempting suicide. Officer Alan Howard was wading through rush hour traffic on Bee Caves Road when he got the call and flipped on his lights and siren. He arrived at the gated house for the second time just as Officer Toby Miller pulled up.

Kristina opened the front door. Justin was with her. Earlier in the day, Celeste had tried to stab herself with her keys. She'd done it in front of Steve. Now she'd grabbed a framed photograph, smashed it, and cut at her wrists with the broken glass as she stood in the red, black, and white Oriental-themed guest bedroom.

The officers walked down the hallway to the bedroom where Celeste had locked herself inside. "That fucking asshole Howard and Wines better not be here," she yelled.

Howard looked over at Miller. "Don't let her know I'm here," he whispered. He moved to the kitchen where he talked with Justin and Kristina, while Miller communicated with Celeste through the closed door.

"Just fucking go away," she griped. "I don't want to talk to anybody."

In the kitchen, Kristina cried, much more upset than she had been on the day Steve Beard was shot.

"I didn't do anything," Celeste yelled. "Nothing's going on. I'm not trying to kill myself!"

The deputy threatened to bust down the door. Eventually, the bedroom door opened. Superficial scratches on her wrists marked Celeste's wounds.

To the mental health deputy who had arrived on the scene, Celeste bitterly complained that Steve used to do the grocery shopping and pay all the bills.

She turned to Kristina and told her exactly what Craig Bratcher had looked like when he "blew his brains out" with a shotgun. "Blew his brains out"—it was the exact phrase Celeste had used to her daughter.

The mental health deputy escorted Celeste to St. David's.

But Celeste didn't want to be there. "If I wanted to kill myself, I would have!" She was so angry that she refused to fill out the forms or put on the hospital I.D. bracelet. When she was asked her sexual orientation, she simply replied, "I don't have sex."

She refused a urine test. She got on the phone and threatened to kick her daughter out of the house and disown her. The date was December 22, 1999, the day Celeste had argued with her recuperating husband about money.

"No, there was no suicide attempt. Um, I got really—I'm trying to think—I got really upset—oh! The, the invoices for, um, Jimmy, that was about Christmas time. When I—the bank wasn't giving me any money. I mean, not like I thought I should have. And I was working, you know, doing all this stuff to do the house, so I inflated Jimmy's invoice by $75,000—fifty or seventy-five thousand dollars.

"And so—and plus I was doing all those repairs to the house. I thought, you know, Steve was gonna be pleased."

DeGuerin pointed out to Kuperman that in December 1999, Steve said he didn't want a divorce.

"That's right."

"It's clear to you that Steve cared for Celeste."

"That's a fair statement." In 1997 and 1998, Steve increased Celeste's share of the estate. The 1998 increase, Kuperman said, was at Celeste's request. Then in November 1999, at Kuperman's suggestion, Steve again increased Celeste's inheritance by giving her his share of the second phase of Davenport Village shopping center. Otherwise it would be a mess to probate, Kuperman had told Steve.

When DeGuerin pointed out that that increase was a pretty good indication that Steve didn't think Celeste had anything to do with his shooting, Wetzel objected and was sustained.

Kuperman and DeGuerin argued back and forth about whether Celeste had complete access to Steve's trust after his death. DeGuerin argued she didn't, since she had to get the approval of the estate's trustee, the bank. Therefore she was better off with Steve alive. Kuperman argued otherwise—the bank *had* to give her income at least once a year *and* she could request additional funds that even ate into the principal.

Allison Wetzel knew how to keep her jurors awake—bore them almost into drifting off with financial or medical details, then zing them awake with tawdry Celeste stories, preferably involving sex.

The jurors were about to get their sex when Brandy Whitten; her husband, Rick Klaw; Peggy Hailey; and Jill Bailey, all of whom had worked with Tracey at BookPeople, were sworn in.

Brandy was a short, heavy-set young woman with a sweet round face and dirty-blonde hair twisted into a single, long, Mother Earth braid down her back.

Gary Cobb tried to ask about Tracey's "relationship" with Celeste, but DeGuerin kept objecting to the word "relationship."

The more he objected, the more Brandy's voice shook. Only three BookPeople staffers knew Tracey had been hospitalized—Brandy, Rick, and Peggy. They'd all gone to eat together and figure out how they were going to talk about it with the entire staff once Tracey returned to work.

By the time they'd finished eating and walked into the store, Tracey stood in the coffee shop area in the back right-hand corner of the store with a woman they'd never seen before. Tracey introduced them to Celeste Beard. Peggy had thought Celeste worked for the hospital, while Rick had thought she was Tracey's handler because Tracey was obviously overmedicated. She slurred. Her body swayed. Her eyes were dilated. She was confrontational. They wanted her off the sales floor fast.

They ushered the couple through aisles of books and the few yards to the back elevator where they slipped them upstairs to the private fourth-floor offices. There, they learned Tracey had come from the hospital. And they noticed Celeste was controlling.

Celeste came in to BookPeople several other times, visiting Tracey on the fourth floor. When she did, Tracey, who always kept her office door open, would suddenly close it. Other times, Celeste picked up Tracey and they left for lunch together.

The more time they spent with each other, the more Tracey seemed to change. She carried a cell phone that, in those days, was too pricey for BookPeople salaries. She started carrying a small, black leather purse. She'd never carried a purse before. She wore a watch that looked like jewelry. She started getting manicures. She styled her hair differently and had it colored.

Then, Tracey invited the staff out to Celeste's lake house for a party. She was calling it a Fashion Victims Party. Tracey wasn't the type to throw theme parties.

But on July 9, 1999, about forty BookPeople employees and friends trekked out to Spicewood, followed the long, winding directions to Windemere, and finally pulled up in front of a fancy house on a corner. It wasn't some weekend lake shack. It was a full-fledged home that was far out of the price range of a BookPeople employee.

Jill Bailey, Honey Smith, and Emily Basham were some of the first to arrive. A professional photographer snapped everyone's pictures as soon as they walked through the front door. The guests were instructed to toss their keys into a bowl, a hint that it might be a swinging sex party.

Within thirty minutes, Jill, Honey, and Emily wandered into the master bedroom, checking out the house, and accidentally caught Celeste and Tracey in an extended hug and full-mouth "passionate" kiss.

"Sorry," Emily oopsed to the couple. Tracey and Celeste giggled.

"It was not platonic," Honey stated. In fact, she was so embarrassed that she didn't want to look at the couple.

When Brandy and Rick arrived at the party, Tracey and Celeste, acting like a couple, showed them around the home Celeste had redecorated three times. There was a stone fireplace in the living room, Chinese red walls in the gourmet kitchen, and hand-painted tiles even under the desk where the dog slept.

They walked out to the landscaped backyard dotted with a stone pathway, Christmas lights in the trees, and a hot tub that soon was filled with BookPeople employees. There was catered food, a keg of beer, and an open bar. BookPeople people didn't have catered parties; they had potlucks.

They looked at Tracey, who held hands with Celeste. The couple appeared to be sharing inside jokes. Some BookPeople employees thought Tracey acted more relaxed that summer evening. She grinned. Celeste crawled into her lap and nuzzled her neck. They kissed. They gave each other longing looks.

On one of the wrought-iron picnic tables, Brandy set the pot brownies she'd baked at Tracey's request.

At that, DeGuerin fired out of his seat like a hot match. He wanted to know where Brandy had gotten the marijuana, how much it had cost, and how much she had had.

The jurors just stared at him. Didn't he know he was in Austin, Texas? The town where he grew up? The town where he went to college? The home of old hippies, young college students, and proud pot-smoker Willie Nelson? Weed, in Austin, was as common as Starbucks. And got about the same reaction.

But Brandy gave the lawyer what he wanted—she'd made two 8x8 containers of pot brownies of average strength from a recipe out of a book she'd gotten for free at BookPeople. It was about the third time in her life she'd made marijuana brownies.

With a disgusted, judgmental look on his face, DeGuerin kept harping on the strength of the brownies, insinuating that Brandy had eaten some before she got to the party and was intoxicated when she arrived.

Repeatedly, Brandy denied his accusation.

He argued that she was resentful of the opulently decorated house.

"No, I was taken aback." She did admit that "pretty soon" after she'd met Celeste, she didn't like her. She thought she was manipulative.

Again, DeGuerin proclaimed that that was out of resentment because Celeste was of a different class.

Brandy pointed out that *resent* and *not like* are two different things.

DeGuerin wouldn't leave it be.

As the various BookPeople people testified, Celeste cocked her head to the left as though she were irritated. Under Rick Klaw's testimony, Cobb entered into evidence photographs from the party, including one of Celeste sitting in Tracey's lap, another of Celeste eating a marijuana brownie and looking happy about it.

The photos were passed over to the jurors, who flipped through them. DeGuerin didn't want to begin his cross-examination while the jurors were distracted by the photos.

Kocurek gave him a minute, then said, "Let's go. I think this jury can multi-task."

Dick DeGuerin wasn't nearly as hard on the bearded and bespectacled man as he had been on the wife.

Nearly two hours later, the head buyer of BookPeople, Peggy Hailey, took the stand. An obese woman wearing a purple tunic and wire-rimmed glasses, with slightly graying hair parted straight down the middle, Peggy was a cross between Janis Joplin and Mama Cass Elliot. She'd also appeared on CSPAN-2 with Tracey.

When Peggy was asked to identify Celeste, she described her the exact same way as every BookPeople employee did—the one in the black shirt. She told Wetzel that she'd thought Tracey and Celeste were in a romantic relationship because Tracey had told her they were.

Objection, DeGuerin called. He wanted Peggy's statement struck from the record because it was hearsay. So she added that she'd also thought it was romantic because Celeste would come up to the fourth floor, where they had very few visitors. And at the lake house party, she said, "They interacted like any other couple." They were arm in arm and hand in hand.

When DeGuerin asked Peggy about her marijuana use that night, she stated she didn't eat any brownies or even drink any alcohol that night for fear that she wouldn't be able to find her way out of Windemere. And she left early, around 10 or 11 P.M.

"Giving the party for Tracey at the lake house was no big deal because I gave Dawn an expensive and elaborate 30th birthday party at Barton Creek Country Club. I gave Dana a 40th birthday party in Marble Falls. I gave Darlene Brooks a . . . party in Spicewood. I had 4 open houses at my home and the party for Tracey was no big deal. I enjoyed giving parties and was good at it.

"Steve came up to the lake house the day after and we spent the remainder of the weekend at the lake house. He paid the bills, so he knew about the party.

"I did not act any different with Tracey than I did with my heterosexual friends. My bunco parties would get kind of wild and we were all married women. I did not realize that I was leading Tracey on, because I treated her the same as I treated Dawn.

"I did not sleep with her, nor did I intimately kiss her."

. . .

Dr. Robert Coscia, Steve's trauma doctor, sat in the witness chair on Monday, February 10, 2003, a day of blue skies and wispy clouds.

When he spoke to Celeste the day Steve was shot, "She asked me if he said anything." But the doctor's concern was infection. Steve had a 50 percent chance of survival, "at best." Four and a half months later, Steve was discharged, although he had a "significant yeast infection."

DeGuerin griped that he couldn't read the doctor's notes. He griped that the prosecution was whispering. He showed Coscia exhibits trying to prove that Steve hadn't had an infection because he hadn't been running a fever. The doctor argued back, disagreeing with the lawyer.

The jurors were antsy.

Septic shock, DeGuerin announced. "That's what he died of, isn't it?"

"No." Steve Beard had died of a blood clot to his lungs related to his injuries and his long stay in the hospital, Coscia stated.

"I was at the infamous marijuana brownie party, but I did not swallow," Nancy Pierson cracked. The jurors smiled— one of them had brought brownies, potless of course, to the jury room after Brandy Whitten's testimony.

Nancy was a tall woman with short, well-cut, blonde hair who walked like an athlete and testified that Tracey was the best goalie in soccer because "she could fly through the air like no one else would."

Nancy, a smiling, happy massage therapist in a Hawaiian-looking shirt, and an oversized watch wrapped around her wrist, had known Tracey since her sophomore year in college. She'd been around Tracey and Celeste numerous times—at her house, at Tracey's house, at breakfasts. She "definitely" thought they were in a romantic relationship, and it wasn't one-sided.

At the BookPeople party, she said, they were acting "very affectionate."

DeGuerin passionately objected. Her testimony was cumulative.

But Nancy continued. Tracey and Celeste announced to their guests that they were retiring for the night, but everyone was welcomed to stay as long as they were on the back patio with the keg of beer. Tracey and Celeste then walked into the bedroom and shut the door.

The guests left the patio a mess—red plastic cups tossed everywhere, Kendall-Jackson wine bottles on the table, liquor bottles, a keg of beer that was shockingly full, leftover food, including a few bites of pot brownies, and rolling papers.

The next morning, Justin snapped photos of everything as though he were a crime-scene investigator recording the evidence. And Celeste and Tracey emerged from the bedroom, with Celeste relishing that the party was a bit wild and they had had a great time, and bragging about how many marijuana brownies she'd eaten.

DeGuerin quickly struck back trying to indicate that Nancy was a wild slut. She'd had sex on a rug that night—with a woman. With a sly grin, Nancy didn't deny it.

Sounding like he knew a little too much about marijuana brownies, DeGuerin went on and on about how the effect of pot brownies hit about thirty minutes or later after eating them. Then he began obsessing about how masculine Tracey was and how feminine Celeste was.

Finally, Nancy stated that she objected to his monologue about male/female roles. That, she said, was from the 1950s.

Again, DeGuerin seemed to forget that he was in Austin, where numerous Christian churches accepted gay members. And that he had gays in the courtroom.

At barely 8:00 in the morning on Tuesday, February 11, 2003, the sixth day of the trial, Allison Wetzel was already questioning Christopher Doose, and Dick DeGuerin was already objecting.

Chris wore a three-button navy blue suit, a dark blue shirt, and a striped tie that matched both of the blues. Admittedly, he'd dressed for the cameras—he didn't want folks to think he was a slob.

Wetzel moved Christopher back, before the night of the shooting, to the days and nights when Celeste had drugged Steve.

Chris stated he'd gone with Celeste to Twin Liquors in Westlake to buy the Everclear. Located in a strip center next to a discount dry cleaner and Popeyes fried chicken, it was a chain frequented by the heavy-drinking Westlakers.

He'd seen Celeste replace the vodka with Everclear. After Steve passed out, Celeste would go "out on the town," to the lake house, Tracey's or Jimmy's. Steve wasn't to know about Jimmy "because Steve would divorce her," Christopher stated. "She would get only a certain stipend of money and lose everything else." Celeste seemed to run scared about that. She sometimes called Steve "Daddy Warbucks."

But when Steve did find out about the affair, Celeste seemed to have an I-don't-care-anymore attitude, Christopher testified.

He remembered the day well, even though Steve had talked to Chris all the time about Celeste. Steve stood in the kitchen and said he was thinking about getting a divorce. His voice sounded hurt and helpless, not angry. What more could he do? He cancelled the Sunday Suck for a while.

But even that seemed irrelevant—Celeste had told Christopher that she'd gotten a doctor to write a note that she couldn't perform the Sunday Suck anymore because of TMJ.

26

"How the Sunday Suck came up, I have no idea. I never said that. It sounds like something one of the kids came up with. I talked with Dawn & Marilou about the difficulties of sex and maybe the girls overheard, but I never referred to it in that way."

• • •

Celeste scribbled busily on her notepad, as the jury seemed enwrapped in Christopher's testimony, interrupted only by DeGuerin's continuing objections. "Leading and suggestive."

Kocurek repeatedly overruled the defense attorney.

DeGuerin repeatedly refused to accept her ruling and wouldn't sit down.

Kocurek sent the jury out of the room, turned to DeGuerin and pointed out that he'd griped that Wetzel's questions were too leading or that they were too broad. It didn't matter how Wetzel phrased the question, DeGuerin was still going to gripe. Kocurek brought the jury back in to the sound of a flushing toilet and the jurors giggling.

In the summer of 1999, Celeste planned a driving trip to Washington State to pick up Craig Bratcher's possessions, which had been in storage almost since the day he'd died. All that time, Celeste had been fighting his family, primarily Kathy, over Craig's paltry estate.

Celeste had hoped for a trip that included herself, Kris and Justin, and Jennifer and Christopher. But Steve wanted to go too. The kids would ride in the Expedition, and Steve and Celeste would take the Cadillac. Celeste couldn't tolerate that—being in a slow-moving car alone with Steve for hours upon hours.

Justin suggested they alternate.

That wasn't good enough.

Steve bought a new Suburban for the trip, complete with captains' chairs for him and a TV for Celeste so that she could watch movies. She liked comedies and what Christopher referred to as "fucked-up movies," such as *The Silence of the Lambs*.

In Ogden, Utah, Steve paid the hotel bill while everyone else walked over to a restaurant for breakfast, where Celeste slipped sleeping pills into Steve's orange juice. When Steve joined them and took a sip of his juice, he said, "This tastes funny." He wanted to order another one.

"Drink it. Don't be wasteful," Celeste shamed him.

He drank it and turned to her. "Are you happy now?"

"Yes, thank you."

Later that day, they stopped at a Sizzler in Oregon. There, she slipped sleeping pills into his potatoes because Steve was irritating the hell out of her. With Steve passed out, Celeste talked freely on the telephone to Dawn Madigan and Tracey.

Steve phoned Dr. George Handley and said he was having trouble breathing. Handley told him he needed to get to a lower altitude. So once they got to Seattle, they dropped Steve at the airport. He was to fly to Phoenix and they'd meet him there in three days, and pick him up for the rest of the drive home. He handed Celeste a fistful of cash to get the kids to Arizona.

With money in her designer purse and Steve out of the way, Celeste declared, "Yes, yes, yes, yes! We can do our own trip. We don't have to drive slow. Now, we can have fun!"

Ten minutes later, she phoned Tracey and claimed the kids were being mean to her. Celeste then turned to the kids, stated that they were in trouble and Tracey wanted to speak to them. The phone passed from kid to kid. Tracey yelled so loudly that her voice could be heard throughout the car despite the tires pounding the asphalt at much more than 80 mph. "Be nicer to her! Treat her better!"

Christopher didn't know what the hell they'd done wrong.

Celeste got in a better mood when they hit a Cole Haan shoe outlet. She spent all the cash, and Christopher had to start picking up some of the bills. That wasn't anything new for him. He and Amy regularly paid the twins' way because Celeste would take the money Steve had given them. Regularly, Celeste took a check Steve had signed, pressed it against a sunlit window, put a blank check over it, and traced Steve's signature in order to pay bills.

Whatever money the girls did have, Christopher urged Jen to lock in his sister's safety deposit box. She did. It's what they lived on after the twins went into hiding.

• • •

Wetzel presented Christopher with the numerous cards, letters, and journals he'd found during the December cleanout of the house.

On April 26, 1999, Tracey wrote Celeste: "Celeste, you are so beautiful. I think about your long, silky body and your incredible, long legs and I just can't stand it. And then I think of your incredible face and I want to get into my car & drive to Dallas, and stand outside your building and wail, until I get arrested. We won't even talk about what happens when I think about your sweet, tough, sexy voice! We are talking *hard time* now!" And she thanked Celeste for phoning her every day.

DeGuerin went on another tirade of objections. The defense attorney appeared utterly stunned that an irritated and tired-looking Kocurek was just as repeatedly overruling him.

Wetzel presented a card depicting two women, their arms around each other, and a big dog about the size of Wren, standing in front of them. In that May 12, 1999, card, Tracey wrote: "I know that at times I don't contain myself well; that my feelings explode up through the surface, and I end up bleeding all over places where I don't belong. Like today, I woke up missing you with a fever better reserved for the dying. . . . Feeling like that, I would lay down & die just to smell your skin. . . . I know that this is letting my feelings run a little too deep. But, surely, it will help when I can see you, for just a little more. Or when I can wake up with you on some rare occasions. . . . I will not give up my desire for you, or my hold you have on my heart. Those are special things that belong to both of us, and should be cherished."

Wetzel read one of Celeste's writings for Dr. Gotway about what she'd had a right to expect as a child—"a safe, caring & loving environment" without abuse.

Celeste wept as Wetzel quoted her words. ". . . When I got home it was like living in a jail that offered no security." She went straight to her room, did her homework, cooked dinner, washed the clothes, and cleaned house. "I tried to be perfect so that they would love me enough not to fight." Still, they fought, so Celeste slept with her mother.

". . . I would sleep with her praying to God that when he [her father] got me out of her bed at night she would save me. It never happened. This went on for 8 years."

"He always said he would kill us if I ever said anything so I complied. It made me feel dirty—lonely—like I had no control."

She wrote that she had had no friends. "According to my mom they were all bad. I see now she was afraid they might know something. . . . The shame I grew up with was overwhelming.

"My father used to tell me as I got older I enjoyed it otherwise I would fight him like I used to. But, I would just block it out like going into a box. . . .

"I don't feel good about myself—I feel ugly, dirty, like I have no control over my life and extremely hopeless."

The afternoon of the shooting, Celeste, the twins, and the boys checked into the downtown Marriott hotel close to the hospital, at the girls' insistence. They were terrified Tracey would come back.

At the Marriott, Celeste sat down with Phil Presse and another defense attorney. After the meeting, she came out and told the kids that the lawyer would be representing them all—they wouldn't need to hire attorneys. She repeated "Don't mention Tracey's name," and ordered the kids not to talk to the investigators, "period." Eventually, she told them Steve didn't want them to help the prosecution—he didn't want to put the girls through that.

Christopher didn't buy her story about the attorney representing him. He was a teenager who'd just had his hands swabbed for gunpowder. He was scared. He'd already phoned his attorney.

The day Steve came home from the hospital, Christopher testified, he and Kristina—not Jennifer as Donna had stated and Celeste agreed—had driven to Studio 29, where Celeste dropped off the wheelchair-bound Steve, got into the car Christopher and Kris had driven, and left.

At the house, Christopher and Kris tried to ease Steve to

his room. He made it halfway up the stairs, when he couldn't climb another step. He had to sit down. Christopher and Kris got Doug Byers, Celeste's Fox Services handyman, and the three of them lifted Steve, who was in "excruciating pain," from his wheelchair and maneuvered him to his bedroom via a different route.

Celeste was nowhere around and didn't show for three hours. When she did show, they asked her where she'd been. "None of your business," she answered. In the past, they'd always known where she was. Celeste practically refused to be alone. Then she started disappearing for hours, always telling the kids it was "none of their business" where she'd been.

A limousine pulled up at the Toro Canyon house the day of the funeral. Celeste, Dawn Madigan, Kristina, Justin, Jennifer, and Christopher crowded in, all wearing black, Celeste's hair swept into an up-do. A heavy gold coin on a heavy gold chain hung around her neck as she laughed and cracked jokes with Dawn—Celeste sure was glad she'd bought trip insurance. But on the way to Cook-Walden, they made a brief side trip to Northwest Hills Pharmacy in the Davenport Village. Dawn needed pantyhose.

They walked into the second-floor pharmacy where the rich perfume of fresh flowers scented the air and the store was crowded with upscale gift items. Celeste turned to an employee and loudly proclaimed, "Now that I own the place, it's time for you to kiss my ass like you kissed Steve's."

She climbed in the limousine and laughed.

When they arrived at the cemetery, Celeste took a moment, then stepped out, her demeanor "changed completely." She began to cry.

The jurors' heads were bent down as they wrote notes.

Christopher described Celeste putting a bottle of Wolfschmidt vodka in Steve's coffin. A teddy bear, a fez, and photos were also tucked into the casket.

Later that same day, Christopher stood with Justin on the back drive of the Beard house. Still dressed in their funeral suits, Justin showed Christopher a "secret cell phone." Chris may not have ever seen the phone before, but he'd seen the phone number that was in the call history.

DeGuerin flipped out with objections. The judge had to overrule him at least twice each time before he'd sit down.

The phone number Christopher recognized was Tracey Tarlton's.

Celeste raced out the garage door, frantically rummaged through the Cadillac, looked in the console, and screamed, "Where is it?"

"Where is what?" Justin replied.

"You have it! Give it to me!"

Justin denied having anything.

Celeste searched the car again.

With her eyes diverted, Justin tossed the phone under the Cadillac.

"I know you have it!"

"Search me," he said.

She patted him down as Chris and the girls watched. She went back into the house and searched the guest room, where she was sleeping each night.

Justin climbed under the car, retrieved the phone, turned to Kristina and said, "I think she's asking for this?"

"What is it?"

He showed the phone to Kris, who took it, walked inside, and gave it to her mother, who locked herself in the guestroom.

That, Christopher stated, was the turning point for him. Adding to his suspicion were the strange men who were spending the night at the house with Celeste, the fact that Celeste had gotten Steve to change his will when he was in the hospital so that she would get more and his three natural-born children would get less, and the fact that she'd bragged about how much she would get—$10 million, a "modest sum," Christopher said.

He knew he had to go to the authorities. It just took him a while to convince the other kids to go with him.

· · ·

Wetzel mentioned Studio 29.

DeGuerin objected. The attorneys marched up to Kocurek's bench.

Celeste, her long hair swept back by a hair band, con-
fabbed with Catherine Baen, her lips moving rapidly. In the
second week of the trial, rather than sitting primly at the defense table, her hands neatly tucked under the table, as she
had done the first few days of the trial, she was beginning to
relax. She laughed some.

About ten minutes later, Christopher said that on February 9, 2000, he, Celeste, Kristina, and Jennifer were in the
back lobby of Studio 29. Kristina sat on a bench next to her
mother. People were gossiping that Celeste was involved
with Tracey. People were saying she'd played a part in
Steve's death. Celeste bent over wailing.

"Celeste, don't cry. It's going to be okay," Christopher
said, as he and Jen knelt at Celeste's feet.

Celeste couldn't breathe. She shook violently. She
looked the kids straight in the eyes. "I want to kill myself.
And I want y'all to kill yourselves with me."

A juror covered his mouth with his hand.

"There was no response. She was too hysterical. It was
just a subject change," Christopher testified.

At 11:30 A.M., Wetzel passed the witness.

DeGuerin looked at his watch as if he wanted to wait until
after lunch to start his cross-examination. "Mr. Doose," he
said, "you claim to be a friend of Steve Beard's."

"Yes, I was."

Yet, DeGuerin pointed out, Christopher had played
along with all the horrible deeds.

"There was no choice—"

He declared Christopher an accomplice. He lashed at the
young, hopeful politician that Christopher had never told
Steve anything about what was going on, including that Celeste was having an affair with Jimmy Martinez.

The jurors leaned back in their chairs, not taking notes.

DeGuerin insisted that Amy had arranged for the male
strippers at the girls' 18th birthday party.

"No, that's incorrect," Christopher replied.

DeGuerin suddenly was quiet, as he tried to get organized. Apparently, he *hadn't* planned on doing cross until after lunch. Finally, he flashed up photographs of the birthday party. He was red-faced and acted disgusted as he talked about the male strippers and showed pictures of the twins, the strippers' groins in their faces and the guys' bare buns in the direct eye of the camera.

Three jurors—one male and two female—strained to hold in their laughter.

Again, DeGuerin maintained that Amy had gotten the strippers.

Celeste did, Christopher answered.

DeGuerin accused him of lying and proclaimed Amy had testified that she got the strippers.

Judge Kocurek leaned her head back against her chair.

Celeste had gotten drunk and was angry at the kids for drinking. She'd handed Jimmy a credit card to pay the tab—$2,000 for food, $8,000 for liquor. There'd been more of Celeste's adult friends at the party than kids. Jimmy then drove Celeste to his house for the night.

After lunch, with arms crossed, DeGuerin continued attacking Christopher. He flashed up a photo of Christopher dancing with Celeste at the twins' graduation party—the Celeste you *claimed* you had seen spike his drink, the Celeste you *claim* you had seen grinding up sleeping pills. So you say you're not an accomplice? Not playing along?

DeGuerin went through Christopher's testimony, line by line, trying to confound and madden the young man. DeGuerin looked like a short-necked snapping turtle, flipped on his back, desperately trying to upright himself.

The angrier DeGuerin got, the calmer Christopher got—his palms that had sweated when he first took the stand, no longer did. When DeGuerin twisted two of Christopher's previous answers into one statement, Christopher replied, ". . . you're combining two different instances."

Every time Christopher made a statement, DeGuerin said it was Christopher's "claim."

No, Christopher responded. It was what he knew.

Celeste shook her head at Christopher.

DeGuerin brought up a trip Christopher and Jennifer had planned to take to Canada. DeGuerin said there was a stipulation to that trip.

No, Christopher replied.

DeGuerin introduced a check written by Celeste for nearly $4,000 that Christopher deposited on January 27, 2000, the day after Steve's funeral. Celeste had written a memo on the check saying Jennifer could go to Canada only if she didn't get any Cs on her report card, followed by three exclamation marks.

Celeste smirked at Christopher.

Again, Christopher said no.

The courtroom steamed. Becky Beard fanned herself. Some spectators fell asleep.

Allison Wetzel asked Christopher Doose why he never told Steve all the things he knew.

"I was young, and I didn't understand what was really going on and the implications they had."

The jurors leaned forward while he spoke.

"Do you wish you'd told Steve Beard?"

"Absolutely. Every day of my life."

27

February 13, 2003, was a humid, drizzly, foggy Thursday. The long ends of Celeste's colored ponytail were frizzy, brittle and broken. Her demeanor seemed different—sadder.

Gary Cobb called Wanda B. Jenkins, M.S.W., a case manager at Health South. On January 19, 2000, a "very upset" Celeste Beard phoned Health South complaining about Steve's discharge. At home, she said, he'd had " 'difficulty ascending the steps.' " " 'He did not sleep well.' " He required people to help him to the bathroom. "She stated, 'He shouldn't have discharged in this condition.'"

Celeste demanded a meeting with everyone involved in her husband's care.

Twenty-five minutes later, Celeste and Steve were at the hospital. By 2:45 P.M., Celeste made it clear that she wanted Steve readmitted. She didn't think he was ready for home. She made it clear again at 4 P.M. and by 5 she'd taken Steve to the Brackenridge ER.

Three days passed without hearing from Celeste. Then there was a page at 11:30 A.M. on January 22, 2000. Celeste raged that Steve was in Brackenridge due to an infection from his heart, a severe yeast infection, and possibly heart failure. She blamed Health South for the yeast infection.

"She indicated that she's not threatening a lawsuit now but it 'may be different if my husband dies.'" Celeste said that three times.

Gary Cobb wanted to know if Celeste Beard had ever come to Jenkins on January 18, 2000, and said she didn't want Steve discharged.

"No."

The jurors who'd been leaning forward with interest during direct were immediately lost to Dick DeGuerin as soon as he began his cross.

The night of January 26, 2000, just hours after Steve's funeral, Celeste "was in a very good mood," as she packed some of Steve's things, TCSO Deputy Brett Spicer testified. He'd worked off-duty security at the Beard house that night.

And that night, Celeste turned to Spicer, who looked like he belonged on a pinup calendar, and asked him if he liked "natural women."

The deputy shrugged his shoulders.

She repeated her question, specifically asking if Spicer liked women who didn't shave their armpits and pubic area, because Tracey Tarlton didn't. She later told Spicer that Jimmy Martinez had phoned her around Christmas saying he wanted to give Celeste a present in person—to sleep with her.

Dick DeGuerin's cross consisted of anger, condescension, and twisting of testimony. He stood and yelled so loudly that the jury woke from their DeGuerin-induced stupor. But his point was lost in his tirade.

Justin Grimm entered the too-warm courtroom around 1:45 P.M. He certainly looked nothing like the slim young man Kristina had started dating in January 1999.

Before Justin came into the picture, Kristina, Jennifer, Christopher, and Amy had been a happy clique of four. When Kristina started dating Justin, the happy foursome became a threesome with a satellite clique of two, Kristina and Justin, who seemed like a troublemaker, always with the covert plan—"I know your code."

But Justin refused to spill any details of his own life— with the exception of hinting that his family had been and maybe still was in the CIA. The twins reveled in his mysterious hint. As Amy knew, they were easily influenced.

Kristina did whatever her boyfriend wanted. He even kept her driver's license and money, which infuriated Steve.

"Who the hell is he?" Steve barked at Kristina. "You have a wallet and a purse. Why is *he* holding on to your car keys and your money?"

Steve hated the nerdy bastard. He didn't trust him and he didn't want him in the Beard house alone. "I don't give a shit . . . if you continue to be with Justin," he yelled. "You can go on welfare for all I care. I'm not supporting you." Steve knew the boy was trouble.

Regularly, Justin snapped Celeste's car keys out of her hands. "I'm driving."

"No, you little twerp! You're not driving. I'm twenty years older than you. Give me my goddamned keys."

Sometimes, she dug into his pocket to get her keys back. Justin thought it was a game and funny.

That's what Steve Beard didn't like about his new daughter's boyfriend. Justin Grimm was a control freak.

On top of that, whenever Celeste wanted her daughter to spend time with her, Kristina looked at Justin. If he shook his head no, Kristina turned to her mother and said, "No, I don't want to go with you." When Justin came into Kristina's life, everything changed for Celeste.

"It's because of Justin. He's a bastard. He is a bastard."

Celeste kept her head down as Justin was sworn in in his dark suit, white shirt, and blue tie. Under oath, and under Gary Cobb's questioning, Justin swore that his father was a real estate developer, his mother was a housewife, and his sister was a lawyer.

Justin had frequently spent the night at the Beard house, he said. He didn't know if Steve knew he was there, but Celeste certainly did—she was the one who'd first invited him to stay overnight. She'd never told him he couldn't sleep there until October 1, 1999.

Celeste stared straight at Justin.

Mr. Beard, Justin said, had been packing for the trip to Europe. Celeste had watched TV rather than pack, so Justin offered to help her pack. She turned him down. He saw nothing to suggest she was going on a trip, he swore.

Around 3:15 A.M., on October 2, he got a call from Kristina. He told his parents he was leaving and drove over to the Toro Canyon house. He spotted Celeste and Kristina in a cop car and he got word that they were on their way to Brackenridge and wanted him to meet them there. Not until he got to the hospital, he said, did he learn that Steve had been shot.

Celeste never said she was looking for men, but that's what the kids knew she was doing whenever she put on the "good Celeste." And they went along to watch.

Celeste got herself rich, honky-tonk perfect in heavy makeup and enough jewelry to fill a store window, pulled on a short black skirt, a white blouse with ruffles along its plunging neckline, and high heels, and let her hair loose and let it flow in good ole country-western-singer fashion.

Justin, Kristina, Celeste, Amy, Christopher, and a friend

of Celeste's simply known as "Gay Val" parked in front of La Zona Rosa, an old rust-colored brick bar and concert venue with flaming red neon lights on a street littered with leaves and liquor bottles. Behind the venue's chain link fence, Jerry Jeff Walker pounded his worn cowboy boots on the stage as he sang "Up Against the Wall, Redneck Mother."

Celeste climbed up on the stage, crossed her legs in a display of femininity, propped up her big silicone and saline boobs, and flashed her diamonds. She wanted Jerry Jeff. But Jerry Jeff had ignored her, so she wanted to go to Jimmy Martinez's house.

They piled into their vehicle and then fell out of it in front of Jimmy's two-story home, which resembled every other house in the neighborhood. A very drunk Celeste banged on the front door, demanding he let her in.

Jimmy wouldn't.

Celeste banged on the door more. Furious, she threw her cell phone at the house, then peed on his lawn.

The jury erupted into laughter.

Dick DeGuerin jumped to his feet and objected.

Judge Kocurek sustained his objection and directed the attorneys to the bench. As she instructed, "Stop, stop," the jurors couldn't stop snickering. One older woman giggled so hard that she held a file folder in front of her face to try to hide from the judge.

At that, Kocurek sent the jurors out of the courtroom.

Catherine Baen sat with Celeste, both of them laughing.

Justin Grimm grinned with pride.

As DeGuerin walked back to the defense table, he smiled and growled, "Let's get it on. He's talking about papering the yard. Jesus Christ!"

Celeste closed her hand into a fist, lifted it into the air, and knocked knuckles with one of her young attorneys. Celeste got her birthday present that day with the "peeing on the lawn" comment. She loved it!

With his hands clasped in front of him, Justin Grimm walked into the courtroom and sat down in the witness chair on Tuesday morning, February 18, 2003. While the judge wore preppie pearls around her neck, DeGuerin wore a dour look on his face.

Gary Cobb questioned Justin about the Seattle road trip.

Kristina had cried in the hotel room, he said, while Celeste had yelled at her, "Just do it!" She wanted Kristina to prep the sleeping pills to slip into Steve's orange juice. As they drove, Steve thought he was having breathing problems and asked for his medicine. Celeste rolled down the window, air rushed into the car, she punched a few pills from Steve's antibiotic and steroid dose pack, tossed them into the wind while chuckling a bit, rolled up the window, and handed Steve two sleeping pills.

As he began drifting out, he asked for his oxygen and turned it on. Just as he began to come around, when Steve wasn't looking, Celeste turned off his oxygen.

"Mr. Grimm, isn't it true that Steve Beard didn't like you at all?" Dick DeGuerin attacked.

28

One of the things that had turned Christopher Doose against Justin Grimm was that the day Steve died, as Christopher and Justin stood next to Steve's Cadillac, Justin said, "Why are you so sad? You never liked him either."

"No," Justin answered DeGuerin. Steve did like him.

"He called you a loser to your face."

"No."

DeGuerin said Justin had to sneak around to spend the night at the Toro Canyon home.

"Yes."

And just as DeGuerin did with Christopher Doose, he blamed Justin for not reporting to Steve his "claim" that Celeste was drugging Steve, turning off his oxygen, and all the other bad things Justin "claimed."

"You participated in them all." Then with an extra swipe at Christopher, DeGuerin demanded, "You're not going to blame it on your youth, are you?"

DeGuerin's cross was faster paced than usual, and though Justin's *I don't remember*s and denials were quicker than those in November, his responses still did not come across as utterly believable.

With DeGuerin's tone accusatory when he spoke of Justin's actions, and praising when he spoke of Celeste's, he ranted on about the "hit man" tape and Justin's ability to tape record phone conversations.

Celeste had been begging, screaming, crying, and trying to find her girls, DeGuerin stated, doing more of the testifying than Justin, who quietly sat in the witness chair. Justin, he said, had lied under oath to Judge Kocurek when he told her he didn't know where the girls were living, when in fact they were living with Peggy Farley, Kristina's therapist, and Justin was living there with them.

Justin denied it all.

But DeGuerin didn't let him, his voice growing more and more attacking and disdainful as he continued to declare that Justin had lied. And then, to Justin's supposedly outlandish statement that he offered to help Celeste pack for Europe, DeGuerin demanded, "What were you going to help her pack, Justin?" Her slips? Her panties? Her pantyhose?

DeGuerin stated that Steve had found out about Celeste and Jimmy Martinez in February 1999 and that was why she'd gone into St. David's.

He moved to the post-shooting days, when Justin was nineteen, a "computer nerd," and overseeing the home's security upgrade. He handed Justin a red spiral notebook.

Very slowly Justin flipped through it as DeGuerin still looked disgusted and asked Justin if that was his handwriting. Justin still flipped through the notebook, his tortoise-like pace insinuating that he couldn't even recognize his own handwriting.

The notebook was Justin's jottings on the home's security system. DeGuerin read from Justin's own words. Page 12. "'I feel that Mr. Beard will feel these corrections are essential.'" But Justin hadn't talked to Mr. Beard, he'd just "invoked his name," DeGuerin said.

Celeste wasn't looking happy, as if she'd partied too hard over the weekend, as she sipped from a Styrofoam cup.

The jurors were getting bored again. The questions were numbing; the answers were redundant: "I guess." "I don't remember." "It appears that way." "I'm not sure."

But DeGuerin had one big point he could make—if Celeste got convicted, and Kristina got the money, then Kristina and Justin got married, Justin would be pretty well off. "You have financial stake in the outcome of this case."

"You could say that. But my stake would be for justice."

"Not for Justin?"

"No."

Justin later said Celeste had threatened him with holding a press conference where she would announce that Kristina and Jennifer had disappeared because Justin had murdered them.

DeGuerin's response was simple: "Do you really think someone in a psycho ward could call a press conference?"

"The State calls Jennifer Beard."

Her heartbeat raced frighteningly as she took the stand on what should have been Steve and Celeste's eighth wedding anniversary. Jennifer was so nervous that she couldn't recall why Celeste had entered St. David's. But after hearing so much about Celeste's lesbian friend from St. David's, Tracey Tarlton, Steve had asked Celeste if she was a lesbian.

"'I can't believe you're asking me. No,'" Jennifer quoted her mother. Celeste then left in a huff.

Jen's voice began to crack as her testimony approached October 1, 1999. She and Christopher were planning to stick around the Toro Canyon house, since Celeste and Steve were about to leave for a month. Then the Tuesday or

Wednesday before the shooting, Jen and Celeste were standing in the kitchen when Celeste brought up the idea of Jen and Christopher spending the night at the lake house, which had been nicknamed the "fuck house."

Celeste cocked her head to the left as she watched her daughter. Jennifer never looked at her mother.

When Steve came home from the hospital, he, Celeste, and the dog stayed in the master bedroom watching TV. The next thing Jennifer knew, Steve was back in the hospital while she and Christopher were in Galveston buying $10,000 of decorative African masks for Celeste and in Houston for a funeral for a relative of Christopher's.

They were on their way to the funeral, when they got the call telling them to get home. They skipped the funeral and raced back to Austin, receiving a second call on the way. "Steve died," Justin said. And Jennifer's voice began breaking with tears again.

Celeste glared at Jennifer as her daughter entered the courtroom on February 19, 2003, a warm, cloudy, and drizzly day. Once situated in the witness chair, Jen glanced everywhere in the room but toward her mother, who, in spite of the weather, was in a seashell-pink sweater set. Every day since her birthday, Celeste had been sporting new sweater sets.

Jen's voice shook as she talked about the phone call she'd received from Celeste in early April 2000. "She demanded me to come pick her up. . . . I just did what she said."

With Christopher driving and Jennifer in the back seat, Celeste phoned Kristina's cell and talked to her. After Celeste hung up from Kris, "She said she could physically kill her."

In the courtroom, Celeste leaned on her left arm, watching Jennifer.

Jennifer had wanted to leave her mother the day Steve was shot. But she wouldn't do it. She couldn't do it. She had to stay with her sister and make sure Kris was safe.

But "little things just kept adding up," and they scared

her. So she decided not to have a relationship with her mother.

With her left hand, Wetzel began writing on a flip chart all the phone numbers connected to the Beard family. She jotted at least sixteen phone numbers and asked Jennifer to identify as many of them as she could.

Celeste's cell, Steve's car, Kristina's cell, her own cell that she'd shared for a while with Kris, and the main house, Jennifer pointed out.

Wetzel only had three more questions for her witness. Was Jennifer still afraid of Celeste?

"Yes."

Was Celeste in the courtroom?

Without looking at her mother, Jennifer said, "Yes."

Would you identify the defendant?

Jennifer looked out of the left corners of her eyes to glance at her mother.

As a Bratcher, Jennifer was thought of as the more loving and outgoing of the twins. As a Beard, she was considered the quieter, more guarded of the two.

Just before 9 A.M., Dick DeGuerin harped on Jennifer. He stated she hadn't wanted to be adopted by Steve, she hadn't liked Steve, and Steve hadn't liked her. She and Steve had had fights, she'd called him names, and she'd thought he was a drunk.

DeGuerin sat in his usual arms-crossed, cocky way, a grimace on his face. He scratched his head, then continued, doing all the testifying. He stated Steve hadn't been using his oxygen when they were driving to Seattle because Celeste was a chain smoker.

Jennifer countered that Celeste had smoked outside the car and Steve had used his oxygen.

He argued that among all the trips they'd taken that summer, Celeste didn't see Tracey for five out of eight weeks.

She talked to her on the phone a lot, Jennifer responded.

"I didn't ask you that." He asked about the graduation party and said Celeste was drunk.

That wasn't clear to Jennifer, she said. "I drank too much myself." She had vodka and tequila shooters, then woke up in one of the bedrooms.

He argued that Celeste hadn't spent the night at Tracey's. She'd only stayed until Tracey went to sleep and Tracey wrote that in her journal.

Again, Jennifer offered testimony otherwise.

He read the words from Tracey's diary: *Celeste was so sweet. . . . She stayed until I was ready to fall asleep.* With that, DeGuerin denounced as false the idea that Celeste had spent the night at Tracey's.

"She told us she did."

Over and over, DeGuerin asked the same question.

Each time, Jennifer gave the same answer—she told us she did.

Celeste's eyes lowered.

Christopher Doose knew that look. Whenever Celeste lowered her eyes, she was trying to put something over on him.

DeGuerin stated that Tracey was stalking Celeste.

"I don't remember that."

"You don't deny that," DeGuerin retaliated.

Jennifer didn't deny it.

DeGuerin read again from Tracey's journal, May 31, 1999. Celeste was returning to Timberlawn, and Tracey wrote, "It makes me so jealous." "Why do I get jealous?" "That's the picture of the obsessive woman that you saw . . ."

He grew angrier and more argumentative as he insisted that Jennifer hadn't seen Celeste with Tracey. He stated that Tracey had made threats with a shotgun in September.

Jennifer said she'd threatened suicide.

However, out of the courtroom, Jennifer admitted that she and Celeste knew Tracey had a shotgun because one time Tracey was on speakerphone as they drove back from the lake house. Over the speakerphone Tracey said she had the shotgun and, "Let's just kill ourselves."

DeGuerin claimed Tracey threatened suicide over the trip to Europe and Jennifer told that to Charlie Burton.

Jen didn't remember that.

DeGuerin still ranted in his angry, accusatory voice saying that Jennifer had gone to the Toro Canyon house around 4:30 or 5 P.M. on October 1, and gotten the lake house key from Celeste, and at that time, Celeste had told her daughter she was coming out to the lake house that night.

Jennifer denied that.

DeGuerin returned to Charlie Burton—Jennifer had supported her mother when she'd talked to Charlie Burton.

She'd said things in front of Celeste because she was scared.

He moved to the Studio 29 suicide pact and talked about how Celeste had mutilated herself.

"She's done that her whole life." Jennifer slowly swiveled in her chair.

He pronounced that Dawn Madigan had said Jennifer laughed in the funeral limousine and that Dawn didn't have any reason to lie.

She's friends with Celeste, Jen retorted.

He asked if Jennifer had signed a check with Celeste's name.

No, she replied. Kristina told her that she did, "but that's hearsay."

The jurors laughed. DeGuerin sustained her. Judge Kocurek stated, "You're not the judge, Mr. DeGuerin."

He moved to a James Avery gold and silver ring that Christopher had given Jennifer, pointing out that it was just like one Kristina had bought on December 17, 1999, and was the same size as the identical ring owned by Tracey Tarlton.

Jennifer called that "coincidence."

DeGuerin questioned, " 'Coincidence'?"

"You can size Tracey's finger."

Jennifer Beard got some jurors to smile as DeGuerin frantically looked for paperwork and Jennifer pointed out where he'd left it.

He asked her about the coffins and stated that Steve had bought burial packages for everyone.

Pink was Celeste's signature color, Jennifer said, and Steve was buying a mausoleum.

He asked her where she got her money, particularly enough to buy a $250,000 home.

She supported herself. If she couldn't meet her expenses, the bank gave her money. The home was really a triplex and they rented out two of the units. She'd traded in her Cadillac for a BMW convertible sports car and took out a loan for the rest of it.

He asked her if she was planning on filing another lawsuit against her mother.

"No."

29

In September 1999, Tracey Tarlton walked into Phil Presse's office—at Celeste's recommendation—for help with a driving-while-intoxicated charge. Presse offered her a glass of wine. After all, he was having one. And he went on and on about Steve and Celeste—what a joke their marriage was. "Steve doesn't know anything about what she's doing," he boasted. "She's always having these parties and he doesn't know anything about them. We always go to them."

So on Saturday afternoon, October 2, 1999, as soon as Tracey walked through her door after getting home from giving Detective Wines her statement, she dialed Phil Presse's number. "I need a criminal attorney," she said.

"For what?"

"Because they're gonna do a ballistics test on my gun, and I talked to these investigators."

He told her to call the guy upstairs in his building, Keith Hampton.

She called him, and before the day was over, she was sitting in Keith's office. Only a few minutes passed before she knew she liked Keith. He was sharp. He was upfront. And if there was one trait Tracey admired, it was people being upfront and honest. Speak your piece, whether it's good or bad, and move on.

"I'm gonna tell you what happened," she said.

She told him everything. "I don't want her implicated," Tracey insisted.

Just after 11:30 A.M., on February 19, 2003, Tracey Tarlton walked into Judge Kocurek's 390th courtroom. She looked at the gallery, frowned, and sat down. She wore her maximum security jailhouse clothes, an orange scrub top over a long-sleeved white shirt and green scrub pants.

About ten days before, Tracey had been moved from her maximum security home for the past two years to F tank, a minimum security tank filled with young misdemeanor and drug offenders—all strangers who watched television and harshly informed Tracey that they couldn't believe she was snitching against Celeste.

Tracey cried—one of the officers had told her she'd been moved at Dick DeGuerin's request. She wanted to know why he had more power and influence than the DA's office and why he got whatever he wanted. She already knew he was getting Celeste special treatment.

As soon as Wetzel heard about it, she was on the phone to Del Valle and got Tracey returned to maximum. At that, Tracey calmed down—the DA's office *could* get something done. It wasn't powerless in the face of the almighty Dick DeGuerin.

As Tracey sat in the witness chair, the jurors filed in, at first not noticing her, then taking a shocked second glance. Wetzel had hoped that Tracey, in her jailhouse scrubs, would force the jurors to glare over at Celeste, in her little twin sweater sets, long blonde hair pushed by hair bands out of her lightly made up face, and think, *Look what she's done to Tracey*. Tracey would be sympathetic.

Besides, Wetzel had spent seven hours with Tracey on Saturday. And Tracey was as ready as she'd ever be. Wetzel thought her premiere witness would do great. Then, on Sunday, members of Westlake Presbyterian Church said they were praying for Allison, and Allison was praying for Tracey. "She needs all the help she can get."

"I had a breakdown of sorts," Tracey explained of her 1999 admittance to St. David's Pavilion.

Kocurek's father-in-law was president and CEO of St. David's Health Care System.

Tracey and Celeste stood downstairs at St. David's, in the cool of winter, smoking and chatting. Though she looked like what the kids called the "destroyed" Celeste with too much old hairspray caking and matting her hair, Celeste was animated, funny, and very attentive to Tracey. "She was flirtatious from the first time I met her . . . and, you know, it was a compatible interchange."

"Did it appear to you that she was attracted to you in some manner from her behavior?"

"Yes, it did."

They connected immediately as Celeste told Tracey she was there because of her husband, who was controlling. From then on, they spent all their free time together, sitting with each other, smoking together, doing "everything together," as Celeste continually talked about Steve, made fun of him, made derogatory remarks about him, telling Tracey how he mistreated her.

Steve would "urge" and "coax" Celeste to commit suicide, Tracey testified. "And when she would fail, he would chastise her for that . . . he would demean her and belittle her . . . he thought she was stupid . . . He was real critical of the way she dressed. You know, he would make sure she had on what he wanted her to have on before she went out of the house, she said. So it seemed reasonable to me that she would not feel good about him."

"After a couple of years, I told him I no longer wanted him picking out my clothes. I told him St. John's was the only clothes I would continue to wear that he picked out. He didn't seem to mind. I think he realized I was nothing like Elise."

. . .

Tracey swayed slightly in her chair. Her Texas accent was thick and hard.

Soon, Celeste followed Tracey into her hospital room, wrapped her arms around the lesbian, and kissed her. Tracey kissed back. Their hands explored each other's bodies as they fondled one another "mostly" over their clothes.

Next thing Tracey knew they were discussing long-term care facilities where they could both go for additional treatment. "Because we wanted to continue this dalliance."

Celeste, wearing feminine pink, leaned on her arm as she listened.

Tracey briefly ended up at the Menninger Clinic in Kansas, but she and Celeste spoke every day by phone. Through those conversations, Tracey let Celeste know that Menninger wasn't the place for them. Tracey didn't like the doctors. They'd initially diagnosed Tracey as schizophrenic. "And when they ran their tests, they said absolutely not—bipolar." But life at Menninger just never fell into place for Tracey.

So she and Celeste decided to go to Timberlawn in Dallas. "And we arrived within an hour of each other, I think, and we did get in the same room." While other patients drooled on their torn T-shirts, Celeste decked herself in her fine clothes and expensive jewelry. And her makeup and hair were always perfect.

Tracey remained inpatient at Timberlawn for four weeks, then went outpatient, staying at the nearby Red Roof Inn. Celeste also went outpatient "ostensibly staying at the condo" Steve had rented for his wife.

"He was very involved in her treatment." He wanted notes from all her therapy sessions, he wanted to talk to her therapists, he wanted to talk to her doctors. It was a sore subject with Celeste that Steve wouldn't let her express what was going on with her since he was the one who had driven her to depression, Tracey said.

"I believed everything she told me."

Over Dick DeGuerin's objection, Tracey stated, "When we went to Timberlawn and became roommates, then we became sexual . . ." She noted the massage episode when she was giving a topless Celeste a backrub and they were interrupted by a scolding nurse.

According to Celeste, Tracey testified, the staffers told Steve about it, who then requested Tracey be removed as Celeste's roommate. Tracey first was relocated down the hall and later moved to another unit. Tracey blamed Steve for the roommate breakup. But she "felt nervous for Celeste."

Celeste had said that she felt she was sinking in her depression because Steve was always with her therapists. "She expressed to me at the time that her relationship with me, her friendship with me was an important hold that she had on something besides just going down the drain. So I felt afraid for her."

Tracey also believed Steve was a rich man who "pushed" his way through the staff, "pushed" his wife, "grabbed here and grabbed there and didn't have any concern at all for anybody else, including her."

Easily Tracey could believe she was important to Celeste. Celeste told Tracey that it was her first lesbian affair. And at Timberlawn, Tracey testified, they went well beyond fondling each other over their clothes. They stripped naked and had sex that climaxed with orgasms.

"And once we were outpatients, we stayed together a lot at my little motel room and we explored that sexual relationship much more fully." There was a compatibility, a passion, a grace between Tracey and Celeste. Tracey could see something wonderful in Celeste. And she thought Celeste saw the same in her. Celeste sparkled. Plus the Red Roof Inn was downright romantic compared to the psych facility.

They began having oral sex.

". . . When we first started having sex to orgasm, she was right with that and seemed to enjoy it." Celeste was perhaps a little timid at first—only in that way that a woman who'd never been with a woman could be. Still, Celeste did everything to make Tracey think she wanted it, she liked it. Tracey wasn't the only one who initiated sex.

"But . . . it didn't take long before she started sort of

pulling up right before she had an orgasm, stopping. And she said that she'd been sexually abused by her father and she couldn't stand to have sex with men and she really liked better having sex with me because I was not a man, but that it still made her feel guilty to have an orgasm.

"And she would pull up from that and not want to go there and at the same time she would—it would tear her up not to go there. She would cry and cry and it would be a big thing."

DeGuerin objected.

"It was very upsetting, and it was something that we sort of worked with and worked on for several months and even went to see somebody about it."

DeGuerin objected again.

"I'd go to her work and visit her. I mean, she was my friend.

"It was different, because Dawn and I were best friends and were really close. I could talk to Dawn about anything, but I didn't feel comfortable talking to her about the abuse in my family. And with Tracey, I could. She was like the first person that I felt comfortable talking—talking about it with."

Once Tracey left Timberlawn in May 1999, she and Celeste continued their dalliance. Sometimes, Tracey flew to Dallas on Fridays to see Celeste. Sometimes, they stayed in Dallas for the weekend. Other times, they drove in Celeste's Cadillac straight back to Austin where Celeste spent the first night at Tracey's, before going to Toro Canyon the next day.

Other times, they stopped in Waco, checked in at the nearly thirty-year-old, run-down La Quinta Inn that bordered the Southern Baptist university, Baylor. After spending the night having lesbian sex next to the Baptist chapels and steeples, they drove to Austin, where Celeste would either go back to the elegance of Toro Canyon or slum with Tracey on Wilson Street, before returning to Timberlawn on Sunday.

When Celeste got out of Timberlawn that summer, three or four times a week she drove over to Tracey's to spend the night, after knocking Steve out with Everclear and sleeping pills. "She also said that sooner or later it was going to kill him." Celeste looked forward to that day. "It was a point of release for her."

In fact, as far back as St. David's, Celeste had talked about feeding her husband Everclear and sleeping pills. ". . . She said, 'He's an old man, he's going to die soon, but not soon enough, and I'm just going to help him along wherever I can.' "

Tracey believed Celeste hadn't married Steve for his money. "So when I asked her why didn't she divorce him, she first said to me it was because she would only get five hundred thousand dollars."

When Tracey pointed out that Celeste wasn't in the marriage for money, Celeste told her, "It's because he would never let me leave. He would hunt me down, he would chase me down, he would never let me get out of his sight. It wouldn't be any better if I divorced him than if I didn't divorce him."

Still, Tracey and Celeste talked about the two women ending up together for the rest of their lives, Celeste saying that they'd live at the lake house. "We went back and forth about it."

Then Celeste told Tracey to get a cell phone "so I can find you when I want to find you." Kristina programmed the phone for Tracey by punching in all of Celeste's numbers, as well as Kristina's.

Testimony returned to Steve and Celeste. Celeste said she had given Steve a blow job once and told him afterwards she'd never have sexual contact with him again. She loved to imitate Steve, including Steve passing out in his closet. "She, you know, she thought he was disgusting."

Wetzel moved to the various social events Celeste and Tracey attended together—breakfast with Tracey's friends, dinner with Tracey's friends, and a Club Skirt benefit at Scholz's beer garden.

Scholz's, in between the University of Texas and the Capitol, was a historic building in which Judge Kocurek had eaten barbecue just before she walked over to the Capitol and was sworn in as judge by Governor George W. Bush, her second swearing-in in one week.

Six months earlier, in the spring of 1999, the beer garden had been full of lesbians in Western wear, including Tracey and Celeste. "I remember that Celeste wore, you know, sort of a little Dale Evans kind of Western skirt outfit."

"Did she get you an outfit to wear?" Wetzel asked.

"I don't recall what I wore. I know that I didn't wear a Dale Evans outfit."

Tracey's friend Pat Brooks recalled, though. Tracey wore a Western shirt that Celeste had bought for Tracey because it coordinated with Celeste's skirt. Everyone who saw Tracey and Celeste at Scholz's thought they were a couple. Tracey got Celeste her drinks and lighted her Marlboro Light 100s. The scent of cigarette smoke mixed with Dolce Vita perfume always curled around Celeste. She and Tracey danced together. It appeared to be a reciprocal relationship. At least that's what Tracey's friends saw—as well as Celeste's bare breasts when she opened her shirt and flashed them.

"I didn't really—I felt like—I felt uncomfortable around them. I felt like they didn't like me. They made me feel like she's the heterosexual. You know, I'm serious, that's how I felt. I mean, like, my friends wouldn't say you're the lesbian, you know? But I felt like you're the heterosexual. So that's the way they made me feel.

"But they were real nice to Kristina."

Wetzel moved to the BookPeople party.

Tracey had planned on doing her usual thing—getting a keg of beer, having her friend and caterer Pat Brooks create a spread of not-fancy food, and having her employees come over to her house. She did it about every six months as a reward for their hard work.

"I want to do this at the lake house," Celeste said.

"It's too far to go. People will be drinking," Tracey returned.

But Celeste was excited and insistent. And once Tracey got on board with the idea, she thought it was pretty good too. Celeste came up with the theme—the 1970s. Everyone was supposed to dress in '70s attire. Celeste hired the caterer, the photographer, and the bartender. She got the liquor. She gave Tracey money and asked her to get Brandy to buy some weed and bake the pot brownies.

"Did the defendant appear embarrassed that her children were there the next morning, having spent the night in bed with you?"

"No. . . . She always maintained that . . . they didn't know or care."

They moved to the couples counseling session with Barbara Grant. "It was both of our ideas," Tracey said.

The jurors kept eyeing the gallery. It was packed. Sitting there was Ray McEachern. He clearly remembered the day Steve and Celeste married. He and Darrold Cannan stood in the ACC men's restroom when Ray turned around and looked at Darrold. Darrold's bottom lip shook.

"Ray, you look like you're about to throw up."

"We're fixin' to witness the biggest train wreck you've ever seen."

Ray McEachern believed every word to which Tracey Tarlton testified.

She and Celeste spoke several times a day with Celeste usually being the one to dial the numbers, when Celeste was on the driving trip to the Pacific Northwest.

By then, Celeste was growing more and more anxious about living in a loveless marriage with an old man, Tracey reported. She asked Tracey to get her ten tablets of Ecstasy, grind them up, they'd go to a jazz club, and slip the drug into Steve's drink so he'd overdose and it'd look like an accident at the hands of a stranger.

Kocurek interrupted and ordered the attorneys to the bench.

She stared straight at DeGuerin. "Your client is laughing and rolling her eyes. When the witness first came in the first time, she stared her down. I don't want any of that going on or we're going to stop and she'll be taken out."

DeGuerin protested—he hadn't seen anything like that.

"I have, and it had better stop right now."

Wetzel asked Tracey what Celeste did with the X tablets.

"She said she ground them up, put them in his drink, and he drank the whole drink and nothing happened to him. Just acted normal."

Tracey, at Celeste's request, ordered *The Poisoner's Handbook*. Eventually she ordered other books for her—*The Poor Man's James Bond*, *The Anarchist Cookbook*, and books on lesbian sex.

After reading *The Poisoner's Handbook*, Celeste came to Tracey with a recipe for botulism. She wanted Tracey to whip up a batch so she could feed it to Steve.

While Celeste was in Australia, Tracey got some hamburger meat, dirt containing botulism spores, and water, mixed it all up and sealed it tight in a jar, which she set in the August Texas sun to bake and grow.

In two to three weeks, about the time Celeste was to return from Australia, the poison would be ready. Tracey also bought some mice on which to test the toxin.

Every two or three days, Celeste phoned Tracey from Australia wanting to know how the botulism was growing, and did the mice die?

They didn't. Tracey let them loose in a field. And Celeste still wanted to try the foul-smelling mixture on Steve.

She told Tracey she'd asked Steve to make some chili dogs. He did. She mixed the botulism in with the chili. "She said he ate it up to the last drop." And he didn't even get a sick stomach.

"Uh, you know, as far as poisoning him and giving him botulism and stuff, I didn't cook, so how did I do that? And Steven is not gonna make, uh, chili cheese dogs, or whatever she said he made." Celeste sounded disgusted. *"Chili dogs. He was a gourmet cook. He would not eat chili dogs. And he*

*wouldn't even make them. I guarantee that would have been
'Forget it.' "*

"She felt like that I must have not done it right, and so she
mixed her own batch out at the lake house." Tracey helped.
But someone found the wide-mouth jar and took the lid off.
"And so the whole idea sort of disintegrated for her at that
point."

Allison Wetzel wanted to enter into evidence another
edition of *The Poisoner's Handbook* that included a recipe
for botulism.

DeGuerin objected, calling it false logic.

The attorneys stood at the bench.

Again DeGuerin said, "It's false logic. There's an old
story—"

"I don't need to hear the whole story," Kocurek interrupted.

"Daniel Boone," DeGuerin persisted.

"I don't need to hear about Daniel Boone right now.
State your objection."

"It's just a book."

He was overruled.

Tracey Tarlton read the recipe in court. "As twenty-
eighth of a millionth of one gram will kill a man . . ."

Celeste leaned close to Catherine Baen.

"Botulism is fun and easy to make."

Wetzel asked Tracey how she felt knowing she could
help kill a man with the poison.

". . . I believed what she told me about what had happened to her . . . so I was willing to help her. I was willing to
help her. I wasn't at that point willing to actually step in and
do anything directly about it, but I was willing to support
her."

Tracey believed Celeste had married Steve because it was
the only way she could get back Jennifer from Craig—
Steve would do that for her if she'd just marry him.

"You're full of it," Tracey told her at St. David's. "You

married this man for his money. How could you even pretend that you didn't do that?"

"Oh, no, no, no," Celeste said.

"I was moved. I mean, I thought, *Somebody is going to give up their life to get their kid back to where they think she's going to be safe or safer.* You are going to give up your life to do that? I was really touched. I felt like it was noble."

Celeste also told Tracey she'd given up a baby girl for adoption, only after she'd interviewed many people before finally selecting a lesbian mother. She told the kids she'd given the baby to a very rich family. The Bratchers believed she'd sold the baby for $10,000.

In August 1999, Tracey met Steve Beard at the girls' graduation. She showed up with her hair fixed and wearing an elegant cream-colored suit that Celeste had bought for her. She grinned while holding a baby. Steve was nice, gracious, thanked her for being a supportive friend to Celeste, and invited Tracey to the graduation dinner at ACC. Tracey looked to Celeste for an okay or no. Silently, Celeste signaled yes.

Steve also invited Tracey to hamburger night, where she saw what she'd only heard about—Celeste pouring Steve's Everclear drinks for him. She'd heard about it because Kristina had brought the vodka over to Tracey's so that Tracey would buy the Everclear for her and then substitute it for vodka.

But that hamburger night, as Tracey thought only she and Celeste were on the front porch, Tracey kissed Celeste and kissed her more than once. No one said anything about it and no one asked her to leave.

"Please, please come," Celeste pleaded, when she invited Tracey to the twins' graduation party at Jimmy Martinez's house. "I'm not going to know anybody. It's going to be all the girls' friends. I'm not going to know anybody there."

Tracey relented. Celeste had told her that when she and Steve had separated, she'd begged Jimmy to remarry her. But he'd refused and they were just good friends.

The party, though, just like the twins' 18th birthday, was filled with Celeste's friends. Marilou watched football on Jimmy's big TV. Most guests sat eating at picnic tables in the backyard. Celeste, Amy, Christopher, and Tracey danced. Celeste's friend Val slipped liquor to the kids, and they got drunk, despite the fact that Celeste had had a stamp made for the party identifying those who were underage. Everyone was getting drunk, except for Kristina and Justin, who were running their usual shuttle service and missing the party.

Jimmy knocked back beer after beer. Tracey was slugging back drinks too, while Celeste swigged down the vodka. Then Celeste seemed to disappear.

One of the girls came and got Tracey and told her their mom was upstairs in the bathroom throwing up. "You need to go up there and help her."

Tracey found Celeste sitting on the bathroom floor, vomiting into the toilet, "sick as a dog." She got Celeste a cold rag and pressed it to her pale forehead.

"Okay, I'm fine," Celeste said. "I'll be down in a second."

Tracey went back downstairs and out to the backyard. When Celeste didn't follow, Tracey worried. She went back upstairs, opened the bedroom door, and found Celeste in bed with Jimmy. They were both clothed, and they were just talking. But Tracey recognized that intimate embrace. Anger rolled with disgust roiled through her. She snapped a few words to the loving couple and left.

"It was the first time that I had come face to face with something that she had told me that ended up not being true."

Tracey didn't want to have anything to do with Celeste ever again—not after all they'd been through, not after Tracey had been so devoted to Celeste, not after Tracey had listened to all the things Celeste had told her about Jimmy—and men.

"And did you start to wonder whether many of those things were true?" Wetzel asked.

"Right," Tracey answered.

Tracey jumped in her SUV and sped for south Austin, but the police stopped her for driving while intoxicated. She may have intended never to see Celeste again, "but then I got thrown in jail, which puts a kink in that for the moment. I needed help, so I called her—"

Tracey explained, "She was my partner. . . . That's the person that I talked to all day every day. That's the person that I confided in. That's the person that confided in me. That's the person I relied on."

After a multitude of calls, Tracey finally reached either Kris or Justin. She couldn't remember which. She then phoned Jimmy's several times before getting Celeste on the line. Celeste came and picked her up.

"I'm not doing this," Tracey stormed to Celeste. "I'm not gonna go for this. You've been lying to me all this time about him."

"No, that's not how it was." She and Jimmy weren't really doing anything, Celeste swore. "You know, we were married, so of course we're going to have an intimate way of dealing with each other. It looks intimate, but it's not intimate." They only looked like they were doing something because Tracey was too drunk to see. Jimmy really was just an ex.

Tracey fell right back into believing.

And Celeste hooked her up with Phil Presse, who Tracey understood was the twins' godfather.

A few days later, Celeste told Tracey that Steve had found out about her DWI arrest and said, "I knew she was south Austin trash in the first place. I don't want her to come over here anymore."

She and Celeste laughed about it.

Her ringing phone woke Tracey from sound sleep in September 1999.

"I need you to come over here now," Celeste said. "I need help."

"Are you okay?" Tracey asked.

"No, I'm not okay. Come over here now. I need some help."

Traffic was light at that time of night—11 P.M. or midnight. So Tracey flew over to Celeste's, jumped out of her

SUV, raced up to the door, and inside. She saw Steve's head flat down on the dining table—passed out cold.

"Let's get him on the floor," Celeste said.

They grabbed the side of the chair, pulled, and dumped him on the floor. He fell face down. Steve didn't move a muscle.

Celeste got a towel and a plastic garbage bag from the kitchen. She wrapped the towel around Steve's throat. She always said she knew how to pull off any crime because she'd read so many mystery novels and true crime books. She'd received five true crime books in just the first week of the trial.

She put the plastic bag over Steve's head and held it shut tight until her hands tired. "You hold it. I can't hold it anymore."

Tracey wrapped her hands around Steve's neck and the bag. The plastic sucked in and blew out with Steve's every breath. Then he moved. It wasn't much, but he moved. Tracey couldn't do it. She left.

In the courtroom, Celeste frantically scribbled on her notepad.

Throughout September she continually talked about the dreaded trip to Europe. "She felt like this—she was not going to survive it, that she would never return from it, that she would kill herself there, that he would not let her do anything but that. . . . This was a constant theme for us."

After Dick DeGuerin objected, Tracey continued. "She had always been fragile and vulnerable . . . She seemed to be getting more delicate and weaker, and she credited that to him and his abuse." So when Celeste repeatedly talked to Tracey and told her that Steve would leave her no choice but to kill herself in Europe, Tracey took Celeste's words "very seriously."

"I believed her absolutely," she told the courtroom.

Then the week before Celeste was to leave for Europe, she asked Tracey to do something for her—to shoot Steve.

30

Celeste knew Tracey recently had gotten back her shotgun that she'd asked a friend to keep when she was suicidal. So on the Wednesday before October 2, 1999, a shaking and inconsolable Celeste came over to Tracey's house.

"I can't make it," Celeste said. "I can't do this. I can't not go because he'll make me go. I won't come back. He will kill me in Europe." So many times, Celeste had run to Tracey sobbing, wailing, flailing, so desperate over Steve that she curled her hands into fists and beat on Tracey's chest. "He'll get me. I'm not going to make it back. You might as well just shoot me."

Celeste and Tracey had talked about it so many times.

Over and over Tracey had asked, "Isn't there some other way? Can't you do something different? Can't you leave? Just divorce him? Is it so bad? Are you sure this is about him?"

Celeste swore it wasn't about the money, at least not about her getting the money. But Steve had so much money that he would track her down wherever she hid and force her back to him, which would force her to kill herself.

But that Wednesday, they didn't talk about that. "I just saw this woman that I loved in a desperate situation trying to find a way to survive this man that was so awful."

"I don't want to do this," Tracey told Celeste. "I can't do this. This is too far. We have gone too far."

Celeste lowered her eyes. "If it's not him, it's me. There's nothing left. I might as well just take it right now and shoot myself."

I am the one she trusts. I'm in this relationship with her. I'm her lover. I'm the person that she thinks she wants to be with forever. I have a responsibility to her. It wasn't a matter of right or wrong. If she didn't kill Steve, then Steve would "kill" Celeste. Tracey didn't feel she had a choice.

"I'll do it. But if something happens, if I get caught, I need for you to take care of three things." She needed Celeste to take good care of her cats and dog, or find them good homes; pay her legal bills; and support her in jail.

Celeste agreed.

But Tracey hadn't fired her shotgun in Lord knows how long.

"Go find a way to shoot it," Celeste said. "And I'll get the rest figured out."

The kids always called Celeste "the Master Manipulator."

"It'll be fine," Celeste assured. "It'll be just fine."

The next night, Thursday, the Lily Tomlin concert that they had planned to attend would have to wait. Tracey drove out to Austin Skeet Range and tested her shotgun. Its sight was fine. Its firing was fine.

She reported back to Celeste, who told Tracey she'd phone her at BookPeople on Friday to come over to the Toro Canyon house when Steve wasn't around and she'd lay out the plan for her trigger woman.

Just as she promised, Celeste called Tracey at work on Friday, told her when Steve would be at the Country Club, and instructed her to come over then. The deed had to be done that night, around 2 or 2:30 in the morning, because they were leaving for Europe.

That afternoon, Tracey dropped by the house. Celeste walked her around the yard and house pointing out where she wanted Tracey to enter the grounds—via the Toro Canyon entrance where the electric gate wasn't working, where she wanted her to park that night—in the drive on the that same side of the house.

She told her how she wanted her to exit her vehicle, where she wanted her to walk and enter the house, how she wanted her to approach the bedroom—go to the front, to the left, up the side and back to the brick enclosed courtyard, and through the sliding glass doors into the bedroom. Tracey stood at the foot of Steve's bed and looked at where she'd be firing. Shoot him in the stomach, Celeste said. "I don't want blood splatter on the walls." She wanted to be able to stay in the room and didn't want to have to redecorate.

The gallery chuckled.

"If I shoot him in the stomach," Tracey warned, "he's going to linger here for a little bit. You know, we don't want that."

"I read these books. I know what happens. He'll bleed to death. I won't call anybody until he does," Celeste assured.

She showed Tracey how she wanted her to exit the house and grounds—the exact same way she came in. Steve, Celeste said, passed out every night either in his closet or bedroom. She would let Tracey know where he was.

Celeste handed her plastic gloves and plastic to put on the seat and floorboard of Tracey's Pathfinder. She told Tracey what to wear—her black high-top sneakers, dark jeans, black turtleneck, and a black stocking cap. She specifically told Tracey not to drink—so Tracey wouldn't do something stupid to Celeste. She told Tracey where to dump the bloody plastic afterwards—a convenience store Dumpster on South First and Ben White Boulevard, where Celeste exited when going to Tracey's. Celeste knew that the Dumpster couldn't be seen from inside the store.

Tracey was nervous. She didn't know the layout of the Beard house that well and yet she was going to be traipsing through it in the middle of the night without benefit of any light and toting a shotgun with her name engraved on it. She knew her shotgun would eject its shell onto the bedroom carpet and she worried whether she'd be able to find it in the dark.

"Look for it," Celeste said. "Grab it if you can find it. But don't worry about it because I'll pick it up."

Celeste wanted all the kids out of the house—Jen and Christopher at the lake house, Kris and Justin at Justin's. But Kristina didn't want to spend the night at Justin's, Celeste said. There was no reason to worry, though. She'd take care of it. She'd be in the girls' bedroom with Kris.

Later that day, Tracey and Celeste spoke on the phone.

Around 11 that night, Celeste knocked on Tracey's door. It was just three and a half hours before gun time, and Celeste changed the plan. Come through the Westlake gate, rather than Toro Canyon. She was worried about the neighbors. They could see the front drive. She'd have the gate open. Park at the top of the driveway, go around by the pool, and enter by the door close to Steve's bedroom on the poolside.

Tracey had never entered the house that way. She wasn't even really sure where that entrance was. Her nerves quavered.

Steve, Celeste said, was already in bed. The doors would be unlocked. The security system would be off. Megan was out at the lake house.

Tracey hadn't been worried about Megan. Then Celeste told her Megan barked at the least bit of noise.

Celeste was all business that night. She said she'd taken Steve's ring, watch, and money clip—took the money out of the clip—and threw everything else into the lake so that his murder would look like part of a robbery.

Twenty to thirty minutes later, Celeste walked out Tracey's door.

As she did, Tracey leaned over to kiss her.

"We've got time for that later!"

You know, it wouldn't take all that much time right now. Tracey sort of laughed.

Two-thirty A.M. slipped close to 3, and as she parked near the girls' bedroom, Tracey worried about Kristina hearing. *But Celeste said she wouldn't hear it. It'll be all right. She'll be back there, and she'll take care of it.*

Tracey barely pushed the car door closed and listened. *I was absolutely sensitive to disturbance. It was, you know, it was horrifying—it was frightening.* Her sneaker-clad feet stepped onto the grass.

She walked through a gate toward the pool, stopped, leaned for a moment against the house, and wondered what the hell she was about to do. She focused on Celeste. She thought about all the torment and terror Celeste had suffered the past months. *Look, you know what? You gotta do this here.* Tracey pushed herself.

She walked past the pool that gurgled in the night and opened the door that Celeste had promised would be unlocked.

In Steve's room, there was just enough light to see his large, sleeping silhouette. His sleep apnea machine was on the nightstand. Steve lay on his back, his stomach facing Tracey. She walked up to the foot of the bed. She stood just her height away from the man. She couldn't stop. She couldn't look. She couldn't do anything but squeeze the trigger and leave.

She heard an *umph*, then the wad hitting the pillow. Steve sat up and reached over the bedside. Tracey didn't know for what. A gun? A phone? An alarm?

She glanced around for the shell, but Steve seemed so active. She had to get out of there. And she knew Celeste would pick up the shell. She exited out the sliding patio door, walked with "brisk and directed motion" to her car, and got on 360, making sure to go the speed limit, and headed straight for the convenience store Dumpster. She tossed the plastic from her floorboard and seat, her gloves, her cap, and her high-tops.

She got home, washed her clothes, cleaned her gun, and put it back in her closet. She drank a beer and showered. And she waited. And she waited. Sleep eluded her.

Just about the time she got up and poured herself a cup of coffee, there was a knock at her door—Detective Rick Wines and Sergeant Paul Knight.

Celeste and Tracey stayed in touch throughout the fall, using their phones to set up face-to-face meetings. Sometimes Celeste used the pay phones at the hospital. Sometimes Tracey used the pay phones between BookPeople and Whole Foods. Sometimes she used the pay phones at the convenience stores on South First and South Congress, close to her house. Rarely did they speak over Tracey's home phone. They feared her line was tapped.

Still, two or three times a week, they met in the park near BookPeople, between Ninth and Tenth Streets, quick conversations when Celeste was downtown meeting her attorneys, quick meetings when Celeste left the hospital just for a moment. Celeste never wanted to leave Steve for very long; she didn't want anyone planting a bug in his ear that she might be involved.

But to Tracey, Celeste often talked about the shooting. First it was what everyone had told the detectives and what she had told them, too. Then it was the status of the investigation.

Sometimes, Celeste seemed strung out by the stress and saddened by the pain Steve suffered. "I hate that. It's hard to watch him in so much pain."

To Tracey it seemed a spiritual strain on Celeste.

Celeste told Tracey to go buy a new cell phone and give it to her so that they could talk to each other without Steve and the kids knowing.

Celeste wanted to have all of Steve's "stolen" belongings replaced, because if the detectives thought the items were stolen it raised the crime to capital murder with a possible death penalty punishment.

Late in the afternoon on December 27, 1999, Tracey walked out of BookPeople, past the multi-story parking lot with the giant fruits and vegetables on top—promotion for Whole Foods—and over to the nearby park to meet Celeste.

Tracey carried in her hands Christmas gifts for Celeste, elegant bookends in the design of whippets like Wren. Celeste arrived in her Cadillac with a small box from James Avery Craftsman, the same Kerrville jeweler that made the jewelry for Camp Longhorn.

Tracey untied the ribbon and opened the pearl gray box with the embossed JA and signature candelabra on the top. Inside, she found a gold and silver wedding band.

"This is so you'll always remember where you belong," Celeste said to Tracey.

Tracey thought Celeste was saying she would always belong to Celeste, and felt that little flutter in the stomach that happens when sexual attraction and love collide.

"And did the defendant indicate whether she was going to have anyone helping her when Steve Beard was released from the hospital?"

"She said she wasn't going to bring home health care with her. She was going to do it herself because she was going to reinfect the wound."

"Did she say why she was going to reinfect the wound?"

". . . She felt like that she would bring him home and create some toxicity in the wound and kill him and it would be on the onus of the hospital because it would have looked like he picked up the infection in the hospital and not from the wound.

"I said, 'I'm already charged with assault. If you kill him, they are going to charge me with murder. Don't do this.'"

"It will be fine," Celeste defended. "We can take care of it."

"I didn't win that argument at all."

Celeste didn't wash her hands before dealing with Steve's wound. She didn't clean out the tubing. And when his fever spiked, she phoned Tracey before calling the hospital.

After that, Celeste said she lost her new cell phone and she and Tracey started speaking solely on pay phones. Then their conversations became more and more infrequent. When they did talk, Celeste was in hysterics about the kids suspecting her.

But after Rick Wines phoned Tracey's attorney, at Bill Mange's direction after meeting the kids, Tracey told Celeste she knew there was a hit out on her.

At that DeGuerin objected.

Kocurek had to tell him three times he was overruled before he sat down.

Tracey asked Celeste who would do that to her—put a hit on her?

"It's the girls. The girls did that," Celeste answered. "They are so upset about their father, they put a hit out on you. I'll take care of it."

Tracey believed her.

Allison Wetzel pulled out a clear plastic bag containing a watch and a ring.

Tracey took the ring and slipped it on her finger. It fit perfectly. She'd worn it, she said, from the moment Celeste gave it to her until June 15, 2000.

With just that ring, Allison Wetzel had felt she could win a conviction.

Wetzel showed Tracey photographs of the twins that Celeste had given Tracey. She showed her cards that Tracey had sent Celeste and Celeste had sent Tracey. "My hopes are to see you soon and explore our *friendship*," Celeste wrote.

"And *friendship* is underlined. Did that underlining of the word *friendship* have any meaning to you?"

Over a multitude of overruled objections from DeGuerin, Tracey finally answered. "When I read that statement and *friendship* was highlighted like that, what it meant to me was that it was an inversion." Celeste was taking a word, turning it around, and highlighting it so that it would be read the opposite way. Tracey didn't even consider the possibility that Celeste meant a platonic relationship. They'd already started flirting at St. David's.

As the very long day drew toward a close, Wetzel returned to 2000 and Tracey's contact with Celeste.

A couple of times, Celeste, sobbing, phoned Tracey in the middle of the night and told her she was going to walk down Westlake Drive and to come pick her up. Tracey did. They then drove to the shopping center, where they sat in the back seat of Tracey's Pathfinder, Celeste in Tracey's lap, crying with guilt over what they'd done and about the girls leaving her.

Another time, Celeste phoned and left a message. "I'm sorry. I'm sorry. They are coming to get me to take me to the hospital now. Don't be mad at me. Please forgive me."

A couple of days later, Tracey tried to check on Celeste at St. David's. She knew Celeste had been there because Celeste had called her and told her. The staff rebuffed Tracey from visiting.

"They know who you are," Celeste later told her. "They are really freaked out that you came up here. Don't come up here."

The last time Tracey and Celeste met in the park near BookPeople, in the spring of 2000, Celeste came undone. She cried that the girls had left her. She cried that she had breast cancer. She was going to go live with Caresse, she said.

"But you haven't spoken with your sister in years."

"Well, now I have, and I'm going to go live with her and they are going to have to operate. It's really bad. It's progressed."

Two, three weeks passed without Tracey hearing from Celeste. It was the longest they'd been without talking in almost a year and a half.

On June 15, 2000, Tracey couldn't take it anymore. She called Celeste. "You can't go for three weeks and not talk to me. If I don't know what is going on with you, I'm too worried. You give me this bombshell and you disappear."

"Fine," Celeste retorted. "Don't talk to me anymore." And she hung up.

Tracey swerved into the Gardens of Westlake, right behind Celeste. As Bob Dennison watched, they drove to the top of the drive. Celeste got out of her car shaking her head. Backwards and forwards, she took tiny steps.

"Stop! Let's talk about this," Tracey yelled.

"They are going to see you. They are going to see you." Celeste kept stepping forward and then back. "Just go! Just go! I don't care what you tell them. Tell them whatever you want."

Like a shot to the gut, it hit Tracey. Celeste was only keeping her around so that she wouldn't go to the cops and tell the truth. "I'll see you. I won't be back. Don't worry." She climbed in her Pathfinder and left.

Tracey Tarlton went home and started drinking.

31

Allison Wetzel drove home that night so giddy over Tracey's testimony that she was even nice to Catherine Baen when Catherine phoned her at 6:30 that night wanting Allison's witness list for the next day.

Allison and Catherine were more than courtroom foes.

From the first day they stared eye to eye at each other—and they could, since they were about the same height—they seemed to abhor each other all the way down their long bodies, long legs and to the tips of their toes.

Still, Allison was in such a good mood that night that she apologized for the previous week's sniping.

By the time Allison hung up from Catherine, got the kids fed, bathed, and read to, and sat down to work on the next day's testimony, she was too exhausted to be giddy any longer. But if she replayed in her memory Tracey testifying about Celeste's orgasms and fantasized about Celeste's husband, Cole Johnson, sitting there in the courtroom listening to that testimony, a grin couldn't help but creep back onto her face, dog-tired or not. Celeste had orgasms with Tracey—it was Allison's favorite part of the day. Too bad Cole wasn't allowed in the courtroom.

Thursday, February 20, 2003, Wetzel had just a few more questions, then all she had to do was sit back and watch DeGuerin infuriate the jury again by dragging out the trial with his desperate search for one tiny hole into which he could dive and swim to Celeste's rescue.

It was storming outside, but inside, the watering hole seemed to be drying up. The jury had laughed at Tracey's crack about how she didn't wear a Dale Evans skirt. Wetzel had warned Tracey not to do that again. It didn't look good for a killer to be making jokes, even when it was obvious the jurors appreciated the moment of comic relief.

Tracey sat in the witness chair and poured herself a cup of water.

Celeste watched in a navy blue business suit, her hair pulled back by a barrette.

"Was there ever any discussion about you throwing away the shotgun or disposing of it in any way?" Wetzel asked Tracey.

"Yes, there was." A plate engraved with Tracey's signature was bolted into her gun so that the plate couldn't be removed. "And so I felt like that if we tried to throw the gun away, if it was recovered, it would be even more suspicious that I had thrown this relatively expensive shotgun away and it would obviously be traced back to me."

Besides, Tracey had no fear—Celeste was going to pick up the shotgun shell. There wouldn't be anything to trace back to the gun.

Wetzel introduced the documents relating to Tracey's plea agreement with the State.

"Hearsay, self-serving and bolstering," DeGuerin objected.

He was overruled.

Constantly, DeGuerin's staff moaned and groaned about the judge's rulings—she was Wetzel's former boss, so the judge was ruling for Wetzel. Wetzel and Kocurek had applied for the same judgeship that Kocurek got, and then Wetzel had campaigned for Kocurek and helped her win her return to the bench, so the rulings in Wetzel's favor were payback by the judge, they argued.

Wetzel and her team were equally angry about the rulings. They felt they were all going DeGuerin's way.

But in fact, DeGuerin won the little rulings. The State won the big rulings.

And for Kocurek's part, she believed if the ruling was obvious, she made the obvious ruling. If there was a bit of gray area between the black and white written laws and legal codes, she ruled in favor of the defense to prevent an appeal. Kocurek definitely didn't want to do this again. And they were only in the third week of the trial.

Briefly, Wetzel returned to the previous day's discussion of Celeste's secret cell phone.

At first, Celeste kept the phone with her, Tracey explained. Then the kids became suspicious, so Celeste put it in a drawer, but checked it at night and throughout the day to see if Tracey had called.

During one of their phone conversations the spring after Steve died, Celeste cried that she'd watched her dogs, Nikki and Kaci, get run over. Celeste was out of control as she recounted every gory detail of their deaths.

Tracey was heartbroken for her friend—Celeste had already been through so much, and now both of her dogs were dead.

Wetzel asked again about the last time Tracey saw Celeste on June 15, 2000.

"I went home and I started drinking a bottle of vodka that was—her vodka's in the freezer. It was sort of an angry, you know, I'll just drink your vodka, you are gone."

Three weeks later, "I read an article in the paper . . . that Celeste was not present at the hearing because she was on her honeymoon in Aspen with her new husband."

Tracey was dumbfounded. "Everything started falling apart in my mind, that, you know, I realized within a couple of months that everything that she had told me was not—was untrue." Her voice was a low groan.

Court recessed while the attorneys gathered at the bench. DeGuerin pouted that Tracey Tarlton was crazy. "She sees things that aren't there."

"We're seeing a lot of craziness in this trial all around," Kocurek responded. And she soon picked up a large green folder. "I think both of you know I have had this sitting up here the whole time, so behave."

"What's that?"

The folder read CONTEMPT OF COURT. "I've done it before. . . . All I'm saying is, follow the rules."

At 9:40 A.M., Dick DeGuerin stood, walked over near Tracey, took a black marker in his hand, and began writing on the giant flip pad that rested on an aluminum easel.

"Suicidal," he printed in big letters. "Homicidal. Delusional."

He turned to Tracey. "You would agree with me that you have frequently been suicidal?"

"Yes, sir." Tracey always made sure she put a "sir" or a "ma'am" with her yeses and nos.

"You would agree with me that you have been homicidal?"

"Yes, sir."

"You would agree with me that you have been delusional?"

Tracey wasn't so ready to agree with that one. She wanted to know what DeGuerin was referring to.

DeGuerin wanted her to admit that she was delusional when she believed Steve Beard had been the one to separate her from Celeste at Timberlawn, despite the fact that her therapist told her otherwise.

"What Celeste told me I believed before what my therapist told me."

He still insisted she was delusional about that.

"No, sir."

DeGuerin whipped a smirk of gloating on his face when he pulled out a journal of Tracey's that she'd kept during her three hospital stays. "You haven't seen that journal in a while, have you?" He acted as though he'd just won his case. "You know that Kristina took it out of your house back in ninety-nine, don't you?"

"No, I didn't know that."

The State apparently didn't know either. They'd never seen the journal and wanted a look. After a meeting at the bench, Catherine Baen handed Wetzel a copy.

DeGuerin pointed to an April 7, 1999, note in Tracey's journal, about the time she was moved into the adult psychiatric unit. "That's where the real psychos are, isn't it?"

"That's where the truly suicidal people are, right."

Her one paragraph note that so interested DeGuerin was nearly illegible because Tracey was so heavily medicated. "Celeste has decided to leave me. She had a meeting with her doctor and she has already moved her clothes to her new room. She will not look at me and she will only say that I was too pushy," DeGuerin read, then pointed out that that was long after Tracey *claimed* her sexual relationship with Celeste had started.

DeGuerin had trouble deciphering the next sentence.

"She wanted to take the relationship 1 day at a time, but I can tell she will not be interacting with me. I believe that she is strongly attracted to me and it has created a tremendous amount of confusion for her."

DeGuerin never could figure out "created." But he understood that Tracey believed Celeste was attracted to her. "This is the same time that Susan Milholland is telling you you're delusional, isn't it?"

Tracey had no recollection of who Susan Millholland was.

"I noticed how sad Celeste is today," Tracey wrote in slightly better penmanship on April 8. "I have told her that it is okay, that I won't hold hard feelings. If she wants my friendship, I will give her my friendship without any sexual overtones. She said yes, but I remember now that she has so much trouble saying no, so I will have to check it out."

DeGuerin saved for later the remainder of the sadly pathetic entry. "It is hard now watching Celeste being protected from talking to me by her new roommate and companion. She told me to just give her some space & time, so that is what I will do. She is in terrible pain & grief and I don't understand what that is about! I think it must be about losing me, but I don't know. If it hurts that bad why does she want to stay away? Remember, it is probably <u>not about me</u>," Tracey quoted the typical therapist line, "so go on with <u>my own issues at therapy</u>. She is having a great time sitting between two really cool people—one is someone I used to sit with. She is now her roommate. It is so hard for me—I need to take better care of myself in group—I just really haven't communicated with anybody else. HELP ME FEEL BETTER & GIVE ME CONFIDENCE. Give me Integrity & Courage."

Her yearning journaling went on for another page.

DeGuerin pulled out notes passed between the two patients as they sat in group therapy. Tracey asked if Celeste had said yes because it was hard for her to say no.

"Of course not, I just need you as a friend, nothing more," Celeste wrote back. It was a phrase DeGuerin would return to time and time again—"a friend, nothing more." But at that moment, he still gloated that Tracey had forgotten about the journal. He acted as though it were the shotgun with Tracey's engraved nameplate—case solved, we can go home now, just like the sheriff's department had done.

Tracey tried to explain repeatedly that she couldn't recall what she'd written in a journal four years ago when she was so heavily medicated that she could barely scribble.

But DeGuerin refused to buy her explanation. He picked and poked at a few of the phrases she'd written that he hadn't previously read: "It is hard now watching Celeste being protected from talking to me by her new roommate and companions."

"You were jealous of her new roommate, weren't you?"

Tracey couldn't remember the roommate.

He read about Celeste asking for space and time, and used that to insist that Celeste wasn't the aggressor Tracey had said, Tracey was the true aggressor. "I think it must be about losing me . . ." DeGuerin proclaimed that that was delusional thinking.

"No, sir. It's speculation."

Throughout, DeGuerin complained non-stop that Tracey wasn't being responsive, while the judge argued she was, he just wasn't letting her answer his questions.

He continued to whine.

"If you argue with me one more time when I make a ruling, you're going to be very embarrassed, Mr. DeGuerin. Don't argue with me."

"Yes, ma'am."

"Sit down and ask your next question."

He moved to Susan Milholland's notes from April 7, 1999. "Worked with patient to reality test delusional thinking." Tracey had told Milholland, "my peer's husband has influence and money and has arranged for me to be transferred to [adult psychiatric unit]."

DeGuerin continued ranting that Tracey was delusional because she thought Steve had had her moved to another unit.

"I believed Celeste," Tracey insisted. "I mean, I wish I had listened to Susan Milholland then. People told me later on the same thing Susan Milholland told me about Celeste, and I didn't listen to them either. That's why I'm here now."

DeGuerin kept trying to condemn the self-admitted killer with her own words.

"That's what the therapeutic journal is for, to explore these feelings, to see what's coming up and to try and figure out what's really going on. It's an exploration. It really is not meant to be a historical restoration of facts."

But he divided her words into such tiny phrases and sentences that the impact of the whole was mitigated. Her hurt wasn't seen, just her insanity—exactly what DeGuerin wanted. He moved to the second page of Tracey's April 8 journal entry.

"Wow, my treatment team has decided to move me over to the adult psychiatric unit . . . I had been scheduled to check in at the Red Roof and do outpatient there. I think that it all has something to do with the Celeste issue, that [her] husband got wind of it and didn't want me around during Celeste's recovery."

They argued again over the credibility of the journal—it being fact or feeling, Tracey repeatedly explaining that it was about her feelings. "What I'm doing here sitting in the stand is telling the truth about what happened with relation to my ending up shooting Steve Beard."

DeGuerin objected to her comment and was sustained.

"I feel like I have lost so much—not just Celeste, but my chance at closure in the trauma unit. I set it all up. I let Celeste be the building block upon which I based my therapy. And when she pulled loose, my entire empire came tumbling down.

"When all that happened in the room," Tracey explained, "he wanted her to move to another room. She pulled back and said, 'I can't do this anymore. Let's—let's stop.'"

"He wanted her to—"

"Steve Beard," Tracey answered. "And so—"

"Wait a minute," DeGuerin interrupted. He asked her if she'd talked to Steve.

"No, it's just what Celeste told me."

DeGuerin insisted, "Actually, it was what was in your head—"

"No, sir."

"—In your delusional head, isn't it?"

Tracey denied it, and DeGuerin kept exposing to the courtroom the patient's most personal thoughts.

"I'm having such a bad night!! I am lonely for familiar faces & maybe even a few that love me. And I am so afraid that I am not doing the right thing & I don't think I can get that answer until tomorrow—and even then it will be clouded. . . . I just feel so frustrated & mad—I have used up all my insurance $ and I feel like I am just a little more stirred up. I feel like if I went home now that I would get drunk. I feel like I am falling in this big hole & can't get out. I will meet with the doctors tomorrow and see about this plan—if it is good, I will stay a few days, & if not I will go home (against medical advice)."

From the beginning of that entry to the end, Tracey's handwriting deteriorated greatly. Neither Tracey nor DeGuerin could interpret the last few lines, but it mentioned home and family.

Tracey poured herself a cup of water and put it to her lips, her hand curled above the top of the cup like a thirsty carpenter.

He turned to more of intern Milholland's notes about the patient DeGuerin called delusional. "Worked with patient to expand call list to include therapy goals as well as relationship/sex addicts group."

That was news to Tracey. She didn't know anyone considered her a sex addict. But she also didn't deny it. "I was in treatment."

"Patient shared feelings of fear and shame 'if others found out what she had done.' Patient did disclose a peer comes to the hotel and they go to dinner with a group and she and this peer flirt with each other."

Tracey had a pattern of going from one doomed-to-fail relationship to another doomed-to-fail relationship, DeGuerin said. "For instance, Celeste told you that she had never had a lesbian relationship before, didn't she?"

"Yes." It was one of the few times Tracey didn't add "sir."

"You had entered into other relationships with people who had never been lesbians, right?"

"Right."

". . . Weren't you trying to convince Celeste that she must be a lesbian because all of her marriages failed?"

"No, sir."

DeGuerin pointed out that Tracey had heard Celeste tell therapist Barbara Grant, "I don't believe I'm a lesbian."

"That's right," Tracey answered. "But she was involved with a lesbian and I knew that firsthand. So whether or not she called herself a lesbian really was no concern to me at that point."

As Tracey had told various people in the DA's office, "Celeste was lesbian enough."

DeGuerin returned to Milholland's notes. "Advised patient to become honest with self and others, be accountable for self and stop protecting others." Then he read, "Patient stated this would be solved if certain people met with untimely deaths."

"You were talking in Timberlawn about killing Steve Beard, weren't you?"

"Yes, sir. As I said, in St. David's, Celeste had already started talking to me about that. So by the time we got to Timberlawn, we had been talking about it for weeks."

She clarified, "What I was referring to was that my feeling like I needed to worry about Celeste would be alleviated. The untimely death at that point was in reference to the spiked drinks and the sleeping pills that went in his—in his food.

"At that point there had been no discussion at all of, you know, actively killing him in some other way." She passed off the phrase "untimely deaths" as a flip statement. "I don't have any history with—with this kind of crime, and I—it wasn't really in my consciousness to censor a remark like that."

Kocurek ordered a ten-minute break while the attorneys approached the bench and DeGuerin and Kocurek wondered whether Tracey had "opened the door." They both believed she had.

"I'm probably going to allow it," Kocurek said, "but it looks kind of silly if she's eight years old."

Tracey returned to the courtroom, stood before Kocurek and explained a note in her medical records that stated she had once been homicidal. When she was 11, her brothers, 20 and 18, had said, "Wouldn't it save our father if we could just hire a hit man to kill her?" They were speaking of their abusive, alcoholic mother. And Tracey responded, "Yeah."

"Y'all are just stupid," her sister-in-law intervened.

Tracey carried the guilt of that for thirty years and finally tried to release it in treatment.

Kocurek ruled that the thirty-year-old moment in time would be allowed into evidence.

"As long as we're talking about this," DeGuerin added, "I think she's also opened the door to the Reginald Breaux incident where she tried to run him down in her car."

"She ran over him. She hit him and ran over him," Baen inserted.

"She was arrested and she was never charged," Wetzel protested.

Kocurek wanted to hear Tracey's version.

She said she'd picked up a homeless man and taken him to his brother's house, but he couldn't go in. So she dropped him off at a convenience store. "And when I'm backing out, he yells at me about something because I'm leaving. And I said, 'No, no, I'm going. I'm not going to take you anywhere else.' And he threw a beer can at my car in the window. . . . And then I put it in forward and he jumps out in front of my car and he gets hit. And I stopped and I go wait for the police to come." The police arrested her. "And when the detective talked to me, she said, 'I don't even know why they arrested you.' "

"That's different from murder," Kocurek stated. "I'm not going to allow it."

When testimony resumed, DeGuerin brought up the hit man discussion from more than thirty years before, then probed into her days of playing Russian roulette. She'd heard voices telling her to kill herself.

"Yes, that's right."

"And when you backed off from killing yourself, the voices would tell you that you're being chicken?"

"Something like that, yeah." Tracey admitted to auditory hallucinations, and she eventually admitted to delusions. Then she backed off of the delusions. "That's why I thought that they were probably delusions, because I knew that they weren't real."

DeGuerin reached for Tracey's journal again where she complained that the program was "terrible" and filled with nothing but "drunks and misfits." He pointed out that Tracey was a drunk and a misfit, too. He read on. "I believe that they moved me over here because of Celeste—I think her husband found out. Money talks. He seems to get just about everything he wants, even her. God, I wish I didn't feel in love with her."

Tracey had briefly stopped writing in her journal to look through the doorway. She watched Steve and Celeste walk by. With a blank face, Celeste stared straight at Tracey, as though she didn't know her.

"I am numb—stunned," Tracey wrote. "Celeste looked at me and went over to a seat and sat down. If I didn't think that something was up, I do now. When I mentioned it this morning Susan said I was delusional, so I let it drop—but I'm not."

As DeGuerin began to ask about Tracey's "story" that she and Celeste had had sex at the Red Roof Inn after Tracey's journal indicated that they had split, he seemed to wobble in his boots when he walked.

Tracey appeared rock-solid, less nervous and less verbose. Again, she tried to explain to the defense attorney the purpose of a therapeutic journal.

But DeGuerin backed up to Tracey's writings while she was in St. David's and stressed that although Tracey testified they that were already "feeling up" each other, Tracey never mentioned Celeste in her journal.

Court recessed so that the jurors could enjoy a barbecue buffet they'd ordered in.

There was a juror or two who had a crush on the pretty, young judge who walked into the courtroom every morning looking charmingly disheveled—like she'd just jumped out of bed and grabbed a graham cracker breakfast with her toddlers, forgetting to brush her own hair, before rushing downtown. So when the jurors returned to the courtroom just after 1 P.M., one of them smiled to her, "We left you some."

DeGuerin, though, never acted like he bothered to listen to the jurors' comments or read their facial expressions and body language. He seemed more focused on hearing his own voice and posturing with his arms crossed in a judgmental fashion as if he were an all-knowing god. He moved into Tracey's brief stay at Menninger.

"And they put you in a ward with a bunch of psychos?" he said.

"Well, I think the entire facility might be said to have a bunch of psychos, but this particular ward was for schizophrenics and people with Tourette's mostly."

". . . See if I read this correctly. 'Delusions, hallucinations, thought miniature men were stretching wires onto seats of airplane.' Is that some delusion that you were having as you were flying up to Menninger?"

"I don't recall. I don't recall the delusions. I really don't recall the flight."

He read from her psychosocial assessment: " 'Patient is bright, but manipulative.' " He read from her psychological test report. " 'She is apt to be given not only to hallucinatory experiences, but serious, even delusional misinterpretations of other people and reality.' "

He stated, "What happened at Menninger's is that they got your number up there, didn't they? And you didn't like it?"

Wetzel objected and was sustained.

DeGuerin repeatedly quoted Tracey's discharge summary—" 'bipolar disorder, recurrent, mixed, depressed with psychotic features.' "

Tracey agreed with that final diagnosis.

". . . You agree with psychotic as accurately describing you, correct?"

For the first time, DeGuerin was getting to Tracey. She wouldn't even look at the red-faced attorney as she tried to hold in her anger. "Well, I do think that I had a bipolar disorder and that is characterized as a psychotic illness, yes." She swiveled harder in her chair.

He read further: "' . . . Without external structure and when involved in interpersonal relationships, her thinking is overcome by severe psychotic delusions.'" He quipped, "If that's accurate, what that means is, you could have very well imagined that Celeste was reciprocal in her attraction to you as you were in your attraction to her. We can't trust your word on that, can we?"

She firmly replied, "I believe that you can trust my word on that, actually."

But there was no way DeGuerin was going to trust her word. If the doctors at St. David's, at Menninger, at Timberlawn were correct, Tracey's thinking was "overcome by severe psychotic disruptions in interpersonal relationships," he repeated.

Tracey readily agreed that she had problems with relationships. "I'm just saying I don't see anywhere in there that it says I have no cognitive ability to recognize when someone is in a relationship with me."

He stressed that the Menninger staff wrote that Tracey could "give in to swells of anger aimed either at herself or other people." He insisted that that "hit the nail on the head."

Tracey lowered her head a bit like a goat about to butt heads.

After much discourse and questioning, DeGuerin returned to Timberlawn and pointed out that Celeste did not arrive the same day as Tracey, as Tracey had testified. Celeste checked in to Timberlawn on Tracey's third day there.

"I don't remember my flight back to Timberlawn, so I just don't remember much about arriving there and getting there."

"Have you, over the years since this has happened," DeGuerin pressed, "deluded yourself into thinking that Celeste came and met you within hours of the time that you got there?"

Tracey denied that and admitted she was just wrong.

He read again from her journal where someone had overheard Tracey and Celeste talking and thought it "sounded like a lovers' spat. It really pisses me off and scares me because I am afraid that they will make us switch rooms."

He noted that Tracey once wrote that she was over her "infatuation" with Celeste. "And an infatuation is not a consummated affair, is it?"

Tracey argued that she and Celeste had had a fight, she was angry, and that phrase was her way of throwing up her hands and saying, "I don't need this."

But Tracey later wrote that she feared Celeste was going to leave Timberlawn—she'd signed herself out three times—and Tracey wouldn't feel safe without her.

Tracey's notes to Celeste were of a sexual nature, but Celeste's notes to Tracey were not of sexual themes, DeGuerin stated. "Why would it be that I am wanting to have an affair with a woman who is married and who I will only be able to see maybe once a week?" DeGuerin insisted that was a proclamation that an affair hadn't started.

"I'm wanting myself to put on the brakes, and I'm not putting on the brakes."

DeGuerin refused to buy her explanation.

Around 2:30 P.M., the judge took a break for a restless jury to race to the restroom. In the gallery, spectators mumbled that DeGuerin had "met his match" in Tracey Tarlton.

When testimony continued, he returned to intern Milholland's notes that stated Tracey's "dream" was to have an affair with Celeste. At the time, Tracey was suicidal. "I just want to drink a bottle of beer, break the bottle and kill myself with the glass. I don't want to live."

He read more of Tracey's words to the learning therapist. " 'I fall in love with married heterosexual women. The women leave and/or divorce their husbands. We have a relationship for one or two years and then I leave or act out, forcing them to leave me.' "

At that, DeGuerin stated, "What you do is, you convince them that they should try lesbianism, isn't that right?"

"No, sir. I've never recruited anybody."

The courtroom laughed, including Celeste. After which Tracey added, "Up until now."

DeGuerin had to approach the bench. "She recruited Zan Ray," he said to the judge. He insisted that during his interview with Zan, she'd said, "Tracey moved in on her."

"That's not what she said," Wetzel rebutted. She'd listened to the audiotape of the defense's interview with Zan.

The attorneys walked back to their places. DeGuerin bored his eyes into Tracey and stated, "It's true, isn't it, that you recruited, to use your term, Zan Ray, the woman with whom you had a relationship—"

"No, sir. It's not."

"Wasn't Zan Ray a heterosexual woman before you began your relationship with her?"

"Yes."

"Wasn't Celeste Beard, to your knowledge, a heterosexual woman before you sought out a relationship with her?"

32

"Yes, sir," Tracey answered. Celeste was heterosexual, just like Zan Ray. "But these women both came voluntarily into the relationship. They were not coerced."

DeGuerin suggested they were "persuaded."

"They weren't persuaded in an overt way. They were persuaded by their feelings for me."

Once again, DeGuerin resorted to Tracey's journal. April 24, 1999, she wrote, "I feel so jumbled up, like I can't get my footing. My heart and head are off with Celeste. It is no wonder that I don't feel like I'm here. I must let go of her and concentrate on the things in front of me."

May 30: "The dam is broken. After not being able to cry for almost two months, I am crying this morning. Celeste was supposed to come here to go to breakfast, and not only did she not come, but she slept right through. I talked to Kris and she couldn't wake her. I started crying. I feel so alone and lonely."

DeGuerin stated that that didn't sound like Celeste was pursuing a relationship with Tracey. Tracey never wrote in her journal that Celeste spent the night, only that "Celeste was so sweet . . . After we went to the movie, she came over and stayed until I was ready to fall asleep."

That was because that wasn't a problem for her, Tracey said. She only journaled about things with which she had issues.

"Is there a single journal entry in which you say, 'It finally happened. We finally had sex'?"

"No."

" 'I will allow her to come to a physical relationship with me in her own time,' " he quoted her journal.

". . . We were sputtering and starting . . . backing up and going forward," Tracey responded. Celeste had been comfortable with the sex at first, then backed off. "We needed to work on it and that's when all of this happened."

Eventually, DeGuerin returned to the BookPeople party and his obsession with the marijuana brownies.

Tracey testified she hadn't smoked pot since the 1970s, then Celeste had asked her to get some. "And I started keeping marijuana at the house and Celeste would smoke it with me. . . . She liked marijuana . . ."

Again, DeGuerin emphasized that it was harder to tell how much marijuana one had had when it was eaten as opposed to smoked "until it's too late." "And Celeste had too much, didn't she?"

"Several people told Celeste to stop," Tracey answered. "And Celeste was flagrantly eating too many."

"Ended up kind of kicking her—" DeGuerin started to say ass, but on second thought, he toned it down for the courtroom. "Ended up kind of getting her, didn't it?"

"Well, she was very high, yes."

"And she was also drinking heavily?"

"Yes."

"And that was a good opportunity for you to take advantage of her, wasn't it?"

"I—I didn't take advantage of her."

DeGuerin insisted that Tracey had attempted suicide on August 4, 1999, just before Celeste and the twins left for Australia. Tracey had no recollection of the suicide attempt.

The judge let the jury take a stand-up stretch break. Tracey joined them, and as she stood, with DeGuerin's back to her, she tried to make eye contact with Celeste. Celeste didn't look back.

DeGuerin showed Tracey an emergency department report stating she had gone to South Austin hospital on August 4, 1999, and had to have her stomach pumped due to a drug overdose.

Tracey still didn't recall the event.

No one on the jury bothered to take notes.

He stated Tracey overdosed again on October 10, 1999, eight days after she shot Steve Beard.

"I don't remember that either."

"Is it possible you were delusional at the time?"

"I have no reason to suspect that I was delusional at the time."

He brought up *The Poisoner's Handbook* and insisted it was a joke.

". . . I don't think it was intended as a joke book. It's not placed in that section."

In a condescending voice, DeGuerin read samples from the book to verify it was a joke book. As he did, Celeste tried unsuccessfully to hold in her snickers.

"It wasn't a joke to Steve Beard. I know that," Tracey replied.

DeGuerin retorted that Tracey had testified that Steve liked the "horrible-smelling" botulism so much that "he licked his plate clean."

"And that's kind of a delusional thought, isn't it?"

"Argumentative," Wetzel protested.

Around 4 P.M., Kocurek allowed one last restroom break for the day.

Wetzel leaned against the railing that separated the attorneys from the spectators and talked to her mother, who asked how long Tracey was going to be testifying.

"I think until she makes a suicide attempt on the stand."

When testimony continued, DeGuerin focused on Tracey's jealousy over Steve and her anxiety about the trips Celeste was scheduled to take. May 30, Tracey journaled, "It gets so hard to pretend that I have a girlfriend who wants to see me and spend time with me." DeGuerin jumped on the word "pretend."

"That wasn't a literal statement."

For another hour, DeGuerin interrogated Tracey—about the kids, about the mice, about her drug use, about putting the bag over Steve's head. It was as though DeGuerin were trying to call a square dance and dance it too. *Swing your partner do-si-do.* He was so revved up and enthralled with his own finally fast-paced calling, his own little steps, that he never noticed he was the only one dancing.

"You're not trying to tell this jury that you didn't have the intelligence to intellectualize and say, 'This is wrong. I can't go kill Steve Beard?' "

"Sure, I had the intelligence to do that, but this was my partner and she was intelligent also, and I had watched her for months suffer in this dilemma and she had struggled with it and fought against it all this time. You've got to understand," Tracey pled with desperate urgency in her voice, "I believed her. I really believed her. . . . I was there to help her. She was my partner."

Tracey had just finished calling DeGuerin's dance, and she wasn't even wearing a Dale Evans skirt.

But one way or the other, Dick DeGuerin was gonna make that crazy killer dance. He called for the shotgun. He told Tracey to step down. He placed the shotgun into her hand and told her to show the jury how she carried it when she'd walked into Steve Beard's darkened bedroom to the sound of his breathing.

Tracey put the gun in her right hand and hesitantly walked, her voice getting thicker as she forcibly narrated, her shadow and the gun reflecting hauntingly on the overhead screen.

"If you'll imagine," DeGuerin instructed, "that the bed is over there and Steve is on the bed, show us how you shot him."

"I walked down to the end of the bed and I saw him and I pulled up and shot him." She briefly lifted the gun toward her shoulder.

Becky Beard held her hand over her mouth.

Tracey quickly set down the gun. She folded her hands in fig leaf position and lowered her head.

"And you saw him move, right?"

She only nodded.

"Psycho." "Misfit." The negative vibrations of the words still hung in the courtroom on another rainy day in Austin, Texas.

At 9 A.M., Celeste entered the courtroom in another new sweater set—sea-foam green. Her daily sweater twin sets, along with her daily sobs were a topic of court gossip. Rarely did any observers see tears, just a pull of the lower lid, a wipe at the skin and a tissue swipe of the eye, turning the eyeball red.

DeGuerin continued his cross-examination with backhanded swipes at the gay community, insisting that Tracey was "recruiting" straight women even in jail.

Straight men apparently were blind to what straight women saw in Tracey—a woman who wanted to love deeply, encourage and be supportive of, laugh with, take care of, and spend time with her mate.

Add that to the fact that she was smart, well educated, well read, and hardworking with a good, high-profile job, Tracey Tarlton was what every straight woman looked for in a good, straight man. Her only drawback—besides the fact that she wasn't male—was that she was a bipolar recovering addict who occasionally heard voices when she wasn't properly medicated.

DeGuerin insisted that Tracey was at Tramps salon on Burnet Road getting her hair and nails done at the very time she said she was across town at Celeste's doing the walk-through.

"That would be impossible."

He purported that Celeste couldn't have been at Tracey's home at 11 P.M. on the Friday of the shooting because Jennifer had testified that Celeste was at the lake house until 11:30 P.M.

"Assumes facts not in evidence," Wetzel objected. "That's not what Jennifer's testimony was."

"Sustained."

Still, DeGuerin repeated several more times that Celeste was at the lake house until 11:30 P.M., with Wetzel objecting again, and the judge sustaining, again.

And again, DeGuerin seemed to ignore his jury makeup. There were corporate officers, high tech executive workers, well-educated men and women who paid attention in the courtroom, took fastidious notes, and on breaks hit their computers and cell phones to take care of their real world jobs.

He argued that when Tracey had testified the day before, she didn't bother to include her claim of 11 P.M. as being Celeste's arrival time at her Wilson Street home.

"It seems that I have stated in this courtroom that Celeste came by after she was at the lake house at eleven," Tracey responded.

"You have on direct exam," DeGuerin noted. "But when I asked you about it yesterday, you left it out, didn't you?"

He pointed out that she had told Detective Wines that she'd been drinking that night, but had told the court she didn't drink until after she'd pulled the trigger and gotten home.

"That version that I gave the police, I was lying to the police. I was trying to protect Celeste. I was trying to protect myself and so I—Unfortunately I can't stand behind what I told the police on that day."

"So you would lie to protect yourself?" DeGuerin shot back.

"I would lie—I would lie to protect—Yes, I lied to protect myself in that instance and to protect Celeste."

"Did you, shortly before you shot Steven Beard, say to Terry Meyer, 'If Steven Beard ever hurts Celeste, I will kill him'? Did you?"

The jurors wrote that down.

"I was told that later that I had said that. I don't recall saying that right now."

He asked her the same question again, only inserting the name Denise Renfield. Both Meyer and Renfield worked at Tramps.

Tracey gave him the same answer too—if she'd said it, she'd forgotten it. "I was told later that I had said that to her by Celeste."

"Did you tell Katina Lofton while you were in jail, while she was your roommate, that you were going to lie about Celeste being involved?"

"No."

"Did you tell Katina Lofton while you were in jail that Celeste had nothing to do with the shooting of Steven Beard?"

"No, I admitted that she had something to do with it."

"Did you tell Katina Lofton that you and one of the daughters continued to talk after the shooting?"

"No, I did not."

"Did you tell Katina Lofton that Celeste did not know you were going to shoot Steve?"

"No."

He went on with more questions about Katina, all of which Tracey denied. "Katina and I didn't talk on that level."

And he continued on, always receiving a "No" response from Tracey.

Celeste Beard Johnson looked worried that Friday morning.

When Allison Wetzel finally began her redirect at 10:30, she pulled out Celeste's personal calendar to prove Celeste had had contact with Tracey after August 1999. Celeste was scheduled to go to the birthday party of Nancy Pierson, Tracey's friend, on September 4, 1999. Celeste cancelled, but sent a present and phoned during the party. Also on Celeste's calendar was a September 21, 1999 dermatologist appointment for Tracey that Celeste had made for her with her own doctor.

Wetzel asked Tracey about the comment she'd allegedly made at Tramps—that she'd kill Steve if he hurt Celeste, pointing out that Celeste had told Tracey she'd said that.

"I remember that, because we had a discussion. I said, 'I don't think I said I would kill him'. . . . She said, 'Well, that's what they said.'"

Wetzel asked Tracey why it had taken her so long to decide to plead guilty and testify against Celeste.

At first, Tracey didn't want to "just throw [Celeste] in with this." But as time passed, "it weighed heavier and heavier" on her that she'd shot Steve Beard "under false pretenses." She thought he was a "monster," when he wasn't. "And then, as time went by with that, I started feeling really kindredness with Steve Beard more than with Celeste."

DeGuerin continually objected to Tracey's words—self-serving, not responsive, not relevant, narrative, leading, and suggestive.

"The kindredness stemmed from the fact that we had both been used by the same woman to get at his money."

DeGuerin kept objecting.

"And I had the sense that I wanted to think that if the tables were turned, that he would testify on my behalf. So I decided to testify on his."

"Do you feel any remorse for your part in this crime?"

"Every hour of every day, tremendous remorse, yes."

"The real reason you're testifying is not out of some kindred spirit with Steve Beard," DeGuerin offered, "but it's because you got a sweetheart deal, twenty years, of which you will probably only have to serve ten, isn't that right?"

33

"No," Tracey answered DeGuerin about her testifying just to get a reduced sentence, "that's not the primary reason."

By then, Becky Beard knew she wanted to meet with Tracey after the trial—to thank her for testifying.

Just after lunch on Friday, February 21, 2003, which Celeste had spent teary-eyed at the defense table, Kristina Beard walked down the center aisle of the courtroom gallery.

Everyone turned and stared at the young woman in the red, black, gray, and diamond print skirt that resembled an Indian blanket, and coordinating black, v-neck sweater. She kept her eyes focused straight ahead, certainly not a glance to the right and her mother.

By then, all the kids had their courtroom demeanor down pat. Rigid, serious, and frightened. But outside, when Celeste wasn't staring them down, they were full of life and giggles. Kristina, particularly, had a laugh that rose from her belly, lighted her face, and made a room glow warm and happy. And when she left, her light was missed.

Celeste watched her daughter as Wetzel asked the young witness what Celeste had told her about Steve Beard.

DeGuerin objected and argued that the prosecution was piling on the same testimony again and again.

Wetzel countered that Kristina knew more about some things than anyone else.

Kocurek allowed the question despite warning that the prosecution was "on the brink."

"Well," Kristina answered, her voice soft and scared, "she said . . . that he had a lot of money. He lived in a big nice house and that he was going to pay to bring Jen and I back to live with her."

At the time, they lived in the Terrace Mountain house, and Caresse, Celeste's sister, and her kids had come for a visit. Kristina stood in the kitchen, keeping one eye out for Caresse and her kids while keeping another eye on Celeste as she slipped sleeping pills into Steve's food. "I think it was a like a chicken kiev or something like that."

When they moved to the lake house while the Toro Canyon house was being built, Celeste began to switch Steve's vodka with Everclear. "It started off where she would pour [out] like half the bottle and then she would pour Everclear into the other half of the bottle and then it got to the point where it was more and more Everclear than vodka and then it was just all Everclear."

Kristina continued, "She said something like, 'This would ruin his liver,' you know. This would make his liver happy."

She told Kristina if Steve died, Celeste "would get it all."

Kristina thought Steve was a nice man, but never expected him to be in her life for very long because Celeste never stayed married for long. And, yes, Kristina and Steve argued sometimes. "Normal teenage stuff. I mean, sometimes I didn't like food that he liked and he would say, 'You don't know what you're talking about. You like it.'"

As Wetzel delved into Kristina's high school years, Kristina stated that she'd graduated early because of taking summer school classes in Hawaii, which contradicted her August 2000 testimony where she admitted to her graduation being pushed back.

Wetzel moved the witness into her mother's affair with Jimmy Martinez.

"She had told my dad that she was chaperoning our prom, and really she was going out with Jimmy."

Steve had been the parent who took the girls to buy their prom dresses at St. Thomas. He sat in a chair, holding a glass of water, Amy and her mom running in and out of the dressing room, the girls modeling for Steve, and Steve lovingly yeaing or naying the dresses. He just wanted some normalcy for the girls.

• • •

Wetzel asked Kristina what kind of comments Celeste had made about Steve.

Kristina looked down. "We had this dog that she would say—our dog Nikki—she would point at Steve and go, 'Nikki, look at the cow.'"

Before Celeste entered St. David's, she had spent a lot of money. Steve found out about it and asked, "Where did all the money go?"

"Just stuff," Celeste answered and laughed, thinking it was funny.

But that didn't please Steve. He didn't care she'd spent the money. He just wanted something to show for it.

Still, Celeste dug through Steve's possessions until she found his handgun. She then watched for him. And as he came up the driveway, she put the pistol to her head. Kristina cried and dialed 911. Cops and mental health officers arrived, took the gun away from Celeste, gave Steve a case number to get it back, and left.

Shortly thereafter, Celeste entered St. David's Pavilion. She then confessed to Kristina that she spent money because she was depressed. And she was depressed because she'd started thinking about the sexual abuse she'd suffered, when she was a child, by her father.

That was the first time Kristina ever heard her mother accuse Johnny Johnson of molesting her.

"The depression when I went to St. David's was caused because of my childhood. My mother had just moved to Texas and it triggered the memories to come flooding back."

Once Celeste completed her treatment at Timberlawn, she went over to Tracey's house to watch videos and smoke cigarettes on the back porch as Wren ran around. And sometimes, Kristina drove over to Tracey's early in the morning to wake her mother or pick her up after she'd spent the night.

Kristina knew Celeste didn't sleep in Tracey's guest room. It was filled with boxes. And there was only one bed in Tracey's bedroom. So Kristina asked her mother where she slept. "She said she slept on the couch." But Kristina never saw Tracey's couch covered in blankets and pillows as though someone had slept there.

Usually, she and her mother talked on the phone the night before with Celeste asking Kris to give her a wake-up call so that she could get back to Toro Canyon before Steve got up. But sometimes, when she phoned Celeste, no one answered. So Kristina went to wake up her mother in person.

Kristina drove down Loop 360 to Tracey's south Austin home, parked her vehicle, walked up to the front door, and unlocked it, as she had her own key—which she'd first denied in August 2000, then reluctantly admitted.

Celeste and Tracey heard Kristina as she opened and closed the front door and walked down the hallway to Tracey's bedroom, where Kris found her mother in bed with Tracey. Celeste was in her pajamas. Tracey's shoulder appeared to be bare under the covers.

When Celeste spent the night at Toro Canyon, she usually slept in the master bedroom with Steve and only occasionally slept in her room, Kristina swore.

"I always slept on the floor or in the kids' bed."

Celeste also asked her to lie and say she was at the lake house when she was really somewhere else. "It was kind of hard to keep up because she was always lying about something."

She talked about the errands she had to run for Celeste— like picking up the mail and coordinating a fundraising gala for a Montessori school affiliated with Willie Nelson. Celeste had agreed to organize it.

"Did she have some kind of nickname that she used for you when you were doing all these things for her?" Wetzel asked.

Dick DeGuerin butted in and objected. The attorneys approached the bench. The jurors madly whispered among themselves.

"What was the name?" Kocurek asked.

"Her little niglet."

"Oh, my God," DeGuerin gasped.

The objection was sustained.

But Wetzel argued, turning to DeGuerin and demanding, "Why don't you ask your client if it's true?"

"That's not proper for her to make insulting remarks to me directly." DeGuerin pouted. "I always address myself to the court."

"Don't make remarks," Kocurek scolded her former boss.

DeGuerin griped that Kristina was "not responsive. She's not under control—not in this hearing, but in other hearings."

"No, she hasn't," Kocurek defended. "In this courtroom she ha[s] been perfectly—that's my experience. I'm going to tell her to move on to the next question."

Wetzel moved to the large portrait of the three Bratcher/Beard women by Katy Nail, which hung over a buffet in the living room. In the background of the painting, Kristina said, there was a fountain. And in the fountain, about the size of a silver dollar, was a painting of Steve's face.

"Did the defendant say whether she wanted to have the face in the painting?"

"I don't think she wanted to because she said it was like a Father's Day present for him and Katy Nail really wanted to put him in the family portrait because he was the only one missing in it. So they decided on something small that was kind of discreet."

"Did the defendant tell you about any plans for changing that painting at any point?"

"Yes. She said that when our dad died, that she was just going to paint over his face."

No one had ever told Katy Nail about painting over Steve, though Katy had painted over that portrait time and again. First, trying to get Celeste just right—every time she painted Celeste's face, Celeste came out looking like a psycho nurse.

And later, after Jen moved to Austin, she worked on the

portrait again, squeezing Jen into the painting. Originally, the picture had depicted only Celeste, Kris, and Steve. Celeste told Katy that Jen didn't need to be in it because she was never going to see it.

In September of 1996, just after Jen had joined the household, Steve ate dinner, sat down to watch TV, and started to pet Megan when he got up to go to the bathroom. The next thing he knew, it was two days later and he was waking up at home.

Steve had fainted while on the commode, fallen forward, cut his head on the doorframe, and urinated on himself. Celeste found him unconscious as blood poured from the three-inch-long gash that traveled down the right side of his forehead, across the eyebrow, and into the eyelid. He was airlifted to Brackenridge Hospital.

Celeste turned to Kris and in a concerned tone asked the teenager whether she thought the doctors would be testing Steve's blood and find alcohol or sleeping pills.

Wetzel asked if Kristina had ever found any lesbian books in the house after Celeste met Tracey.

Kristina admitted she had, on a desk in her own bedroom. Quickly and defensively, she added, "But I didn't flip through them or anything. I read the titles." Yet she said next, "If you read the back of the book, I don't remember the title, but it seemed like women with family and children coming out, things like that."

"I vote we go home now," DeGuerin huffed, during a break.

But Wetzel continued her direct examination of Kristina Beard, asking about the graduation party at Jimmy's.

Kristina stood in the living room, with Jimmy, and near his pool table when she watched her mother go upstairs.

"Hey," Jimmy said, his beloved beer nearby, "I think Tracey is upstairs." He didn't like the woman. She was just too butch for his comfort. He looked at Kris. "Why don't you go see what is going on?"

So Kristina walked up the steps to Jimmy's bedroom, where she opened the door to find Tracey on top of her mother as though she were making out with her in Jimmy's bed. After three seconds of stunned staring, Kristina spun on her heels, fled downstairs and to Jimmy. "Tracey's on top of Mom!"

Jimmy rushed up the stairs.

Shortly, Tracey walked down the stairs, looked for her keys, and hurried out the door. Kristina returned to Jimmy's room to find her mother getting ready for bed and commenting that she was going to have sex with Jimmy that night. No one mentioned Tracey.

Finally, Kris and Justin got back to Toro Canyon and were just about to drop off to sleep, when the phone rang.

Kristina sighed in the courtroom.

She picked up the phone, heard something about it being Tracey calling collect from jail, and hung up. The phone rang and rang again. Kristina dialed her mother at Jimmy's and told her what was going on.

"Oh, don't worry about it," Celeste assured. "We'll take care of it tomorrow."

The next morning, Celeste picked up Tracey from jail.

As far as Kristina knew, Steve hadn't told Celeste to bail out her friend.

Wetzel asked Kristina about Wednesday hamburger nights, specifically the night near graduation when Tracey had come over.

Her voice a bit softer, finally more relaxed, but sounding tired, Kristina said that that particular hamburger night the kids ate around the bar in the kitchen and the adults ate in the dining room.

After dinner, the adults moved out to the rocking chairs on the front porch, where Celeste and Tracey sat in chairs next to each other. Kristina moseyed out to the porch, too, and leaned against the wood railing while Steve walked inside.

Celeste and Tracey teased Kristina about her relationship with Justin. Then, Tracey leaned over to Celeste and kissed her, seconds long and open-mouth. As she sat back in her chair, the three were silent, no reaction at all. Finally, Celeste got up and walked inside the house toward the kitchen.

Kristina followed her.

Celeste stood in front of Steve and matter-of-factly said, "Tracey just kissed me."

Steve's tanned face looked upset. He walked out of the kitchen and onto the porch, closing the door behind him.

Kristina stood in the living room trying to decipher his loud words. She couldn't.

Celeste and Tracey came in the house. Celeste reported that Steve wanted Tracey to go home. That was fine with Tracey; she was ready to go.

"As far as hamburger night, the children are mistaken. I can prove it because they graduated on Aug. 27, 1999. . . . After the ceremony we went to the Country Club for drinks & dinner. . . . We all had drinks at the Club. Steven and Tracey were drunk and continued to drink when we arrived home. They went out on the porch and had a few more strong drinks. I was sitting in one of the rockers when Tracey put each hand on the armrests. Steven had gone to the restroom and to make another cocktail. She started leaning forward getting close to me. It made me uncomfortable and I pushed her away. I chalked it up to her being drunk."

She jumped into her Pathfinder and backed into a tree. Celeste stood there, watched, and laughed. Christopher walked over to the driver's side and banged on the closed window. "You've gotta get out! You've gotta get out!" Tracey was drunk. Kristina yelled with him, "Tracey, you've gotta get out of this car! You can't drive home!"

Christopher opened the door and the two kids pulled Tracey out of her SUV. They maneuvered her into the passenger seat. And Christopher drove her home in her SUV. As he drove, Tracey confessed that she and Celeste were having an affair.

"Oh, no! I shouldn't have told you that." Tracey turned to Christopher. "You won't tell anybody? You won't tell anybody?" She looked pleadingly deep into his eyes.

For months, all the kids had suspected. "Your secret's safe with me."

Kristina followed the SUV in one of the Cadillacs, Celeste riding in the passenger seat until they got about a block from Tracey's home.

"Stop the car," Celeste ordered. "I'm going to jump in the trunk." She didn't want Tracey to know she was there. Celeste climbed into the trunk, Kristina pulled up in front of Tracey's, and Kristina and Christopher helped Tracey up the walk and inside the house.

Tracey shucked off her clothes and paced around the room stark naked while telling the teens that she and Celeste were a couple. It wasn't a pretty sight. She was big. She wasn't "clean cut."

As Tracey paced, she talked about how much she loved Celeste, then said she was depressed and didn't want to live anymore. She wanted to know where her shotgun was.

Kris and Christopher led her into the bedroom. Tracey climbed under the covers. They said goodnight, they'd see her tomorrow.

Kristina giggled slightly in court when she stated that Tracey was naked.

"Where was the defendant this whole time that you were in the house with Tracey walking around naked, talking about suicide and her love for the defendant?"

"She was in the trunk."

Celeste giggled a bit at that.

"And did you periodically go outside and talk to the defendant while she was in the trunk?"

"Yes."

When Kristina told her mother that Tracey was naked and walking around the room, Celeste laughed. "Hurry up. Hurry up. It's hot in here. I'm going to die in the trunk."

But every time they put Tracey in bed, she got up. "Where're my guns? I'm looking for my guns. I need my guns."

"Why do you want to know where your guns are?"

"I just need to know."

They tucked her in numerous times. "Let's go," Kristina said.

"No, we can't," Christopher answered. "We can't leave her. If she kills herself we'll be part of the crime."

Kristina got Tracey to promise she wouldn't kill herself, they tucked her in one last time, and she and Christopher finally left, Christopher letting Celeste out of the trunk.

In mid-September, Celeste and Steve stood in the kitchen as Kristina eavesdropped again.

"I don't want you talking to her anymore," Steve said of Tracey.

Celeste promised she wouldn't.

Kris believed her mother wasn't communicating with Tracey. But one night, when Kris was spending the night away from home, she got a call from Celeste—Steve was having a seizure and EMS was on the way.

"I'm getting up," Kristina replied. "Do you want me to pick you up and take you to the hospital?"

"No," Celeste said. "Tracey is going to take me."

Kristina headed for the hospital, but then she spoke again to Celeste.

"Can you come pick me up? Tracey is just going to go home."

Wetzel moved Kristina to the night of the shooting, and Kristina reiterated that Celeste told her Justin couldn't spend the night that weekend.

"I'm going to need your help, and Justin is a distraction," Celeste had explained.

So when Justin took Kristina home around 11 P.M. on Friday, October 1, 1999, she phoned Jen at the lake house. "Do you know where Mom is?"

Jen said she'd left thirty minutes ago.

Kris expected Celeste home soon. Midnight came, and Kristina was exhausted—she'd worked a full day in the Trilogy mailroom. She walked Justin to the front door. He left, and she went to bed.

The next thing she knew, it was the middle of the night, Celeste was in the bedroom with her but peeking out the bedroom door. "Somebody rang the doorbell." Celeste rushed. "There's somebody at the door. There's somebody at the door."

Freaked, Kris got up and walked over to where her mother stood, with the door barely cracked open. Kristina peeked out to see for herself. Celeste pushed Kristina out the door and said, "Go check it out."

Terrified, Kristina fled into the guest bedroom and called 911. After speaking to 911, Kristina ran back to her room. Celeste was under the covers of Jen's bed.

"Something's wrong with Steve. That's EMS." Kris testified to "Steve," not "Dad."

She raced to the front door to let in EMS and led them to Steve's room, entering the bedroom with them. She turned to Steve. And as she spoke in the courtroom, she almost wept. "EMS is going to take you to the hospital. You're going to be all right. I love you. We all love you."

When court recessed for five minutes, Ellen Halbert whisked Kristina out and guarded the restroom door for her.

Celeste sat in the courtroom and wept.

At the hospital, Sergeant Knight stopped Kristina in the hallway to ask her some questions about phone numbers.

Celeste watched from a few feet away, then warned Kristina, "Stop talking to them. Get over here. Let's go."

Once they checked into the Marriott and Kristina and her mother were alone, Celeste confessed to her favorite daughter that she'd been talking to Tracey when they thought she'd given up communicating with her. "Don't mention it to Jen," Celeste said.

She also told Kris that Phil Presse was coming to the hotel with an attorney.

Afterwards, Celeste informed Kristina that Tracey was implicating Celeste and that's why she needed an attorney. Presse knew that, Celeste said, because he'd spoken to Tracey's attorney, who'd given him the information. "But don't tell anyone." If Kristina did, Celeste said, it'd get Phil in trouble.

Kristina later met with Charlie Burton and talked to him

by herself, but only after Celeste had given her specific instructions about what to say.

"Don't forget to mention—tell him how much I love Steve and that I would never want to hurt him. Don't forget to tell him that I was sleeping in the bed that night."

34

Austin's temperature had been in the 80s on Sunday. On Monday, February 24, 2003, when a few bluebonnets should have been peeking out their heads along Loop 1, the 36-degree cold front, along with a wind chill in the 20s, forced them back into hiding.

Catherine Baen was just about ready to call in sick so that she didn't have to come into court anymore. "This is getting old." DeGuerin was outside the courtroom stomping up and down the hallway as he talked on his cell phone.

Celeste, in another new outfit, a gray business suit, galumphed into the courtroom. She also had a new white cast on her leg, which she'd gotten the week before.

Judge Kocurek ordered Celeste to the bench, where she reprimanded her for making faces and mouthing words such as "That's ridiculous" during Kristina's testimony. The judge threatened to hold Celeste in contempt if it happened again. But when Kristina walked into the courtroom in a skirt and pale lavender sweater, Celeste shook her head.

Wetzel zipped through her questions that morning with Kristina answering them just as quickly.

In December 1999, at Celeste's instruction, Kristina went to James Avery jewelers in Barton Creek Square Mall and picked up a couple of charms and a gold and silver ring similar to the one Christopher had given Jen. Celeste told Kris they were gifts for the Madigans and some other friends.

Kris paid for the gifts with Celeste's credit card and signed her mother's name. That wasn't unusual. Kris carried a couple of her mother's cards to use when she was running errands for Celeste.

The morning of January 22, 2000, Kristina was at Justin's when Celeste called her.

"It doesn't look like Steve's going to make it today," Celeste said. "Could you go by Bank of America and pick up his signature card so we can have him sign it today?" Celeste explained that she wasn't on the account, and she wanted the card signed and notarized that day so that she could pay bills, since it didn't look like Steve was going to live.

Kris got the signature card, but she couldn't find a notary. She took the card to the hospital and gave it to Celeste, who put a pen in Steve's hand and placed the card beside him for him to sign. "But he was unable to do that."

They proceeded to April 2000 and the night Celeste left Timberlawn in a rage at Kristina. Wetzel moved to introduce the tapes, which Kristina swore weren't edited.

DeGuerin objected, again. "It is cumulative and we are way beyond the point where the State is simply making her look bad rather than proving that she committed the crime."

As one of DeGuerin's University of Texas law students sat with his hand on Celeste's back to comfort her, the bailiff passed to the jury Wetzel's transcripts of the tapes. The tape of Celeste screaming and cursing at her favorite daughter was played.

She kept her head down and wrote as the jurors listened to her say, "Did I deserve an old man's dick up my ass when I was four years old, is that what you don't know?"

They didn't even react.

Looking sad, Kristina followed the transcript. So did the judge.

"Well, Justin's not allowed over at our house anymore."

A young male juror began to look grim behind his black-rimmed eyeglasses.

"You and Justin have been so high and mighty. You think that Goddamned house is yours. . . . I can't even trust my own kids to keep their Goddamned mouths shut long enough for me to get out and get everything taken care of."

A young female juror glared at Celeste. Another juror kept her head down with her hand covering her eyes.

"And you're lucky. You didn't have your father sticking his dick in you when you were four years old for eight years. But I'm mean—I'm so mean, I'm, I'm worse than that." When Celeste Beard yelled, her lisp wasn't present in the least. "Well, if you resent it, you little bitch, then you should have said something, instead of just doing it."

Judge Kocurek put her two fists up to her chin, looking upset.

"I was fucking depressed, you Goddamned little bitch."

An older male juror stared at Celeste, who now bowed her head, sometimes covering her face as if crying.

"Do you know what it feels like when you're four years old, you aren't even in kindergarten, and some guy has a big dick sticking in you?"

Wetzel, the child abuse prosecutor who taught Sunday school each week at Westlake Presbyterian Church, glowered at the defendant.

"I protected you and your sister from all that shit. . . . Bring the dog home, if you're not going to stay. I want the dog at the house. And if you don't stay, I don't give a shit."

Kocurek looked at Celeste to see her reaction. Celeste wept.

"I don't think I can ever, ever, ever forgive what you have said to me tonight. Because as soon as I get home, I feel like just fucking sticking a knife down my throat, you bitch."

One of the female deputies guarding Celeste swung nervously in her chair.

"Then why are you doing this? You said you're scared of me. You think I'm going to beat you up or something? I never even laid a hand on you. When have I ever hit you? . . .

"What are you so frightened of?"

Kristina softy said, "'Cause I'm tired of you hurting yourself."

A female juror looked at Kristina.

"I hired somebody to kill Tracey."

The courtroom was silent.

The judge ordered a break.

Kristina walked out stiff-faced.

Celeste blew her nose.

Celeste always planned and thought out everything, Kristina believed—everything but feelings.

During the break, Celeste and Catherine Baen looked at photographs of Celeste with Wynonna Judd.

DeGuerin's face was as red as Wynonna's hair.

"I was hysterical because I felt like . . . that I was in jail because the door was locked and I couldn't get out. . . . And I'm threatening the doctors, you know, I'm gonna get my attorney and you're not keeping me. But someone has to be able to come get you or you're not leaving. And so by the time [Jennifer and Christopher] got there . . . I was panicking that I was going to be stuck in this place and not be able to get out.

"And then when Christopher and Jennifer come get me because Kristina's going, 'No, I'm not gonna come get you,' I was pissed. So I called, and I cussed her out I was so mad, you know, and I'm sorry I did that, but I was just—I was scared. And I didn't want to be in that place anymore. And I knew that something was going on, but I didn't know what.

"And then they talked—they talked me out of it . . . that nothing was going on. And it was really going on—because they were there, you know, stealing stuff out of the house and stealing out of my checking account. And, um, that's when, um, I guess that's when that call with Donna . . ."

At 11:15 A.M., Dick DeGuerin began his cross-examination with what still was on everyone's minds—the audiotape. "You and Justin had started . . . tape recording your mother's conversations with you before this conversation that the jury heard, hadn't you?"

"Pardon me?" After he repeated his question, she said, "I don't recall that."

"Well, for instance, you recorded her calling you and asking you to pick her up at Timberlawn, didn't you?"

"I'm not sure that I did."

"You're not sure that you did?"

"I remember the conversation, but I don't remember if I tape recorded it or not."

DeGuerin *knew* that she had. "Didn't you and Justin start recording conversations with your mother as early as March sixteenth?"

"Not that I remember."

And so began, and would continue, Dick DeGuerin's cross-examination of Kristina Beard—perfectly unimpeachable answers of "I don't recall," "I don't remember," "I don't know."

"Was there a kind of blackmail scheme going on that you know about, where Donna was blackmailing your mother?"

"Not that I knew about." She later added, "I knew there was something fishy going on." Finally, she admitted that Celeste mentioned something to her about Donna trying to blackmail her.

He asked about her cutting off the tape after "I hired somebody to kill Tracey." "But there was more to the conversation than that, wasn't there? . . . And that's when your mother explained to you that Donna . . . had said she was going to tell the police that there was a hit contract on Tracey because your mother was filing charges against Donna [for stealing her jewelry], right?"

"I don't remember that part of the conversation."

"The phone call that the kids altered was me telling Kristina what Donna said she would say, 'that I hired a hit man to kill Tracey,' if I continued to accuse her of taking my jewelry. The '42 diamond ring.' That is why I dropped it."

• • •

Kristina refused to admit that Celeste had revoked the power of attorney in front of Dr. Bernard Gotway on that April Fool's Day, 2000, meeting at Timberlawn. But she confessed to writing thousands of dollars in checks after she knew the POA was revoked.

DeGuerin grilled Kristina about what all she had told Charlie Burton just a few days after Steve was shot—when Celeste got home from the lake house, she woke up Kris; they talked about Kristina's work . . .

Kristina said she didn't remember. And with each "I don't know" and "I don't remember," her voice grew softer.

He quizzed her about Tracey Tarlton. "Did you tell Mr. Burton that Tracey was obsessed with your mother?"

"I don't know."

"Did you tell Mr. Burton that Tracey tried to kiss your mom and your mom was grossed out?"

"I don't know."

"Did you tell Mr. Burton that Tracey had told you that she, Tracey, was in love with your mom but you never told your mom that?"

"I'm not sure."

"Didn't you call Mr. Burton and tell Mr. Burton that Tracey was calling you?"

"I don't know. I don't recall saying that."

DeGuerin said Kristina called Charlie Burton on March 24, 2000, and asked to meet with him about Tracey. She did meet with him on March 29 and played Burton a voice mail from Tracey. DeGuerin wanted to play the tape right then and there to prove himself right.

The judge released the jury for an early lunch so that the lawyers could argue about it. With the jurors out of the room, DeGuerin played the tape. Tracey's voice asked Kristina if she'd called her, if everything was okay, and said that if there was anything Kris needed to tell her, just call.

The judge refused to allow the tape—it hadn't been authenticated.

But after lunch, DeGuerin continued his questioning about the tape and through his own words got in the gist of the recording. He questioned Kristina about all the legal battles she'd put her mother through—the protective order, the probate hearing, the lawsuit. "And you plan to reinstate the lawsuit, don't you, if your mother is convicted?"

"I don't believe so."

He pulled out the transcript of her probate hearing testimony and pointed out where she'd said, "At one time I saw Tracey kiss Mom, and then another time I saw Tracey kissing her in Jimmy Martinez's bedroom."

Several times, Kristina glanced over to her right. It irritated DeGuerin. He asked her who she was looking at, as if she were looking at someone to signal her the answers.

"I'm just looking right," she said. "I'm sorry. I just don't like to look your way." She stared right at him.

"I don't blame you," he answered, "but things are going to get tougher."

DeGuerin kept trying to impeach Kristina via her August 2000 testimony. But Wetzel kept objecting that he wasn't impeaching her the "proper way." Kocurek kept sustaining her. His jumbled attempts at impeachment floated somewhere in the courtroom air like elements of an atom that just couldn't be put together. His potential bomb went off with a thud.

He asked about Jimmy Martinez, saying Kristina was close to him and had gone to live with him when she and Steve were arguing.

"I think it was for two weeks, and I believe Celeste was in Timberlawn at the time . . ."

DeGuerin insisted she ran to Jimmy because Steve had taken her off of Celeste's life insurance policy so that she was no longer the beneficiary.

"I don't know a thing about that."

DeGuerin nagged that Kristina had told Jimmy that Tracey was "molesting" Celeste.

"I don't recall using molesting . . ."

"Have you changed your tune just because you're now against your mom?"

"No."

Each time he claimed something happened, Wetzel ob-

jected—assumes facts not in evidence. Kocurek sustained
her, but that didn't dissuade DeGuerin. Catherine Baen
passed him pages from the August 2000 probate hearing as
Celeste watched, looking sad. DeGuerin handed the pages
to Kristina. With one hand on his hip and his voice sounding huffy, he tried to ask about Kristina's 2000 testimony.

"Hearsay," Wetzel called.

"At some point, you took from Tracey's house a journal,
didn't you?"

"No."

DeGuerin scrambled around searching for the journal.
Finally, he held it in his hand. "Isn't that the journal that
you took to Charles Burton on about October the sixth of
1999?"

"I don't recall doing that."

He asked Kristina about the family planner that she said
Celeste told her she could take.

She said she'd only recently rediscovered it—"before
the pre-trial started." Then she stated she found it "over the
summer after I left."

She left in 2000, so DeGuerin brought out her late August 2000 testimony where she denied having the planners.

"At the time, I didn't know I had them."

"Isn't it true that usually a person's . . . memory is better
sooner after the event than it is several years later?" He
switched to the big blowup in the Beard house when Celeste
found out Kristina was having sex with Justin, which resulted in Justin not being allowed to spend the night at Toro
Canyon anymore. That contradicted Kristina's previous testimony that he was always welcomed to spend the night.

Kristina released a big sigh.

He questioned her up one side and down the other about
seeing Celeste put sleeping pills in Steve's food on their
way to Washington State.

"Did you sit there and watch her put it in his baked potato?"

"No."

"What did she do? Did she say, 'Look over there right
quick while I do this'?"

"I don't remember."

"If you saw it, could you describe it to the jury?"

Despite just saying she hadn't seen it, Kristina described it. "She put it inside his baked potato when he wasn't looking and mushed it around, and then he ate it."

"Well, why was he not looking? Did he leave the table?"

"I don't know why he wasn't looking."

"Did he go to the bathroom?"

"He could have."

"I'm not asking you what could have. I'm asking you what you claim you saw!"

At first, his getting all wound up obviously irritated Kristina. But after a while, the more he postured, the calmer she got, though her body language remained defiant. And she continued answering, "I don't know" and "I don't remember."

Her reluctance to answer didn't faze the jurors. They frowned at DeGuerin.

Celeste looked like she was about to cry.

As testimony dragged on, Kristina glared at DeGuerin when he wasn't looking and angrily cocked her head to the side when speaking.

The judge scolded DeGuerin to hurry up and finish with the witness.

At 4:30 P.M., court abruptly ended. The streets were icing over. The judge wanted everyone to get home safely and early. After all, Austin was in the Hill Country.

Kristina climbed into her dark green, oversized SUV and traversed to the Northwest Hills area of Austin to the two-bedroom apartment she shared with Justin.

Inside their apartment was a leather chair of Steve's, despite the fact that she had testified in August 2000 that she didn't have anything of his. The living room was always clean, except for maybe a spot or two on the beige carpet tracked in by Kaci—the tiny, blonde cocker spaniel they'd given Steve for his last birthday, whom Celeste had repeatedly demanded to be returned to her. The cocker's registered name was Celeste's Kaci Charlene.

Off of their living room was a large deck where they
grilled garlic-filled hamburgers, just like Steve did. The
deck view of tall evergreens rising over a creek would have
been worth millions of dollars in New York City.

Their second bedroom was used as an office. It had two
computers, one for each of them. Justin's had the capability
to download digital tape recordings and burn them onto a
CD. Kristina had the digital recorder.

Tucked in various places were boxes of photographs—
some from their times with Celeste, others from Steve's
days with Elise, including their wedding invitation. They
seemed to have no inclination to give the cherished items to
the natural-born Beards.

A few miles away, in a run-down neighborhood, Jennifer
shared one unit of their $250,000 triplex with a female
friend, who sat in court every day taking notes. They pre-
ferred a life of beer, cigarettes, fast food, and messiness.
But from the front of the triplex, all one could see was a
garage. Formerly a carport, Jennifer and Kristina had transformed it into a garage themselves so that Celeste couldn't
find their cars.

Like their mother, they constantly held cell phones to
their ears. Kris, Jen, and Justin all carried beefy Nextel
phones so that they could communicate via walkie-talkie
speakerphones, sharing their conversations with each other
when the person on the other end thought they were speaking only to one person.

35

Court didn't reconvene until Wednesday, February 26,
2003, and even then it was a treacherous start with still-icy
roads. The prosecutor, the victims' services worker, and at
least one juror lived in the Westlake Hills area, and their ve-

hicles just couldn't safely navigate sloping driveways and hairpin roads.

Kocurek had tried to wait for a bit of a thaw by not starting court until almost 10:30 A.M. Even at that, the natural-born Beards weren't in the courtroom as Kristina sat down in the witness chair, her azure sweater matching DeGuerin's pullover.

He asked Kristina about the night Steve was shot. "Now you've testified that you went to sleep before your mom got home, but you've told Mr. Burton, didn't you, that your mom—you and your mom had a conversation after she got home?"

"I don't remember that."

"You have told this jury, though, that your mom would put Megan in the back room or in your room on Sundays for the, as you called it, the Sunday Suck?"

"Correct."

"So easily she could have put Megan in the back room this night if she was trying to hide Megan or not have Megan around?"

"I guess that's correct."

DeGuerin stated that Celeste slept in Kristina's room more often than Kristina had said and that Celeste kept clothes in Kristina's closet.

Kristina denied both assertions. But both Amy and Christopher believed Celeste spent most nights in Kristina's room—when Celeste spent the night at home. They talked about the clothes Celeste kept in Kristina's and the guest room closets, with Christopher recalling the embarrassing trips he and Jen had taken to return the clothes to the stores.

"Did you falsify your testimony to the probate court?" DeGuerin demanded.

"I don't believe so."

He moved to Steve's time in Brackenridge. "Was there a time when Steve became angry with you and wanted you out of the room?"

"I think I can remember the time, yes." He'd thrown a glass of ice at her.

She went on to testify that the handicap ramps at the Toro house for Steve weren't put in until the day he came home from the hospital, and only that day was the decision made to have them.

DeGuerin stated that Celeste had brought Steve home from Studio 29 that day and had helped him into the house.

Kristina didn't agree with that.

DeGuerin proposed that until Kristina had turned against her mother, she believed Health South had caused Steve's death due to negligence.

Wetzel objected to that, and doing a DeGuerin, she objected more than once. Each time, the judge overruled her.

Kristina didn't voice an objection at that moment, but she objected to anyone saying she and Jen had turned against Celeste. Celeste, she believed, had turned on them.

But, she answered DeGuerin's question, "That might be true and correct."

Suddenly, another fight broke out at the bench among the attorneys. DeGuerin wanted to introduce evidence to which Wetzel objected. "What is the relevance of what this eighteen-year-old, nineteen-year-old kid believed was the cause of her father's death?"

DeGuerin argued that it showed bias and prejudice.

He showed Kristina a bill from Health South with her handwriting and signature on it, which she verified.

And the fight continued. "Your Honor," Wetzel said, "my objection is—"

DeGuerin interrupted her. "Do I understand that—"

"Excuse me," she interrupted him. "Do you mind not interrupting?"

Finally, DeGuerin got before the court the note Kristina had written on the bill—"Don't pay, find out what for. The negelete [sic] by them caused my father's death, Kristina B."

Kristina said she didn't remember writing that on the March 2000 bill.

"You really want the jury to believe that you don't remember receiving a bill from Health South and writing back to Health South, *Don't pay, . . . they caused my father's death*?"

Wetzel objected—argumentative and the defense attorney was making speeches.

She won on both counts.

"Well, do you know how many times on cross-examination you have said 'I don't remember' as compared to how many times you said 'I don't remember' on direct examination when you were being asked questions by Ms. Wetzel?"

"No."

But the jurors took note.

"Have you been told that if you just say, 'Well, I don't know—'"

"Objections. Argumentative."

"—that we can't get in something that is clearly yours?"

"Sustained. The jury is instructed to disregard the last statement by the defense counsel."

He asked her if she phoned a friend in New York from Celeste's cell phone. "I'm talking about calling her from your mom's cell phone because you guys pass cell phones around like party favors, don't you?"

"We did trade phones."

DeGuerin had finally pulled an answer out of her that he'd wanted, so he moved to December 1999 and her trip to James Avery. "And the simplicity wedding band, didn't you give that to Christopher to give to Jennifer?"

"That's incorrect."

He pointed out that Kristina had called Dr. Hauser and asked her to talk to the attorney Kristina was using for the guardianship, Al Golden.

"I'm not sure if I talked to her about that."

He read from Dr. Hauser's notes regarding a phone message from Kristina asking Hauser to call Attorney Golden. "Does that serve to refresh your recollection?"

"No."

They continued their months-, seemingly years-long battle over whether Celeste had revoked Kristina's power of attorney at that April 1, 2000, meeting with Dr. Gotway.

"There was discussion about how I was—how I had to parent Celeste."

He continued with his same ole, same ole—Gotway didn't think it was appropriate that Kristina have POA over Celeste, Celeste told Kristina and sent letters announcing she'd revoked the POA.

Kristina disagreed with the first and didn't remember the latter.

Wetzel started objecting again. It was perhaps her fullest day of objections so far.

At the bench, Kocurek told DeGuerin, "This needs to stop."

He thought she meant his tactics. "Yes, ma'am," DeGuerin said. She'd meant the cross-examination. "If she would quit lying, we could end it now, but she's not going to do that."

Wetzel broke in. "I'm not sure what Mr. DeGuerin is referring to her lying about. I guess that's just characteristic of the way he's been acting all day."

"You've had her up on the stand for five and a half hours now," Kocurek told DeGuerin. "Let's move it along. The jury is getting bored."

DeGuerin showed Kristina another note from Hauser's files where she again wanted to talk to Hauser about the guardianship. The date of the note was April 4, 2000, the day of the big blowup between mother and daughter. DeGuerin stated the message was left for Hauser *after* Jennifer had gone to pick up Celeste at Timberlawn.

"I don't remember that."

He pointed out that after she and Jennifer went into hiding they'd stayed at her therapist Peggy Farley's house, and the two had bought a Jeep, which they had at the same time as their two Cadillacs.

He argued that Kristina had sent her mother an anonymous letter—"Hey, Dike, [sic] nobody loves you anymore. Why don't you do something to go join your husband, Steve?"

Kristina appeared upset by the allegation that she'd told her mother to kill herself. "I did not write that letter."

"Do you have any explanation for how, on the original of this letter, there could be an impression of your name, Kristina B-e, in your handwriting?"

"No, I do not."

• • •

At 2:25 P.M., Allison Wetzel was finally up for redirect.

"Kristina, were there ever times that the defendant, Celeste Beard, attempted to write in your handwriting?"

"Correct." Starting when Kristina was in seventh grade, when she had to stay up so late that she didn't get her homework done, Celeste did the homework, and did it in Kristina's handwriting.

Wetzel asked if the redecorating at the Toro Canyon house was only to make the home handicapped-friendly.

"No." Much of it was just for fun, she said.

"Did Charles Burton say anything at all in the spring of 2000 on the subject of whether his client, the defendant, ought to go to Timberlawn?"

Over DeGuerin's objection, Kristina answered, "He kept saying that, Let's hurry up and get her in.' " It was also his idea that she become Celeste's legal guardian.

The attorneys returned to the bench. They seemed to be spending more time in front of the bench than in front of the jury. And in front of the judge they sniped and carped and spoke to each other like bitter spouses in the midst of a billion-dollar divorce.

Finally, back in front of the jury and witness, Wetzel asked Kristina why Steve had thrown a cup of ice at her.

Steve had asked Celeste if she'd had anything to do with his shooting. At that, Celeste wrote a letter and had Kristina read the letter to him. It was the same letter about which Kuperman had testified. After Kris read the letter, she tried to hug Steve, and he was so upset by the letter that he threw the cup of ice at her. The letter said that Celeste couldn't believe he thought she was involved in his shooting.

Wetzel asked Kristina what she remembered of the very end of the phone call in which Celeste said, "I hired somebody to kill Tracey."

Kris said it only lasted for maybe another ten seconds, during which she told Celeste she didn't want to talk to her. And Kristina hung up.

As far as the cursing and name calling by Celeste,

Kristina said that she'd heard such all of her life, and what the jurors heard wasn't all that bad. "I've heard worse."

"What was the reason you broke off your contact with the defendant?"

"I felt like I was seeing things around the house that were kind of odd along the way. I didn't want to believe the truth at first. And then when she told me about the hiring a hit man for Tracey, it really scared me because I felt like she could do that to me."

The "truth" didn't come easily for Kristina. After Jen cleaned out her cash from Christopher's sister's safe deposit box, they eventually escaped to Christopher's family farm. Christopher, Jen, Justin, and Kris sat in Christopher's Expedition with his mother on the speakerphone talking for an hour, trying to convince Kris that her mother was a killer. His mother pointed out x, y, and z—marrying Steve for his money, wanting him dead, the affairs—and together they spelled capital murder.

Annetta Black, an associate forensic analyst for the Travis County District Attorney's Office, took the stand to testify about the hundreds of pages of phone records she'd analyzed. The records were from May 18, 1999, to July 3, 2000.

The witness looked nervous; the defendant looked stressed.

From May 20, 1999, to August 28, 1999, there were 2,576 minutes of calls between Tracey and Celeste, Black said. Calls from Tracey to Celeste and Celeste to Tracey were about equally divided.

However, between August 29, 1999, and October 1, 1999, near the date Celeste allegedly stopped communicating with Tracey until the day before Steve was shot, there were 336 minutes of calls between the two women. Tracey had phoned Celeste for 96 minutes. Celeste had called Tracey for 240 minutes.

From October 2, 1999, the day Steve was shot, to January 26, 2000, the day he was buried, the women spent 389 minutes talking on the phone to each other. Tracey called

Celeste for 79 minutes. Celeste called Tracey a whopping 310 minutes.

On the day before Steve was shot, two calls were made from Tracey's phone to Celeste, while phones connected to Celeste logged 6 calls to Tracey.

The day Steve died, Celeste phoned Tracey three times beginning at 10:10 that morning and going until 2:11 that afternoon, just about the time Celeste learned her husband had died. The first call that day was for 18 minutes. The last call Celeste made was for 7 minutes.

From the day after Steve was buried to July 15, 2000, there were 276 minutes of calls between Tracey and Celeste, with Celeste doing the dialing for 234 minutes compared to Tracey's 42 minutes.

Just before 6 and a little before 7:30 that night, Tracey called Celeste twice, each call for one minute.

When Matt Hennessy got up to cross the witness, Black gave Hennessy what he wanted—all the phone numbers supposedly assigned to Jennifer, Celeste, and Kristina weren't really their numbers, they were registered to Steve Beard. And Black didn't know truly who had the phones; she only knew who they were subscribed to.

Just after 5:30 P.M., the State called Cathy Kelly. She too was a forensic analyst with the DA's office. She'd reviewed several thousand pages of Bank of America records.

On the day Steve died, sixty-four checks were written on his account. Celeste signed all but three checks, despite the fact that Steve was the only one on the account's signature card. The other three checks didn't have a signature at all.

Dick DeGuerin looked stressed. Allison Wetzel didn't, but in fact, she was concerned. She worried that the prosecution had lost momentum.

Thursday, February 27, 2003, was another cold, cloudy day in Austin. By 8:30 A.M., Wetzel and three of the defense attorneys were already arguing at Judge Kocurek's bench.

When DeGuerin walked over to his client, Celeste Beard Johnson chewed gum and urgently spoke to him. She wore a pale blue sweater set that perfectly matched the blue sweaters DeGuerin and Kristina Beard had worn the day before.

At 8:50, after waiting for one juror to arrive, the jury finally walked single file into the courtroom.

Tall Cathy Kelly explained Celeste and Steve Beard's income and expenses.

From April to November 1999, Celeste Beard received $3,000 to $5,000 a month. But in December 1999, the month before Steve Beard died, she received $19,500. In February 2000, the month after he died, Celeste received more than $15,000.

From April to October 1999, Celeste's checking account averaged deposits of $6,000, primarily transfers from Steve's accounts and the twins' accounts. But from October to November of that year, Celeste received deposits of nearly $64,000. Deposits from February to March 2000 totaled nearly $166,000.

The only living expenses Celeste paid, Kelly said, were the AT&T wireless bill and groceries.

"So what was the money being spent on?" Wetzel asked.

"For the most part, it was spent on shopping—clothes, furniture, jewelry."

When Kelly looked at the children's accounts, she discovered that most of the funds from Kristina's account had been transferred to Jennifer's account and the remainder was transferred to Celeste's account. By the same token, the funds that had gone from Kristina's account to Jennifer's were later transferred to Celeste's account.

Kelly presented a May 6, 1999, payment of approximately $107 to the La Quinta Inn in Waco and a May 11, 1999, payment to the City Grill for $141.77. Both were the weekend of Tracey's birthday.

There was also a May 22, 1999, payment of $379.75 to the Leopard Lounge in Atlanta, two July 4, 1999, payments to the Austin gay bar Oilcan Harry's totaling $64.75, and additional payments to the Rainbow Cattle Co., which was another Austin gay bar, and a payment of over $775 to Pappas, a seafood restaurant on Interstate 35.

On March 6, 2000, Celeste deposited a $2 check payable to the long-deceased Elise Beard.

DeGuerin noted that Steve Beard's account was a joint account.

Kelly responded that Steve and Celeste's names were on some of the checks, but only Steve's name was on the signature card. Celeste's wasn't.

Celeste stopped writing on her notepad during her attorney's cross.

Eventually, DeGuerin asked about the checks written on Steve's death day.

"It's just a large number of checks to be written in one day. It stood out."

DeGuerin promptly read the list of the checks with the list sounding like monthly household expenses, including the mortgage.

Irritated, Kelly emphasized that the mortgage hadn't been paid out of either Celeste's or Steve's accounts for months. But moments later, she was off the stand and out the swinging courtroom doors.

When Donna Goodson walked in around mid-morning, her breasts seemed to fill the witness box. On the camera monitors, her skin looked as though she were wearing whiteface.

Gary Cobb had her point out Celeste Beard.

Goodson was hesitant to look at her former party-pal. "She hated that bastard," Goodson said of Celeste and Steve. When Steve Beard got out of the hospital and came to Studio 29 for a manicure, pedicure, and haircut, Celeste had had to give up her appointment for him. "She was a little put out." Then, when Steve returned to the hospital, Celeste told Donna, "I don't want him to die at the house. I'm putting him in the hospital."

There was little new to Goodson's testimony, but much that was left out—the tawdry details of booze, drugs, sex, and hard living.

. . .

"She would feed me one of my numerous anti-depression or anti-anxiety medications at intervals throughout the day. She made me vodka on the rocks as soon as I got up in the morning. She kept me dazed, which is why I wrote extra checks and didn't notice."

"I was just looking to make some quick money," Goodson explained about her offer to hire a hit man for Celeste.

After going to work for the widow Beard, she sort of "accidentally" moved into the Toro Canyon house. She kept her clothes in Steve Beard's closet, which was empty. Then one day she and Celeste went to the lake house, where they discovered two of Steve's robes. Celeste said, "I thought I got rid of all of his shit."

In the courtroom, Celeste fervently talked to Catherine Baen while Goodson moved on and stated that Celeste slept all day and partied all night and repeated that Celeste had written a $10,000 check for Spiro's manager Nick Gikas.

The jurors' pens scribbled hard on their notepads.

"Here," Celeste had said as she handed Nick the check. "No questions asked."

Cobb moved Goodson to March 21, 2000, when she'd driven Celeste to the airport to catch a plane to Timberlawn. Celeste's attorney, Goodson said, "told her to get to the hospital. Nobody could touch her there."

Toward the last week of March or the first week of April, when Goodson phoned Celeste at Timberlawn to tell her that Kristina was asking a lot of questions about the money Celeste had paid her, Celeste responded, " 'I'll fix that little bitch' and hung up."

In the courtroom, Celeste looked nervous.

Dick DeGuerin immediately zeroed in on Donna Goodson's Louisiana pawn tickets—a ring with a total weight of 7 and a half carats, a 14-karat gold necklace, a Sony digital camera, and a Casio color TV.

An attentive Celeste watched as Donna turned to Dick DeGuerin and stated it was the ring she'd pawned for an alternator in Lake Charles—"Dick."

"*Who* told you you could call me 'Dick!' "

Judge Kocurek grinned. She purposely called Dick "Mr. DeGuerin."

DeGuerin placed photos on the Elmo, which splashed them up on the screen—Goodson in a long, blonde wig at Mardi Gras, her dark-colored blouse unbuttoned to reveal a black bra pulling together cleavage, a diamond-looking necklace with apparently the initials CB in the pendant hanging in the cleavage, animal print sunglasses on her head, an animal print scarf draped over her shoulders, and animal print gloves on her hands, which were on Celeste Beard's bra-covered breasts.

"You were willing to blackmail Celeste just for not returning your phone calls, weren't you?"

"Yes." The topless photos of Celeste that Goodson had snapped six weeks after Steve's death were not just of Celeste. They were of Cole with his arms around the topless Celeste.

DeGuerin flashed up photos of the pawned items, each time with a voice insinuating that the pictures were damningly inflammatory.

"That's a very expensive watch, isn't it?"

"I don't know," Goodson said. "Is it?"

"I'm asking the questions," he barked, as if the honky-tonk-looking hanger-on were usurping his power.

During the lunch break, DeGuerin griped that Goodson had called him "Dick" on purpose. After the break, a wan Celeste hobbled into the courtroom.

"You were swindling Celeste out of money," DeGuerin stated to Donna.

"Absolutely." Her face and jaw line were square like *The Jetsons*' Rosie the Robot.

Gary Cobb asked his witness why she felt safe in jail.

"There was no doubt in my mind that I would be next. It's just Celeste's way."

The State entered Exhibit 199, a photo of Steve Beard. As it flashed on the large screen for the jury to see, Becky Beard wept.

And the State rested—with Steve Beard's photo still smiling at the jury.

One of DeGuerin's former law students slipped over to the Elmo and flipped it off so that Steve could no longer be a reminder to the jury of why they were there.

Dick DeGuerin stood. The State had failed to corroborate Tracey Tarlton's testimony. He requested a mistrial.

36

By Thursday night, with the first stage of the prosecution complete, Allison Wetzel was relieved and ready to relax and laugh a bit.

She grinned her wry grin as she recalled that at the bench, Kocurek had told her to keep it moving. "I could keep it moving a lot faster if I didn't have all these interruptions with frivolous objections."

DeGuerin "got *so* pissed off and hissed, 'Judge, tell her to stop making personal remarks about me!' Hmmm," she smiled, "who's getting under whose skin?"

But Wetzel didn't stop. She was feeling good. The day before, she'd told Gary Cobb that DeGuerin looked like he hadn't washed his hair. "And today his hair looked so greasy it was shining on top. Don't they have free shampoo in the rooms at the Four Seasons? Gee, when we picked the jury, he had a fresh haircut and looked pretty sharp, except for the sweater."

On top of that, she was proud of Donna calling DeGuerin "Dick." "When the jury is laughing with the witness at the expense of the defense attorney, that is wonderful and rare."

Still, she knew no trial, especially this one, which was going so well for her, had a guaranteed guilty ending. She thought of the cameras in the courtroom that would be focusing on Celeste, the family members, and even the lawyers when the verdict was read. "In case of bad news, I will try to remember not to mouth something obscene."

Car wrecks jammed up Austin on Monday morning, March 3, 2003. Rain and chill had drivers losing control. Dick DeGuerin hoped he finally could gain control.

Just before court, in a Hershey chocolate–colored sweater set, Celeste had been laughing with one of DeGuerin's law students. She was on DeGuerin's witness list. By the time court was in session, Celeste looked perfectly angelic.

Across the room, Allison Wetzel wore killer red.

With his poster board exhibit saying "Suicidal, Homicidal, Delusional, Psychotic" already displayed, DeGuerin called Dr. Bernard Gotway.

Looking a bit like a walrus with his graying hair and bushy gray moustache, Gotway often turned toward the jury as he spoke about childhood trauma causing psychological problems. More often, he focused his gaze on DeGuerin, who casually questioned the Ph.D.

DeGuerin asked about Celeste being at the hospital to get away from her husband.

"I think she very much needed treatment," he answered without answering.

Celeste sat behind the defense desk constantly wiping her nose.

Gotway sighed as he stated Steve had been concerned that Celeste was trying to avoid him. She'd had a tendency to pick up trailer trash, according to Steve, and he was upset about that. That comment was nowhere to be found in Gotway's typed notes, which were flashed up on the screen.

As Gotway spoke about how Celeste had wanted the marriage to continue, she grew teary-eyed.

His typed notes said Steve had been "very supportive of treatment. Patient has difficulty 'asking' for things. She says she has trouble asserting herself."

Gotway didn't mention his March 25, 1999, session with Celeste: "She has needs to make things clean, does hand-washing (excessive), refused to go to the bathroom at times for fear of contamination. Discussed with Dr. Miller."

"Don't touch that! A dog might have peed on it," Celeste constantly scolded the twins. But Gotway didn't know that, or that it had turned Kristina, in her own words, into a "germ freak."

"Kristina wouldn't even sit on the same toilet seat as Steve. I'm serious. She—you can ask my mother about that. She bitched if Steve went to the bathroom in the, uh, mud room because she did not want to use that toilet seat if he sat on it."

March 26, 1999, Celeste talked about her sexual abuse, which Gotway saw as her major problem. According to the typed notes, Celeste blamed herself for not telling anyone about her molestation.

On April 1, 1999, Celeste talked about how she felt some responsibility for Craig's suicide and about her "possessive roommate," who was talking about suicide. The roommate, Gotway said, was trying to get all of Celeste's attention and control her. He told Celeste she wasn't responsible for her roommate.

In the courtroom, Celeste looked even more teary-eyed.

Gotway, Celeste, and Steve met for another session of family therapy on April 2. Celeste wanted her own money to control. She was, Gotway said, being "nickeled and dimed." But he later stated that the only reason Celeste got the treatment she needed was because she was self-pay.

On May 11, 1999, Gotway wrote about Celeste's weekend, the weekend that he didn't know she'd spent at the La Quinta, celebrated Tracey's birthday, and wrote Steve about divorce because he'd screamed at her that the girls hadn't turned out the lights.

"Celeste came back early after having a fight with her husband. It appeared to revolve around her not spending time with him . . ."

Gotway and Celeste seemed to believe that her interactions and reactions to Steve were reenactments of her life with her father—she was rebelling against the control.

"Celeste told of having 'funeral clothes' in her closet

ever since the girls were born. She has always wanted to be prepared for their death if anything happened. This relates to a loss of best friend when she was 12–13 years old and patient blamed herself because she refused to go in the car and her friend was killed. She still blames herself," Gotway's June 4 note from his session with Celeste read.

When court recessed for a restroom break, the court watchers grumbled, "What is this accomplishing?"

Upon return, DeGuerin didn't have Gotway go through the details of the remaining 1999 notes including, ". . . Says that she actually replaced the whole toilet because a workman used it one time. She also has used a black light to look for germs when on a trip."

Instead, testimony moved to 2000 and the conversations about guardianship. He told Celeste's attorney, "This is a very bad idea." It would just replicate the situation Celeste had had with Steve—having to ask him for money.

"Celeste is complex," Gotway concluded. She was histrionic, depressed, withdrawn, impulsive, and not a strategic thinker due to post-traumatic stress disorder.

DeGuerin emphasized *not* a strategic thinker and asked if Celeste Beard could have influenced Tracey Tarlton to kill Steve Beard, perhaps as far back as August 1999.

"Objection." Wetzel yelled. "That's for the jury to decide."

Kocurek agreed. And the witness was passed.

Wetzel pointed out how many months Gotway had gone without seeing Celeste, that his information about her was provided by her, that the staff had seen her as demanding, manipulative, feeling entitled, and attention-seeking.

Gotway didn't seem happy with Wetzel's line of questioning. He claimed he was "aware of that side."

Celeste had entered a psychiatric hospital in 1995 and again in 1999 for having an affair with Jimmy Martinez, Wetzel noted.

Gotway didn't know about that either.

He had stated that on March 24, 1999, Celeste had told him that she'd never before mentioned to anyone the sexual abuse. Yet she had—during her 1995 psychiatric hospitalization, Wetzel said.

Gotway tried to explain that away by saying that's what he'd written, but that it might not be literally true.

The jurors leaned forward and listened.

Gotway looked disbelieving as Wetzel asked him if Celeste ever told him that she'd replaced Steve's vodka with Everclear. She pointed out that Celeste talked to Gotway about cutting off her children, and wasn't that an example of her being manipulative?

He admitted it was.

Wetzel told him Celeste had reported her daughters to the cops for stealing her jewelry.

A dumbfounded look covered the Ph.D.'s face.

And, Celeste hadn't told Gotway that she'd threatened to kill Kristina. There was nothing in Gotway's notes about Celeste wanting to hire a hit man to kill Tracey, despite the fact that the patient had mentioned it to the therapist.

DeGuerin's hand went to his mouth.

Gotway said that that wasn't important because it was weeks, months in the past.

He'd had an ethical obligation to report that to the police, and he hadn't, Wetzel argued. She asked the psychologist if he didn't even write it in his notes because he'd wanted to protect Celeste.

Gotway didn't answer.

Wetzel repeated the question.

"Probably, yes."

Celeste Beard Johnson looked forlorn.

On redirect, Gotway stated that Celeste had explained the hit man deal as just someone trying to get money from her, and she'd already decided not to go through with the idea.

Wetzel struck back noting that Gotway had stated Celeste was so grief-stricken over Steve's death that she couldn't even say he was dead. But had she told the therapist that within three weeks of Steve's death she was dating?

No.

She stated that, since Gotway had pronounced Celeste not guilty, there was no need to even have a trial.

DeGuerin bolted out of his chair, jammed his hands on

his hips and objected. He demanded to ask another question, despite the fact that he'd been allowed his two chances at direct.

The judge allowed him one more question.

But DeGuerin couldn't remember it. He had forgotten it because he was so angry.

Just after 2 P.M., former Timberlawn intern Susan Milholland stepped into the witness box. When she'd worked with the very ill Tracey Tarlton, not only was Milholland getting her Masters of Arts in Counseling, but she was also working only part-time.

Dick DeGuerin tried to get the pretty, slender, young blonde with her hair pulled back in a ponytail held by a barrette, and who wore a scooped-neck black shell, to say that Tracey recruited straight women.

Milholland said Tracey reenacted her abandonment from her family. And after Tracey and Celeste were no longer roommates, Tracey had become suicidal. That was why she'd been transferred to the adult psych unit. But when Tracey believed Celeste had gotten her transferred to the new unit, Milholland told her that was very "distorted thinking."

DeGuerin referred to it as "delusional thinking." But DeGuerin had other things on which to focus—Tracey's statement that all would be solved by the "untimely death of a certain person."

"I was very concerned," Milholland said. Tracey played it off as a joke and said she wasn't homicidal then and never had been.

And that, DeGuerin stated, conflicted with other information Milholland had about Tracey. He wanted to get in again that adolescent Tracey Tarlton had wanted to hire a hit man to kill her mother. Instead of that happening, there was another argument at the bench. Not only did the attorneys discuss Tracey's youthful homicide talk, DeGuerin complained that Wetzel and Cobb were whispering.

That was just Allison talking to herself, Cobb said.

Kocurek laughed, and court resumed with Milholland

saying she was so concerned about Tracey's statement, which she knew in her gut to be about Steve Beard, that she'd taken her worry to a team meeting. The threat was so vague, though, the team decided that no further action was needed.

But DeGuerin wanted to know if intern Milholland thought Tracey was homicidal.

She believed Tracey was homicidal and delusional.

Wetzel returned to her same themes on cross—was kissing on the mouth, sleeping in the same bed, going to couples counseling setting boundaries?

Milholland didn't look pleased to be talking to Wetzel. She thought long before responding and tried to give vague answers—the boundaries were down on the first two and "it depends" on the last.

Wetzel asked about the gold and silver wedding band given to Tracey as Celeste said, "So you'll always know where you belong."

That could be evidence of just a close friendship, Milholland said.

Carrying a brown accordion file, Dr. Howard Miller walked into the courtroom. With eyeglasses and graying hair, he resembled Fred Flintstone's boss. He wasn't a forensic psychiatrist and had testified in only one other trial, he stated in a voice that sounded dry and gravelly. He took a sip of water.

His head seemed to sit on his shoulders rather than his neck. His chin jutted out like a caveman's. When Celeste and Tracey were at Timberlawn, he'd served as the medical director of the trauma program. He was Celeste's treating physician in 1999. Celeste, he said, was not faking an illness.

DeGuerin plodded. Jurors yawned. Some looked irritated. Others looked bored. He asked about Celeste's condition in the spring of 1999.

Celeste's personality structure, Miller said, was dependent. She wanted people to like her to a fault. She became demanding, briefly, then quickly became regretful. "Consistency was not her strong suit at all."

Howard moved on to Tracey, whose medical records he'd reviewed. Tracey, he said, suffered bipolar disorder with psychotic features.

Psychotic—DeGuerin had to repeat the word.

With Tracey, Howard said, "she may have been delusional" about her relationship with Celeste. Tracey desperately needed someone to love her and tell her she was worthwhile to heal the pain from her mother's abuse. She had a need to believe she had a relationship with Celeste.

Wetzel scribbled on her notepad as hard and fast as Celeste had written during the State's case.

37

"No sidebars today, Mr. DeGuerin. I'm not in the mood," Kocurek gruffed at the senior attorney on March 4, 2003, the second day of the defense case. Laughter from the jurors gathered in the back hallway filtered into the courtroom as Kocurek joked with everyone but DeGuerin. Be here on time or "we'll be here until Easter," Kocurek grinned at them when they walked in at 8:50 A.M. on the cool, cloudy Tuesday.

DeGuerin's expert witness on Tracey Tarlton, who'd never treated Tracey, continued his testimony about her. She couldn't get straight what was really going on around her, Dr. Howard Miller stated.

DeGuerin stopped his witness. The noise of flipping papers by one of his own law students who was organizing DeGuerin's files was bothering him. DeGuerin ordered his student out of the courtroom.

Tracey made up her own words and created her own language; her illness affected her ability to contain her emotions, Miller continued.

Wetzel interrupted. She walked up to the judge, whispered, and walked back to her seat, glaring at the defense table, while pushing her hair behind her right ear, which she always did when she walked away from the bench.

Miller proceeded to talk about the sexual abuse and daily violence Tracey had experienced growing up. Everything the doctor reported about Tracey Tarlton was also in Celeste Beard's medical records—bipolar, sexually abused, experienced violence in the home. "If there were to be a pattern of violent behavior it would be significant," Miller said, never acknowledging the patients' parallels.

"Is Tracey Tarlton prone to violence?"

"Yes." Even her suicide attempts were violent, the doctor claimed. She played Russian roulette rather than overdosing like most suicidal women did. Apparently, the $300-an-hour, expert witness hadn't read about Tracey's numerous overdoses and hadn't heard DeGuerin argue they were all suicide attempts.

The psychiatrist said he'd sat in on the staff meeting where they'd discussed Tracey's "threat"—if a certain person died . . . "We took this threat seriously." But since Tracey hadn't made a specific or imminent threat, he simply took it upon himself to urge Celeste to limit her relationship with Tracey.

"I believe Tracey sustains a delusional belief that the relationship with Celeste was much more than it was," Miller swore. He stated that innumerable times as DeGuerin read from Tracey's journal the same passages he'd read repeatedly throughout the trial: "I believe she is strongly attracted to me."

In fact, every statement DeGuerin made about Tracey Tarlton, Dr. Miller explained away as a delusional belief by Tracey. And each time he said it was a delusional belief, he punctuated his answers with numerous *um*s and *ah*s.

Some of the jurors looked like they were one breath from dozing off as Miller continued his use of the word *delusional*. With Tracey Tarlton's family history of violence, it was reasonable, he said, that her delusional belief would lead to violence.

Based on the doctor's personal knowledge, DeGuerin

asked, did Tracey Tarlton have the capacity to plan Steve Beard's murder on her own?

"I believe that she was capable of doing such a thing."

DeGuerin wondered if Celeste had the long-range mental capability to manipulate Tracey into killing Steve.

"No, I don't believe she does." Part of her treatment was to help her learn to plan ahead.

DeGuerin brought out letters Tracey had written to another inmate, Felicia Hicks. He claimed that Tracey had been obsessed with Felicia and referred to Felicia as her wife, and that Felicia had tried to sever ties with Tracey and Tracey wouldn't let her.

Tracey had to believe she had a wonderful relationship with someone even when she didn't, Miller stated.

At that, DeGuerin asked if Tracey Tarlton was suicidal, homicidal, delusional and psychotic.

"At times, yes. All of these."

Dr. Howard Miller was reluctant to answer Allison Wetzel's questions. When Wetzel said Tracey didn't hear voices all the time, the defense's expert on Tarlton said he wasn't sure. To other questions, he said he didn't recall or didn't have his notes.

She asked Dr. Miller whether, if ten people had testified that Tracey and Celeste were having a sexual relationship, he would still believe Tracey was delusional at Timberlawn.

Yes, he answered. Miller also stated under oath that Celeste wasn't narcissistic. And despite having been the murder defendant's doctor and the medical director of Timberlawn's trauma program during Celeste's and the admitted shooter's stays at the psychiatrics facility, he swore he had no concerns about liability.

Wetzel inquired about his experience with murderers.

"I have no experience with people who commit murder."

But, he admitted the fact that Celeste trying to kill herself with a gun indicated she was more violent than the average suicidal patient.

. . .

In a navy blue suit over a red mock turtleneck, with a 1960s bouffant do, and hair the same color as Allison Wetzel's, Dr. Michelle Hauser took the stand. Hauser had first sat down with a depressed Celeste Beard on February 24, 1999.

Celeste, who said she'd been on anti-depressants since she was 15 years old, was always unhappy. She could go days without sleeping. She felt so hyper that she ran errands all the time. She was irritable, cried every day, and had just spent $250,000 on clothes and furniture, which was well over her $50,000-a-month budget.

February 24, 1999, eleven days after Celeste's 36th birthday, she had been admitted to St. David's Pavilion for major depression, recurrent, though she didn't want to be put on any medications that caused her to gain weight.

There, Celeste's inappropriate boundaries had become apparent to the doctor. Celeste had bought clothing for a patient; she'd bought pizzas for the entire unit because the food was bad.

Talking fast and breathlessly, as though she were desperate to get out the information, Hauser stated that upon Celeste's March 6, 1999, discharge, Celeste had been diagnosed as suffering major depression, recurrent moderate, rule out personality disorder—meaning a personality disorder hadn't been ruled out.

On March 8, 1999, Hauser reviewed her patient's recent testing by Byron D. Barnes, Ph.D. "I think it takes a lot of guts to go through with it," Celeste told Barnes regarding suicide. When asked to complete the sentence, "I regret . . ." she wrote, "being born—how's that."

"My father," she completed, "hopefully is dead."

When asked to create a story, she told about a man who was sneaking up on his napping wife, while thinking, "I want her dead." He'd feel relief when she was gone, and he killed her, she said.

In neat, legible cursive, Hauser wrote that Celeste's personality was "dependent, narcissistic & histrionic traits."

Hauser recommended long-term, in-patient care. She soon contacted facilities from Arizona to Pennsylvania, ranging in cost from $12,800 to $31,000. But Celeste had been talking to a friend about various hospitals. She wanted to go to Menninger. Hauser tried to talk her out of Menninger—it didn't have a specific trauma program.

Celeste wouldn't hear of it.

"Doesn't want to be around husband," Hauser wrote.

Later that day, Hauser talked on the phone with Steve and Celeste, again urging them away from Menninger and to Timberlawn or a facility called River Oaks because they both had specialized trauma programs.

Celeste became upset at that change of plan, but she agreed not to hurt herself.

Before the workday ended, EMS phoned Dr. Hauser. They'd been called to the Toro Canyon house. Kristina thought Celeste had overdosed on seven to ten pills of Ambien. Through slurred words, Celeste said she'd taken four pills to go to sleep.

Kristina took her mother to the emergency room for an evaluation. That same day, Celeste was readmitted to St. David's. The next day, March 11, Hauser went to the hospital to meet with Steve, Kristina, and a furious Celeste. She didn't overdose, she told everyone again, and she didn't want to be in the hospital. Hauser discharged the patient.

March 12, Celeste told Hauser she was afraid Steve was committing her to a hospital and going to divorce her. Five years before, when she was committed to Charter, Celeste said, Steve had changed the locks on the house and served her with divorce papers.

Ironically, and ignored by the doctor and defense attorney, at Timberlawn, Celeste wrote on her pre-admission form that, after she got out of the hospital, "I plan to temporarily live at my lake house . . . until I can make a decision on whether to continue my marriage."

By July, Celeste was out of Timberlawn and back with Dr. Hauser, ready to work on her relationship with Steve.

But on July 20, two days before she was to leave for the Pacific Northwest, Celeste told Dr. Hauser she was depressed. She was stressed about driving with Steve. She was also upset that she'd found out Kristina had lied to her and was having sex with Justin. Kristina was the only person she'd ever trusted, and Kristina had betrayed her.

Hauser jotted on a Prozac notepad, "Narcissistic injury continue current meds."

That night, Celeste and Kris had a session with Kristina's therapist, Peggy Farley, and Celeste told Kristina that she was the result of a rape by Craig Bratcher. Hauser thought the confession was a good thing. Celeste told Hauser the next day that she hadn't admitted to Kris that her second pregnancy, the baby she'd given up for adoption, was also the result of Craig raping her.

The doctor always looked down from the witness box and at DeGuerin as she spoke. Celeste thought Tracey was trying to manipulate her. Hauser was concerned because she believed Celeste was easily influenced and Tracey could negatively influence Celeste. She talked to Celeste about ending the relationship because the lesbian was unstable and disturbed.

September 15, Celeste missed her appointment with Dr. Hauser. That was the day Steve Beard passed out, for the second time in three days, and was taken to North Austin Medical Center, for the second time in three days, due to, according to Tracey, she and Celeste putting a plastic bag over his head. Hauser and DeGuerin didn't mention that.

September 20, Steve called and left a message for Hauser. They spoke the next day. Steve was worried. Celeste was seeing three to five doctors a week. She acted guilty. And she'd gotten "violently upset" and had thrown a screaming tantrum. She was making plans without consulting him or the twins, and she didn't include him in her weekend plans. Worse, she was using different charge accounts, some in her own name, some in aliases.

On December 1, 1999, Hauser wrote in Celeste's file that Celeste was still feeling overwhelmed by everything, and she'd cleaned out her closets and thrown out things.

On January 26, the day of Steve's funeral, Hauser continued her practice of okaying prescription refills for Celeste, without seeing the patient. But she did actually see Celeste the following day. All Celeste could think about was

Steve. She thought they didn't change his colostomy bag often enough when he was in rehab, which caused wound contamination that led to sepsis. Hauser prescribed 30 mg of Restoril to help Celeste sleep.

Hauser skipped her February 3, 2000, notes about her meeting with Celeste during which Celeste said she had a staph infection on her right index finger and had had to see a hand surgeon for it.

Around 3 P.M. on February 17, 2000, the day after Celeste had stabbed herself in the arm and leg at Studio 29, Dr. M. T. Valls' pager went off. St. David's Pavilion was trying to reach the doctor because "a strange looking woman named Tracey came out to the unit looking for Celeste." Valls, who was covering for Hauser, phoned Celeste to warn her.

Celeste told Valls she'd made a suicide attempt the previous night and had been taken to North Austin Hospital.

The next day, Celeste and Valls spoke again on the phone, with Celeste explaining that she'd been going through Steve's legal and estate papers, which made her feel worse and lose control.

February 21, 2000, a week after Celeste's trek to Houston and Lake Charles with Donna Goodson, Celeste sat in Valls' office, thirty-five minutes late to her appointment. She said she felt "under lock and key." She also felt increasing guilt and sadness over Steve's death and the events that had caused his death. She was second-guessing every move and decision she'd made in the weeks before his death.

At 12:40 P.M. a week later, on February 28, Celeste phoned Dr. Hauser. "Emergency," she wailed. "Call right back." Crying and sad, Celeste said, "I don't want to live without Steve." She was awake all night long thinking about him. She constantly checked his closet to see if was really gone.

Unknown to Hauser, Celeste was already sleeping with Cole Johnson. Unknown to Hauser, Justin Grimm watched Celeste phone in her sessions to Hauser, complain of not sleeping, then hang up and howl with laughter that she wasn't sleeping because she'd been partying all night on Sixth Street.

St. Patrick's Day, the day Celeste, Cole, and Donna went to the Dog & Duck pub, Kristina left a message for Hauser. "Call attorney Al Golden. The guardianship for Celeste can't be arranged today. So Celeste wants to go to Timberlawn on Monday or Tuesday. However, Kristina says guardianship can be done today and wants her to go on Saturday."

But Hauser agreed with Gotway—Celeste was competent. Plus, she felt Kristina had her own emotional problems.

April 4, 2000, Hauser's phone rang again with Kristina on the line. She wanted to have her guardianship over her mother set up as soon as possible. She was concerned about Celeste going to Las Vegas with a "thug."

The doctor and DeGuerin ignored Hauser's next notation regarding Celeste. The very next day, Kristina's therapist, Peggy Farley, called Hauser. Celeste, Farley said, was out of Timberlawn and stalking Kristina. Jennifer had gone to Dallas to get her mother, and Celeste had said that Kristina would "pay" for not coming to get her. "Kristina is scared—Mom will hurt her. Mom is also getting married! Has lied about many things," the message continued.

April 14, Celeste and Hauser spoke for sixty minutes. Abandoned by the twins and Donna, Hauser urged Celeste to return to Timberlawn. She wanted Celeste in a place where she could be more contained. Celeste had said maybe she should just hire a hit man.

"Celeste," the psychiatrist understated, "I would say that's not using good judgment." She told her, "Don't go there"—find another way to deal with anger. Like Gotway, Hauser didn't document Celeste's words. She said she didn't think Celeste was serious.

On cross-examination, Wetzel began by letting the jury know that the good doctor was hostile to the prosecution— she'd refused to return Wetzel's calls and she hadn't given the district attorney's office all of the requested medical records, as she had for the defense.

The jurors could see that for themselves. Hauser, who'd

been eager and verbose for the defense, was calmer but less forthcoming to the prosecution.

Wetzel pulled out Celeste's medical records from St. David's and pointed out where Celeste was verbally abusive and had phoned and fired Hauser on March 11, 1999.

Hauser said she didn't recall that.

Wetzel read Celeste's words from the records: "That's just the kind of bitch I am."

DeGuerin looked up.

Hauser admitted that was typical.

Celeste's medical records showed that she complained to the staff that they weren't knocking on her door before entering her room. When she went to the nurses' desk and wasn't immediately acknowledged, she yelled, "Does anybody work here or are we supposed to all help ourselves!" She screamed that she'd waited an hour and a half for her medications. "I'm paying a lot of money for this!" She griped, "I'm not being a prima donna or anything, but I'm accustomed to living a level above everyone else here."

Wetzel noted that Celeste wanted to bring in her own maid at St. David's.

Hauser confessed that that possibly sounded like something Celeste would say. And she admitted she didn't know about Celeste's affair with Jimmy Martinez, which was ongoing while Celeste was telling the doctor she wanted to work on her marriage with Steve. She couldn't recall if Celeste talked about going to couples counseling with Tracey. She didn't know about Celeste sleeping in the same bed with Tracey, kissing her, giving her a wedding ring.

As Wetzel continued rattling off the details of the relationship, Hauser looked like all of the information was spinning in her head like the reels of a slot machine. DeGuerin wanted to approach the bench, and Celeste wrote hard and fast on her notepad.

Wetzel read from Celeste's 1995 medical records and stay at Charter Hospital where she was diagnosed with borderline personality disorder and depression. She asked the doctor if she believed Celeste was serious about hiring a hit man after hearing the tape—"I hired somebody to kill Tracey."

"I don't know," Hauser answered.

So Wetzel asked her if she would have taken it seriously if Hauser had known Celeste had pointed out Tracey's house to Donna Goodson.

To that, Hauser answered yes.

When court recessed just before 5 P.M., Judge Kocurek announced that there had been a courthouse bomb threat at 9 A.M., but the Travis County Sheriff's Office hadn't taken it seriously.

38

By Wednesday, March 5, 2003, moods were wearying. Jurors had left the courthouse the day before complaining about how boring Monday and Tuesday were. An older female juror began Wednesday by griping at the deputies running the courthouse security screener. "I'm just doing my job," the deputy politely responded. In the courtroom, bailiff Michael Kinkaid tried to ease the tension by handing a normally tardy juror a big gold star for being on time.

Around 8:25 A.M., Jimmy Martinez, seemingly always smiling, schlepped in. He looked casual, relaxed, and confident. But his demeanor belied his mood. His birthday had been the day before, and DeGuerin had not allowed him to get drunk. *Dickhead*, he'd thought.

DeGuerin instructed Martinez to sit down. Martinez sat in a chair right behind DeGuerin. DeGuerin turned to Martinez and ordered him to move, saying that that chair was reserved for attorneys. Martinez moved to the chair Becky Beard normally occupied. Again, DeGuerin told Martinez to move. Finally, Martinez sat down with a network TV producer and laughed and joked that DeGuerin was only going to ask him two questions.

Celeste crutched in five minutes later, wearing a sea foam green sweater set and a black skirt. When she saw Jimmy, her face lighted bright.

Martinez took the stand with a shake of his hands in the air. "Hi, I'm Jimmy Martinez," he said, then laughed. Martinez wore his usual cowboy boots, creased blue jeans, and sport coat. His thick, coal-black hair was combed straight back.

In November 1998, Celeste Beard sat with Dawn Madigan in Katz's, a loud, always busy, New York–style deli that never closed on downtown's Sixth Street. The two phoned Jimmy and convinced him to meet them for drinks. He did, and he and Celeste went back to his house. She didn't stay all night, he swore, and he didn't think of it as an affair. "I looked at it as we were just friends."

Celeste didn't look happy.

They got together a couple of times that month. Sometimes she came to his house; sometimes they met at a tavern on Parmer Lane in north Austin, close to where he lived, far from where Steve lived.

"I started back up with Jimmy, let me think, only for a few months. It was back in like September. No, no, no, no, no. It was, um, we were not doing anything by September. It was back in, I don't know. I don't remember, because in my mind, I didn't look at it as an affair because I was already married to him once. So in my mind that was, like, okay. And he was safe because there wasn't going to be any, you know, going anywhere.

"But Steven and I hadn't had sex in I don't know how many years, I mean, not that that's, you know, that's a reason. Do I feel guilty about it now? Yeah, yeah, I do. Did Steve know about it? Yes, because when we went out, I'd put it on my credit card. And, you know, Steve went over all the bills.

"And I kept it on that side of town. I didn't—I didn't bring anything over to our side of town, to the Country Club, or to anything like that. I felt like, you know, I kept it over there because, you know, Steve wasn't stupid."

• • •

One January night at the Parmer Lane tavern, Jimmy and Celeste talked about the twins' upcoming 18th birthday. Celeste grabbed a napkin and pen, started writing and planning. Once she started planning, Jimmy said, she was pretty much going to see it through.

The graduation party at his house, he said, was his idea. His friends were there, and Celeste's friends were there.

DeGuerin asked if the graduation party was the first time Martinez had met Tracey Tarlton.

"Oh, yes." He chuckled. Earlier, at the first mention of Tracey, Jimmy had laughed and cut his dark eyes to the right as if making fun of her.

"How did she appear to you?"

"Weird," Martinez answered. "She dresses like a guy."

A juror didn't look pleased.

Martinez said he saw Tracey and Celeste dancing and Jennifer and Amy drinking too much. Amy threw up in a trashcan, and Jen threw up too with Christopher trying to take care of her. Martinez put Amy on a daybed. "The room is spinning," she told Jimmy. "Put a foot on the floor," he advised. "That won't work," she said. So he put her foot on the floor for her and she said it worked.

DeGuerin asked if Celeste drank too much.

Yes, Martinez said.

Abruptly DeGuerin turned to the judge and moaned that the prosecutors were making noise. He asked the judge to scold them.

Kocurek replied that she couldn't hear them, and she asked the jurors if it was bothering them. They all shook their heads.

Testimony continued with Martinez saying Kristina came to him and said, " 'Jimmy, would you come get Tracey off my mom?' " He went upstairs to find Celeste sleeping and Tracey on top of her trying to kiss Celeste on the ear and fooling with Celeste's hair.

"Tracey, get out of here!" She ignored him, he swore. He touched Tracey, who then rolled off the other side of the bed, and Celeste mumbled, " 'Tell her I'm not a lesbian. Tell her to leave me alone.' " Jimmy ordered her to leave.

Tracey didn't act like she'd had too much to drink, he testified. In fact, as she left, she turned to him and said, "You tell that Celeste to be at my house in one hour." She stormed out the door, and he locked it behind her.

When the party ended at 3 A.M., Martinez had one more beer and passed out in the backyard, he said.

"The graduation party was talked about in front of Steve at the Club. That is when Kristina invited Tracey to come. The next night was the party. . . . I had way too many cocktails to the point of getting sick. I went upstairs and layed [sic] down on Jimmy's bed (fully clothed). The next thing I know it's the next day and Jimmy & Kristina told me that Tracey tried to molest me. Kristina said that she came upstairs and Tracey was trying to kiss me, but I was passed out. Jimmy said that I was mumbling to him that Tracey wants me to be a lesbian."

Gary Cobb poured himself a cup of water, leaned back in his chair with his legs crossed, and swirled the ice in his cup as if he were lounging around the pool sipping lemonade.

Martinez outlined the security that he and the company High Fidelity had installed for the Beards following Steve's shooting, after discovering some sliding doors that didn't trip the alarm system—four video cameras that became ten at Celeste's urging, four more video cameras at the lake house, two time-lapse recorders at both houses, a video-phone in the doorbell at Toro Canyon.

DeGuerin, with dark bags under his eyes, moved to the $75,000 check Celeste had written Martinez.

Martinez explained it was a tip for doing the job so quickly, and he had signed the check back to Celeste.

Just before 11 A.M., the witness was passed and Machine Gun Gary fired. If Jimmy had had sex with Celeste only six times and if she'd told people that she had a continual sexual relationship with him, did that mean she was delusional? he asked.

"I can't say yes or no about that."

DeGuerin objected over and over again, with Kocurek overruling him again and again, until she ordered him to the bench. Afterwards, Martinez said, "I know I had sex with her, but I never kept count."

Cobb retorted, "Do you have a BMW?"

With his thin lips spreading into a grin, Martinez said, "Yes, I do. It's not a car."

Cobb started to say that BMW was Celeste's pet name for—

"Hold on!" DeGuerin madly cried.

I owe Gary a cheap bottle of wine to reward him for getting that in, Wetzel thought with a smile.

Jimmy probably would have been pleased that Celeste told the kids she had had such hot, rough sex with him that once it threw her into a nightstand and gave her a black eye.

When cross-examination continued, Cobb repeatedly asked if Celeste and Jimmy had been a couple.

DeGuerin cried foul and objected so many times, with Kocurek overruling him so many times that she eventually said, "Over-ruled," slowly and meticulously as if she were talking to a child.

Cobb pointed out that Jimmy and Celeste separated on December 23, 1993, and showed Martinez State's Exhibit 201, his divorce decree from Celeste filed on April 19, 1994. He began to go into the property settlement, but DeGuerin objected on relevancy.

The records stated Celeste had $5,000 of personal effects to Jimmy's $3,000, although Celeste was renowned for moving into Steve's house with a few grocery sacks full of belongings and a bicycle. The divorce papers also stated Celeste moved into Steve's home on December 23, 1993, not New Year's 1994.

Cobb stated that the Martinez family was $20,000 in debt due to loans, credit cards, and the IRS when they divorced.

Martinez responded that those were Celeste's debts.

Astounded, Cobb questioned whether the IRS was Celeste's debt alone. Cobb had to repeat the question many times because DeGuerin objected a multitude of times.

Once more, the attorneys gathered at the bench. DeGuerin's head hung as he returned to his table, and Cobb asked the question again.

Martinez rambled an answer.

"Is that a yes or no?" Cobb retorted, and the spectators laughed. Cobb continued jibing Martinez as he questioned the witness about his affair with Celeste, until he finally asked if Celeste had ever told Martinez that she loved Steve Beard.

"Yes, she loved him," the ex-husband and adulterer said. "I'm sure she loved me, too." While they were having their affair, Celeste probably told him she loved him, but he couldn't remember.

Celeste looked weepy.

Cobb asked Martinez about the witness's testimony that he'd slept outside the night of the graduation party.

Martinez responded by saying that Cobb was looking at him like the prosecutor didn't think he was telling the truth.

With Cobb asking Martinez about money and bills, Martinez stated that in perhaps August 2001, Celeste gave him $9,000 or $10,000 in seed money for his business. He never paid her back the money, though, because she was married to someone else at the time, he said.

Cole Johnson believed Celeste had given the money to Jimmy. "He owes her," he was known to have stated out loud.

"Would you do anything for her?"

"Yes."

Cobb asked if Martinez would be surprised that Celeste and Tracey had gone to couples counseling.

"Yes, that would definitely surprise me." He nervously laughed.

"Sounds like they had a relationship?"

"It sounds like it."

Cobb showed Martinez a photo of Celeste and Tracey dancing together and asked if it looked like Tracey was stalking Celeste.

"Stalking?" he said. "They look like they're laughing."

• • •

A cold rain misted the city while jurors joked over lunch. They wanted to know who was in the gallery, particularly the guy wearing a cross around his neck, with fish and American flag pins stuck in his straw cowboy hat. He was a friend of Jimmy Martinez's.

Moments before court started for the afternoon, Martinez said he needed to tell DeGuerin something.

Celeste got a fistful of tissues from a deputy.

With Martinez back in the witness box, Gary Cobb asked if Martinez stood by his testimony or if he wanted to change any of it.

Martinez briefly hem-hawed about the IRS.

Cobb asked if Celeste liked to read true crime.

"I never saw her read a book."

The prosecutor asked if Celeste was ever afraid or reluctant to have sex.

No, Martinez answered. They'd had sex into August 1999.

The jurors were sent out of the room, and the attorneys, at DeGuerin's request, stood before Judge Kocurek. Celeste's first criminal attorney on the case, Charlie Burton, joined them. He stood there in a navy blue suit and black cowboy boots, carrying a cowboy hat as Cobb and Matt Hennessy cat-fought. Allison Wetzel had thought Burton wouldn't ever actually take the stand and face possible questions like: Did you tell her she could hide from law enforcement as long as she was at Timberlawn? Was the guardianship your idea? Did you think if she appeared incompetent and crazy the DA would be less likely to indict her?

Finally, Judge Kocurek and Cobb laughed; Hennessy did not.

Celeste Beard Johnson had waived her rights to attorney–client confidentiality and Charlie Burton was sworn in.

The jurors returned to the courtroom to see a bearded attorney whose balding head shined under the fluorescent lighting. He had a beak of a nose and heavy bags under his eyes from the years. His deep voice echoed over the microphone as he stated that Kristina, Jennifer, and Celeste were all at the October 4, 1999, meeting held in his office. He interviewed Jennifer alone, he swore, and "she told me a lot."

On October 1, 1999, she drove her mother to her hair appointment, then to Studio 29 to get Celeste's nails done. Jen arrived at the lake house around 5:30 or 6 P.M. Her mother phoned there around 9 P.M. and showed up around 10. Celeste had previously mentioned to Christopher that she might visit the lake house. Celeste left around 11:30, and the kids went to bed at 11:40.

Jennifer said her mother loved Steve, but he could be a pain when he was drinking. He gave her mother everything she wanted, and Celeste was looking forward to the trip to Europe.

Jennifer also told Burton that one night they armed the burglar alarm and turned out the lights because they were afraid Tracey was coming over with a shotgun and they weren't sure whether she was going to shoot them or herself.

Tracey was a bad person and had read a book about how to kill people, Jennifer said. She presented to him that she wanted to go to the lake house, not that she was told to go. And she did not mention anything about Celeste taking a dog there.

Burton also interviewed Kristina alone. Kristina was frequently at his office, sometimes several times a day. "She was almost easier to talk to than her mother, to tell you the truth." In fact, she was the most distressed member of the family.

Kristina told Burton that on October 1, her mother had been at the lake house for about one or one and a half hours and awoke Kristina when she came in around 12:15 A.M. Her mother then slept in the same room with Kristina, just two feet away from her. On October 2, her mother sat up in bed and said "Someone's at the door."

Tracey was psycho, Kristina said.

Both children were on their mother's side until Kristina was appointed Celeste's guardian and there was a fight over money, Burton testified.

DeGuerin corrected Celeste's previous criminal attorney by saying it was a power of attorney Kristina had, not guardianship.

They even made recordings of Tracey calling the house while Celeste was in Timberlawn in March 2000.

DeGuerin set up a tape player and pressed the ON button.

Tracey Tarlton's voice emerged. "Hey, Kristina, you just called me . . ." Tracey asked if everything was okay.

The judge yawned just before Burton said he concurred with the decision for Celeste to be hospitalized. "There was no question in my mind that it was a necessity." Besides, he said, he needed a break from Celeste.

Burton stated that he was the one who suggested they put a sign on Steve's door because Steve was reluctant to have contact with people. Burton thought it best if he knew who was coming and going.

Just after 3 P.M., Celeste sat in the courtroom with her leg propped on a blanket in a chair, and Gary Cobb began his cross. Cobb stressed that Phil Presse had called Burton because Celeste needed a criminal attorney. Cobb repeatedly emphasized that Burton was at the hospital as Celeste Beard's criminal defense attorney in the shooting of Steve Beard and that Burton's obligation was to Celeste, not Steve. Cobb then asked if it wasn't true that Celeste had come up with the idea of putting the sign on Steve's door.

That time, Burton said he and Celeste had come up with the idea together. He was a very distressed man and needed to be left alone, Burton explained.

Cobb brought out that Burton interviewed Kristina on October 5, 1999, before he ever saw Steve, but didn't dictate those notes until November 10. He stressed that Burton didn't know what all Celeste had told Kristina to say.

Burton replied that Kristina didn't appear to be speaking words Celeste had told her to say.

Cobb asked Burton if he knew that Celeste had gone to the hospital in December 1999 after a suicide attempt.

"I probably did. That was a common occurrence."

At ten minutes to four, doctor of psychology Randy Frazier crept into the courtroom in silent black shoes, carrying a black briefcase. A black sport jacket over a V-neck sweater and shirt and tie covered his broad shoulders. He had a moustache and eyeglasses, and his gray hair receded from his forehead. The soft-spoken Dr. Frazier had been Tracey Tarlton's psychologist from June to November 1999.

Tracey's goal, he said, had been to work on her relationship with Celeste.

Wetzel asked to approach the bench. The jurors were excused, and Frazier stated he wasn't clear to what degree the relationship was real despite the fact that he and Tracey had spent a lot of time talking about it. He also said that Tracey was envious of the wealth to which Celeste had access.

The jury returned, and testimony returned to July 26, 1999. With Celeste out of town, Tracey's anxiety had increased, and she admittedly was destructive in her use of alcohol and psychiatric medications when Celeste wasn't around. She said her relationship with Celeste was the best one she'd ever had, they'd loved each other, but it was stolen time. Frazier noted she had a distorted belief system.

DeGuerin asked whether Tracey had truly spent three or four nights a week with Celeste.

She'd said she had infrequent contact, Frazier reported.

August 19, 1999, Tracey told him Celeste was intrusive and controlling but she felt loved by her. Frazier pointed out the inconsistency in her statements. But with Tracey's history, he explained, that type of relationship felt comfortable to her.

When Frazier met with Tracey on August 31, she told him about her DWI and was embarrassed about it. She also said something had happened that she feared would put her relationship with Celeste in jeopardy.

On October 4, the day Tracey's shotgun was sent to ballistics, Frazier and Tracey had phone contact. She called after hours, said she was getting suicidal, but was evasive about the problem. "I would rather kill myself than go to jail again." He wanted to call 911. Instead, he checked on her the following day.

Intoxicated and making insinuations about drinking and an overdose, Tracey phoned Frazier on October 10. EMS picked her up. The next day, Frazier saw Tracey and she said she and her lover were separated.

October 22, Tarlton wondered if she should phone Celeste. She felt like she should wait. At that time, Frazier didn't know his client had shot Steve Beard.

November 3, the day before the newspaper broke the Beard story, Tracey said she'd had no contact with Celeste and was feeling lack of support by her.

Just before 5 P.M., on cross-examination, Frazier said it was common in affairs to have secret meetings, want more time, and feel left out whether the person was mentally ill or not.

Five minutes later, court recessed for the day. Gary Cobb sighed as he walked away.

Wetzel had counted—six times DeGuerin had objected about the IRS questions to Jimmy Martinez. Six times, Kocurek had overruled him. But Kocurek didn't bring out her contempt folder with DeGuerin.

Wetzel told herself to hold in her anger. She had more important concerns. She felt like the defense had made some points with Frazier. She hoped she could neutralize him the next day.

39

By 8:35 A.M. on a chilly and clear Thursday, March 6, Dr. Frazier sat in the witness box as Allison Wetzel sat alone at the prosecution table continuing her cross-examination.

Frazier testified that it was common among sexual abuse victims to have distorted views of love and relationships and believe that was the way they worked—as Tracey did by having a controlling and intrusive girlfriend who made her feel loved.

He didn't notice any psychotic symptoms in Tracey, only disorganized thinking and intoxication when she was suicidal. He didn't find her to be suffering delusions or auditory hallucinations either. Indeed, he was the one who'd sent Tracey and Celeste to couples counseling.

DeGuerin immediately rose to defend his client by saying it was *Tracey* who'd wanted the couples counseling because *she* was worried about the relationship. DeGuerin then delved back into distortions and delusions.

If Tracey felt called upon to kill this man so she could have a relationship, there would be some delusional aspect to that, Frazier explained. If Tracey was getting clear information from Celeste, in words and behavior, that Celeste only wanted a friendship with Tracey, then there could have been some cognitive distortion. "I'm not sure it's a delusion yet." If there was confusion and mixed messages, he said, the person would choose to believe what they wanted to believe.

DeGuerin mentioned the birthday card Celeste had given Tracey that said "To the One I Love" and asked if that would fuel a distorted belief that Tracey had.

"It would certainly fuel the hope," Frazier replied. "That doesn't sound like a distortion."

For thirty minutes, the courtroom doors continually swung open and closed like barroom doors as Dick DeGuerin put on seven bankers to get the Steve Beard, Celeste Beard Johnson, and Cole Johnson bank records into evidence. The Bank of America records filled two boxes with literally thousands of pages.

Wetzel didn't cross a single witness. She only introduced her own Bank of America records.

Certified Fraud Examiner Jeff A. Compton compared Celeste's possible wealth with Steve Beard alive versus Steve Beard dead. With his balding head hanging as he spoke, Compton stated he'd looked at seven bank accounts and Steve Beard's will, talked to David Kuperman, and prepared exhibits.

Most years the Beards spent $1.5 million or less. In 1996, the total annual payments were extraordinarily high because Steve had paid more than $2.4 million in income taxes.

In a somewhat monotone voice that sounded like static on a radio, Compton stated that in 2000, there were $173,000 in estate administrative expenses, which was higher than 1999 because he normalized his graph by removing one-time events. Yet Compton didn't remove the income taxes paid from any year other than 1996.

DeGuerin asked if Celeste Beard was better off with Steve Beard alive or dead.

"I believe she certainly had access to more property with him alive than dead."

Compton argued on cross-examination that owning a half of a house when Steve Beard was alive and owning a whole house when he died was the same for Celeste, because Celeste had access to the whole house when Steve was alive.

Wetzel countered, "Do you agree that having access to something is different than owning it, being able to sell it and keep the money yourself?"

"Yes."

She showed the witness a summary of David Kuperman's testimony of death versus divorce.

Compton got testy. He constantly called Wetzel "ma'am" as she continued to stress that Celeste Beard gained if Steve died rather than divorced his young wife. In return, Compton persistently stated that the prenuptial agreement didn't guarantee what anyone would get, because in a divorce the court decided that. He then got angry at Wetzel and the judge for cutting off his answers. His anger grew so much that he spoke very slowly as if trying to keep himself from exploding.

On redirect by DeGuerin, Compton stated that the Beards annually spent $470,000 on construction and $302,000 at Louis Shanks furniture. The largest expenditure was on the house, which was for both of the Beards, he said.

Some jurors glared at DeGuerin.

• • •

He called Zan Ray. Zan was one of three witnesses De-Guerin desperately wanted on the stand. The other two were Reginald Breaux, the man the defense said Tracey had tried to run over and kill, and Katina Lofton, a former cellmate of Tracey's. Zan, the defense team believed, could prove that Tracey was obsessive about straight women.

Allison Wetzel asked to approach; the jurors were eventually sent out of the room.

Thirty minutes later, the judge ruled Ray's testimony was irrelevant.

At 4:50 P.M., court recessed.

The judge told one local reporter that she was "this close" to fining Dick DeGuerin for contempt.

Promises, promises, Wetzel thought.

Kristina Beard had an easy drive from her apartment just off of Mopac to the downtown courthouse on March 10, 2003. There was almost no traffic on the cool, cloudy morning. Still, she was in a bit of an angry tizzy. She was at the courthouse to be fingerprinted.

"Next, we're going to ask the judge to see if your fingerprints are on 'the letter,'" Dick DeGuerin said to Allison Wetzel in the hallway before court.

"I wore gloves before sending all of the threatening letters I had sent to Celeste," Wetzel replied, her body stiff, her lips straight, and her eyes sarcastic.

Judge Julie Kocurek held a manila envelope in each hand as she leaned forward and stared hard into Katina Lofton's eyes. "I know what you said to the defense, and I know what you told the State," Kocurek scolded.

Lofton, a short, heavy-set woman with attitude responded that she knew what she'd told the defense, but she didn't know what the State had.

"I'm angry because I'm seeing two different stories," Kocurek beefed. "We're not playing games anymore." If she didn't tell the truth, the judge informed the felon, she would be subject to aggravated perjury, a third-degree felony.

DeGuerin interrupted and said he believed Lofton needed an attorney.

Lofton was led out of the courtroom.

"I think it's wrong what you just did," DeGuerin scolded the judge, as he stood relaxed with his left hand in his pocket. "You've done that to no other witness."

"Go ahead and bring Ms. Lofton out," a livid Kocurek ordered.

Katina Lofton once again stood in front of Judge Kocurek's bench.

Kocurek reached for a black Bible, pushed it toward Lofton, instructed the woman to place her hand on the book, and swore in the inmate.

Just after 8:35 A.M. on Monday, March 10, 2003, the jurors took their places in the jury box.

"Mr. DeGuerin, please call your next witness," Kocurek said.

"Dr. Terry Satterwhite," he said.

"Mr. DeGuerin, you said you were calling Katina Lofton."

"No, I did not."

She ordered the attorneys to the bench, and soon the jury was sent out of the room. DeGuerin accused the judge of intimidating Lofton and griped that he couldn't get into the holding tank to talk to her.

"Sheriff, go ahead and take her back to Del Valle," the judge countered.

"Are you saying I don't have the right to talk to a witness?" He was indignant.

Kocurek answered that she was keeping Lofton away from everyone so that she would tell the truth. Every day, DeGuerin sent one of his attorneys to visit Lofton.

Finally, Dr. Terry Satterwhite, a frail man and professor of infectious disease at the University of Texas Medical Branch in Houston, moved slowly in the witness chair. He peered through wire-rimmed glasses as he read his notes and stated that Steven Beard had died from an infection.

DeGuerin asked the doctor what that had to do with Beard's gunshot.

"I don't think it had any relation to that," Satterwhite answered, and added that the bloodstream infection did not usually come from a gunshot wound. His lips barely moved under a graying moustache, his thinning hair combed over his balding head. Satterwhite's brow wrinkled, and he spoke softly.

DeGuerin asked if the infection could have been caused by someone changing Beard's ileostomy bag with dirty hands.

"No, I don't think that would be very likely."

On cross-examination, Gary Cobb talked about how Dr. Roberto Bayardo had sectioned the lungs and found a death-causing blood clot. He emphasized that there were autopsy photographs that showed the clot.

"I'm not really qualified to interpret the photographs," Satterwhite answered, his voice wimpy and mumbling, so much so that his words were often unintelligible. He seemed like he was straight out of Mayberry. But he agreed with Bayardo, "The blood clot's there." He admitted that a blood clot had some of the same symptoms of strep A.

Cobb asked if Beard could have had both strep A and a blood clot.

"There's no doubt he had both of those," the doctor said.

Cobb showed the witness a photograph of Celeste Beard's infected fingers. Justin Grimm had taken the picture in late January of 2000, just after Steve had died.

The doctor reluctantly admitted those fingers changing a colostomy bag could have passed an infection to Steve Beard, although it was not likely.

Dr. Charles Petty was a professor of forensics at the University of Texas Southwestern and in Dallas alone he'd performed 13,000 autopsies. Petty looked like a bumbling professor straight out of a B movie—the teacher everyone loved, but made fun of. He was distinguished, disheveled, and professorial with thinning hair on top, flyaway white hair on the sides, wire-rimmed glasses, a dark green jacket,

white shirt, striped bow tie messily tied, and silent black
shoes.

"He died, in my opinion, by an overwhelming infection . . ." Petty said with arms crossed.

DeGuerin emphasized that, unlike Dr. Roberto Bayardo,
Petty had studied all of Beard's records.

To that, Petty plainly and loudly said, with his hands in
prayer position, that that was significant because he had
possession of a lot more information than Bayardo when
Bayardo "made up" his autopsy report.

DeGuerin inquired whether the gunshot wound could
have caused Beard's death.

"There was no reason to suspect that he would die of that
at all."

On cross-examination, prosecutor Gary Cobb asked the
expert—who had just admitted to performing only two or
three autopsies since 1991, the last one of which was
seven years ago—if he found any fault with Bayardo's autopsy report.

Petty paused at length before finally admitting, "No."

Cobb tried to delve into the seminars that the doctor had
conducted with Dick DeGuerin, specifically one taught in
Tucson, Arizona, in 2000 entitled "The Chili or the Bullet."

With his arms crossed once again, Petty tried to blow off
the query.

The doctor, who claimed he had a hearing problem, repeatedly indicated he couldn't hear Cobb, despite the fact
that Cobb was yelling his questions. Petty had had no trouble hearing DeGuerin.

Bayardo's autopsy could be correct, Cobb probed.

"I suppose one could interpret it either way," Petty conceded, as the defense team frowned.

Cobb blatantly stated that "in the end," the gunshot was
the cause of Steve Beard's death.

Yes, the defense witness answered.

Dr. Christine Warmann breathed heavily as she sat down in
the witness chair. She had short brown hair, pale skin, and

broad shoulders. Her voice was deep, but so soft that she could barely be heard.

When the attorneys gathered at Judge Kocurek's bench, Warmann cocked her head like a bird looking around the room—her eyes wide, her eyebrows constantly raised.

Dr. Warmann had treated Tracey Tarlton from July 30, 1999, until January 23, 2001. On August 3, 1999, Tarlton had been taken to South Austin hospital for a serious drug ingestion. Tracey was on a respirator and had nearly died, the doctor reported, but there was debate over whether the overdose was a suicide attempt.

"I was just trying to go to sleep," Tracey had said at the time. The stressor, the doctor said, was that Tracey didn't want to deal with the two-week absence of her girlfriend, who was going to Australia.

DeGuerin insinuated that Tracey had overdosed to keep Celeste from going on the trip.

Warmann disagreed. "I don't recall" and "I don't know" repeatedly came from the mouth of the obviously reluctant witness, until DeGuerin asked if Tracey suffered auditory hallucinations.

A couple of times, the doctor said.

He asked if Tracey ever suffered delusions.

"Never," Warmann answered.

Around 2:15 P.M., a slimmer, white version of Jimmy Martinez entered the courtroom—Doug Byers, Celeste's handpicked repairman with Fox Services. His voice was hoarse and raspy like marbles were rattling in his throat as he talked about preparing the house for Steve's home-coming.

He'd built the handicapped ramp, skid-proofed it, and had made special trips to get the stain just right. "We were planning on it being there for a while." He'd hung a TV stand on the wall of the master bedroom so Steve could lie in bed and watch TV. Celeste had even lain down on the bed to make sure the TV position was just right.

Contradicting the kids, Doug swore that Celeste was at

the house when Steve arrived from the hospital, and that he and Justin, rather than Christopher, had carried Steve into the house.

The jurors listened carefully as Byers recalled finding Justin "rifling" through Celeste's papers. One moment, Doug said the event had happened after Steve died. Then he said that it might have been when Celeste was going back and forth to Brackenridge to see Steve. Then he corrected himself and said it had happened after Steve died.

He also changed his testimony regarding whether one could have parked next to Kristina's bedroom as Tracey said she did. First he said yes, then he said no, which was the answer DeGuerin wanted.

On cross-examination, Cobb pointed out Byers' latest change in answer.

"I was mistaken by the question."

But after Cobb inquired about when Byers began preparing the house for Steve's return home, Doug couldn't figure out his answer again—first he said not until January 2000, then he said before then, then he said he hadn't been approached about doing the work for Steve until January 3, 2000.

Cobb accused Byers of socializing with Celeste at Chuy's Tex-Mex restaurant. Doug denied that, but admitted Celeste had sent him a thank-you card for attending another court appearance, and he considered them to be friends.

Then, Cobb pointed out there were bank records that proved Celeste had been shopping when Steve arrived home from the hospital, so she couldn't have been there as Byers swore.

As Doug Byers began to leave the courtroom, he paused at the defense table and reached over to shake hands with Celeste. The guard stepped up; Catherine Baen waved Doug away. Celeste believed Doug was important to her defense. And all the way down to his soul, he knew she was innocent.

. . .

By 4 P.M., the courtroom was hot and miserable. The sun had come out by lunchtime and heated the day. The jurors sat in their box fanning themselves and waited . . . and waited. Katina Lofton trudged in.

She was a 26-year-old with big hips and tight cornrows. She looked more like an angry child than a ten-time felon. And, like a nervous child swinging back and forth in her chair, Lofton testified that she was spending six years in prison for theft, forgery, and tampering with government records. As proof to the jury, she wore green jailhouse scrubs over a long-sleeved gray T-shirt, matching gray socks, and black jellies.

She swore that from March to April of 2002, at the Del Valle jail, she had been housed in maximum security with Tracey Tarlton, who was a trustee. Katina pouted that she wanted to be a trustee too.

DeGuerin began to question his witness about Tracey and Celeste; Allison Wetzel continually objected. "Sustained," Judge Kocurek repeatedly said, until Wetzel asked to approach the bench. Lofton buried her chin in her chest. Neither Wetzel nor DeGuerin smiled as they left the judge's bench.

DeGuerin asked what Tracey had said about Celeste's involvement in the shooting.

"She said Celeste was going to live happily ever after while she rotted in jail." Lofton elaborated that Tracey said she'd called the Beard house after she shot Steve Beard and told Celeste to get the shotgun shell. Celeste became hysterical and said, "What are you talking about?"

DeGuerin inquired whether Tracey had said Celeste never knew she was going to shoot her husband.

"Hm?" Lofton replied.

The defense attorney pointed out that previously, under oath, Katina had stated Celeste didn't know Tracey was going to shoot Steve.

Lofton said Celeste's daughter and Tracey had talked after Tracey was jailed, but she didn't know what kind of contact they'd had.

DeGuerin read from the sworn interview he'd had with Lofton to refresh her memory.

At that, Lofton said one of Celeste's daughters had always told Tracey where Celeste was, once mentioning that Celeste was somewhere cold, like Aspen. Tracey had wanted Celeste to be her girlfriend, though she'd never said Celeste was gay. With that, Lofton boldly volunteered, "I'm not a lesbian." Tracey only said she and Celeste were friends—Celeste had helped her out with a cell phone and a party.

A blonde female juror who almost always took a corner seat in the jury box looked disgusted.

DeGuerin asked again if Tracey Tarlton had ever said that his client was responsible for the shooting in any way.

"No, sir." Tracey had said she was going to lie so she could get a 20-year sentence and she'd taken a lie detector test and passed it.

DeGuerin tried to stop his witness, but Lofton added that Tracey had taken two lie detector tests and passed them both.

DeGuerin interrupted and asked what Tracey had said about making bacteria. He meant botulism.

Lofton understood otherwise—Tracey had shot Steve Beard and had said something about his colostomy bag.

Judge Kocurek reached her hand up to her neck and rubbed.

DeGuerin read from Lofton's statement where she'd said that Tracey had told her she'd made bacteria.

With that, Lofton suddenly said she'd been confused. Yes, it was true, she answered.

But DeGuerin read that Lofton had previously said it wasn't true.

A male juror with tiny, black rectangular eyeglasses smirked behind his hand as he scribbled notes.

DeGuerin pointedly asked if Tracey had said she was going to lie about Celeste.

"Yes."

He asked if Tracey ever said why she'd shot Steve Beard.

40

"She just said he never really cared for her," Lofton said in explaining why Tracey had shot Steve Beard.

Just before 5 P.M., Allison Wetzel questioned Katina about Charlie Burton.

Lofton stated she'd met with Burton, who'd told her he'd help her with her case if she'd help Celeste. The attorneys soon returned to the bench to confer with Kocurek. Lofton swung in her chair and quizzically watched the proceedings. A few minutes later, Kocurek recessed court.

DeGuerin then griped that the prosecutor was signaling with facial expressions, rolling her eyes, and whispering.

Kocurek told Wetzel that if she did that anymore, she'd be fined $100. She ordered DeGuerin to get his client's facial expressions under control, too.

Wetzel wondered if Matt Hennessy had made up that rolling-of-the-eyes story just to jack with her. *It's not going to work,* she told herself.

March 11, 2003, was the second day of spring break. The morning was foggy and misty as live music wafted through the Four Seasons hotel. South by Southwest, an internationally renowned week-long live music conference, had the hotels crammed with bands trying to create their big break.

The Celeste Beard Johnson defense team, which was residing at the Four Seasons, also hoped for a big break in the form of a Kristina Beard handwriting sample handed to DeGuerin by Kocurek.

Already, an Easter-looking Celeste had hobbled in wearing a periwinkle-purple twin set. DeGuerin lightly patted her on the back as she sat down. She was still on his witness list, but by then Wetzel was thinking, *I'll believe it when I see it.*

By 8:40 A.M., the jury was in and Wetzel stood before Katina Lofton. "Is Celeste your friend?" Wetzel asked.

"Yes."

The prosecutor noted that Celeste had sent 'Tina $200 on July 10, 2002, Dana Whatley had sent her $50 the following October, which was the same month that Wetzel and Sergeant Debra Smith had visited the prison-residing Lofton. Lofton had told Dick DeGuerin that Wetzel asked "a shitload of questions" at that meeting and Celeste had asked Lofton to tear up her letters, which Lofton didn't do.

Wetzel read from a letter the felon had written Celeste on June 22, 2002—'Tina was there to support Celeste, she wasn't like Donna Goodson, Celeste shouldn't worry, her attorneys weren't worth a shit, 'Tina had no paper or stationery, and it sucked being indigent. And, there was a reference to Tracey Tarlton, to which DeGuerin objected.

On July 10, 2002, the day Katina received the $200, she wrote a letter to "Dimples," Celeste's jailhouse nickname, and said, "There is no limit to what I wouldn't do for you."

The State produced a July 23, 2002, letter, also to "Dimples." That letter said Katina had something "very, very important" to tell Celeste. She also said she couldn't go to college because she didn't have the $400 it cost per semester.

Responding to Celeste's query as to whether Katina was going to testify against her, Lofton wrote, "How in the fuck could I testify against you when I willingly helped you to the best of my ability, even volunteered to talk to your lawyer." She enclosed a prison money slip so Celeste would know how to send her money. And Lofton wrote that she had nothing but love for Celeste.

Katina interrupted the prosecutor to make sure everyone in the courtroom knew she meant only platonic love.

Wetzel continued through more of the letters, as Celeste yawned.

To help get paroled, Katina asked if Dana Whatley

would write a letter of support on company letterhead saying Dana would offer 'Tina a job, as Celeste had told her she would. Included in the letter was a poem about Celeste's and Katina's friendship—Celeste was "a great friend and a good woman." The letter was written after Lofton had received the $50 from Whatley. She closed by saying she missed and loved Celeste "dearly."

On October 14, 2002, Lofton wrote Celeste that she had "some shit" that Celeste's attorneys needed to know ASAP. She said she loved Celeste like a sister and she needed Celeste's friend to find on the Internet a good dentist and a good plastic surgeon in Houston, Dallas, or San Antonio who didn't ask questions. She needed the best in the business for body contouring and facial work.

Lofton broke in and said that those questions were for a friend. She also explained that the information she had had to do with lies Tracey was making up.

However, on October 23, 2002, Katina wrote Celeste that *she* needed the surgery, to trust her on that. She added that Celeste wouldn't lose her life and to trust her on that. Again, Katina asked Celeste to get her attorneys to do some work for her so that she could get out of prison.

On the witness stand, Katina's bottom lip jutted out in a constant pout. Her face always looked strained as if she were thinking hard. That look continued as Wetzel recounted that Lofton had told Sergeant Debra Smith and herself that Tracey had said she and Celeste planned the shooting. Lofton denied that statement. But Wetzel repeated the statement and that time Lofton agreed that she'd said that.

"Now is that different from what you told the jury yesterday?"

"No," Lofton said—Tracey had lied and had said she was going to lie about it. Katina looked straight at Allison Wetzel and directed her words to the prosecutor. "You said, 'Why did she tell you this?' You put your hand through your hair and put your head down."

"I put my head down?" Wetzel said in disbelief.

"Yeah, you did this." Lofton sank her head into her hands.

"Do you think that's what Debra Smith saw too?"

"Well, I was there, and I know that's what happened."

Almost everything Wetzel repeated in the courtroom regarding information Katina Lofton had provided to Debra Smith and herself, Lofton denied.

Wetzel pointed out that after she and Smith had interviewed her, Lofton wrote the prosecutor two letters asking for legal help, including a divorce and name change. Wetzel didn't reply to either letter.

Later, Katina asked to see Wetzel. Debra Smith went to visit instead. During that meeting, Wetzel stated, Katina said Celeste had promised her $50,000 for testifying.

Katina denied that.

Then, on February 9, 2003, just days after the trial had started, Katina wrote Celeste another letter—she didn't want to be standing next to Celeste when the walls came tumbling down. She told Celeste not to write her anymore, that having her as a witness would only make matters worse, Celeste had lied to her, and all Celeste cared about was herself. Katina said she wouldn't get on the stand to testify to bullshit about who did what, Tracey saying one thing, Celeste saying another, the newspaper another. She would no longer allow Celeste to poison her mind with bullshit.

On February 13, 2003, Katina wrote Celeste a profanity-filled letter firmly informing her that she wasn't into "pussy," she "loved dick."

Wetzel calmly looked at the witness. With a straight face and a pleasant voice she said, "You're not talking about Mr. DeGuerin are you?"

Wetzel then noted Katina's ten felony convictions.

"I don't keep count," Lofton stated, her cornrows looking like a herringbone pattern.

Forgery, credit card abuse, theft, false name, false information, Wetzel read.

Lofton countered that Wetzel didn't care about that when she'd interviewed her, so "what's your point?"

Tampering with government records, Wetzel continued, before making her point—all the felonies involved dishonesty. She next noted for the jury that Lofton had lost custody of her children in a court proceeding prosecuted by Wetzel—Katina's husband had slammed a child to the ground.

DeGuerin rose from his chair and called for a mistrial, which was denied.

Wetzel stated that just one week before the start of Celeste Beard Johnson's trial, Katina had asked her mother to phone the prosecutor—Katina wanted to testify for the State.

And that—Katina Lofton—was one of the three witnesses Dick DeGuerin believed could prove that his client, Celeste Beard Johnson, was not guilty of murdering her fourth husband, Steven F. Beard, Jr.

A woman in a cowgirl costume turned heads as she walked up to the witness stand. Kristina Beard's former therapist, Peggy Farley Honaker, sat in the criminal district courtroom in a Western vest, denim skirt, and cowboy boots. Her shoulder-length blonde hair parted on the left and flipped under. Her face was tan behind wire-rimmed glasses.

In April 2000, Kristina had phoned at 3 A.M. saying she and her sister had no place to stay, Honaker testified. Soon, Kristina and Jen, with their clothes, and Christopher and Justin were on her doorstep with Peggy explaining she couldn't be Kristina's therapist if the teen stayed even one night at her house.

Kristina and Jen stayed through the Fourth of July weekend, Peggy swore. Christopher left after a couple of days, but Justin wanted to stay. She wouldn't let him. Justin wouldn't help around the house. He wouldn't eat leftovers. He was hard to deal with.

Still, every day he returned to her house. And every day, she said, he obsessed over whether Celeste had been involved in Steve's murder and he wrote it all down, planning on turning his "tome" into a book. The girls got so sick of hearing Justin talk and write about the murder that they told him to shut up.

Meanwhile, the twins bought a Jeep to pull their Jet Skis

and spent their days playing on Lake Travis, driving the
Jeep around the ranch, and partying. Peggy wanted the girls
to get jobs, have chores, and reconcile with Celeste.

Kristina refused to meet with Peggy and Celeste. She refused to phone her mother. She refused to write her a letter.
But every day, Kris was on the phone to the bank, Honaker
swore.

In therapy, Kristina had called Steve fat, stupid, old,
and a drunk, and she referred to him as "Steve," not
"Dad." She complained that Steve was disappointed in her,
was jealous of her relationship with Celeste, and picked on
her. Steve Beard had even called Peggy and expressed the
same complaints.

DeGuerin asked if Kristina ever spoke of Celeste spik-
ing Steve's drinks.

No, Honaker answered, she only complained of his
drinking.

On cross-examination, Honaker admitted that when the
twins had arrived at her house they were afraid for their
lives because Celeste had hired a hit man. She also acknowledged that Kristina's complaints against Steve
seemed like typical adolescent conflict and Kristina had
also said bad things about Celeste.

However, when Kristina's former therapist spoke of her,
she called her Kristine. Allison Wetzel corrected the
woman—Kristina.

Reluctantly, Honaker admitted that the twins had offered
to loan her $20,000. She'd turned it down, she claimed, but
her then-husband had accepted it.

DeGuerin's day didn't seem to get any better when he
called two expert witnesses to prove that the threatening letter sent to Celeste in August 2000 was written by Kristina.
"Hey, Dike [sic]," DeGuerin read. The letter stated that the
only way anyone would like Celeste would be if she proved
her love for Steve by joining him.

But DeGuerin's fingerprint expert couldn't match
Kristina's fingerprints to the partial print on the letter. And

his handwriting expert could only say that Kristina had "probably" written the letter.

Matt Hennessy wouldn't even smile on his way into court on Wednesday, March 12, 2003, another warm, foggy, and misty day in Austin, Texas. Katina Lofton and Celeste were on the witness list again. Despite Wetzel's reservations that Celeste would testify, everyone in the courtroom hoped and prayed she would. Reginald Breaux was also on the day's witness list.

At the bench, Judge Kocurek refused to let the transcript of Katina Lofton's interview with Dick DeGuerin be admitted into evidence. It was something he'd been arguing for days, and a battle he'd been losing equally as long.

But Celeste and Steve Beard's prescription drug records from the Northwest Hills Pharmacy were entered when DeGuerin called Judy Cantu, a raven-haired pharmacist at the Davenport Village location.

Once again, DeGuerin's witness sounded like a backfire as Cantu enumerated the multitude of sleeping pills prescribed for the Beard family.

Celeste received twelve pills of temazepam on July 28, 1999 and a second prescription for them on January 27, 2000. From March 6, 1999 to February 10, 2000, Celeste filled seven prescriptions of the sleeping pill Ambien, five of which were filled prior to October 1, 1999.

From October 1998 to September 1999, Steve Beard had had three prescriptions of temazepam filled, thirty pills each. The last prescription filled was on September 9, 1999, just days before he passed out and Celeste and Tracey had held a plastic bag over his head.

DeGuerin asked her about the day of Steve Beard's funeral.

Cantu swore Celeste Beard hadn't said to her that she would have to kiss Celeste's ass like Cantu had kissed Steve's.

On cross, Cantu noted four other prescriptions for medicine that could have made Steve Beard drowsy. She named off approximately sixty prescriptions for drowse-inducing drugs filled for Celeste, when Wetzel abruptly stopped the witness and simply stated that the list went on for many more pages. Indeed, Celeste often had five different prescriptions filled on a single day.

Celeste Beard was getting "a whole lot" of drugs that could make a person drowsy, Wetzel said.

"Yes," Cantu replied.

The witness also noted that within mere days of Steve's funeral, Celeste had had two prescriptions filled for antibiotics that could treat both staph and strep infections. And Celeste did visit the pharmacy on the day of her husband's funeral. Afterwards the pharmacy staff talked about her visit, and Celeste had spoken to another employee besides Cantu.

After Cantu was excused and the jury released for a break, Ellen Halbert leaned over and whispered that the twins had stayed at therapist Peggy Farley's house for one night after fleeing from Celeste, then went to Anita Ashton's place in West Texas for two weeks, where Christopher broke up with Jennifer.

Only then did they return to Peggy's, where they stayed and worked for her, doing everything from drywall to painting. That was how they learned to build their own garage, which they did so Celeste couldn't do anything to their cars.

And Kristina swore they'd bought the Jeep Wrangler only so they could see the DA without Celeste knowing, since Charlie Burton's office was across the street from the DA's office. At one point, they'd even planned on putting the Jeep in Peggy's name so that Celeste wouldn't know about it.

Peggy, Halbert said, did take $20,000 from the girls. They'd sent her a certified letter trying to get back their money.

The defense rebuttal was a simple question—"What motive did Peggy have to lie?" It was the same thing the defense said about Katina Lofton. "What motive did Katina have to lie?"

41

Down to the tips of his custom made cowboy boots Dick DeGuerin believed Kristina Beard had a motive to lie—a multimillion-dollar motive. The jury was brought in, then released again so that DeGuerin could argue about inconsistent statements made by Kristina.

His argument seemed to go nowhere with the judge as Terry Meyer, a Celeste friend, traveling companion, partygoer, and Tramps salon manicurist, entered the courtroom.

Terry was perfectly done, perhaps even perfectly overdone. Black-rimmed eyeglasses hung just below perfectly waxed eyebrows. Perfect lipstick colored lips on a smooth, olive-toned face, which one could barely see due to perfectly overly fluffed, dark, shoulder-length hair.

Tracey Tarlton had phoned Tramps, Terry testified, saying she was a friend of Celeste's, and made an appointment with Terry for July 16, 1999. From then on, Tracey walked into the Burnet Road salon with black wrought-iron over glass doors about every seven to ten days for a manicure and sometimes a pedicure.

Despite Terry stating she'd seen Tracey regularly until the end of August, DeGuerin focused on September 1999— in September 1999 did Tracey Tarlton say if Steve Beard did anything to hurt Celeste, she would kill him?

Yes, Terry answered. "It scared me."

"Did you think she was serious?"

"Definitely." When Terry had mentioned that Tracey's hands were shaking, Tracey had called Steve a pig. That was when Tracey said she'd kill Steve, Meyer stated. She noted that on October 1, 1999, around 5 P.M., Tracey had arrived at Tramps for a manicure. When Terry heard the next day that Steve had been shot, she immediately thought Tracey had done it.

On cross, Wetzel asked the defense witness if she'd ever seen Tracey stalking or "bird-dogging" Celeste.

No. She knew they were friends, but seemingly like every one of Celeste's adult friends, she didn't know they went to dinner with other lesbian couples, didn't know that they went to concerts together, didn't know about the BookPeople party and the hugs and kisses shared there, and didn't know that Tracey and Celeste slept in the same bed.

Despite the statement that Terry believed Tracey was serious about killing Steve, she didn't tell Celeste about Tracey's words prior to the shooting and she couldn't remember whether she'd even told Celeste after the shooting. But she knew she'd told Dick DeGuerin and Bill Mange. And she said she'd probably told her husband.

She swore she did tell Celeste that she believed Tracey had shot Steve, and when she said that, Celeste looked surprised.

On redirect, Terry said that right after she first met Tracey in July of 1999, she'd told Celeste that Tracey was in love with her. Again, Celeste seemed surprised. Terry swore she didn't think the love was mutual. She also stated that Tracey was a little intimidating.

DeGuerin said "spooky."

Westlake hairdresser Joseph Prete was a prissy young man with closely cropped facial hair, graying hair on his head, blue jeans, and a collarless shirt of the same color.

DeGuerin got right to the point. Did Celeste ever say, "I don't know how I'm going to last for three months. I wish the fat bastard was dead?"

"No," Prete answered. She called him a fat teddy bear, because he collected teddy bears.

Pass the witness.

In a soft voice, Prete explained that he had his own private area with a beautiful view at the salon. So, he didn't know what Celeste may have said to the manicurist.

Upon return to questioning, DeGuerin asked about the graduation party.

Every photo he took, Joseph said, Tracey was crouching

in the background. "She's just everywhere." He and his partner left the party early because his partner felt uncomfortable with Tracey there.

At 1:30 P.M., pretty Dawn Madigan walked into the courtroom.

"I considered her one of my closest friends, if not the closest," Dawn testified of Celeste, who Dawn also vowed was not a lesbian . . . to her knowledge. Indeed, Dawn and Celeste had hugged and kissed. And Celeste and Steve had a good, loving relationship. They were devoted and gave each other what the other needed. Celeste took care of his demands.

About 10 or 10:30 on the morning on October 2, 1999, Dawn's cell phone rang as she drove her son Cole from Spicewood, Texas, into Austin. Kristina was on the phone and said Steve had been shot.

At the hospital, Dawn was comforting Celeste when Travis County Sheriff's Office detective Rick Wines walked up. Kristina and Jennifer joined them, and Kristina asked who had taken Steve's wallet and ring.

Wines said he didn't know.

The smooth-skinned teen leaned in to the wiry old detective and demanded, "You don't really know who shot him, do you?" She leaned in closer, close enough to smell the cigarette smoke in his striped shirt, glared right into the detective's tanned face and repeated, "You don't really know who shot him, do you?"

Her words and actions made Dawn Madigan shiver uncomfortably. Kristina's behavior, she thought, didn't seem appropriate.

Celeste didn't say anything.

But Dawn had always been uncomfortable with Celeste and Kristina's relationship. She felt Celeste needed to give her daughter more guidance. Instead, Kristina made her own rules.

Celeste cried in the courtroom.

· · ·

"I wanted them to be my friend. I never said 'no' to them, because I was afraid they would hate me. I was too busy being a friend so I couldn't be a mother."

Dawn stayed at the hospital all that day and saw Steve with Celeste and Kristina. Kristina grabbed Steve's hand. Steve *pushed* her out of the way and pulled Celeste to him, Dawn said.

She then rode to the Marriott with the family in the Beard Suburban. Dawn didn't see an Everclear bottle, she testified, but she watched Celeste, sitting behind the driver's seat, throw out a book and say, "I need to get rid of this." They asked her why. She seemed embarrassed. The book was about self-mutilation and harming oneself.

Dawn munched ice on the stand, then said she wasn't surprised to see the book. Celeste read a lot and was a great researcher.

Then, as they sat in Dawn's Suburban for a cigarette, Celeste's phone rang. "Tracey, I can't talk to you now," Celeste said. "Well, they're at your house because Steve has been shot." And Celeste hung up.

"Don't you think she had something to do with this?" Dawn said.

" 'No, she would never do something like this,' " Celeste replied.

As soon as Dawn heard that Steve had died, she rushed to the Toro Canyon house. Celeste was so upset and distraught that Dawn had stayed there that evening, spent the night, stayed with Celeste the next day, gone to the funeral home with them, and ridden in the limousine with Celeste to the funeral.

"It was a very tense and emotional situation." They laughed in the limousine, she said, only to ease the tension.

Becky Beard rose out of her courtroom seat and walked out the door.

Celeste and the kids had a talk in the limousine, to which Celeste said she couldn't have that conversation—she couldn't hear that right then.

The prosecution managed to keep out the hearsay testimony that in the limousine the twins had asked, "When do we get our money?"

In fact, as Celeste had walked through the house pointing out things she wanted to give Steve's children, Kristina objected, Dawn swore, particularly about a painting, and Kristina kept talking about the money.

DeGuerin asked again about Kristina's relationship with Steve.

"She mocked him. Made fun of him," Dawn answered—his weight, his cooking, his cleaning, his drinking. And Kristina called him "Fatso."

Five minutes after 3, Gary Cobb took over. He casually looked at the woman who wore a scarf tossed around her neck and had colored blonde hair that looked like it had been swept permanently to the left in a windstorm.

Seemingly backing away from the close friendship she'd just reported to DeGuerin, Madigan stated that she hadn't seen Celeste since May 2002 and she'd told Celeste's previous attorneys she didn't want to be involved in the trial. Before May 2002, she said, Celeste would stop by and visit, and on occasion they'd go to clubs. Then she said they'd gone to a club only once, the night they met Jimmy Martinez.

That night, Jennifer had taken her home because Dawn had been drinking, and Kristina had taken Celeste home, which contradicted Martinez's testimony. So Cobb had her state two more times that Celeste had gone with Kristina.

Cobb asked the witness to tell the jury what Celeste had said about her relationship with Tracey Tarlton.

At first Dawn indicated she didn't understand the question.

So Cobb outlined Celeste and Tracey's life together.

Celeste was never afraid of Tracey and had never expressed any concern over Tracey hurting Celeste or anyone in the Beard family, Dawn said. If she had been, Dawn swore, she felt Celeste would have told her, due to their close friendship.

Cobb noted the romantic kisses between Celeste and Tracey.

Dawn didn't think Celeste would do that.

Cobb insisted that the witness didn't know Celeste as well as she thought.

Madigan disagreed.

Cobb showed her two photographs of Celeste's staph-infected fingers and passed the photos to the jury.

Cobb stressed that Celeste had set up a scholarship fund for Dawn's son.

Dawn admitted Celeste had bought her furniture, a pink pearl necklace and earrings, more earrings, and the framed antique pillow.

Around 4:15 that afternoon, wearing a black pantsuit and beads, her cross notably missing, Marilou Gibbs stepped into the witness chair. Steve had given Celeste something she'd never had—security and unconditional love, Marilou vowed. He'd been like an overindulgent father who'd laughed about how much money Celeste spent.

Celeste grinned at Marilou.

Steve cursed a lot and thought it was funny when Celeste dished it out as good as he gave it. But he tried to control Celeste's appearance and laid down rules for the girls—they were expected to be at dinner. Kris and Jen didn't like his cooking, though, and didn't want to be there. So Celeste had told them that as Steve gave them everything they wanted, the least they could do was come home and eat his meals.

"They disliked Steven's cooking so much that I would get them fast food after school and at dinnertime they just pretended they were not hungry."

Without one bit of prodding by DeGuerin, Marilou tossed in that Celeste frequently drove out to the lake house with both dogs.

When DeGuerin asked about the twins' 18th birthday party, Marilou replied, "Oh, yes. Steve knew about the party." She and Steve had talked about it on the phone.

" 'Truthfully,' " he'd said, " 'you and I are both too old for that sort of thing.' "

"Speak for yourself," Marilou had shot back.

"Of course," Marilou stated, Steve had known about Jimmy Martinez. She'd even heard Steve say that Kristina had gone over to Jimmy's.

Almost every time DeGuerin asked Marilou a question, her response was an "Oh, yes!" or an "Of course!" as she rattled on about her close friendship with Steve and Celeste Beard, although she hadn't attended their wedding. She hadn't visited Celeste in St. David's—Steve didn't think it was a good idea. And she hadn't visited Celeste at Timberlawn.

Marilou said Celeste's emotional problems were due in part to troubles with Kristina as well as Celeste's mother and stepfather moving into the lake house. Celeste and Tracey connected through their similar history of sexual abuse. But Tracey, she said, was a really sick person. Celeste just wanted to do everything she could to help Tracey.

DeGuerin asked if it surprised her that Celeste wanted to help Tracey.

"Not at all—because that's the type of person Celeste is."

But she also talked about how Celeste would give Steve "the finger." Steve simply replied, "Here's two for you." Marilou quickly and smoothly shot both of her forefingers into the air and grinned.

42

When Marilou Gibbs took the stand and said her first few words, everyone began to think like Allison Wetzel—Celeste Beard Johnson wasn't going to testify. Marilou was speaking for Celeste. Still, everyone hoped . . . after Marilou . . . maybe . . .

. . .

Marilou returned to the stand just after 8:30 in the morning on March 13, 2003. As he'd done with so many of his witnesses, DeGuerin had her focus on Steve's drinking.

"I would think he were an alcoholic," Marilou said of the man she constantly described as her contemporary and friend. "He drank every day and he drank until he passed out."

DeGuerin asked how Celeste coped.

"She put water in his Wolfschmidt."

Regarding Amy Cozart, Christopher Doose, and Steve, Marilou insisted there wasn't much of a relationship there—Steve wasn't big into talking to teenagers. He didn't confide in them. But he'd confided in her. Steve had talked to her about Tracey.

And just a few days before the graduation party at Jimmy's, she spoke to Steve on the phone. At the time, she wasn't planning on attending the party, "and he said, 'Smart decision.'" But Marilou did go, and there she met Tracey Tarlton.

"I thought she was very rude and tried to call Celeste away from the conversation." Tracey said, " 'Celeste, c'me here!' " Marilou imitated Tracey in a tough, butch sort of way.

"Tracey, I'm talking," Celeste replied. Marilou mimicked Celeste sweetly.

Tracey got mad, walked away, and slammed a door, Marilou swore.

Another time, Tracey had yelled, "Celeste, come 're," and Celeste didn't come. So Tracey walked into the kitchen and rattled dishes. Then Tracey watched Celeste hug and kiss Marilou and Dawn. "She did not take that very well." Tracey "gave long glaring looks."

During halftime of the football game that was on the big screen TV during the party, everyone stopped to eat. Tracey stomped up and said, "Where am I supposed to sit?"

"Well, there are plenty of places," Celeste said.

An elderly male juror seemed charmed by Marilou.

Marilou claimed she talked to Kristina about finding Tracey in bed with Celeste that night and Steve's feelings over the event. "He was very concerned about it," she said of Tracey and Celeste's relationship. He felt Tracey had become dependent on Celeste, and he wanted them apart. In fact, he put his foot down. No more being around Tracey, and Celeste had agreed.

Marilou claimed Steve had known about the Tarlton family wedding in Atlanta. And he'd told Celeste to go, Marilou swore, so that she could start letting Tracey down easily. Steve, Marilou insisted, was the one who'd sent Tracey and Celeste to couples counseling so that Tracey would understand that Celeste was a married woman and that the friendship wasn't going to go any further. "He wanted to get rid of that damned dyke."

Marilou went on and on with her tales. Celeste was "very, very enthusiastic" about the trip to Europe because she could do plenty of shopping. After Steve was shot, Celeste was nervous and upset about Tracey calling all the time. She tried to avoid Tracey's calls. She changed their phone numbers, but Tracey faxed her instead.

Celeste spent Thanksgiving 1999 with Marilou and her family, while the girls spent the day with their boyfriends. And as time passed, Kristina and Justin became more and more "take-charge."

DeGuerin asked Marilou to tell the court about Celeste's feelings.

At first, Celeste couldn't believe Tracey had shot Steve. But once she believed it, Celeste was riddled with guilt for bringing Tracey into her household.

"Celeste rarely drank," Marilou said. Drugs were foreign to her. Then Steve died. "Celeste became a changed person." Justin was driving Celeste's car when she never let anyone drive her. And she couldn't be reached. A "strange person" answered the phone and said Celeste couldn't talk, she was ill.

Marilou asked if she needed to come in and help Celeste. The person said no and hung up.

Marilou phoned in mid-February, and Celeste answered. But the phone was jerked out of Celeste's hand and Donna Goodson said, "I told you she can't talk."

"Celeste was just nearly out of her mind," when she and Kristina stopped communicating.

Marilou became weepy. Then Celeste began sobbing as Marilou said that ignoring medical advice, Celeste had come home from Timberlawn to try to mend things with her daughters. Marilou told her to go back to Dallas—she'd be better able to mend things if she was healthy.

Some jurors looked disgusted. Some looked blank-faced.

Celeste was a "basket case" when she got the "Dike" letter encouraging her to kill herself, Marilou testified. "To me, it was Kristina's writing."

"I consider myself her foster mother," Marilou said on cross. "She's given me her love, affection, and trust."

Gary Cobb tried to prove Celeste had given Marilou much more than that—$4,000.

Marilou stressed that Celeste had loaned her $4,000 in April 2001, but Marilou had paid it back in less than a week.

Cobb insisted that Marilou had lived rent-free at the Beard lake house.

Marilou denied that, too. She also denied ever receiving a letter directly from Celeste.

But Cobb had Marilou read a letter written on October 25, 2002, by Celeste and addressed to Marilou and her daughter Dana. In it, Celeste asked them to get some stationery to Katina. "She is the one working with Dick."

At that, Marilou said she occasionally got a letter from Celeste.

He asked her about Jimmy Martinez and Tracey.

She said she didn't notice or know about a sexual relationship with Celeste and Jimmy. And she wouldn't believe Celeste was sexual with Tracey unless she saw it with her own eyes.

Mere moments later, Marilou seemed to contradict her own testimony when she stated Celeste had told Steve that she'd had an affair with Jimmy in November 1999.

Cobb asked if Celeste had ever given Marilou any bedroom furniture.

Marilou thought at length before answering no.

DeGuerin sat with his face in his hands.

Then she admitted Celeste had given her a mattress and box springs, a vase, and some earrings for Christmas. "Certainly no large items."

Cobb delved into Marilou's relationship with Steve. He pressed her about how often she saw him.

"I'm sorry, sir. I don't know how to answer that."

He tried to pin her down about Steve knowing about Celeste and Jimmy.

All she answered was that Steve and Celeste had given Jimmy a refrigerator as a housewarming gift.

"You don't know anything about her relationship with Jimmy Martinez," Cobb declared. He pointed out that Marilou Gibbs was the only person to testify that Steve had known about the graduation party at Jimmy's.

The cross-examination was painstaking. Judge Kocurek glanced at the clock on the wall.

Finally, reluctantly, Marilou admitted that she'd seen Steve frequently when the Beards lived at the lake house, but after they'd moved to Toro Canyon, she saw him perhaps once a month.

And lastly, Cobb had Marilou repeat that Steve had said Celeste could go to Atlanta and to counseling with Tracey in order to distance herself from Tracey.

When the kids heard what all Marilou had testified to under oath, they didn't call them tales. They called them lies. They had video of Thanksgiving morning and Celeste lying on a mattress on the floor of the Beard house, the carpet pulled up for the redecorating. The video continued that day at the Grimm family home with tape of Steve's birthday cocker Kaci, Celeste, and a roasted turkey ready to be carved.

The kids claimed Steve hadn't liked Marilou and thought she was lake trash. And they had a videotape of the birthday party Celeste threw for Dawn Madigan at Barton Creek Country Club. There wasn't one split second of video of Steve with Marilou. But there was video of all the women in the restroom with Marilou holding some sort of cigarette.

The kids also laughed that Celeste nicknamed Marilou "Snaggletooth," a name they called her too.

They wanted to know, if Marilou was such good buddies with Steve, how come he told them he didn't like her? Why wasn't she at Steve and Celeste's wedding? And why didn't she visit him even once in the hospital? And why wasn't she at the funeral?

Marilou had answers for all their questions. They just disagreed on the truthfulness of the answers.

A mere twenty minutes before noon, a rotund, bearded man with gray hair walked into the courtroom and took the witness seat. He introduced himself as Gus Voelzel, Steve Beard's architect. Voelzel appeared to be a jolly man whose eyes sparkled when he laughed. But that day, he was irritated. DeGuerin had kept him waiting for too damned long. And like Steve Beard, Voelzel wasn't pleasant when he was irritated.

When DeGuerin asked Voelzel about Megan, he replied, "That dog was absolutely his companion all the time." When a stranger approached Steve, Megan growled. She growled frighteningly so. Steve scolded Megan and swatted her, but never did anything vicious to her.

Dick DeGuerin's witness wasn't turning out to be so good for the defense. For everything DeGuerin proposed about the house—trying to contradict Tracey Tarlton's testimony—Voelzel had an answer, and that answer backed Tarlton's story. The doors from the pool into the house couldn't be unlocked from the outside, only the inside. And one could park pretty close to Kristina's bedroom.

Dick DeGuerin called Bonita Thompson, an employee of Cook-Walden funeral home. Thompson was a large woman with a round face and a shoulder-length shag haircut, who breathed heavily due to illness. She'd gotten out of bed to testify.

Two years before he died, Steve had wanted a family room attached to the mausoleum. He'd told Celeste to take care of caskets for herself and the girls, and three different times, the girls were told that Steve had taken care of their caskets, Thompson swore.

On January 28, 2000, two days after the funeral, Thompson drove over to Toro Canyon, arriving at 10:30 A.M. During that time, Celeste talked about the arrangements she wanted made for her and her daughters' funerals and worked out a payment plan.

Testily, Thompson told Gary Cobb that they were just honoring Mr. Beard's wishes to prearrange the funerals, although he hadn't paid for the arrangements before he'd died. And, the twins signed the forms for their funeral arrangements and caskets.

Cobb stated that Celeste had picked out the coffins.

Thompson disagreed.

Cobb had Thompson read a Cook-Walden letter that stated the mother had purchased the caskets.

And at that, as well as a smile from Bonita to Celeste as Bonita exited the courtroom, the defense rested.

The courtroom went eerily silent, seemingly stunned that Celeste truly hadn't testified.

The twins were certainly stunned. They figured her ego would get her to testify.

Indeed, Celeste had desperately wanted and intended to be on that stand.

She ached to tell her story, with her doing the talking. For weeks, the defense team had prepped her for testimony. They'd planned on her testifying.

But two nights before, Celeste had sat down with her attorneys. "I trust you. You tell me what you think."

Judge Kocurek wanted her convicted and wouldn't give her a fair chance, was what they thought. Look at what she'd let in—the extraneous motion, the audiotapes, the phone records. Look what she'd kept out—Zan Ray, Reginald Breaux, and $100,000 the defense claimed the twins had stolen from Celeste.

Celeste reluctantly accepted their advice.

Though the jury was released, the defense still wasn't

finished. Dick DeGuerin tried one more time to get into evidence his transcript of his interview with Katina Lofton. Kocurek denied him again.

Around 4 P.M., in jailhouse black-and-white stripes, and shackles that clanked when he walked, the much-talked-about Reginald Breaux entered the room. He was a nice looking man with a moustache who was in jail on a domestic violence charge. But Breaux, in an intelligent-sounding voice, talked about his fall 1998 encounter with Tracey Tarlton.

At first, his story was similar to Tracey's. But in his version, Tracey went for a knife in her glove compartment. At that, he told her he was getting out of the car. Tracey started going after him. He responded with profanity, grabbed her knife, got out of her vehicle, laughed at her, and called her a "crazy bitch."

She left, but circled back into the parking lot. As he looked her right in her face, she hit him with the front, driver side bumper, and knocked him down. She started coming back, he said, when the cops showed up, stopped her, and arrested her.

"I thought she was nuts."

Breaux swiveled in his chair. He'd sustained a deep thigh bruise and some scrapes.

Allison Wetzel introduced the police report on the offense and immediately noted that Breaux never mentioned a knife to the cops and didn't pursue the case.

He'd gone to the wrong police station, he explained, called about the case a couple of times, gotten no response, and moved on.

Wetzel reeled off his previous convictions—burglary, theft by check, assault, cocaine possession, and more.

Kocurek again denied DeGuerin's request to allow Reginald Breaux to testify before the jury.

But he needed it, he argued, to show Tracey Tarlton's aggressive nature.

43

By Friday, March 14, 2003, the Celeste Beard Johnson trial was closing out its sixth week and becoming the longest non–death penalty criminal trial in the history of Travis County. Just the night before, Kocurek's 3-year-old daughter had asked her mother if she'd had a bad day sitting in the chair. Everyone, from judge to jury, wanted to go home.

But the State introduced Dr. Richard Coons, a noted forensic psychiatrist and attorney. Many court watchers considered him Travis County's hired gun; he was known for frequently testifying against the insanity plea and for the death penalty. The State's rebuttal witness purposely took a liberal stance on that hot, sunny payday.

He pointedly began by stating that he'd testified in previous cases for both Wetzel and DeGuerin. Then he moved to the more pertinent—he'd met with Tracey Tarlton three times in 2003. She was bipolar, and he stressed he knew judges and doctors who were bipolar, but functioned well when properly treated.

In early 1999, Tracey's bipolar illness was untreated. But at the time of Steve's shooting she was in remission, not suffering any symptoms, and certainly wasn't hallucinating. Coons stressed that he firmly disagreed with Dr. Howard Miller—Tracey Tarlton was not delusional. He based that "mainly on my interview with her."

The actual shooting, he said, didn't involve long-range planning—only Wednesday through Friday. And even then, the plan was changed at the last minute.

He spoke about whether heterosexuals ever had sex with homosexuals and vice versa, saying of course it happened. But he focused on asexuals, which the prosecution believed Celeste to be. Asexuals did have sex, he said. In fact, asexuals used sex to get what they wanted.

With her head down, Celeste listened.

The person in love with the asexual would want to protect her and could be manipulated into doing whatever the asexual wanted. The sex that happened between Tracey and Celeste was consistent with someone who didn't like sex but used it to get what she wanted. In fact, Tracey's family history would have made her vulnerable to a kiss on the mouth.

Dick DeGuerin looked at the large, senior citizen who sat with his shoulders hunched and persisted that Tracey was delusional—Celeste had told Tracey she didn't want a sexual relationship, Tracey's therapist had told her Steve didn't have anything to do with Celeste changing rooms.

"It *could* be delusional, but I don't see it that way," Coons responded, watching the defense attorney through wire-rimmed glasses.

DeGuerin repeatedly tried to shame Coons, first, for not recalling every detail of Tracey's medical records, and, second, for not studying her trial testimony.

Coons then shocked the courtroom. Tracey Tarlton, he said, wasn't obsessed with Celeste Beard. She simply was in love, and pursuing that love was a big part of her life—but not obsessive.

DeGuerin jumped on that, emphasizing that Tracey had a pattern of pursuing heterosexual women.

Coons agreed.

DeGuerin insisted that was obsessive.

Coons relented that it was obsessive before backing off and trying to recover by saying it was a pattern.

Kocurek recessed court to give the jurors a break. Less than thirty minutes later, with the jurors still out, she stood in her courtroom and announced another bomb threat, this one being taken seriously. Kocurek instructed everyone to evacuate immediately.

About forty minutes later court was back in session—the bomb hadn't been a bomb. And Dick DeGuerin was back to his own obsession—Tracey Tarlton tried to recruit straight women.

"It can happen," Coons answered.

As testimony crawled along, Celeste looked angry as

DeGuerin spoke about the card she'd sent Tracey—"For the One I Love." DeGuerin claimed that when one was buying a card one took what one could get.

"I wouldn't send you a card like that," Coons fired. And the courtroom erupted into laughter.

On redirect, Wetzel tried to salvage her expert witness's credibility by asking if Tracey Tarlton was pathologically obsessed.

No, he answered.

She asked if Tracey had shot Steve because he was in the way.

Tracey was trying to protect Celeste from suicide, he answered.

The jury was excused around noontime, but DeGuerin kept Coons on the stand to ask him about Tracey's involvement with Zan Ray and her alleged attempt to kill Reginald Breaux. DeGuerin insisted that that history was important.

Coons countered that Tracey was symptomatic at those times, suffering an untreated bipolar illness, and intoxicated; but she wasn't symptomatic when she shot Steve— she was under treatment, and she wasn't intoxicated.

Kocurek told DeGuerin to wrap it up; DeGuerin asked to revisit the Breaux situation. Kocurek stuck with her ruling.

By 2:30 that afternoon, the State closed.

Less than ten minutes later, DeGuerin called psychologist Dr. Jerome Brown, a balding man with tufts of gray hair sprouting over his ears, a face so red that he looked like a bearded plum tomato, and a gut so large that he looked like he belonged on the old TV show *Jake and the Fat Man*.

Swaying in his chair as he spoke in a soft voice that didn't match his body, Brown explained that he'd studied Tracey's medical records, journals, cards, letters, and three volumes of her testimony, and he'd listened to Dr. Howard's and Dr. Coons' testimonies. He pronounced Tracey's interest in Celeste as "a pathological obsessive attachment." When it reached the extreme, one could be violent toward the object of obsession, violent toward oneself, violent to others to impress the object, or violent toward those the obsessed perceived as keeping her away from her object of obsession.

Tracey's belief that Celeste had started flirting with her right away was a common misinterpretation. Her longing or fantasy was only reinforced by their continuing contact, which made it even more difficult for Tracey to let go. He compared it to a wife who wanted a divorce, so her husband killed her.

"Maybe some sex happened," DeGuerin conceded. "Would that make it any different?"

That would make it worse, Brown stated. Plus, Tracey's bipolar illness and history greatly increased her chance of violence. Brown's eyes got lost in his face.

DeGuerin wanted to know how Tracey could come before a jury and lie.

She was angry at Celeste and wanted to hurt her, Brown answered.

Allison Wetzel asked if Tracey and Celeste had had sex.

"Honestly," he said, "I can't figure it out."

But when Dick DeGuerin had asked Celeste time and again whether she and Tracey had had sex, Celeste finally stopped DeGuerin's questioning of her with one sentence: "Dick, I don't eat at the Y."

Wetzel wanted to know if it was significant that Celeste gave a wedding ring to Tracey *after* the shooting.

"I don't know what to make of that."

Wetzel asked what Brown thought of Tracey saying she shot Steve to protect Celeste.

"I think Miss Tarlton believes that." And she believed that, he said, because she was delusional.

Court recessed for the weekend, but Dick DeGuerin tried once again to get Reginald Breaux on the stand.

Kocurek chuckled. "I was wondering if you could get the Reginald Breaux request in one more time."

"All rise." Monday, March 17, 2003, was the first time since the beginning of the trial that Judge Julie Kocurek formally took the bench rather than slipping quietly and unnoticed into her black leather chair.

The courtroom was packed on the three-year anniversary of Celeste's first St. Patrick's Day spent with her most recent husband, Cole Johnson, and her one and only St. Patrick's Day with her nemesis Donna Goodson. Celeste's trial for the solicitation of Tracey's murder still hadn't been set. No one wanted to think about that. Everyone just hoped it would mysteriously go away. They were thinking about closing arguments and, they hoped, a quick verdict.

First, though, DeGuerin had to try one last time to get into evidence the transcription of his interview with Katina Lofton.

Appearing impatient, Kocurek ruled against him again. Then, at 10:15 A.M., the State reopened its case and called Bob Powell, the natural-born Beard kids' tall, elderly civil attorney with a mortician-thin face and complexion from the dead. He was there to introduce Celeste Beard Johnson's August 2000 videotaped deposition.

In a staccato voice, he read from the deposition transcript.

"Did you ever have a romantic involvement with Tracey Tarlton?"

"No, I did not."

"Did you have any kind of intimate physical relationship with Tracey Tarlton?"

"No, I did not."

Dick DeGuerin objected. He wanted the videotape introduced.

Kocurek overruled him, and Powell resumed reading.

"Did you ever engage in a kiss in any passionate way with Tracey Tarlton?"

"No, I did not."

"Or she with you?"

"No."

Celeste glared at Powell, but as he continued reading, some jurors glared equally hard at Celeste while spectators in the gallery softly harrumphed.

"Was there any other reason that you had grown increasingly uncomfortable with Tracey Tarlton, other than the incident at Jimmy Martinez's house in the last week of August?"

"Yes." She explained, "It was when Steven and Tracey were drinking out front." She thought it was the Wednesday hamburger night before graduation.

"Kristina, myself, Tracey, and Steven were on the front porch, and I was sitting in one of the chairs on the left-hand side if you're facing Toro Canyon, and Steve and Tracey were sitting in the two chairs on the right-hand side, and Kristina was leaning up against the fence or the—not the—yeah, the fence. It's a little courtyard. And when Steven went to use the restroom, Tracey came over to talk to me, and I felt like she was, you know, leaning into me, and it made me feel uncomfortable."

"Did you say anything to her?"

"No. I just, you know, pushed her away because I felt uncomfortable." Celeste waited until the next morning to tell Steve "because he was pretty drunk."

"And what did he say the next morning?"

"I don't know what his exact words were, but I felt, after telling him, that it was in my imagination."

"That what was in your imagination?"

"That she was in my space."

About half of the jurors held one of their hands over their mouths. The others took notes. Celeste and DeGuerin whispered. And Powell read about Celeste contacting Tracey in "May or June 2000."

"Did you tell her that she was the cause of what you were going through?"

"No, I don't believe so."

"Did you ask her why she shot Steven Beard?"

"No, I don't think so."

"Did you ask her if she shot Steven Beard?"

"No, I don't think so."

"Did you say, 'Why have you done this to me, Tracey?'"

"I don't know what I said to her exactly."

"Did she deny shooting Steven Beard?"

"I don't think that came up."

On cross-examination, Dick DeGuerin emphasized that that deposition had been taken in August 2000, before Tracey Tarlton was charged with murder, before Celeste

Beard Johnson was charged with anything, and that the lawsuit had been dropped the day before Justin Grimm was to be deposed.

DeGuerin asked Powell if he and the children were planning on filing suit against Celeste again "after" Celeste was convicted.

"No, sir."

At 11:15 A.M., the State closed again.

Dick DeGuerin called Boone Almanza.

The natural-born Beard children got up and walked out of the courtroom.

Almanza declared that "most definitely" he believed the children and Bank of America would file suit again against Celeste.

Ten minutes after Almanza took the stand, DeGuerin introduced the actual videotape of Celeste's August 2000 deposition.

The camera focused on a prim, proper, and demure Celeste Beard Johnson dressed all in white, her shoulders slumped, her hands under the table, and her voice sweet and soft as she answered each question.

"Did Tracey Tarlton own a shotgun?"

"I have no personal knowledge that she owned a shotgun." Celeste sounded tired, just as Kristina had on the hit man tape.

She was asked if her friendship with Tracey ever changed.

Celeste paused at length before saying, "We remained friends."

"Did you know that Tracey Tarlton would be at Timberlawn before you arrived at Timberlawn?"

"I don't recall," she quickly stated.

"Did you ever pay for a trip for Tracey Tarlton?"

"Did I?" Her voice was downy soft. "I don't think so."

"Did you ever spend the night at Tracey Tarlton's home?"

"No, I did not," she answered with speed.

"Did you ever, on any occasion, place sleeping pills in Steven Beard's food in the evening?"

"No, I did not."

She stated that on "quite a few" occasions Tracey visited the Beard house at Kristina's, Steve's, or Celeste's invitation to have cocktails with Steve. She cocked her head over her left shoulder and claimed that Kristina was as close to Tracey as she was.

"Was there ever any occasion where Steven Beard told you that he did not want Tracey Tarlton coming back to the house at twenty-nine hundred [sic] Toro Canyon again?"

"No, not that I know of." And he never inferred it either.

As Celeste continued, her posture became less prim and she sometimes wiped at her eyes. And the questioning eased to the night Steve was shot.

"Why did you leave Megan at the lake house?"

"Because Amy specifically begged me to leave her."

"And what was the reason that you drove to the lake house that night?"

"Because Steven had gone to sleep and I was by myself, and I always went somewhere to—either shopping with Kristina at Wal-Mart in the middle of the night or out to the lake house if one of the kids were there if I was at home by myself."

"Did you suggest to Justin and/or Kristina that Justin should not spend the night that night?"

"No. Justin was not allowed to spend the night at our house."

As the jurors paid close attention in the courtroom, on the video Celeste said she didn't recall talking to Tracey on Friday, October 1, 1999. And, she started becoming testy. She came home from the lake house, checked on Steve, changed into her pajamas, went outside and smoked a cigarette, then climbed into bed with Kristina, and fell asleep around 1 A.M.

Celeste began to cry, became upset, shed more tears, blotted her eyes, and sniffled as she explained about the cops coming in, the Dennisons coming over, and the gunpowder residue test at the hospital.

"Had you been told at this point that your husband had been shot?"

"I was told when they were wheeling my husband out of the house. I think Bob Dennison told me."

"And did you ask who did it?"

Passionately, loudly, and still crying, Celeste proclaimed, "I was in shock and I was hysterical, and my thoughts weren't—excuse me. My thoughts were not on who could have done it but just that my husband—was he going to *die*? That's all I cared about."

By then, the courtroom gallery was butt-to-butt seating and tempers were flaring. Everyone wanted to hear Celeste's "testimony."

On the tape she admitted to initiating that May or June 2000 contact with Tracey by calling her on a pay phone from a downtown restaurant. "I think I just told her I needed to talk to her." They then met behind BookPeople.

"What did you say to Tracey?"

"All I remember is that I was hysterically crying because I was upset about my children."

"And you were seeking comfort from her?"

"I was not seeking comfort from Tracey," Celeste said, her voice touchy.

"What were you seeking?"

"I don't know what I was seeking. I was distraught and I was upset, and I just wanted her to know what I was going through."

Many of the jurors looked up and at Celeste.

"When you called Tracey from the restaurant downtown, you made reference to your family and you were distraught about your family. What was it in particular that you were distraught about, about your family?"

"Because I had lost my *entire* family in less than six months." Celeste was emotional.

"And were you blaming Tracey for that?"

"I don't know. I don't know what my intention was on calling her. I don't know. I don't. I can't explain why I did what I did. I shouldn't have done it, but I did it. And I don't know why I did it. I was just upset."

Questioning eventually moved to money—Celeste inflating invoices, checks forged with Celeste's signature. The

more they discussed money, the more irritated Celeste became. And just as she'd done at the November pre-trial
hearing, her irritation and anger turned to tears, then to
tiredness. Repeatedly, she yawned to indicate her exhaustion. The exhaustion resulted in a nearly inaudible voice as
Celeste, on the videotape, looked down, and spoke about
her various hospitalizations.

"Have you had any other medical treatment than those
hospitalizations that you've described to me?"

"I started treatment for breast cancer"—several heads
flipped around on that—"and then I didn't follow through
with it, but I'm starting again on Monday."

After the videotape ended, Celeste wept.

*"I was on Xanax for that deposition. That's why my answers
were so slow like that. I thought the kids were going to be
there. You know, I didn't know who was going to be there, so
that's why I took the sedative."*

"A lot of people think the Bible says that money is the root
of all evil. And what the Bible actually says is that the love
of money is the root of all evil. Celeste Beard loved money
more than she loved anything else," Gary Cobb proclaimed
in closing arguments. "Because of that, she had Steve Beard
killed."

Cobb pointed to a chart that outlined the millions Celeste would inherit if Steve died. Then he flipped over the
chart. "On the back. Look closely." The back side was
blank. That, he said, is what Celeste would have gotten if
she and Steve had divorced—"a big pocket full of nothing."

Catherine Baen, for the first time in the trial, stood before the jury. Attempting to do a PowerPoint presentation,
she couldn't get her words and exhibits in sync. She droned
on and on, eating into DeGuerin's time, his face turning
redder with each minute that passed.

Finally, just after 5:30 that evening, Dick DeGuerin began his closing argument. "Celeste Beard is not a saint. But
she is a caring person who . . . picks up strays," he said.
"Celeste Beard did not do this. She was better off with

Steve Beard alive. Lifestyle is not guilt."

Passionately, he declared that Tracey Tarlton killed Steven Beard out of her own sick, selfish reasons. And he showed the jury a photograph of Tracey, in the courtroom, holding the killer shotgun. "She's a crazy woman!"

When the judge gave DeGuerin a five-minute warning, he begged for ten and got it. Tracey Tarlton didn't shoot Steve Beard in the stomach because she didn't want to make a mess, he said. He reached for a pillow and shook out a white sheet.

Groans emitted from the gallery.

He stretched out on the already cleared defense table, balanced the pillow on his gut, covered himself with the big sheet, and declared that Tracey had shot Steve Beard in the stomach because that's all she could see. "Can you see my head?"

Celeste giggled. The jurors watched her giggle. They didn't laugh with her.

At 6:45 P.M., Allison Wetzel stood. She noted that the defense had conceded there was a sexual relationship with Tracey. She pointed out that Amy and Christopher had no reason to lie. She mentioned the Sunday Suck—"I gotta go make some money."

"Money," she declared, "is what this whole case is about." She brought out the bank's copy of the check Celeste had given Christopher Doose for the trip to Canada, the one DeGuerin had proclaimed could only be cashed if Jennifer made no Cs. On the bank's copy, there was no notation at all about grades. It had been added *after* Christopher cashed the check, and it was out of his hands.

She showed the jury Jennifer's ring and Tracey's identical ring.

She emphasized Celeste's infected fingers. She "made a beeline for his colostomy bag." She talked about the hit man tape and how Celeste had spoken to Kristina—cursing her, threatening her. "That's the real Celeste Beard. Not this little butter-melt-in-your-mouth."

44

"I was kinda overwhelmed when [Tracey] said in court that, um, that I was flirting with her because I didn't see me flirting with her. I didn't look at her as a lesbian. I just looked at her as a person. And, um, the fact that she was lesbian never entered the picture for me, at the beginning of the friendship."

As dusk fell into dark and the jurors deliberated, the Beard family and friends didn't seem to want to leave the courthouse. They chatted, they hugged, they cried, until they spotted Dick DeGuerin talking to the press. At that, they scooted for the elevators, the TV cameras swung off of DeGuerin and followed them. As the elevator doors closed, the kids giggled—they thought it was cool that they'd taken the cameras off of Dick.

Finally, the exhausted jury collapsed in a nearby hotel, while Allison Wetzel was on the phone, seemingly needing to talk, while Celeste Beard Johnson sat in her cell.

"I wished I had been allowed to testify. I pondered how I had lived my life and reflected on things I could have done differently. I wondered how many people could withstand a microscopic investigation of their life. I thought about how I never stood a chance in this family against millions of dollars. I prayed that Steve wasn't turning over in his grave because of what was happening to me. He had done everything he could to protect me."

The verdict watch continued into Tuesday, March 18, 2003. Becky Beard woke early that morning, reached for the telephone in her Holiday Inn room, and started calling others to have someone to talk to. She woke almost everyone she phoned.

By 10:30 that morning, the jury room smelled with sweat from too many stressed people in too small of a room for too many weeks. And the jurors wanted some of the court reporter's notes read to them.

Kocurek said they could only have portions read if they disagreed on the witness's statement.

Already, the jury had had delivered to their room the tapes of Celeste talking to Kristina, floor plans of the house, phone records, letters from Katina Lofton, the entire Kilimanjaro of medical records, Celeste's personal date book, the family planner, the book on poisoning, and a three-hole punch.

"I was a nervous wreck all alone in that cell. I have heard, the longer the jury is out, the greater the chance of a guilty verdict. I kept rehashing the trial."

• • •

A verdict didn't seem like it was close, so Becky Beard and her niece Kelly did a bit of shopping, while Paul and Kim camped in their Extended StayAmerica hotel room watching TV and nervously smoking cigarette after cigarette. At least they were comfortable in shorts and T-shirts while they sat in front of the television.

DeGuerin spent much of the day in the judge's outer office chewing the fat with one of the alternates who was relishing spending time with "the" Dick DeGuerin. As Megan had never left Steve's side, the alternate—who wasn't convinced that Celeste was guilty—never left DeGuerin's.

The press spent the day staring out the windows watching the clouds and thunderstorms that morning and the sun come out in the afternoon. They meandered in and out of the courtroom, the pressroom, the restrooms, any place they could think to go, looking more exhausted than the family members.

The kids hid in the victims' services conference room in the DA's office, next door to Ellen's office. They swapped Steve Beard stories and laughed.

Celeste still waited in the holding tank. In the dark, tiny, rectangle of a cell with one bench and one toilet. And one small, rectangle of glass at standing eye-level. If only she could have testified . . .

"I'm trying to remember. I remember the day of the shooting. Let me think about the week of the shooting. I mean, we were, you know, trying to get ready, uh, for Europe. Steve was sick. The travel agent was, uh, harassing me about getting travel insurance. So I went down and did that. I don't know if Steve was in—Steve was—he was okay to travel. We had to get, um, his oxygen and stuff like that. I mean, we were just running around to get ready for the trip.

"Um, and then the kids came and asked about going to— one of them going to the lake house. I think it was Jennifer and Christopher. Yeah, I'm thinking it was in the middle of the week. It was quite a few days before. And, um, so that meant that Kristina had to stay at home, because one of them always had to stay at home, if the other one went to the lake house—because I ended up being alone in the house. And I didn't like it.

"I mean, Steve was there, but he was passed out all the time, you know, after a certain time at night. And so—and I slept in the girls' bedroom, in Kristina's bedroom. She had two twin beds at the time. And I didn't want to be alone so that was just the deal. That's the way it worked out. Only one of them could go to the lake house.

"And so that—Kristina asked I think that day if she could go to, um, the movies with Justin. And I said yes. And she said she'd be home at I believe at midnight. She came home, and I was still there. No, she came home—when she was gone I had driven out to the lake house with the dogs. And I left Megan there."

"So, anyway, I went out to the lake house, which, that wasn't unusual, and saw the kids. And, uh, I left Megan for Amy—because it was Christopher and Jennifer and then Amy was by herself. She was like the odd man out."

• • •

Amy's appearance explained why she was odd man out, Celeste said.

"And she loved Megan. Like when she slept over at our house, Megan would sleep with her. And she had Megan at her house before. And so anyway, I left Megan. I wasn't that close to Megan.

"And so then I came home and Kristina was already home. And she was in bed, and I talked to her for a little bit about the movies. And then I got ready for bed."

But Kristina testified that she never talked to or saw her mother before Celeste woke her up as the sheriff's lights flashed through her windows.

". . . She did before she turned against me."

"And I had checked on Steve. And, um . . . probably— this is all around midnight—'cause when Steve gets drunk he takes his, uh, breathing mask off of his face, when he gets drunk. And so that's why I checked on him—to make sure he still had his mask on. And everything was fine, so then I went into Kristina's room.

"My pa-jam-as and stuff were in there, which were left in there. I had a drawer that had my p.j.s in it. And I got ready for bed and went to bed. And then the next thing I know we're being awakened by these bright lights. I think Nikki was probably growling because she slept up above my head on my pillow.

"And there's these bright lights just going through the slates on the blinds. And Kristina and I got up at the same time. Nikki was already at the door, and so we opened the door a little bit. And pulled on Nikki, you know, made sure that Nikki didn't get out the door. And we went into the guest bedroom and shut the door to Kristina's bedroom. But you could see these lights coming through the sliding glass doors in the hallway. And so we went in the guest bedroom."

Kristina stated that when she woke, Celeste was already standing at the foot of her bed. And it was Celeste who woke her.

"I'm a very hard—heavy sleeper. She always has to wake me up in the morning. The girls would have to wake—get me up in the morning. If they had to go somewhere, they'd have to come wake me up."

But that 3 a.m., they moved from Kristina's room to the guestroom.

". . . Because we were trying to see what it was. And, um, then when we got out into the hallway, we got scared.

"We kept Nikki in the bedroom. She was scratching on the door. We kept Nikki in Kristina's bedroom."

"And I was like—I mean, this—I'm embarrassed to say, but she was in front of me, and I'm like pushing her—like when, um, there was a bug in the house, you know, I pushed Jennifer to kill the bug. I mean, that's embarrassing to say, but I was pushing her [Kristina] in front of me, you know, go, go. And then we went into the guest bedroom. And called 911."

Kristina did the dialing.

"And this must be when 911 is calling our house, because Steve was calling—we didn't hear the phone ringing. One line in her—on her desk in her bedroom had the house phone, but we were in the next bedroom and so we didn't hear the phone ringing.

"But the guest bedroom had only one phone line and it didn't have the house phone line. It had a separate phone number. Nine-one-one told us that the police were already in our house, that it was the police. So we hung up the phone and we went in there.

"We had hung up the phone and, um, and I went down that long hallway, and then past the butler's pantry and then through the kitchen and through the breakfast room, and then, you know, down the stairs where that you could either go into the dining room or the bar. Um, I was coming right

there, right past the bar, when the sheriff was coming down the steps off of my wing.

"And he kept asking me, um, 'Did your husband just have surgery? Did your husband just have surgery?' Well, that's freakin' me out because Steve at the lake house a few years ago Steven had fallen and cut his head open and there was blood everywhere. And so I was panicking because he's asking me that question, and I kept saying, 'What's wrong with him?' you know, 'Don't let him die,' because I didn't know what was wrong with him. I just thought the worst because they wouldn't tell me. They just kept asking if he had surgery.

"And then they're pushing us out the front door as they're talking to me. You know, they're not letting me go see how he is—or what's wrong. And so I just freak out because, you know, I just imagine the worst.

"And then our neighbors, Dr. Dennison and Bess came over, and Bess was hugging me. And I was sitting on the steps—the front steps, and, um, she was holding on to me. And I asked Bob to go find out what was wrong with Steven, since he was a doctor.

"And I don't know at what point—Kristina had gone back in the house to get me shoes and, um, 'cause I had my pa-jam-as on. And, um, she got those out of her side of the—their side of the house because that's where I kept all my casual clothes was on that side of the house because I slept over there. Um, I didn't sleep in my bedroom.

"And then she had also gone back in the house. She was over, um, by—I don't know if she actually went in our bedroom or just by our bedroom, but, um, and she came out. And I don't—I think it was her that told me that, um, Steven had been shot.

"And then not too long after that, they wheeled Steven down the front steps and, um, I—I—I was able to tell him that I loved him.

"I stayed in my pajamas. They're actually see-through basically. They were real—they were pink and summer pajamas. And, um, the sheriff—the woman took us—took Kristina and I to the hospital, I sat up in the front seat with her, and Kristina sat in the back. So there was no—Kristina said that

I told her, 'Don't mention Tracey's name' on the way to the hospital, there's absolutely no way that that was possible because I sat in the front seat with the officer. So there's no way I could have communicated anything with Kristina.

"And I thought that they [the cops] were doing me a favor because I was so distraught, you know, by driving me to the hospital. I didn't realize . . . I did not realize until, um, Philip [Presse] was there that they were actually thinking I was a suspect. I mean, I thought they were doing me a favor.

"Well, actually it was right before Philip got there. It was when they swabbed my hands. I asked them, 'Am I a suspect?' because I start thinking why are they doing that.

"It made me feel like they thought that I had some—that I had shot Steve, you know, had something to do with it.

"And then Philip came. Kristina's the one that called Philip. And then Philip told me not to talk. But she also—but Kristina also called Bailey Elliott [their house builder] and Gus Voelzel.

"But the weird part when we were pulling out with the sheriff was Justin was there. And he was parked on Toro Canyon, and, um, how did he know that that happened?"

Kristina, however, said she phoned Justin.

"From what—phone? Yeah, because we couldn't find it on the cell phone records. And we thought that that was really odd."

Another thing she and her supporters thought was "strange" was the shotgun found in the attic.

"It was the same gauge and everything. And Christopher exchanged it somewhere, and he doesn't remember where. So, my attorney had a hard time finding it. I mean, he couldn't find it.

"But we were trying to figure out—Kristina and Justin were the only ones that knew what kind of guns Tracey had. They knew she had a shotgun, and they knew what kind of *shotgun and everything. Kristina took that one gun from Tracey and gave it to the police. And Kristina and Justin had access to Tracey's house. So we were thinking that maybe if they were—if that gun wasn't going to work they got the other gun, you know. I mean it's just odd that—I mean that's just an odd thing for Jennifer to buy and keep it hidden in the attic."*

She returned to the scene at the hospital on the day Steve was shot.

"And then I'm, I'm freezing. I'm—I'm distraught and Ana [Presse] gave me some Valiums. And I'm just laying [sic] on the floor. I can't even sleep, you know, waiting for Steve's surgery. And then they all pile their jackets on top of me, everybody in there.

"I was just—I just remember I was cold. And I couldn't stop crying. I mean they all piled their jac—I just remember laying [sic] in the middle of the floor with all these jackets on top of me. I think Steve's surgery took like fourteen hours.

"And the doctors—they were all so nice to me. Yeah, and um, when Steve—every day Steve would get a little bit better, you know, do a little bit better. And at one point, Dr. Coscia was like buy wine, bring him wine, I don't care, bring him any kind of food, just get him to eat anything. So I was bringing him all of his favorite foods from, you know, outside. I'd even get him his chicken 'n' dumplings from . . ."

She couldn't remember the name of the place, but she could remember it was off Dessau Road.

"She has the best. I mean, it's soul food. It's a black lady that cooks it, and the place doesn't look real clean, but it's the best chicken 'n' dumplings you've ever had. Dot's! It is so good."

She brought him his favorite soaps. She brought him wine, even though Steve didn't drink wine.

"I just went everywhere.

". . . In the trial, they were saying how I didn't hire anybody to take care of him at home, and that was because he asked me not to. He asked me to take care of him. And I was thinking, you know, that it's my fault—" Celeste started to cry. *"Yeah, because if I never would have brought Tracey into our lives, then none of this would have happened."*

Tears filled her throat. *"So I was—I was—I learned how to change his dressing. I took all those classes, you know, and did everything. And all I was supposed to do was take him back and forth to get his dressing changed."* She sniffed back her tears.

"Well, not class classes, but, I mean, like I'd have to come in at a certain time and the nurses would show me how to—how to do things, how to care for him, but I didn't have to do because it was scheduled for him to have a dressing change every day, so I had to—you know, all I'd have to do is bathe him and take care of him and, um, you know, if the stuff—if his bag, uh, exploded or something on him, all I'd have to do is, you know, change it. I knew how to do that—his ileostomy bag. But basically it was just, you know, as far as the other stuff, I just had to make sure he got in the car, you know, helped him into the car and took him down there once a day, seven days a week for his wound care, is what they called it."

She returned to those first few days at Brackenridge Hospital and the sign on Steve's hospital door that warned away cops, long-time friends and long-time relatives.

"And Steve used the phone and called people. He conducted business out of the hospital. He worked on our house. We were building the maid's quarters. You know, all of that stuff was done out of the—when he was, I think, on the sixth floor. And, um, if he wanted to talk to the police, he could've called. And if they wanted to talk to him, they

could've called. But they chose not to. And they chose not to call Charles Burton. And now they're blaming me."

"After we left the hotel room, I don't even remember how long we stayed at the, um, the first hotel and then we moved to La Quinta, because I think the first hotel was like two hundred dollar a night or something.

"And, um, after we finally moved back home, I was going—the visits are like every couple of hours. And I was going to every visit, and I was exhausted. I wasn't getting any sleep. And I'd go up there—"

She was silent for ten seconds, then cried again.

Around four that afternoon, the jury made more requests—the financial spreadsheet, records regarding stays at the La Quinta Inn in Waco, photos of the lake house, the letter from Cook-Walden funeral home, and phone bills that indicated Celeste had paid for Tracey's cell phone.

Steven Beard III chatted with Dana Whatley. Later, Dana quietly talked into a micro-cassette recorder. She appeared exhausted. In contrast, Cole Johnson looked just fine. Later, Steven III joked with the press and prosecutors while Dana, Marilou, and Cole sat quietly on the front row of the courtroom, reading and waiting.

That night he and his family went to Threadgill's restaurant, one of Austin's landmarks from the days of Janis Joplin, for some down-home cooking. Kim and Paul got takeout from Pok-e-Jo's, an inexpensive barbecue joint on Fifth Street near their motel, and ate in their room. They weren't big on socializing with the rest of the family.

Celeste fondly recalled her last Christmas with Steve—just the two of them together. The girls were with their boyfriends.

"You know what Steve had made for me? The most beautiful, um, opal and diamond—um, it was a black opal and diamond ring with, uh, . . . the band and everything was, uh, . . . platinum. And it was—the stone was about that big."

She circled her fingers between a nickel and quarter size.

"It was buuu*-tiful. It was all filigree. He had, um, he had Kirk Root make it for me. And he also had, um, commissioned Kirk to make this* huge *ruby set for me for my birthday and anniversary—or, no, my birthday and Valentine's Day—which, uh, Kristina took.*

"I didn't even know about it until I saw it on the bank stuff. She went and picked it up from Kirk Root when I was in the hospital." Celeste stuttered briefly. *"That's what I mean that Steve was doing business and stuff, conducting his affairs while he was in the hospital. So if he wanted to call the police or talk to them, there would have been no problem."*

She very loudly blew her nose. *"And he gave that ring to me Christmas day when we were at the hospital—the black opal. . . . It's gorgeous.*

"I gave him—I had another ring made for him by Kirk. I think I had a jade ring made. It's hard for me to remember because I gave all this jewelry to the kids.

"Steve and I had just a private little dinner. . . . In the hospital—I bought, uh, his favorite steak and potato from Ruth's Chris. Salad, and we ate in his room. At that time I believe he was in South Austin."

By Wednesday, Paul and Kim looked bushed; Allison Wetzel hadn't slept. When the jurors paraded into the courtroom just before 10 A.M., a few were smiling. Most appeared stressed, worried, exhausted, as though they'd taken a big exam.

Outside, where life went on, the sun shined, the March winds blew and the United States went to war—Operation Iraqi Freedom. But in Judge Korcurek's 390th Courtroom, no one noticed. Dana Whatley didn't smile all day, while most of the Beard family still gathered in the first-floor conference room laughing, playing cards, and telling stories, the kids mimicking Celeste frying in an electric chair.

· · ·

Around 4:40 that afternoon, the long awaited announcement came—a verdict had been rendered. The courtroom immediately filled.

Twenty minutes later, the Beard family arrived. Kristina, looking near tears, walked in holding Ellen's hand. She, Jennifer, Christopher, and a weeping Amy all touched.

A Kleenex box was passed among the natural-born Beards.

Sheriff Margo Frasier, in an animal print blouse, walked into the courtroom, followed by the sheriff's department public information officer. Four deputies stood in the courtroom's one aisle. At least two more stood near the door closest to Celeste.

Anita Ashton and her husband Jerry Inglis entered as Sheriff Frasier spoke with the twins.

"And so now [Anita's] taking my children as her own children. That's what it is. She's giving them all the hugs that they never got from me because they're saying, you know, that I didn't hug them enough. I mean, hell, I did everything for them."

At 5:05, Allison Wetzel entered.

As the jurors entered the courtroom, some looked at Celeste Beard Johnson. All were dry-eyed. By then, more deputies had entered the courtroom. One stood near the jurors' door, two stood near the twins, and seven stood near Celeste.

Stevie Beard, Steve's grandson, kissed his father Steven III, and the capital murder verdict was read.

Like a shockwave of electricity it bolted through the family—"Guilty."

45

When the verdict came back, it felt like a dagger went straight through my heart. My face showed no emotion. I refused to let them see me suffering. I was terrified of going to prison. When I got back to my cell, I was placed under suicide watch for seventy-two hours. I wasn't able to stop crying because the fear overwhelmed me.

Celeste quietly cried as Kocurek called the attorneys to the bench.

At 5:20 P.M., court was recessed until 10 A.M., Thursday.

The large, blindingly dark lounge of the Spaghetti Warehouse restaurant on Austin's Fourth Street was reputed to be haunted by ghosts, just as was the mausoleum where Steve Beard rested in his crypt.

Wednesday night, while air strikes continued in Iraq, the Beard clan and friends and supporters walked across the wooden plank sidewalk into the Warehouse, turned a quick right through the curtains and entered the lounge. As a TV crew filmed them, the group drank, smoked cigars, watched the news on overhead TVs, and erupted in a cheering roar as the verdict was aired.

That night many of the kids got drunk.

Allison Wetzel was at home with her children and preparing for the sentencing phase. Sitting on her desk at the office was a pair of brass balls that had suddenly appeared after the verdict was announced, an honor given by the DA's office.

On Thursday, March 20, 2003, folks were rustled out of bed by frantic phone calls—court was starting at 8:30 A.M.

rather than 10. Judge Kocurek had wanted to send the jurors home and let them get some rest. Dick DeGuerin had refused to agree. He wanted them sequestered again, despite the fact that during the trial he'd stated he didn't want the jury sequestered.

So as Celeste wore her favorite pink, and matched Catherine Baen, who was in pink too, her fingers were rolled in black ink pressed against a fingerprint card. Cole stood nearby. Celeste cried.

"While I was being fingerprinted, I told myself to think of something beautiful. I thought of my dogs, Nikki and Orly. For me, that is the only way to endure the unbearable. Instead of being humiliated, I thought about my husband and my friends and family. No matter what, these people have stood by me. Because of this I was able to hold my head up."

Becky Beard took the stand. Wetzel couldn't ask a question and Becky couldn't answer without DeGuerin objecting. Still, the jurors heard that her father had been her Rock of Gibraltar, her financial adviser, her everything. He listened; he gave advice. Suddenly, he wasn't there to talk to.

DeGuerin continued objecting, but objecting quietly, as Becky joked that she'd wanted a Cadillac for her 50th birthday, but she'd had a good party that the twins had attended. Becky began to cry. She and Jennifer had bonded that night.

She recounted Celeste telling her that Steve didn't love her, Becky responding that when her father got better she'd tell him what Celeste had said, and Celeste getting "very, very angry." Celeste told Becky that she would not tell him. Becky retorted that she would.

And Becky remembered the night before Steve died, when she spoke to him for ten or fifteen minutes, and her dad frantically repeating, "I love you, Becky. I love you."

"And I'd get to spend like ten minutes with him, which is why I fought with his daughter, because she wanted to take

*my visits. And I said, 'Why can't we split them?' Or share
them? And she wanted them all for herself, and I was like,
"No!" So, you know, I'm like the big bitch because—"*

Paul Beard briefly stepped into the witness box to recall the
hunting trips and fishing trips he'd taken with his dad, as well
as their driving trip to the 1964 World's Fair in New York City.

His dad had been proud of him, Paul said, for joining the
Navy. On April 30, 2003, Paul would retire from the military, but he wasn't going to have a retirement ceremony because his dad wouldn't be there. At that, Paul Beard broke
down and couldn't continue.

At 10:30 A.M., the girls walked into the courtroom. Dana
Whatley wrapped her arm around her mother as the charges
against Celeste were read, and the jury received its instructions. Already, Celeste was guaranteed life on the capital
murder charge. They were to consider her injury-to-an-el-
derly-individual sentence.

Barely fifteen minutes after the girls arrived, Gary
Cobb stood before the jury to present his closing argument. He asked for the maximum punishment—life. And
talked about what a schemer Celeste was, clear back to her
days in Arizona.

As Cobb delved more into Arizona, DeGuerin objected
and moved for a mistrial.

Celeste listened intently.

"This case has never been about the money for this family. It will never be about the money."

The courtroom was quiet and subdued except for the
weeping of Paul, his wife Kim, and Steve's granddaughter,
Kelly.

DeGuerin stepped up to the jury. At first, he spoke softly.
"I tried to be candid and honest with you throughout this
trial . . . and I failed." Then he raged, "By God! I disagree
with your verdict. I disagree with it strongly!"

He seemed to be shaming the jurors, and the looks on
their faces did not remotely hint that they were co-
dependent people who would respond to shaming.

DeGuerin vowed that he knew there was reasonable doubt and demanded that the jurors who knew that too stand up and be heard.

The jurors were hard-faced.

DeGuerin stated that he'd made a mistake in not pointing out that Tracey had lied. He talked about Studio 29, Dawn Madigan, and Joseph Prete. He said Celeste had been at the lake house at 11 P.M. on October 1, 1999.

Wetzel objected—that wasn't what was in evidence.

And again DeGuerin resorted to shame. He disagreed with the jury's decision. He disagreed with their ruling.

"Punishment is different from guilt or innocence," Wetzel began. Celeste Beard Johnson's fraudulent behavior reflected her behavior in the murder of Steve Beard.

She asked the jury to recall the "anonymous" letter Celeste wrote newspaper reporter Laylan Copelin. "I want you to see Celeste as the victim she is," Celeste had written.

She's over there in her pink sweater, Wetzel continued, white tissue and little tears, but she is not the victim. She wanted that big, ole pot of money. "She couldn't wait another five years." She wanted it right now!

As Wetzel spoke about the twins—they have both lost the only parent who cared about them because of the greed of this woman—Kristina looked over at Celeste.

Wetzel talked about Tracey being vulnerable and just wanting someone to love her. "But folks, Tracey Tarlton did not do this on her own," and she would not have done it on her own.

Wetzel moved to DeGuerin's pillow-and-sheet trick, "sorta a made-for-TV moment." But Wetzel said it was a reminder of how vulnerable Steve was just moments before he died.

Do not lose sight of who planned the murder down to the last detail, Wetzel said. It would have been more humane to shoot him in the head and get it over with.

She mentioned how Steve had called out to Celeste via his 911 call.

Dick DeGuerin, she said, wanted the jury to negate all

he hard work they'd done and be a hung jury. Don't do it. Punishment puts meaning to the verdict. Give Celeste Beard Johnson, Wetzel said, "what she's earned and what she richly deserves."

Court watchers barely had time to grab a lunch snack before the jury returned. And the majority of that time the jurors simply spent trying to calm their anger at Dick DeGuerin's insulting arguments. Celeste Beard Johnson was sentenced to life, plus a $10,000 fine.

The following day Steven Beard III stepped into the witness stand for elocution. He turned to Celeste and roared, "I hope you burn in hell!"

"When Steven III was up on the stand, it didn't affect me at all. I just looked at him as the pathetic person he is. I just recalled that he never visited his father while he was in the hospital. He only came to Texas for money."

"What did I ever do to you, or Jen, except love you?" Kristina, sitting in the witness chair, glared straight into her mother's eyes. "And this is how you treated us, like trash. We'll go on. Everybody will get to go home but you."

Anger clogged deep in the daughter's throat. "You say we turned on you. Well, you turned on us. You turned on the whole Beard family. He let you into his home, loved you, honored, obeyed you, and you violated him and murdered him. You *are guilty*! . . . *Shame* on *you*!"

"When Kristina was on the stand, I could see the hate in her eyes and facial expressions. I realized that she was now looking at me how she always looked at Steven. I had a mantra that I would quietly repeat over and over: 'This is my beloved daughter. I love her and she can't hurt me unless I let her.' This allowed me to completely tune out what she said."

After facing Celeste one last time, the Beard family members, including Kristina, the girl who said she knew how to fake-pray with the best of them, and Jennifer, the girl who said she didn't know how to pray, gathered in a prayer circle, held hands, and thanked God as they stood in the courtroom. They'd done the same thing just before the verdict was announced.

The Beards walked out of the courtroom and went to meet with Tracey Tarlton—to thank her and hug her.

That night, Allison Wetzel was just glad to be home, in her sweats, folding clothes, giving baths, and eating Teddy Grahams. After seeing the wrecked lives of the people in the trial, she had a renewed appreciation for her own life.

"I still can't believe I got convicted. I mean, did you see any evidence? Except they made me look like a horrible person?"

46

The day after the trial ended, Dick DeGuerin sent a letter to Judge Kocurek asking for a free transcript of the trial. Celeste, he said, was indigent. Four days after the trial, Kristina Beard felt bad that her mother was in jail, and miserable that she'd helped put her there. "Jen quit loving Celeste so long ago," she said. "I wish I could."

"When they were on the witness stand, they blew everything out of proportion. They cut me up, down, and sideways right into my bone marrow. But somehow, someway, I still cared for them more than anybody else ever would. I love them and wanted them to still love me. I am the only mother they will ever have; maybe someday they will realize that."

Whenever Kristina Beard was stressed about Celeste, she had nightmares—frequently of giant bugs bigger than she.

Kristina woke from a nightmare on Wednesday morning, May 7, 2003. In that dream, she was at the Toro Canyon house when Steve appeared. He'd walked home from the hospital and was fully recovered. They were thrilled to see each other.

But the dream turned into a nightmare—Steve stabbed Celeste to death for what she had done to him.

Kristina woke thinking the dream was reality. After a few minutes, she realized Steve was still dead.

"I would be much happier if she was dead," Kristina Beard said on May 18, 2003. She still watched over her shoulder for Celeste, believing she'd seen that look in her mother's eyes—that look that said Celeste wanted them dead. "I'd just rather not think about her." She didn't even want anyone to tell her when Celeste died.

Jennifer was suffering nightmares of being bitten by snakes.

By then, Celeste's attorneys were asking for money from the estate to fund her appeal. Bank of America had sued Steve Beard's heirs. And the children, including Kristina and Jennifer, had sued Celeste.

After three days of thundershowers, the Austin sky was a dull blue. Hurricane Claudette had barely sideswiped the city, but sand from the Sahara Desert was blowing in on Friday, July 17, 2003 and tainting the azure with gray. Still, the sun shined hotly in the hallway to Judge Julie Kocurek's chambers, while Celeste Beard Johnson sat alone in the tiny, dark cubicle of a holding cell wearing black-and-white jail stripes, her leg still in a white cast.

The 390th courtroom was unusually quiet and empty. Kocurek was away on business in Washington, D.C. But Judge Charles Campbell, an obese man with a feedbag-sized waddle, who was filling in for her, entered the courtroom at 9 A.M., looked over at Matt Hennessy, the only lawyer present for Celeste, and asked the solo attorney where his client was.

A reporter or two, a photographer without equipment—Campbell had ordered no cameras—a dowdy civil attorney for the Beard children, Dana Whatley with her ever-present notepad, her mother Marilou Gibbs, who was slimmer than usual, and Cole Johnson, who was beefier of belly than usual, sat in the gallery as deputies wheeled in Celeste. She did not even glance at her husband and friends. She spoke briefly to Hennessy and slowly and awkwardly climbed into a chair. She wore a rubber jailhouse shower shoe on her left foot and the bold black-and-white stripes on her baggy pants didn't match.

Allison Wetzel, sitting alone and wearing a new outfit that she'd been showing off moments before, was psyched. She was finally going to have her chance to cross-examine Celeste. Her giddy demeanor suddenly reversed when she growled, "How many indigent people have a goddamn forensic accountant?" She waved a fresh affidavit from accountant Jeffrey A. Compton in which he stated Celeste and Cole "own $8,200 in assets consisting of a bedroom suite, twin bed set, side tables, computer and office machines, TV, stereo equipment, and tools for work" and therefore his client could not "pay legal fees beyond the amount of approximately $1,500."

"It pisses me off," Wetzel snapped before taking her chair behind the prosecution table.

Celeste Beard Johnson crept back into her wheelchair and was rolled up to the witness stand, the sheriff's department deputies looking like her wait staff. "Thank you," she sweetly whispered to them. She was in the witness seat hoping to be declared indigent and get that free copy of the $41,700 trial transcript that DeGuerin had requested.

"Good morning," Allison Wetzel began her cross-examination. "Are you still married to Spencer Cole Johnson?" And with an affirmative answer to that, the prosecutor and felon grew antagonistic.

"There's nothing left," Celeste pleaded. "The credit cards are in arrears, and the money is gone." That included $26,000 worth of jewelry and furs. As she fumbled with figures until she said she'd paid $800,000 to DeGuerin for the capital murder trial, her tone became touchy. "I have sold every single thing that I have ever owned or was ever in my house, so the money would go straight from the sales first to those attorneys."

She still had to pay $250,000 for the solicitation for murder trial. She knew she had to pay another $250,000 for her appeal. "I don't know. I don't know how much I owe in expenses. I don't know."

The prosecutor and witness went back and forth until an angry Celeste, sucking on her lip, clarified that she "owed" the money, she hadn't "paid" the money for the solicitation case and appeal.

Wetzel asked the price of the expenses.

"Not to be flip," Celeste returned, "but you heard all the testimony of the expert witnesses and you asked each one how much they were getting paid, so all of those—another lawyer—I don't know. I would assume over two hundred thousand."

"Not to be flip, ma'am," Wetzel responded, "but Judge Campbell wasn't here to hear all that testimony, so just for—"

"Well, I don't know. I honestly, if I knew, I would tell you. I don't know."

So Wetzel ticked off the list of experts as Celeste kept her head down or cocked to the side as she boredly answered yes or no.

"They also conducted some mock trials with some jurors from the community, some mock jurors?"

"I have no knowledge of that," Celeste claimed, "but they might have."

Celeste's team of attorneys was reluctant to admit that, much less talk about it. But Wetzel knew the facts simply because she knew too many people in town—church, book club, Cub Scouts, basketball, volunteering at her sons' schools. And through those connections, Wetzel had discovered the facts of the mock trial—DeGuerin had won the fake case.

"You said that you got sued, and I just wanted to make it clear that it was a declaratory judgment that the bank filed after your lawyer made a demand for some money. Do you recall that?"

"I believe I was sued first," Celeste insisted. "I was sued

by the children and then by Bank of America and then he
filed something. I don't know what he filed, but I know I
was sued first because they had said here that they weren't
going to sue me. And then as soon as I got convicted, they
sued me."

With Wetzel quizzing Celeste again about the timeline,
and with Celeste acting more and more tired, she clarified,
". . . It's my understanding that the bank filed a lawsuit first
on behalf of the children, wanting to distribute the remainder of the trust fund immediately to all five kids.

"And then the kids also filed through Steven's son,
Steven III, they also filed a lawsuit against me for the remaining personal property, which there isn't any, but they
wanted to make sure that they filed that against me. And
that's I guess what you're talking about. And then—"

"Do you remember telling us in November that you had
three hundred purses?"

"They are all gone," Celeste said.

"Really?" Wetzel responded.

"Really." Celeste countered that all of that had been sold
and she had less than $300 in her inmate trust fund.

"I recall that during the trial and while you were incarcerated before your conviction that you made gifts of
money to other inmates. Are you continuing to do that?"

"Of course not."

"Is it true that there is a group of female inmates in the
Texas Department of Criminal Justice who call themselves
'Celeste's Posse'?"

"I have no idea," she said. "I don't—"

The judge stopped the prosecutor from asking about Celeste's Posse, which reputedly roamed the cellblocks of the
Hobby Unit that housed Tracey Tarlton.

And Celeste defended herself. "The letters and everything that we had in the trial were inmates asking me for
money to buy hygiene and stuff like that. There was never
any payment for any testimony or anything like that. I felt
sorry for people. I mean, it's sad when you're incarcerated
and you don't even have a stick of deodorant or toothpaste.
And the reason why I'm not giving anybody any money in

TDC is because I don't have any money to give. And, number two, I don't talk to anybody there. So no, this Celeste's Posse, I have never heard of it."

"Pass the witness," Wetzel said, as Celeste began to weep. Her nose was red. She grabbed for a tissue.

Hennessy asked, "Do you hold out any hope that you will be getting any money from either the bank or Steven Beard's children or the estate created by your dead husband?"

"As I said, I think that they will spend all the money they can to make sure I don't get any money."

"So do you have any hope that you will get it?"

"No."

The judge, speaking so slowly that one often thought he was finished with a sentence when he wasn't, wanted to know just what percentage of Celeste Beard Johnson's assets were being held by Bank of America due to the lawsuit.

". . . Somewhere over three million dollars . . ." Wetzel answered, as Celeste sat with her legs crossed, the leg with the cast on top and nervously bouncing.

And the judge ruled, "This defendant is not indigent as I understand the term indigency."

Throughout the spring, summer, fall, and winter months of 2003, Celeste's attorneys negotiated with the Bank of America attorneys and the kids' lawyers in hopes of getting enough money from the trust to pay for her appeal. In return, she would give up claim to Steven Beard's estate and trust.

By October, Celeste's team was talking $1 million. And the Beard kids' solidarity began showing a few hair fractures. It was a crack between natural-borns who were ready to move on and twins who didn't want to give in.

"I don't let people push me around," Kristina had said a month after the trial. "I have a GIANT set of balls now after standing up to Celeste. Everything seems so petty now after you take her on."

November 7, 2003, Amy Cozart stood in Christopher Doose's apartment just off of Interstate 35 and watched

Chris make hamburgers. He poured on the garlic just like Steve Beard. In fact, the burgers were probably as big as Steve's bear paw of a fist.

Amy and Christopher had become so close that they were like an old married couple, completing each other's thoughts and sentences. But Amy was no longer friends with Jennifer and Kristina. She couldn't handle that much unhealthiness in her life.

Chris remained in contact with Jen. Sometimes, he even longed to get back together with her. But when he thought about what she wanted—a life of fun, no kids, no responsibilities—and what he wanted—a life in politics, making change for the good, a wife who could campaign, kids—reality and practicality won out.

Amy cracked open the sliding glass door to the deck and lighted a cigarette. Cool air from the fall slipped through the open door as Christopher turned to her, his thoughts on Celeste. "Do you think she really did it?"

Epilogue

For a split second the living room went dead silent as shock flashed over Amy's round face. Of course she did, Amy said. Megan. The dog. That was the key. That was the proof, Amy argued.

Stillness filled the room, as silence blew in again.

Just after January 10, 2004, less than a year after Dick DeGuerin had questioned Justin Grimm about how Justin would benefit financially if Celeste were convicted and Justin and Kristina married, Justin and Kristina did marry, in a fairy-tale wedding in Grand Cayman.

Christopher and Amy, the only two who didn't benefit financially from Celeste's conviction, weren't invited. Paul, Kim, and Becky Beard attended. Steven III didn't.

Two and a half months later, Celeste sat meekly in her chair, her crutches propped on the wall beside her. She was embarrassed—her chin was broken out with strawberry-colored pimples. It'd been a stressful week, she explained, but she wouldn't elaborate. Her now-mousy blonde hair was pulled back tight. Still the grease in its strands was visible as though too-old petroleum jelly had been rubbed in, then toweled off.

There seemed to be a gray cast over her hair, her skin, and the room. Outside, wispy clouds streaked the blue sky. Bluebonnets dotted the farmyards where cattle lazily munched the fresh grass of spring. Guards in gray, mounted on sorrel horses watched the women prisoners hoe their rows.

It'd been one year since she'd been convicted. She whispered through her tears, "I'm scared to death that I'm not going to get out of here." She had to raise high or duck low to say her words. Otherwise, a black bar covered her face. When she dipped low, her acne stress couldn't be seen.

She wanted to share the document she'd recently signed revealing the split of the estate, but she wanted her attorney's approval first. "Because I think everybody should know how much money they just collected when, um, if they would have waited to see if I got convicted in my appeal, then they would get everything. But they're so greedy that they all wanted the cash now. And thank God my attorneys got paid. Everything got paid. The appeal, everything's paid for now. But, it just makes me sick that that's all they cared about."

Talk of the document was already all over Austin. Celeste was to receive almost $800,000 from the trust— $750,000 for Dick DeGuerin, plus $42,000 to pay for the trial transcript, so that he could finally begin Celeste's appeals process.

Her interest in the Davenport Village shopping center would be divided six ways with each of the children and Celeste receiving an equal share. If Celeste's appeal was successful, and if she was acquitted at a retrial, she then would receive her one-sixth share. If she lost, she received nothing and the kids would divide her sixth.

But Cole Johnson, the husband who Celeste said saved her life, had asked Marilou Gibbs if he'd get Celeste's share if she remained jailed. Marilou was dumbfounded that he'd even asked. "No," she answered. He didn't understand why not. It was never his, she'd explained.

Since then, Celeste hadn't been hearing from Cole as much, and he wasn't doing the things she requested of him like getting her courtroom clothes out of storage and giving them to Marilou to keep for the retrial she longed for.

"I can't live in here forty years," she said.

Celeste demanded that she be able to wear street clothes and makeup and that no press be allowed in the 390th District courtroom on Friday, September 10, 2004. Judge Kocurek denied Celeste's requests. But when the TDCJ prisoner crept into the courtroom that late summer afternoon, still on silver-toned crutches, she was in new khaki-colored pants and a pink scrub top, neither of which were prison or jail issue. Her old courtroom, street clothes probably wouldn't have fit—she looked like she ate her favorite chicken-fried steak and potatoes every day.

Her hair was long and frizzy like a dried horse's tail, but freshly and neatly clipped on the ends. Her skin was corn silk smooth, clear and ready for a TV camera close-up as though she were doing a cosmetic commercial. Celeste hadn't been seen in public wearing eyeglasses since her March 2003 trial.

And she didn't glance at her husband Cole. Nor did she smile to Dick DeGuerin, who accompanied her to the Judge's bench, where two deputies stood behind her as she plead no contest to the first degree felony for the solicitation of Tracey Tarlton's murder.

In return, Celeste was sentenced to five years in prison, out of a possible five to 99 years. The time was to be served concurrently with her two life sentences, and she would be given credit for the days she'd spent incarcerated since her March 28, 2002 arrest.

DeGuerin constantly repeated to the judge that Celeste wasn't admitting guilt and didn't believe she was guilty. She was pleading no contest simply because she didn't want to go to trial.

Her supporters believed she'd be out on appeal, granted a new trial, and found not guilty just about the time those five years had been completely served.

But if Celeste Beard didn't help Tracey Tarlton in the shooting of Steve, how did Tracey get into the Beard house in the wee hours of October 2, 1999?

"I honestly think it was just a fluke. I mean, I think that she came over there that night mad is what I really believe—that she was angry when she came over there. Otherwise, if she wasn't angry, she would have remembered the walk-through, supposedly, you know, if there really was a walk-through, she would have remembered it. But I think that she just—she knew our habits, that Steve was drunk and passed out.

"But I think she was hoping to find me there. I don't know. Who knows?"